The Mythological State and its Empire

Routledge Studies in Social and Political Thought

For a full list of titles in this series, please visit www.routledge.com

19. The Reading of Theoretical Texts
Peter Ekegren

20. The Nature of Capital
Marx after Foucault
Richard Marsden

21. The Age of Chance
Gambling in Western Culture
Gerda Reith

22. Reflexive Historical Sociology
Arpad Szakolczai

23. Durkheim and Representations
Edited by W. S. F. Pickering

24. The Social and Political Thought of Noam Chomsky
Alison Edgley

25. Hayek's Liberalism and Its Origins
His Idea of Spontaneous Order and the Scottish Enlightenment
Christina Petsoulas

26. Metaphor and the Dynamics of Knowledge
Sabine Maasen and Peter Weingart

27. Living with Markets
Jeremy Shearmur

28. Durkheim's Suicide
A Century of Research and Debate
Edited by W.S.F. Pickering and Geoffrey Walford

29. Post-Marxism
An Intellectual History
Stuart Sim

30. The Intellectual as Stranger
Studies in Spokespersonship
Dick Pels

31. Hermeneutic Dialogue and Social Science
A Critique of Gadamer and Habermas
Austin Harrington

32. Methodological Individualism
Background, History and Meaning
Lars Udehn

33. John Stuart Mill and Freedom of Expression
The Genesis of a Theory
K.C. O'Rourke

34. The Politics of Atrocity and Reconciliation
From Terror to Trauma
Michael Humphrey

35. Marx and Wittgenstein
Knowledge, Morality, Politics
Edited by Gavin Kitching and Nigel Pleasants

36. The Genesis of Modernity
Arpad Szakolczai

37. Ignorance and Liberty
Lorenzo Infantino

38. **Deleuze, Marx and Politics**
Nicholas Thoburn

39. **The Structure of Social Theory**
Anthony King

40. **Adorno, Habermas and the Search for a Rational Society**
Deborah Cook

41. **Tocqueville's Moral and Political Thought**
New Liberalism
M.R.R. Ossewaarde

42. **Adam Smith's Political Philosophy**
The Invisible Hand and Spontaneous Order
Craig Smith

43. **Social and Political Ideas of Mahatma Gandi**
Bidyut Chakrabarty

44. **Counter-Enlightenments**
From the Eighteenth Century to the Present
Graeme Garrard

45. **The Social and Political Thought of George Orwell**
A Reassessment
Stephen Ingle

46. **Habermas**
Rescuing the Public Sphere
Pauline Johnson

47. **The Politics and Philosophy of Michael Oakeshott**
Stuart Isaacs

48. **Pareto and Political Theory**
Joseph Femia

49. **German Political Philosophy**
The Metaphysics of Law
Chris Thornhill

50. **The Sociology of Elites**
Michael Hartmann

51. **Deconstructing Habermas**
Lasse Thomassen

52. **Young Citizens and New Media**
Learning for Democractic Participation
Edited by Peter Dahlgren

53. **Gambling, Freedom and Democracy**
Peter Adams

54. **The Quest for Jewish Assimilation in Modern Social Science**
Amos Morris-Reich

55. **Frankfurt School Perspectives on Globalization, Democracy, and the Law**
William E. Scheuerman

56. **Hegemony**
Studies in Consensus and Coercion
Edited by Richard Howson and Kylie Smith

57. **Governmentality, Biopower, and Everyday Life**
Majia Holmer Nadesan

58. **Sustainability and Security within Liberal Societies**
Learning to Live with the Future
Edited by Stephen Gough and Andrew Stables

59. **The Mythological State and its Empire**
David Grant

The Mythological State and its Empire

David Grant

Routledge
Taylor & Francis Group
New York London

First published 2009
by Routledge
711 Third Ave, New York, NY 10017

Simultaneously published in the UK
by Routledge
2 Park Square, Milton Park, Abingdon, Oxon OX14 4RN

Routledge is an imprint of the Taylor & Francis Group, an informa business

First issued in paperback 2012

© 2009 Taylor & Francis

Typeset in Sabon by IBT Global.

All rights reserved. No part of this book may be reprinted or reproduced or utilised in any form or by any electronic, mechanical, or other means, now known or hereafter invented, including photocopying and recording, or in any information storage or retrieval system, without permission in writing from the publishers.

Trademark Notice: Product or corporate names may be trademarks or registered trademarks, and are used only for identification and explanation without intent to infringe.

Library of Congress Cataloging in Publication Data
Grant, David, 1947–
 The mythological state and its empire / by David Grant.
  p. cm. — (Routledge studies in social and political thought ; 59)
 "Simultaneously published in the UK by Routledge."
 Includes bibliographical references and index.
 1. State, The. 2. Political science—Philosophy. I. Title.
 JC131.G73 2008
 320.1—dc22

ISBN13: 978-0-415-98875-9 (hbk)
ISBN13: 978-0-415-54239-5 (pbk)
ISBN13: 978-0-203-89198-8 (ebk)

Contents

Preface ix
Acknowledgements xi

PART I
The Nature of Political Mythology

1 Introduction 3
2 The Past as a Figure of the Present and Future 19

PART II
Establishment and Refinement

3 The Leviathan, the Calling and Their Separation 43
4 Imagining a General Will 78
5 The Reason of Protestant Politics 100

PART III
Modernisation

6 Reason and the Myth of Justice 123
7 The Liberalism of the Market 146
8 Freedom is the State 166
9 Defending the State against Scepticism 187

PART IV
Embodiment

10 The State as Civilisation   201

11 Governmentality, the Market and Liberalism   221

Notes   253
Bibliography   281
Index   285

Preface

During a long career in Justice administration in Australia, I was constantly confronted with legislative, judicial and prison practices that were heavily disposed to a punitive regime.

My attempts to understand the foundation of these practices, resilient in the face of their failure to deal with the issues involved, repeatedly came up against well-established explanations. In the end, these explanations almost always translated into inferences of habituated behaviour by marginalised people and the need for the political and justice institutions to accept that habituation and do the best it could within its established regimes to deal with it. In this, there often seemed to be a strong sense that there was some inherent characteristic that contributed to that habituation.

This raised the question for me whether this was a fatalism that was at least understandable in the face of seemingly intractable social problems or whether this fatalism was blind to deeper issues that went to such matters as the instrumental role of the institutions of the State and, finally, to the nature of the State itself. This book emerged out of an attempt to understand these broader questions. It has led me into a consideration of certain dominant traditions of thought and their embodiment in practice, an investigation to which the book is devoted. In this regard it takes further the work I commenced with *Prisons—The Continuing Crisis*.

Acknowledgments

One is fortunate to meet even one genuinely inspirational person in life. In pursuing my studies, I have met two. Foremost has been Martin Krygier, whose quiet wisdom and intellectual elegance has repeatedly shown why wit is usually of more value than just being on the mark. If there is an invisible hand in this work—not just through his observations about content but more so in tone—it is his. The other is Stephen Gaukroger, who first encouraged an artless mind to the point where some of the trees could be made out through the fog. I should also like to express my appreciation for the support and constructive comments made by Jeremy Webber, Scott Veitch and Robert van Krieken on what was in effect an earlier draft of this work.

Part I

The Nature of Political Mythology

1 Introduction

PREAMBLE

The modern State is not modern. It is a mythological entity created and sustained to satisfy our deepest instincts, fear and the desire for sympathetic conditions of existence. It is not the product of reason but of reason in the service of myth. Emerging from this condition into political modernity would mean understanding the mythological nature of our fundamental political presumptions, including the idea of the State, in their long passage through the political tradition from Hobbes to Hayek and Pettit. This would also mean seeing liberalism and republicanism as mythological strategies, the function of which is to repair and sustain this myth of the State. Yet facing this challenge and modernising our political presumptions might bring an end to the manufacture of the docile and productive individual and establish Enlightened self-responsibility as the dominant personal code.

This work is an exploration of the meaning and implications of the connections between these ideas. Its primary focus is therefore an extensive examination of political mythological thinking and it will undertake this through a consideration of the emergence and persistence of the State as the pre-eminent example of the kind of mythological entity described by Blumenberg. In doing so, this work sets out to explain and test a particular three-part proposition. The first part is that strategic variations in the application of liberal principles have sustained the idea of the mythological State, the foundation of this idea being that forgoing responsibility for oneself to the State will ensure that our fear and desire are dealt with through the creation of freedom, autonomy and responsibility to others. The second part is that, while the variations in the idea have been pursued over time, strategic variations in the application of liberal practices have actually dealt with fear and desire through the manufacture of docility and productivity. The third part is that individuals typically forgo their self-responsibility willingly and submit to such practices due to the seductive power of the mythological idea of the State.

This exploration shall be undertaken by looking at a range of key thinkers within and outside the political tradition, but often against the grain of the usual readings of them. One argument here is that it is the contributors to the modern political tradition from Hobbes to Hayek and Pettit who have, unaware of the mythological presumptions of their respective political philosophies, engaged and perpetuated such thinking in their interleaved accounts of politics and the State. In doing so, the tradition has perpetuated a notion of modernity which is characterised by pre-Enlightenment presumptions. This is not to say that the modern State is not legitimate, but that it is not truly modern. This lack of true modernity, therefore, is due to the persistence of pre-Enlightenment, in fact of mythological, thinking.

The consideration of the work of the chosen thinkers will be undertaken through the prisms of liberalism and republicanism, portrayed here as mythological strategies. These strategies are mythological by virtue of their two component trajectories, the first claiming to establish an idea of freedom that satisfies these instincts, but which disguises the other, which induces or imposes the acceptance of normalising regimes on typically willing individuals. The social ontology of Wittgenstein is used here as the model of normalisation and the nature of such regimes has been revealed by Elias' account of civilisation and by Foucault's study of discipline and governmentality. These trajectories have, repeatedly over time, offered not only critiques but also positive proposals by which the long course of the political myth at least from Hobbes has been repeatedly repaired and so sustained. Thus through liberalism and republicanism we examine the political implications of the intersection of the ontological thought of Blumenberg, Wittgenstein, Elias and Foucault.

In this context, this work argues that the honoured notion of individual responsibility is highly problematic and that it reflects a range of deep flaws that inhabit our central political presumptions and arrangements. Despite the apparent similarity between them, but an appearance which hides a vast difference, it will be argued that a new notion of self-responsibility should take its place as a core personal code. In this, it will also be made clear how key principles of the Enlightenment remain of value and that they may be realised by adopting the arrangements and practices upon which self-responsibility is founded. Self-responsibility is principally denied by mythological thinking. Such thinking pervades the foundations of our political thought and makes the highly reassuring but false claim that, by creating widely empowered entities and inducing individual subjection to them, these instincts will be satisfied. It will be shown how such thinking thereby becomes the basis of the honoured notion of individual responsibility.

In effect, we are exploring the causal connection between human instinct and the nature of the arrangements of the modern State, a deep connection which prevents the realisation of Enlightened self-responsibility. This is a synthetic approach towards a new understanding of the modern State, the foundation of which is no longer faith but neither is it reason. It is reason in the service of fear and desire, and of mythology.

To enable a better navigation of this terrain, this chapter will now provide a somewhat wider view of the range of interconnected ideas that comprise this work. Because the Enlightenment has been put forward as a valuable reference point, we shall first explore its significance for the broad argument. This will be followed by an outline of the notion of self-responsibility, a foundational idea within any newly Enlightened approach, based on the acceptance of existential fear and on the optimal self-determination of one's conditions of existence. We shall then examine the grounds, drawn from the consideration of questions of the legitimacy and modernity of the State, on which political mythology has been established and sustained and how this denies the realisation of self-responsibility. These are grounds adopted and promoted by the political tradition through their construction and reworking of the idea of the mythological State and on which are built their ideas of reason, freedom, autonomy and responsibility but which disguise the manufacture of docility and productivity. The chapter will conclude with a broader outline of the notion of liberalism used here as the mythological tool with which we explore this wide landscape, and then with a statement that makes it clear how, in the end, this work is a consideration of the political implications of the continuing dominance of myth over reason.

ENLIGHTENMENT

The Aspirations of the Enlightenment

Since the Enlightenment has been presented as an aspirational reference point for this work, it is important first to say a few things about the sense in which that term is understood here and the extent to which this is drawn from the Enlightenment as a wide current in the cultural and intellectual history of Europe, as an historical reality. As the bulk of this work will show, there is no adoption here of the range of universalist, rationalist arguments and inferences from that historical reality. Nor, certainly, is there any general endorsement of the political philosophies produced by Locke, Montesquieu, Rousseau or Kant as they might be argued to be Enlightenment figures.[1] In fact, the arguments presented here are substantially a rejection of key political arguments of those thinkers and their successors within the tradition.

However, neither is there any simple acceptance of the external criticisms that have been made of the Enlightenment, whether by conservative reactionaries, Romantics or by radical political and social reformers.[2] Rather, it is argued here that there is a way to look at the Enlightenment which draws out a sustainable intellectual theme and by which, at the same time, the presumptions that are displayed in the political theories of those key thinkers from Locke to Kant can be seen afresh.

This way of looking at the Enlightenment is to see it in its aspiration to be a liberating force. This is to say that provisional, rational incremental progress can be made in human affairs, one effect of which would be the gradual realisation of Enlightened political individuality. This sense of progress would result from the promotion of respectful self-responsibility rather than from continuing to address political questions inherited from medieval Christian ways of thinking and which are based on myth not reason.[3] Although there is no endorsement here of the political theory that he developed from it, this is the sense given to Enlightenment by Kant: '*Enlightenment is the human being's emergence from his self-incurred minority. Minority* is inability to make use of one's own understanding without direction from another.... Have courage to make use of your *own* understanding! is thus the motto of enlightenment.' He continues: 'For this enlightenment, however, nothing is required but *freedom*, and indeed the least harmful of anything that could even be called freedom: namely, freedom to make public use of one's reason in all matters.... The *public use* of one's reason must always be free, and it alone can bring about enlightenment among human beings.'[4]

Conservative Criticism of the Enlightenment

Seeing Enlightenment in this way helps to address certain criticisms levelled at it, especially by conservatives and Romantics. Nisbet gives some insight into the way that conservatives, generally against the arguments of radicals and liberals, responded to what they saw as the inevitably destructive implications of the Enlightenment and the modernity which it heralded. What Nisbet saw is that, whereas nineteenth century liberals sustained the faith of the Enlightenment by promoting the emancipation of man's mind from religious and traditional bonds[5] and radicals saw in it the dismantling of the institutional structures of oppression, conservative thought regarded the Reformation and the Industrial and French Revolutions that consequentially followed as having largely socially destructive effects.

These effects included the equalitarianism that ended traditional hierarchy and authority, the excesses of centralised popular power, the substitution of passion for the restraints of tradition, the replacement of sacred values with impersonal norms of contract, the decline of religious and political authority in favour of power, the loss of liberty not as freedom but as principled right, the debasement of culture through mass dissemination and the sense of progress that saw the past as bad and the future as best.[6] In saying so, conservatives rejected the Enlightenment claim that individuality, progress, contract, nature and reason were means by which the oppressions of traditional arrangements, which they saw as good, could be relieved. They preferred the traditionalism of the Middle Ages to the analytical reason of the Enlightenment, as they did its communalism and kinship to later individualism. The main reasons were that the claimed progress only brought, to their eyes, the tyranny of popular sovereignty, the poverty and degradation of the working class, the instability that came from the conversion of landed property into capital, the alienation that came with industrial cities and the growth of technology.[7] They also saw the instability that came with the abolition of the guilds and corporations, the undermining of the patriarchialism of the family and the loss of moral influence that came with the subjugation of the Catholic Church to the State, which took control of education and welfare, one manifestation of which was the slide into Jacobin terror.[8]

It might well be said in response that to visit on the idea of Enlightenment the sins of those who took improper advantage of its loosening of the oppressive bonds of tradition is misjudged, even unfair. It might also be said that the proper response to such sin, where there was sin, was not to revert to oppressive tradition, or 'myth' in terms that will be explored here, but to seek a new way, a radicalisation of the originating sentiments of Enlightenment, of those sentiments expressed by Kant.

Criticism of the Enlightenment from Romanticism

A different attack on Enlightenment comes in the name of Romanticism. Berlin's argument is that this tradition dealt a blow to the Enlightenment from which it could not, and did not, recover. This is an argument with which this work disagrees, so long as one takes the Kantian aspiration of the free public use of one's own understanding to be the touchstone of the Enlightenment. Berlin refers to the impact of the arguments of Herder and, interestingly, of Kant, whom he sees as a father of Romanticism. From Herder he gathers three criticisms: first, the fundamental importance to being human that individuals express themselves; second, the notion of belonging, what it means to belong to a group; and third the notion that ideals are both often incompatible with one another and are irreconcilable.[9] Berlin's claim is that the importance of each of these is denied by Enlightenment thinking. In response, it may be said that, to the extent that Enlightenment thinkers denied the importance of these arguments, they were themselves wrong. However, Herder's attack makes no mark on the primary Enlightened Kantian notion of the free public use of one's own understanding.

Regarding Kant, Berlin attempts to co-opt him in his criticism of the Enlightenment by portraying him as the father of Romanticism. He acknowledged that Kant was someone who 'hated romanticism. He detested every form of extravagance, fantasy, what he called *Schwarmerie,* any form of exaggeration, mysticism, vagueness, confusion. Nevertheless, he is justly regarded as one of the fathers of romanticism.'[10] Berlin's argument comes from his claim that 'Kant was virtually intoxicated by the idea of human freedom' and 'In the case of Kant it became an obsessive central principle.[11] For Berlin, 'This was, of course, to assert the primacy of the will. In a certain sense Kant was still a child of eighteenth century enlightenment, because he thought that all men, if their hearts were pure, and when they asked themselves what it was right to do, would in similar circumstances arrive at identical conclusions, because to all questions reason in all men gives the selfsame answer.'[12] However, Berlin is saying that, despite his enlightenment rationalism, Kant's emphasis on the independence of the will makes him a 'restrained' Romantic.

The problem for this argument of Berlin is that the Kantian will is not the Romantic will, say of Schiller. He as much as admits this himself. Schiller's theory of tragedy, Berlin claims, 'is founded upon this notion of (spiritual) freedom . . . and this is the way in which, perhaps more than through direct reading of Kant, it had such a powerful effect upon romantic art.'[13] Berlin also identifies the contrast between nature and the moral individual as 'the central doctrine in Schiller' but says 'Schiller rejected the Kantian solution, fundamentally because it seemed to him that though Kant's will liberates us from nature, he puts us on a very narrow moral road, into too grim, too confining a Calvinist world, where the only alternatives are either being the plaything of nature or following this grim path of Lutheran duty which Kant thought in terms of.'[14]

In fact, Kant does not indulge but constrains the free use of reason and in a way that the Romantic Schiller would resist. As Blumenberg points out, 'For Kant, the hypertrophy of the appetite for knowledge is the root of all the spiritual phenomena whose negation is called "enlightenment." "Passive reason," in its instinct to go beyond what has been achieved without regard to what can be achieved, must be helplessly inclined towards prejudice and superstition. Enlightenment . . . is more than "thinking for oneself"; it is the removal, as it were, of the opportunities for the passivity and thus the seduceability of reason.'[15] Further, it is the intervention of the political process into this problem by which freedom of thought 'finally destroys itself.'[16]

Kant's promotion of reason and the will is not the Romantic will and Kant cannot himself be used convincingly, as Berlin attempts to do to strengthen his Romantic criticism of Enlightenment, as a father of Romanticism, even as a 'restrained' member of that party. The Kantian aspiration for the elaborated but consistent use of one's reason, understood as denying unfettered freedom of thought, remains as the touchstone of the Enlightenment, not of Romanticism. Where Kant falters is the way that he does fetter this use of reason through political arguments and processes which, as will be extensively examined below, reveal him as having a mythological disposition. By this strategy, Kant compromises his own aspiration by employing what is properly seen as a full mythological strategy. It might also be noted that although Berlin sees Romanticism as having left a positive legacy,[17] it has much in common with 'many (if not all) of the prominent theories of myth'[18] and, as will be argued to have been Kant's mythological politics, is in itself highly problematic for that.[19] Where Romanticism can be seen as having made a positive contribution is where it was not mythological, that is where it promotes at least the principles of self-responsibility and self-creation.[20]

The general point to be made is that the Kantian sense of Enlightenment adopted here stands its ground against the criticisms of both conservatives and Romantics. Used in this sense, it is a principal reference point for what follows.

SELF-RESPONSIBILITY

Responsibility and Self-responsibility

Self-responsibility is presented here as a reflection of this notion of Enlightenment within the lives of individuals and thereby as a reference point for preferred political arrangements, including of the State.

The distinction between the two alternative meanings of 'responsible' made in introducing this chapter may be seen as reflecting different ways of understanding the modern State. If the notion of self-responsibility now applied, it would be taken to mean that one's behaviour reflects the arrangements of a State that promotes the respectful self-reliance of the individual and his wide engagement in the rational processes of the State. In the alternative account, that is of the honoured notion of individual responsibility, it would mean that one's behaviour reflects the prescriptions of a mythological State which does not promote, in fact denies, the widest proper engagement of the rational individual because it is essentially concerned with his induced demands to eliminate the fearsomeness at least of all other individuals and with creating for him desirous conditions of existence. It would do this rather than promote his capacity to accept the inevitability of, and deal respectfully with, fear and to significantly create the conditions of his own existence. Because this second account is taken seriously here, it is argued that the meaning of 'responsible' which reflects the ideals of the Enlightenment, a 'self-responsibility' that ultimately reflects rather than denies the capacity of the individual to be concerned first with behaving rationally, remains to be established and for mythological reasons. If this latter perception of the State can be demonstrated by argument, then the former perception does not describe present arrangements.

Nature of Self-responsibility

The proposal here is that the rationality of self-responsibility is one in which the individual is responsible to and for himself and, therefore, responsible to or for no other capable individual. No other should be responsible to or for him and he would accept and deal with his fear in a manner respectful of others, with the support of social institutions and practices redesigned to promote that. In this, respect is such that he would allow others to be self-responsible, that he does not assume responsibility for others, either by inducement or force. Until the State begins to promote the individual as self-responsible in this sense rather than be first concerned about him as fearful and desirous, it is argued that the ideal of the Enlightenment preferred here cannot be realised.

Complementing self-responsibility as a personal code, it is possible to conceive of a State which is of a very different kind from that with which we are familiar, the practices of which would promote the rationality and wide engagement of respectful, self-responsible individuals. In fact, the role of the State would be central in helping individuals to establish such a condition. The establishment of self-responsibility would be first concerned with the promotion, including by re-arrangement of the State form, of respectful self-reliance rather than promoting the importance of the fear-desire nexus. This is to say that the State may not intrude except minimally and only for the purpose of promoting self-responsibility. The self-responsible individual by definition will not intrude into the lives of others but the State will be justified to intrude into the lives of those who intrude into others' lives when they do not act responsibly in this sense. But this State intrusion may only be for the first purpose of promoting self-responsible behaviour through constructive engagement with those who offend against this principle. It may not be guided by the elimination of fear and the creation of sympathetic conditions, each of which relegates engagement low on the list of preferred means and outcomes.

Under the umbrella of such a reconstituted State form, none would rule or be ruled, except in the sense intended here. Self-responsibility would promote respect and therefore peace, since a self-responsible person would not take responsibility for, that is determine the conditions of existence of, others when every sentient and able adult is encouraged and readied to become responsible only to and for himself. This requires a State the purpose of which is to promote responsibility in this sense rather than one that promotes its forgoing. So, fear may be dealt with without being fearsome and the conditions of one's existence could be created without forgoing one's responsibility to the State or its dominant interests. So would the aspirations of the Enlightenment, in the Kantian sense outlined above, begin to be fulfilled. None of this is to say that, due to the nature of this embedded mythological arrangement and the normalisation and certainty it entails, there would be any easy way to establish non-mythological arrangements.

In anticipation of expected doubts about the practicability or wisdom of promoting non-mythological practices, there is the obvious but important caveat. The claim for self-responsibility is not based on an assertion that it is a quality which individuals could assume overnight, particularly when it's forgoing will be argued here to have been common at least since the emergence of the modern State with Hobbes. Even with redesigned social institutions and practices, there will be slow learners. It is a characteristic to be acquired over time throughout a community and from an early age for the individual, through reconfigured State and social institutions whose charge is to increasingly broker outcomes of engagement and self-responsibility rather than determine or deny them.

Given that self-responsibility is established incrementally through respectful, agonistic processes, an argument for it is not an argument for the notion of autonomous individuality, free from the heteronomous influences of existence. It is an argument for the possibility of political and other arrangements that honour reflective decision-making for an increasingly self-determined form of life which accepts the inescapability of fear. This is so despite an unsurprising but resistible disposition to create mythological magnitudes and despite the effect of early and continuous training of individuals to adopt mythological practices.

Without intending any elaborate architecture for the future but so that there is an early sense of the field being explored here, some broad examples can be put forward as indicative of the 'compared to what' of this work. In politics, there are categorical differences between democratic arrangements dominated by the corporate interests of political organisations and their influential allies, on the one hand, and, on the other, those which promote sensible, wide participation in political decision-making. In matters of criminal justice, there is a difference in kind between the progressively amended but still commanding punitive practices of judicial officer and correctional institution, on the one hand, and, on the other, one in which the primary concern is the genuine engagement with offender and victim in which judicial and institutional roles would be to facilitate respect and self-reliance. Similarly, there is wide difference in indigenous affairs between arrangements which sustain indigenous people on lifetime welfare, in the claimed hope that they will acquire marketable skills, on the one hand, and, on the other, the return of viable amounts of traditional land for their own sustenance or sustainable exploitation. The latter in each case is taken to be indicative of the principle of self-responsibility. In these broad examples, this principle would be progressively applied in political decision-making, in justice and in indigenous affairs: there would be carefully extended but widespread participation in political decision-making; a focus on reconciliation and the provision of negotiated developmental offender programmes in justice; and the return of traditional lands to indigenous owners along with the sensible withdrawal of welfare support.

Beyond these indicative examples, it should be said that to provide a comprehensive elaboration here would be an excessive burden. Indeed, it would be another work. More importantly, it is something which cannot be substantially prescribed, since self-responsibility by its nature is founded on the working out of alternative social arrangements by different kinds of individuals with the support of different State practices.

It is not being claimed here that the forgoing of self-responsibility upon which present mythological political arrangements are founded is total. What is forgone is the individual opportunity to deal with fear without being fearsome and to attempt to create the conditions of one's own existence rather than have this undertaken by the State in its mythological condition and through its dominant interests. Secondary responsibilities are still retained by individuals, for example the raising of children or the periodic casting of votes as to which dominant interests should have the role of dealing with the fear-sympathy nexus, so long as the individual satisfies certain minimum requirements of the State. These secondary responsibilities are at their most extensive in a liberal State but restricted in a communitarian society and effectively eliminated in a totalitarian State. But neither does this imply that secondary responsibilities may have no mythological content. On the contrary, child-rearing typically, although not inevitably, comprises training offspring to have expectations of the State that encourage the forgoing of responsibility and one's attitude to voting can be merely an intention to legitimise the actions of alternative dominant interests.

Neither should it be taken that self-responsibility is being set up here as an absolute reference point against which the ongoing efforts of liberalism or republicanism are too easily criticised or dismissed. Arrangements based on the principle of self-responsibility would themselves require efforts of the kind that liberal or republican arrangements have comprised. They would be progressively established by degree. But the starting point is different, liberalism and republicanism argued here to be first and foremost concerned with claiming that fear can be eliminated and sympathetic conditions are best created by others, while self-responsibility is first concerned with accepting fear as unable to be eliminated but rationally manageable through the establishment of respectful responsibility to and for oneself. As the bulk of this work argues, most of the interesting debate about the political theories of Hobbes, Locke, Montesquieu, Rousseau, Kant, Rawls, Hayek and Pettit occurs around the axis of liberal or republican thought and the significant amount they have in common within the political tradition.

What is being put here is an argument that it is along this axis where our modern mythological presumptions can be seen. So it is that an alternative axis, one concerned with an agonistic promotion of respectful self-responsibility that is not infused with responses to pre-Enlightenment questions but takes the Kantian notion of Enlightenment seriously, can provide an alternative starting point for debate and practice which is not mythological.

LEGITIMACY, MODERNITY AND MYTH

Yet there are reasons why self-responsibility, in the sense just described, has not taken root. It is because, in the argument here, the State has assumed responsibility for individuals in return for promises about fear and desire. Because of the force of these instincts, the State has typically done this with our complicity.

This 'positioning' of the State emerged as a result of the social and political turmoil caused by the religious wars in Europe, especially in the seventeenth century. It was the Treaty of Westphalia (1648) which both formed the system of States and characterised their absolutist nature to protect the life and property of subjects. This was a time of widespread fear, even existential fear, where the conditions of one's existence were precarious. These were circumstances that were compelling. It was in this context that Hobbes published *Leviathan* in 1651, by which he conceived and thus initiated the slow refinement by his intellectual successors of what was to become the modern State. More broadly this was where liberalism and modern republicanism found their soil. Seen in this way, the creation of the conditions which denied self-responsibility is the history of the modern State.

It will be argued here that the core elements of the absolutist, Hobbesian State remain today, although they have been refined by the political tradition. This is not a claim that the modern State is illegitimate but it is a claim that the modern State is not modern. Blumenberg has rejected the position of Lowith in *Meaning in History* regarding the modern age generally and against Schmitt regarding the modern State in particular, arguing that neither are the result of a secularisation of the eschatological pattern established by Christian religion. It was his critique of this thesis that Blumenberg presented in *The Legitimacy of the Modern Age*.[21] There he accepted that there had been a reoccupation of Christian positions, through a process of inducement caused by the breakdown of the absolute religious positions within the State, which produced a mirror-image of certain Christian positions. One example was the replacement of theological with political absolutism.[22] However, for him reoccupation was not secularisation. A threshold had been crossed in this, as it had also been across a range of other issues,[23] so the modern age is legitimate.[24]

But he also acknowledged that the modern State is not modern, as it has reoccupied Christian positions and tried to answer Christian questions, specifically by this creation of a political absolutism which is a mirror-image of theological absolutism. Reinforcing this position was his argument that there is a difference between 'sovereignty, raison d'état, will, decision, friend-enemy' and 'contract, consent, liberty, law and rights.'[25] The latter typify the self-assertion[26] which characterises modernity but they are overridden by the State, which is characterised by the former, whenever its interests are threatened. True modernity and the realisation of Enlightenment are thereby denied. The State needs to be radically criticised for these modern notions to be realised.

The lesson here regarding this overriding is not so much the sad loss of libertarian progress but that it is a pointer to the relationship between the nature of the State and these presumed conditions of liberty. It points to the fragility of these conditions, a fragility due to their location on the same axis as the sovereign State, on which they are founded, of which they are a manifestation and so to which they are subsidiary: there can be rights but these are conditioned by the kind of subjection to the State that requires the forgoing of our responsibility to and for ourselves. This axis reveals a different continuity, other than secularisation. That is, beneath the apparent discontinuity between 'sovereignty, raison d'état, will, decision, friend and enemy,' on the one hand, and 'contract, consent, liberty, law and rights,' on the other, there is a continuity. This continuity exists also beneath Lowith's secularisation and Blumenberg's induced reoccupation, as well as beneath the difference between them. The question is to identify its substance and then to determine its connection to modern political thought.

We can see a credible candidate for this other continuity in Blumenberg's *Work on Myth*. It is mythology. In that work, he explores the disposition in mankind to imagine absolute mythological entities, magnitudes the function of which is to satisfy a foundational, informal, uneasy but strong contract with individuals. This contract is for the elimination of fear and the satisfaction of desire for sympathetic conditions, in return for the subjection which is the forgoing of self-responsibility and which, once conceived, is the subject of ongoing work and refinement to ensure it can claim to perform these functions.

The question then is how these principles of mythology are connected to modern political thought. The answer is found in the modern political tradition[27] and the political magnitudes they imagine. It is argued here that this tradition commenced with Hobbes and that he conceived the absolutist State in response to the disintegration of the unitary theological absolute, thereby ensuring continuity from the theological to the political absolute, although one which denies its modernity not its legitimacy. It will be argued here that the work by the tradition on this magnitude has continued from Locke through to Rawls, Hayek and Pettit. It will also be argued that the Hobbesian State, as gradually refined by the tradition over time, has all the key mythological characteristics, including that its function is to satisfy an informal but strong contract, quietening our fears and desires in return for the forgoing of self-responsibility, or at least to be seen to be doing so. In short, the mythological magnitude and the magnitude of the State share the key characteristic of fearsomeness as the basis of a contract with each individual to deal with fear and desire on condition of the forgoing of self-responsibility. Given that the unitary absolute State has replaced the unitary theological absolute, there is continuity. While the State is not 'continuous' through secularisation, it is 'continuous' through being mythological. So it is not modern.

The claim for the State is that it deals with fear and desire for sympathetic conditions by promoting freedom, autonomy and responsibility. For example, individual rights are said to be the means by which our fear is dealt with and by which we can readily pursue our aspirations regarding the conditions of our existence. But there is a crucial twist at this point. It is the argument here that the instincts are satisfied not by establishing conditions of freedom but through the manufacture of docility and productivity which subjection allows: docility is a key contributor to the reduction of fear and productivity mitigates want. This is a subversion by the State and its interests, agents and allies. The State has adopted a strategy to achieve its contractual outcomes which is very different from that which it claims. So it has two trajectories: first, the idea of the State as promoting freedom, autonomy and responsibility; and second, the manufacture of docility and productivity. It is a subversive process because, of necessity, the first disguises the second. It is a 'necessity' so that the latter is made palatable and thereby affirms our typically willing forgoing of self-responsibility.

The contributors to the tradition have been able to persist in this subversive strategy over the long time since Hobbes because of the uncomfortable, tectonic alliance between the fearful, dominant minority and the individuals of the fearful majority, an ironically mutual commitment to deal with these instincts through the mythological State by subversively refining this idea and urging its transformation into a State real in the world. Until this disguise, this subversion and their foundation in the mythology of the State ceases, the State will avoid modernity and self-responsibility will be denied.

This is the conceptual sequence by which the State has been established as a mythological idea and by which self-responsibility has been denied. The means by which we will in this work explore these concepts is through a particular notion of liberalism.

LIBERALISM

The relationship between these sets of concepts, and the means by which we will understand their varying mythological characteristics, will be examined through a particular notion of liberalism. This is not liberalism in the sense of an ideology of individual civil or economic freedom, except as a reflection of a deeper sense of that notion.

The interpretation of liberalism developed here takes its starting point from Foucault's argument that one must always suspect that one governs too much. So liberal thought starts with society and considers what makes it necessary for there to be a government. Consequently, governmentality[28] should not be exercised without a critique that presumes that question. Liberalism is that critique. The position adopted here is that Foucault is correct, as far as he goes. There is the production of an ideology of individual freedom but it is only the popular myth of freedom behind which, and disguised by it, is another process of liberalism. This other process accepts that liberalism is a process of critique but it goes on to say that it typically adds a new, reforming, positive programme. The historical purpose of this dual strategy, reflected in separate but connected trajectories, is to identify and correct weaknesses in whatever is the then-contemporary phase of liberal political arrangements. We will see this dual strategy at work in the trajectory of the idea of the mythological State from Hobbes through Locke and Kant to Rawls and Hayek, disguising the trajectory of the embedding of mythological practices from the pastoral practices of the sovereign State to governmentality and then to the market. These two evolving trajectories of idea and practice, which will be seen to converge in the work of Hayek but are also suggested in that of Locke, Rousseau and Kant, are the two principal elements of the political myth, so liberalism, as a critique and proposer of amended programmes, is a mythological strategy.

REASON AND MYTH

Standing behind but also infiltrating the broad argument presented here is that reason and myth are closely and positively connected in the thought of those in the political tradition, despite what would be their assertions to the contrary. Such assertions can be given a feather weight because their respective political philosophies will be seen to have demonstrably mythological foundations.

Reason is connected to mythology by them in one of two ways, either as a justification for entry into political arrangements that are mythological or as an incentive for a supposed departure from such arrangements. The former are typified by claims about the rational nature of the decisions taken by individuals to depart from the irrational state of nature or its equivalent. Hobbes, Locke, Rousseau, Kant and Rawls are in this category, as key figures in the thought and practice of liberalism, in the sense intended here by that term. The latter are typified by arguments that it is the supposed departure from the oppressive government of the State that will allow the development of liberal freedom, autonomy and responsibility. Hayek is in this category.

In both cases, I will argue that reason is used in the service of mythological practice, principally as a disguise for it, the effect being a mere eclipse of the real mythology that continues to thrive in its shadow. This is clear in both Parts I–III and Part IV. Parts I–III are an extended exploration of the phased trajectory of the idea of the State as a mythological entity and so extensively canvass this issue in the political tradition from Hobbes to Rawls, Hayek and Pettit. Part IV is an examination of the phased trajectory of the embedding of political mythology in the lives of men and women. In both cases, this relationship between reason and myth, and how reason plays this subversive role as the myth is embedded, is foundational. In fact, given that it is our instincts that are at the heart of political mythology, then instinct and not reason is the key to a proper understanding of the State. So it is that reason takes a secondary, although important, role in this picture, acting as this disguise to prevent what might otherwise be greater questioning of the disposition to subject oneself to the mythological State.

IMPLICATIONS

If it can be convincingly argued that the slow refinements of the idea and practices of the State since Hobbes are the refinements of the mythology of the State, then certain implications will be argued to follow. First, the 'modern' State cannot be regarded as modern, despite certain apparently modern features, but is an entity primarily concerned to sustain the forgoing of individual self-responsibility, that it is a mythological entity. It promotes 'contract, consent, liberty, law and rights' but only in the service of 'sovereignty, *raison d'état,* will, decision and friend/enemy.' Second, individuals are the subject of inducement but are substantially complicit in this, for the purpose of the relief of fear and the creation of sympathetic conditions of existence. Otherwise, especially for those who are either not compliant or who are unwilling to forgo self-responsibility, subjection is imposed by strategies of the State, by its dominant interests and by its agents and allies. Third, the political theorists who have conceived and refined this idea of the State are part of a tradition whose key presumptions are mythological and whose work has comprised the repair and maintenance of the dominant political myth. Fourth, pre-Enlightenment State practice applies mythologically across social space through the universal forgoing of self-responsibility and the establishment of regimes to fine-tune compliance.

These are the implications of seeing that our key political presumptions are not primarily rational but instinctual, and that our principal political ideologies, liberalism and republicanism, are strategies which have functioned to create and sustain the political mythology, at the epicentre of which is the mythological State.

OUTLINE

The three principal elements of this work are: first, an argument for the phased trajectory of the idea of the mythological State; second, irrespective of the intentions of the thinkers considered but within the long tradition of political theorising, an argument for the establishment and slow emergence of this idea of the State into its present form through 'work on myth'; and third, an argument for the phased trajectory of the embedding or, literally, the embodiment of this mythological idea of the State in the material practices of individuals, how individual subjects come to think and behave mythologically. The latter is further 'work on myth.' The balance of the work is structured as follows:

The Nature of Political Mythology

Chapter 2 presents an outline of the theories of myth provided by Plato and Blumenberg. The key features of the latter are identified and a range of amendments are suggested. It is argued that the Western constitutional democratic State features all the key characteristics of a mythological entity.

Establishment and Refinement

Chapter 3 explains how the idea of the State came to be established as a mythological magnitude through the work of Hobbes and was then worked on by Locke and Montesquieu to constitute its power, to begin to bring the fate of the myth into man's hands and to add sympathy to its fearsomeness, as necessary mythological refinements of the absolutist Hobbesian idea.

Chapter 4 examines the significance of Rousseau in identifying a key flaw in the Hobbesian myth, even following its refinement by Locke and Montesquieu, in particular the lack of engagement of its citizens, and the correction of this through the notion of the general will. There follows in Chapter 5 an exploration of how the notion of the general will was taken up by Kant, with the effect of correcting weaknesses in the idea of the mythological State through the application of the imperatives of Reason and through his own political strategies.

Modernisation

Chapters 6 to 9 argue that the disposition to mythologise, that is the disposition to affirm and to work on myth within and beyond the political tradition, has continued into the modern era. This comprises an examination of three contemporary theorists of the State to identify how their work has been profoundly affected by this disposition. Chapter 6 explains how the mythological State of Kant has been transported into contemporary analysis by Rawls, although he unsuccessfully attempts to correct and reprogramme its fear-eliminating and sympathetic nature. Chapter 7 is an exploration of the work of Hayek, in which his argument to depose the State is better seen as having it govern at a distance, so varying but retaining its mythological credentials. In Chapter 8, Pettit's republicanism is examined as being subject to this broad disposition. Chapter 9 considers and responds to the case put by Loader and Walker in defence of the State, that the State can in fact eliminate fear, and which is therefore against the broad argument put here.

Embodiment

Chapters 10 and 11 explore how this continually refined idea of the State as myth has been realised subversively through changes in the material practices of individuals, how myth has become the way we live politically as well as the way we think. The intersection of the work of Wittgenstein, Elias and Foucault is examined in this regard. Drawing on an elaborated account of liberalism initially inspired by Foucault, the work is completed by briefly revisiting the practical effect of the work of Hayek, seen here as connecting the trajectory of the idea of the mythological State (Parts I–III) with that of evolved, embedded practice (Part IV). Through this it is argued that the idea of the mythological State has disguised the production of docile and productive individuals as free, autonomous and responsible, thereby allowing a claim that it despatches the problems of fear and desire, respectively. Thus has the idea of the mythological State been created, sustained and embodied.

2 The Past as a Figure of the Present and Future

THE DISPOSITION TO MYTH: PLATO AND BLUMENBERG

The argument to be presented here is that, from within the long tradition of political theorising about the State and by refashioning elements manufactured by his predecessors in that tradition, Hobbes fabricated a new idea of the State. Further, it will be argued that this idea has been worked on in turn by his successors within that tradition even up to now. It will be argued that the Hobbesian idea of the State was mythological.

These claims require an outline of the model of myth being tested here, by comparison with which the work of Hobbes may be considered mythological. This outline is the principal focus of this chapter. This is not an examination of mythological theory generally, only of the particular approach used here, that proposed especially by Hans Blumenberg. Some attention is also given to a particular reading of the Platonic notion of myth which has an interesting resonance with the work of Blumenberg. The reason for selecting Blumenberg from among the wide number of theorists of myth is that his approach provides particular opportunities for insights into the political tradition. Later, we will look at the extent to which the notion of the State that has emerged from Hobbes and his successors in the tradition can be considered to be a sustained mythological entity. If this notion of the State does satisfy such an assessment, it will allow a judgement to be made about the extent to which Hobbes and the others have been mythological in their thinking. That is, the extent to which this tradition is mythological.

Although the work of Blumenberg is the principal theoretical reference point of this analysis, it will be argued that there are important intersections with the Platonic notion of myth, especially as it is explored by the work of Brisson. Further, apart from its broad explanatory force regarding the Hobbesian notion of the State, the choice of Blumenberg's mythological work is made here because he has offered, along with significant praise, telling criticisms of the work of Ernst Cassirer, whose work *The Myth of the State* remains a benchmark for the application of mythological theory to the State. The arguments presented here are therefore proposed as an advance on the work of Cassirer, principally because, first, his concept of myth is oppositionist regarding forms of rule rather than having features that are conserved and reconfigured in response to the varying demands of different eras, and, second, because he cannot see myth as working in tandem with reason. In this context, neither is the work of Blumenberg accepted as flawless. Several significant amendments are made here to both transform and extend the application of his analysis, especially as a basis for an enhanced application of mythological theory to the State.

The Past as a Paradigm for Present and Future—Plato and Myth

Although this work will draw primarily on the mythological theorising of Blumenberg, the intersections of his work with that of Plato will be informative in the elaboration of the model developed here.

For Plato, *muthos* was a message by means of which a community transmits from generation to generation that which it preserves in memory of its past.[1] In that way the past becomes the present whenever it is transmitted and is set apart so it is made the paradigm of the present and future.[2] This is not to say that the story remains the same, since 'a message experiences a certain number of transformations each time it is transmitted' but writing can minimise this by recording the latest version of the tradition on the subject.[3] For Plato, these transformations are fabrications but not from nothing. As Brisson observes: "The poet makes this 'myth,' not by creating something from nothing, but by taking up one of more element(s) of a specific tradition . . . in the manner of a story. This is done to either preserve or recall the memory of these elements, in accordance with a specific context."[4] Regarding 'specific context,' Brisson states: 'In each tragedy, well-known myths are taken up and retold according to the preoccupations of the city of the time. Their context was marked by . . . religious, political and competitive aspects.'[5] That is, myth is engaged as a means of dealing with, among other things, political issues of the day.

Importantly, the communication of myth as a discourse is the transmission of a fabrication or imitation or copy of the reality to which it refers but the process of representing it through language makes reality appear 'albeit in another mode: that of the presence of absence.' It is an illusion. That is, 'By means of this artifice, the myth-tellers and the poets try to make their audience forget the real absence of the god or hero for whom they give up their own identities; not only in word, but also in deed, since they sometimes take on the attitudes which correspond to the words they relate.' The intention of this communication is to provoke a precise spoken and/or acted reaction from the addressee.[6] Myth may be illusory but it is 'formidably effective.' It is intended to persuade children 'and the majority of adults in whom reason has not attained, or will never attain, the ultimate stage of its development' to imitate and thereby 'settle into habits and second nature in the body, the speech and the thought.' Thereby, the communication being so intense, the actual absence is forgotten so that an identification process begins which modifies the physical and moral behaviour of the receiver.[7]

The purposes of all this technique are varied. Certainly, it is to free oneself from the fear of death, as the dialogue between Socrates and Cebes regarding the eschatological myth in the *Phaedo* shows: 'You are afraid, as children are, that when the soul emerges from the body the wind may already puff it away and scatter it,' to which Cebes replies 'Probably even in us there is a little boy who has these childish terrors. Try to persuade him not to be afraid of death as though it were a bogy,' which elicits from Socrates, 'What you should do is to say a magic spell over him every day until you have charmed his fears away.'[8] Myth is curative for an individual. But it is more than that. Myth is comprised of a small number of basic elements yet the relationship between them allows for the fabrication of an almost infinite number of stories. These are stories which, over a long period of time, undergo degradation if there is no poetic intervention.[9] That is, myths require continuous reworking to keep them relevant. One cause of this reworking, another purpose to which this technique is put, is politics: 'the founder of the city must provide the poet with the molds that they must employ to cast, out of the "wax" of sensible things, the artifacts that are myths. These molds (*tupoi*) are the laws (*nomoi*).'[10]

Brisson continues, 'Plato's goal in (opting for persuasion rather than violence) is that the behaviour of the citizens of the city—whether the ones described in the *Republic* or in the *Laws*—may be in accord with the necessities of communal life—myth is used as a preamble to laws which are about to be proclaimed.'[11] Further, '[t]o persuade the citizens to respect such and such a law, the legislator begins by recalling a myth which illustrates the behaviour required by the law . . . myth plays the role of a paradigm, and it is by means not of education but of persuasion that all those who are not philosophers—that is, the majority of human beings—are led to embrace this paradigm in order to adapt their behaviour to it.'[12] That is, myth performs the important function of acting as a persuasive behavioural paradigm in the political context. Myths are not only about an irrecoverable past. In the *Timaeus,* Plato argues that myth can be a model for preferred political arrangements[13]: 'a political model is elaborated which is intended to regulate the foundation of a real city in a future of unspecified proximity.'[14] Myth acts as a paradigm whose elements and framework guide the development of future arrangements of State.

The reading that Brisson gives Plato, therefore, is that mythology works not on an object which is given to it, but on an object which it gives itself. Further, 'Myth thus appears as a discourse through which is communicated everything that a given community conserves in memory and transmits orally from generation to generation, whether or not through the intermediary of a professional and whether or not this discourse was developed by a technician of oral communication like the poet. As the result of redoubled imitation, myth, since it represents a reality inaccessible both to the intellect and the senses, is destined to model or modify in a more or less spectacular way the behaviour of the souls of those who listen to it.'[15]

There are a number of elements of this Platonic notion of myth which are important for the idea of myth to be developed here. Foremost among these is the notion of tradition. Plato might be regarded as the first analyst of the notion that there was a collective speech which was not only communicated from generation to generation but was worked on, that is refabricated through the reconfiguration of its persistent key elements, to ensure its refinement and varying contemporaneous relevance. In this way the past, the features of which cannot be confirmed or denied, is made the paradigm for both present and future. Its purposes include being curative for individuals in their fear of death and being a persuasive model for preferred behaviour. For him, it is effective on children and those adults whose reason is not fully developed, that is the majority of the population and only philosophers were exempted from this condition. Plato might have acknowledged in this regard that it was myth itself that was a real obstacle to that full development. It works through an imitation which settles down into the habits of body, speech and thought as second nature. That it forces forgetfulness of the original absence, that is that one forgets its illusory nature and regards it as real, is a sign of its formidable effectiveness.

Complementing its function in normalising behaviour, myth also plays an important role for Plato regarding the establishment of preferred political arrangements. It acts as a preamble to the laws and persuades citizens that they are brothers in submission to the prescriptions of the legislators and founders of the city. It also elaborates a paradigm of the city that is intended to regulate the foundation of a real city of the future.[16] Finally, myth is a cultural artifact whose relevance to ancient Greece does not prevent it, through 'constant labor,'[17] from being continuously adapted. These features of Platonic myth resonate with key characteristics of the account of myth proposed by Blumenberg.

Existential Anxiety, Mythological Magnitudes and Covenants: Blumenberg

The key notions in Blumenberg's analysis of myth, and which complement these Platonic elements, include the idea of the absolutism of reality; its realisation in a fearsome mythological magnitude; the constitutional arrangement of the power of that entity; the opportunity for its fate to come into man's hands by covenant for the purpose of establishing man's security in the world by eliminating his fear; that there is continuous work on this myth, thereby establishing its persistence in the world of man; that its fate finally comes into man's hands; that this can provide the opportunity for each individual to ultimately take responsibility for himself; and that the notion of myth has contemporary relevance. It is the combination of these

The Past as a Figure of the Present and Future   23

ideas of Blumenberg, intersecting in interesting ways those of Plato, which form the basis of the idea of myth which is used here to argue for its relevance for an understanding of the modern State. These concepts will now be examined in turn.

Of primary importance in Blumenberg's analysis of the nature of myth is his notion that, as a primary strategy in dealing with profound existential anxiety about what he calls the 'absolutism of reality,' mankind has fabricated powerful entities or 'calculable magnitudes' initially illusory but become real. This anxiety, which is the human response to this absolutism, accompanies the profound awareness early in man's existence that he 'came close to not having control of the conditions of his existence and, what is more important, believed that he simply lacked control of them.'[18] Such anxiety is, however, not merely an original condition but continues as a condition of existence of mankind over all time, including to the present, and so for each individual. For Blumenberg it is the very act of the creating through imagination a magnitude that, unlike the source of existential anxiety, can be comprehended or even visualised, which is the first step along the road to reducing this profound anxiety to controllable levels, in the hope of moving towards its elimination.

As it is first conceived, the magnitude is neutral to the interests of man. As a fabrication, it was the distribution of 'a block of opaque powerfulness, which stood over man and opposite him.' But it did not stand alone, as it came to be among many such powers that were progressively and strategically created and 'are played off against one another or even cancel one another out. Not only to be able to shield oneself from one power with the aid of another, but simply to see one as always occupied and entangled with the other, was an encouragement to man deriving from their multiplicity . . . [this is the] confining of a diffusely distributed quality of uncanniness and unmanageability into enclaves limited by strict sanctions.'[19] For Blumenberg, it is naming which creates, that is which selects, the nature of each power. In the early history of man this typically took the form of a God or gods.[20] Man fills the world with such named entities and thereby brings existential anxiety under control.

But for Blumenberg, although myths are powerful, they are not infinitely so. The 'powers of myth cannot be pictured as able to have what they want in whatever way they like. They have to submit to procedures. . . . Without artifice and disguise, without metamorphosis and compromise, without checks to and retardation of arbitrary power, it wouldn't come off. . . . Even the most irate god is forced into circumstantiality.' This is the way that myth operates, that is, always in the context of the antithetical motives of 'the consolidation of the state that the world has arrived at as a "cosmos" and the restriction of the absolutism that arises in this process,' i.e., 'constituting' the features that reflect the nature and limits of its power.[21] For Blumenberg, without such agreed limits to the power of these magnitudes, there would presumably be little to distinguish the effect of the myth on man from the anxiety of the absolutism of reality, apart from its mere conceptualisation. However, it will be the argument presented here that this presumption should be the subject of refinement.

Myth allows man to live by this regulated depletion of power.[22] 'There must be a weakening of the superior power which is not carried out only by man, and there must be proofs of its reliability, at least preliminary forms of lawfulness and of fidelity to agreements. The technique of weakening operates through the division of power; the exclusion of omnipotence; rivalry and entanglement in affairs; the mutual jealousy and envy of the powers; their precinct and department mentality; the complication of their genealogies and successions; and the god's defined weaknesses and capacities for distraction.'[23]

Once created, this power is therefore engaged. This is so that its neutrality can be converted to an interest in man.[24] However, engagement is not only achieved circumstantially but also through the striking of agreement. The ability to enter into a covenant or contract is the foundation of the history of the magnitude with men and those who observe its conditions, including through absolute obedience, can be sure of enjoying what is promised due to the magnitude's unconditional sympathy with man.[25] That is, man's obedience to the prescriptions of the covenant will ensure that the fearsome magnitude will be sympathetic to the obedient. This is not merely for the individual man, since the strife that the magnitude can visit on a community is best prevented if there is collective compliance. So there is a significant inducement for all people to ensure the delivery of this collective compliance. A collective will to comply best ensures peace from the Gods, as well as their active sympathy. But with this comes the pain of self-denial that is born of compliance, and especially so if the behavioural features of compliance are determined by something other than oneself, in which case the benefits of peace from the Gods may be outweighed by the pain of the imposition by others of compliance.

But for Blumenberg, the purpose of constructing such magnitudes is to enable man to deal with the absolutism of reality in the hypothetical state of nature,[26] in which he lacks control over the conditions of his existence and consequently experiences the pure state of indefinite anticipation which is anxiety.[27] The function of myth is therefore centred on man's security in the world.[28] Because anxiety cannot be managed indefinitely, this generalised excitement must always be reduced, that is, anxiety must continuously be rationalised into fear of something, importantly 'both in the history of mankind and in that of the individual.'[29] This occurs primarily, not through experience and knowledge, 'but rather through devices such as the substitution of the familiar for the unfamiliar, of explanations for the inexplicable, of names for the unnameable. Something is put forward, so as to make what is not present into an object of averting, conjuring up, mollifying, or power-depleting action. By means of names, the identity of such an entity is demonstrated and made approachable and a way of dealing with it is generated. What has become identifiable by means of a name is raised out of its unfamiliarity by means of metaphor and is made accessible, in terms of its significance, by telling stories. Panic and paralysis, as the two extremes of anxiety behaviour, are dissolved by the appearance of calculable magnitudes to deal with and regulate ways of dealing with them, even if the results of the magical and ritual *quid pro quo* now and then make a mockery of the intention of gaining the favour of the powers on behalf of man.'[30]

In this way, myth expresses as fact that the world and the powers that hold sway in it are not abandoned to pure arbitrariness. However this may be signified, 'whether by a separation of powers or through a codification of competences or through a "legalization" of relationships, it is a system of the elimination of arbitrariness.'[31] Even the names attributed and the stories associated with myth are told in order 'to kill fear' of what we are not acquainted with, and bestow trust.[32]

But mythologising goes beyond this transformation of existential anxiety, which is the primal fear without a particular source, into fear, which is of something. Myth transforms this anxiety into distance, to elaborate it as something concretely perceptible 'for instance, in the way in which, in ritual, the numinous object is shown, presented, conveyed in a procession, displayed, or touched.' In this way, 'fear [may be] reduced in intensity in the milder forms of awe and reverence, wonder and amazement.' But the numinous is not only reduced in this way. It is also then distributed 'to objects, persons, directions. . . . While the "reduction" function relates to what was originally and involuntarily uncanny, the function of transfer and simulation affects things that of themselves neither have this quality at all nor can attain it, as in the distinction that is accorded to priestly persons, chiefs, and shamans.' In effect, numinousness is converted into a regulated institution through myth, which is also to say that 'myth allows man to live by depleting superior power.'[33]

For Blumenberg, such mythical magnitudes are not created instantaneously. As for Plato, only by persistent work on myth is myth made manifest.[34] This work on myth is first constituted by its conversion from an original bearer to a prototype with higher mythical pregnance, thereby allowing some reliable authority to certify human experience. By this transition, a status of significance as the emergence 'from the diffuse surrounding field of probabilities,' is attained. However, although we may deal with this significance by reverence, astonishment, enthusiasm, obedience, rejection, protective custody or conservation, the charging of parts of the human world as pregnant in this sense is not something we can choose to do or even decisively imagine. An entity evolves into such a status and, having attained it, it becomes capable of resisting effacement or diffusion, for example by 'time, which nevertheless is suspected of being able to produce pregnance through the process of aging.'[35] And so a mythological tradition, which is the persistence of old questions, is established.

This does not prevent later speculation about the primeval origin of the myth.[36] For example, their connection to an original state of nature, whose overcoming is part of the *logos* of myth,[37] means that the evolution of myth has the force of gravity and that the pace of that is necessarily glacial. Although Blumenberg does not specifically say so, by this is meant that this evolution can take place within a community over many generations, as indicated by Plato. It is this which constitutes the tradition within which its interpreters, for example its poets and theorists, exist and work.

As to the question of how myths both emerge and then persist, Blumenberg makes several suggestions. They may have emerged at the behest of those who would benefit most from their creation, in the manner in which the priests were accused during the Enlightenment of having been the inventors of religion,[38] although Blumenberg's own analysis of myth as the primary means of satisfying the human desire to limit fear seems to discourage this as a first cause. This is not to say that their creation for the benefit of particular interests cannot have been an important secondary cause. In a separate argument but one that relates to the persistence of myth, he has argued that the disposition to reoccupy pre-Enlightenment questions is an identifiable feature of post-Enlightenment thought, which is to say that we have not yet fully entered into an age of Enlightenment.[39] Another take on the same explanation would be that the persistence or reoccupation of myth reflects the persistence of existential fear, real or imagined, as a condition of man. This would bring together important themes from his major works, that is *Work on Myth* and *The Legitimacy of the Modern Age*. The implication of this reoccupation is that the mythological perception of the world persists even though 'enlightened' or non-mythologically rational perceptions are available. The consequence of Blumenberg's argument is that the world continues largely to be seen, and beliefs and practices remain, in mythological terms.

Although myth is not infinitely powerful, for Blumenberg its aspiration is finally fulfilled, albeit by theodicy and the speculative philosophy of history. Its fulfilment not only moderates the difference in power between Gods and men, depriving it of its bitterest seriousness, but also reverses it, with the fate of myth coming into man's hands.[40] So, when combined with the absolute obedience towards the magnitude in the context of the covenant, not only is there a mutually formative relationship between man and his mythical magnitudes but it is also one in which there is finally an opportunity for the shift from domination by a created powerful entity to one whose nature comes to be determined by man. Although Blumenberg does not say so, this allows for the possibility that the means by which the magnitude comes 'into man's hands,' first into those of its 'chiefs and shamans,' is a competitive process. That is, this sees the emergence of dominant interests who come to determine the meaning of and the strategy for the minimising of fear and the expression of sympathy. Such interests would therefore be the principal beneficiaries of such strategies, so long as there are means by which all others may be brought to either induced or enforced acceptance of what is determined to constitute fear and sympathy.

However, in this determination, myth should not be projected onto any scheme of Progress. On the contrary, it 'has its own procedure. . . . The world ceases to contain as many monsters. In a sense that initially is not ethical at all, but more nearly physiognomic, the world becomes "friendlier." It approaches what the man who listens to myth needs: to be at home in the world. It is true that the generations of the gods supplant one another, in dominion over the world, by means of deception, cunning and cruelty, but as power becomes more consolidated, its exercise becomes more bearable. . . . What is decisive for the function of myth is that something that one could call the "quality" of the divine is represented as not originally being given, from the beginning or from eternity.'[41] In his search to end existential anxiety, myth becomes the condition of the life of man. That is, man lives not with but within and through myth.

As to its contemporary relevance, Blumenberg indicates that myth has been mistakenly assigned,

> so definitively to an 'epoch' that everything after that can only be a specialty of the histories of literature and art. The identification of myth with 'its' primeval epoch places the accent of theory on the question . . . of its origin. Only if we take into consideration the history of myth, to the extent that it is not primeval, will we be able to approach the question that we naturally ask: What after all does the disposition towards mythical ways of looking at things consist in and why is it not only able to compete with theoretical, dogmatic, and mystical ways, but actually increased in its attractiveness by the needs that they awaken? No one will want to maintain that myth has better arguments than science . . . Nevertheless it has something to offer that . . . still constitutes satisfaction of intelligent expectations. The quality on which this depends can be designated by the term significance.[42]

Finally, as a consequence of all this, Blumenberg sees the *non plus ultra* of myth, which cannot be eliminated since it is a disposition of man, as proposed by Schopenhauer, which is 'the exclusiveness of the subject's responsibility to himself and for himself.'[43] In this, myth has come into man's hands, not in the assumption into the dominant myths determined by the influence of dominant interests, but as the assumption by individuals of the capacity to determine each their own mythology.

THE EXTENSION OF MYTHOLOGICAL THEORY

The internal logic of this broad argument by Blumenberg appears to be robust. He has identified in the absolutism of reality the cause of the creation of fearful mythological magnitudes and therefore of the need for engagement by which the attempt may be made to eliminate, 'to kill' fear. This elimination is attempted especially through the striking of a testable covenant through which submission brings the expression of mythological sympathy towards man through the actions of the magnitude. He argues that the further reduction of fear comes through the dispersal of the magnitude across a network of functions and functionaries, by which there is the weakening of the superior power by which man then lives. He outlines the means by which such magnitudes are constructed through persistent attention and refinement over time, as well as the logic of the evolution of myth such that its future comes to lie in man's hands. He argues that this evolution is not to be seen in any sense as inevitable progress but that myth nonetheless has contemporary relevance. These elements of the broad argument appear to be coherent.

However, there does appear to be at least one troubling matter here. Blumenberg argues that the process of engaging the magnitude must lead to its weakening and that it is by that weakening that man can live. This emphasis does not seem to be right, particularly at the inception of the magnitude but even subsequently. Irrespective of arguments regarding the responsibility for its instigation, the first cause of the creation of the magnitude is its representation of existential anxiety produced by the absolutism of reality, in the history of both the species and of each individual. This 'reality' or anxiety must therefore not only be absolute in its nature but it must also be a profound condition of all human existence. Its representation by myth must therefore be not only absolutely fearsome, that is before the varying strategies are developed to attempt to eliminate this fear, since it is absolutely powerful. It must also be an ever-present condition, persisting in that state over time. Under these circumstances, man must continue to require a means of its representation which is fully empowered. That is, weakening this entity might be an argument for reducing fear, but it denies the premise for its creation. Neither does it make the notion of the need to bring the entity into a state of sympathy for man meaningful: it would be insignificant that a weakened entity is sympathetic to man. A fully empowered but effectively engaged and fully sympathetic magnitude would satisfy the needs of mankind but a weakened magnitude would not. Blumenberg seems to be opting for the latter.

A better way to look at this issue, while remaining within the terms of Blumenberg's broad argument, is that the magnitude remains absolutely fearsome throughout its evolution over time and that the engagement that comes by entering into a covenant seeks to combine, rather than to weaken, that fearsomeness with an equally strong sympathy. In this way, the magnitude remains absolutely fearsome but can still be sympathetic towards mankind. This combination would be effected through continuing and absolute obedience, thereby both inducing self-restraint by the magnitude and generating such sympathy. By the covenant, man draws himself up to the magnitude, the magnitude does not descend. The elimination of fear becomes the aspiration to be absorbed into the fearsome. That at least is the induced belief, built on the anxiety from the absolutism of reality. In effect, mankind generates absolute sympathy from persistent absolute fear through absolute submission to a fabricated absolute power, aspiring to become in the end a part of that absolute fearsomeness. This four-part absolutism will be argued to comprise the archetypal conception of the State, the elements of which provide the material for the subsequent conceptual fabrications of the State by political theorists within the tradition.

Absolutism is thereby not an optional feature of the archetypal concept because to have created an absolutely fearsome entity and then negotiate a covenant to progressively weaken it would trigger the re-emergence of existential fear. This would be a self-defeating strategy. The implication of this is that submission to the magnitude is always conditional. That is, despite existential fear and even at the archetypal level, one forgoes always and only on the belief that fear will be eliminated. Otherwise one's fear may be worsened and even in the state of existential fear we understand that. However, this conditionality also means that, even though we forgo, we always retain some fear, for the entity may either fail its covenant to eliminate fear or be merely fearsome itself.

The implication of this re-drawing of Blumenberg's argument is that the dispersal of the magnitude, through the deployment of functionaries and the proliferation of preferred practices, is not a weakening but an extension and therefore a strengthening of the magnitude across social space. This has two effects. First, this dispersal allows for the expression by individuals of their submissive forgoing of responsibility by becoming themselves part of the magnitude as experts and functionaries. They thereby share 'membership' of the magnitude and aspire to sovereign power and fearsomeness. More importantly, the individual must accept the claim that, in return for this submission, the magnitude does satisfy its three responsibilities: that it does give effect to the conversion of existential anxiety into fear, that it can then effectively eliminate that fear and that it can combine this with the sympathy that submission brings. Becoming part of it allows the exercise of some influence to ensure the fulfilment of these purposes. It is 'some influence' because the 'becoming part of' never fully absorbs the individual, who preserves a modest protective distance from this creation that he expects to limit his existential fear. However, it does motivate the colonisation of the magnitude to ensure, ideally, universal sympathy but, more typically, strong sectional interest. The effect of these two purposes, submissiveness and then gaining control, in combination is that we create what it is that we wish to create us and others: we are submissive, or 'not fearsome,' only on condition that others become so. This interpretation is not inconsistent with Blumenberg's own claim that the first intention of myth is fulfilled in that it finally comes into man's hands, although it does give that outcome a fundamentally different purpose.

The account of myth which emerges from this redrawing of the Blumenberg argument comprises some essential elements. These include that man intentionally created, continues to create and sustains magnitudes as absolutely fearsome, into which he can be incorporated and as a conceptual limit of existential anxiety. Such creation may have been instigated by those legitimately interested in the limiting of fear or by those who would exploit the obedience that its fearsome nature would induce. Either way, absolute obedience is conditional but typically willing on the part of individuals due to the desire to limit existential anxiety by objectifying it and thereby converting it to fear. Fear in this context would especially but not exclusively include fear of others. Such absolute obedience also has the strategic purpose, as the corollary to the limiting of fear, of inducing the magnitude to express an absolute sympathy for mankind as a constraint to the absolute fearsomeness for which it was created.

Importantly, on the condition that the magnitude fulfils its role to radically limit fear, this obedience effectively constitutes an induced but willing forgoing by each individual of responsibility 'to and for oneself', that is the responsibility to eliminate fear without being fearsome because the individual feels, or is made to feel, incapable of realising such responsibility. By 'eliminating fear without being fearsome' is simply meant that individuals who become responsible to and for themselves would not be the cause of fear, as their principal legitimate concern is limited to their own affairs, save for non-selfish action that is guided by respectful agreement. The magnitude would be required to progressively promote such respectful agreement by constructively engaging with any person intruding into the lives of others, who is acting without self-responsibility. Other than through the application of this principle, the magnitude could not itself intrude. The elimination of fear would not be its primary goal. Blumenberg doesn't canvass this issue but it is argued here to be a logical extension of his account of the *non plus ultra* of myth, and one necessary to properly appreciate the significance of the radical critique of myth that he has undertaken.

So, this responsibility is transferred to the magnitude but this transfer cannot be done without making the magnitude absolutely fearsome, even if conditionally so: it is this transfer of responsibility from each individual to the magnitude which constitutes the full empowerment—and thereby generates the inherent fearsomeness—of the magnitude. Further, for the purpose of elaborating the form and practice of this necessary fearsomeness, of this consequential obedience and of the consequential constraint through absolute sympathy, a covenant is reached which must be personal between each individual and the magnitude, since the limiting of fear is ultimately testable only at the individual level. Blumenberg examines but doesn't fully elaborate the notion of this covenant but it is rigorously within his logic. He talks of the need to 'constitute' the nature and limits of the power of the magnitude. This covenant is therefore a 'constitution' of the magnitude, being its form and its relation with each individual, and which can be the subject of refinement, if necessary over an extended period. Importantly, the generation of absolute sympathy is not a weakening of the magnitude but takes place in the context of its extension across social space and is therefore a complementary strengthening of its fearsomeness, the effect of which is balanced by the generation of absolute sympathy through obedience. In the face of questions regarding the need that absolutism be the benchmark here, it is to be remembered that it is a mythological archetype or template being conceived and not a playing out of such an archetype in the world, wherein compromise and qualification would be featured. Hobbes and his successors in the tradition will be argued to have undertaken that playing out.

What constitutes this absolute sympathy, how it takes its form through submission, is the subject of proposal from within the community of individuals over time and is typically subject to competitive strategies and so wide variation, but in its essence it is constituted by a focus on the welfare and sense of security of the individual. The forms which sympathy may therefore take include the forceful constraint of fearsome individuals, the delineation of actively fearsome action by the magnitude itself, the creation of spheres of activity from which the magnitude withdraws except by retaining its responsibility to limit fear, as well as directly sympathetic actions by the magnitude, such as the creation of conditions of existence as self-fulfilment and personal welfare. The creation of spheres of activity from which the magnitude 'excludes' itself, perhaps such as certain theological or economic interests, would not preclude, in fact would positively allow for, alliances between interests active in those areas and the magnitude itself, through which those interests are promoted. In fact, such alliances are likely to be promoted by the magnitude, as much as by those interests, to fill such a vacuum created by 'excluded' activity.

It will also be argued here that these variations of absolute sympathy constitute, apart from material conditions, the concept and forms of individual rights and that absolute obedience is not inconsistent with the notion of individual rights, since the expectation of myth to attempt the elimination of absolute fear is always retained by the individual. This is so even if this expectation always requires absolute obedience to the magnitude. So, obedience to the prescriptions of the magnitude is required, but only to the extent that the magnitude can claim that it satisfies its responsibility to limit fear and be sympathetic. This obedience qualifies individuals for rights and defines the nature of those rights. The issue of such rights will be explored further in this work.

It is an important consequence of this account of myth that, because of this continuous responsibility to limit fear and be the subject of proposals regarding the preferred forms of sympathy, the magnitude is, beyond its original conception, in no respect ever effectively neutral to the interests of man. Further, it is the desire to establish preferred regimes for dealing with the fear-sympathy nexus that induces individuals to 'become part of' the magnitude, for example by adopting the role of expert or functionary or by aligning themselves to potentially dominant interests or simply by adopting its behavioural prescriptions, as means of exercising control over this creation. Importantly, it is through the submission of the individual that the arbitrary exercise of power by the magnitude is constrained. This desire to control the magnitude is symptomatic of the competitive strategies regarding what should constitute absolute sympathy. In short, this gaining control by 'becoming part of' is still the forgoing of responsibility to and for oneself, since the control gained is only to ensure the limiting of fear and the promotion of absolute sympathy. This requires the empowerment that only this forgoing can create.

The full consequence of all this is that this 'becoming part of,' which emerges in the context of the generation and refinement of the covenant and which leads to 'gaining control,' means that the fate of the magnitude finally comes into man's hands, albeit through his own submission. Ironically, this gaining control thereby also allows the possibility that the apparent conceptual flaw and inherent instability of this entire strategy, that is that fear can be limited by creating an absolutely fearsome entity and then constraining this fearsomeness by inducing the entity to be absolutely sympathetic to the obedient, could be eliminated. This elimination would be achieved by creating a non-mythological magnitude that was not inherently fearsome but which actively promoted individual responsibility to and for oneself, in the form of individuals who addressed their fear without themselves becoming fearsome and assumed the responsibility to themselves create the sympathetic conditions of their existence. But this would require an acceptance, rather than a rejection, of existential fear. Courage as the price of self-responsibility.

In summary, the mythology of Plato and especially of Blumenberg, in particular the nature of the magnitudes that are imagined within it for the dual purposes outlined, appears robust, subject to certain amendments or extensions. These are that the magnitude comes into man's hands first through a covenant between each individual and the magnitude and then through a competitive process, producing dominant sectional interests who are the principal beneficiaries of the attempt to eliminate fear and the expression of sympathy; that the fearsomeness of the magnitude is dispersed across social space by coming into man's hands but that this dispersal does not dilute that fearsomeness; and that the evolution of the myth is glacial in the sense that its structural refinement and its coming 'into man's hands' can extend over the life of a series of generations in a community due to a continuing attempt to realise the mythological ideal.

THE STATE AS MYTHOLOGICAL

With the observations of both Plato and Blumenberg as reference points, we will now begin to examine whether it is arguable that the State is characterised by these features, that it can be seen as a mythological magnitude.

Preliminary Comments

As Plato demonstrates, the idea of applying mythological theory to the State is a coherent one, both in relation to preferred political arrangements and preferred individual behaviour. We will recall that for Plato, *muthos* is a preamble to the laws, as well as a means of persuading citizens regarding behaviour, and at the same time elaborates a paradigm of the idea of the city which can be worked on over time. Such an application is best seen in the context of thinking within a tradition, that is there is an original conception of the 'well-known myth,' the elements of which are reconfigured and represented 'according to the preoccupations of the city at the time. Their context was marked by . . . political and competitive aspects.'[44] This points to an aspect which Blumenberg does not emphasise in the manner it will be emphasised here, that is that work on myth not only produces reconfigurations of the elements of the myth but that this can take place over a very extended period, for example over many generations or even centuries, carried forward by tradition. This would only happen in the case of an important myth, such as that of the City or State, as a primary means of attempting to deal with constant anxiety and fear.

To this point we are not yet talking about the State itself but the idea of the State. As has been indicated, there are three identifiably distinct but related elements of the expression of myth: the ideal or archetypal State that rests in the presumptions of the tradition and whose elements are reconfigured over time; those various reconfigured ideas of the State, fabricated for example as institutional arrangements from the elements of that archetype by political theorists working within that tradition; then finally the State itself, real in the world and attempting to realise, for example by its institutional arrangements and by the application of policy and practice, that archetype and those ideas. Here we are still dealing with the first of these elements. It is in subsequent chapters that there will be an examination of the second, that is the various reconfigurations and refinements made by Hobbes and his successors within the tradition down to Hayek and Pettit, then finally an examination of how this traditional idea has been made into practice, the State in the material world, revealed through the work of Elias and Foucault.

Seeing the State within a Mythological Framework

The remainder of this section will comprise an application of the accounts of Plato and Blumenberg, extended and amended in the manner already outlined, from their chosen domain of mythology to that of the State. That is, imagining the State as an example of the mythological magnitudes of which, in particular, Blumenberg speaks. Although Plato does, Blumenberg does not make such an extension, but, with the amendments that have been introduced, it is argued here that this is an appropriate and informative application: it can be fairly argued that mankind is not only disposed to create myths for the purpose of limiting fear through the construction of explanatory systems, for example in the construction of his spiritual apparatus, but that we have also applied this disposition to myth in the construction of social institutions, using the construct of the purely mythological magnitude as the archetypal model. Myth not only has archetypal characteristics but also has something like a collective or 'tectonic' presence in the public and personal affairs of mankind. It is argued here that one such application can be seen in the conception and ongoing work on establishing and refining the State. That is, the State appears to share the essential features of a mythological magnitude and to operate in a manner consistent with that nature.

If this mythological framework is applicable to the understanding of the nature of the State and its relationship to individuals and therefore to the original questions posed here, it should be able to be argued that the idea of the State was established and has been the subject of continuing attempts at reconfiguration and refinement over a long period with the intention that it adopts a form, with an appropriate range of characteristics, which is identifiably mythological in the sense outlined. This process of refinement implies that there is an archetypal State form drawn from this collective or 'tectonic' presence, which would satisfy man's mythological disposition and to which there would be full allegiance, distinct from, but used as a reference for, the variety of actual State forms to which only conditional allegiance is offered. This conditionality is due to the concern that individuals hold about the extent to which the real State form will satisfy the expectations embedded in this archetype. Given the persistent and pervasive effect of fear, there is only formal conditionality regarding the covenant between the individual and the archetypal State: there is absolute obedience to the idea of the absolutely fearsome entity since there is certainty that there will be absolute sympathy in return, to deal with the 'absolutism of reality' in the form of existential fear. This is not to claim that there is an existing form of the State which has fully realised such an archetypal or tectonic form but it is to claim that an examination of the emergence of such existing forms will reveal varying protracted attempts to realise this archetype which rests tectonically in our social, and in particular our political, tradition. Here, it is the emergence of the constitutional parliamentary State that is examined, although by direct implication this argument can be applied to other variations of the State form.

Other key mythological characteristics include that the idea of the State has a form over and opposite man, with an archetypal nature that is absolutely fearsome, and that both its authority and empowerment—and therefore its fearsomeness—are the consequence of the willing forgoing of authority and power of each individual, that is their sovereignty, to the State. This forgoing is formally unconditional or absolute but only because the State's fearsomeness and sympathy are also absolute. The first purpose of the creation of this idea was the radical limiting of fear, as was imagined to exist in an original state of nature, by transferring the responsibility for this limitation to the State. This obedience becomes conditional rather than absolute when it comes to the actualisation of this archetypal State, since subjects will always be expectant but uncertain that the real State will eliminate fear without itself becoming an arbitrary source of fear.

Following this archetypal conception, there was soon, and there remains, the idea that the State must be engaged through the application of various techniques and strategies, the purpose of which is the commitment to the striking and continuing refinement of a testable covenant between each individual and the State. The purpose of such covenants is to ensure the forgoing of individual sovereignty, that is his submission, and then to protect the individual from any arbitrary fearsomeness by the State and of other individuals by various means. These include having it exercise its fearsome power for the welfare of each individual to further reduce the fear of the obedient but also by displaying absolute archetypal sympathy for man without weakening the absolute fearfulness of the State. The endgame in this process is the unrealised, in fact unrealisable, search for an ideal stasis in which there would be perfect balance between this necessary total fearsomeness and this desired absolute sympathy. To the State in this archetypal form, there would be unconditional obedience. What is forgone in this absolute obedience is the responsibility of each individual to undertake measures to eliminate his fear without himself being fearsome and to create for himself sympathetic conditions of existence.

None of this is to say that the obedience to any real State will be unconditional, since the individual will always reserve judgement whether the real State and its incumbent dominant interests are satisfying the expectations of it to eliminate fear and create sympathetic conditions of existence, that is whether the State has realised its full archetypal or mythological form. Neither is it to say that the forgoing of responsibility to the real State is total, for there are 'secondary' or 'derivative' areas of responsibility beyond the two primary areas for which the individual is responsible, depending on the actual State being considered. It is to say, however, that these secondary areas are always to be seen in the context of the forgoing of responsibility in those two fundamental areas. For example, as we have argued, parents will still be expected to carry responsibility for raising children but to do so in a manner that has children understand that they are to forgo these two areas of responsibility to the State. Equally, throughout in its historical refinement but especially in a neo-liberal context, people will generally be expected to contribute to their own welfare and comfort by generating their own income but the State will ultimately be expected to create the conditions, not necessarily imminently, under which that can occur. Where individuals are unable to contribute in this way, it would become the responsibility of the sympathetic State to do so by one hard method or another.

This archetypal covenant is therefore founded on the full individual submission which is required by the nature of existential anxiety objectified as fear. It is this submission that is the basis for the desire that the State adopt an absolutely sympathetic attitude towards man and thereby that it be engaged through obedience and other strategies to focus on man's security in the world. The direct implication is that this obedience is the instinctive but tactical (that is, for the purpose of attaining this security) forgoing to the

State of responsibility of individuals to and for themselves, from which the State derives its authority and power, that is its fearsomeness. Equally, by incorporating himself into the magnitude through this obedience, the individual shares in its fearsomeness and so has less fear. This is the context within which citizenship should begin to be understood, since the forgoing of self-responsibility, which is the submission, is the first step along the road to this form of self-regulation. Thereby does absolutism ultimately share ground with liberalism. Submission is as much the acknowledgement of one's own willingness to change or be changed in a socially preferred manner as it is that others must be subject to the same. Further, this covenant is the means by which the idea of the State is constituted in its form and practice, this requiring persistence over an extended period of time as the desired stasis is sought. As a consequence, it is argued here that the idea of constitutionalism, including separation of powers, representation and other individual rights—whether civil, political or social—is to be seen as a tactic to limit fear, generate sympathy and allow the gaining of control, premised as its elements are on this forgoing of individual responsibility. This does not soften the empowerment of the State, only gives clarity to the exploitation of that power. Constitutionalism therefore embodies key mythological elements, forming the power of the entity through separation and therefore instituting competition between these separated powers, allowing man to take the destiny of the magnitude into his increasingly empowered hands by representation and ensuring sympathetic conditions of existence by establishing a range of protective and assertive individual rights.

In this context, constitutionalism would be before all else the means of giving regulatory form to the otherwise full but arbitrary power of the fearsome magnitude. It would then still be fearsome but would be the subject of two claims, that it was no longer an arbitrary source of fear and that it would ensure the delivery of the covenant which radically limits fear in return for the submission born of this fear. The notion of absolute submission, which would only be due to a fully realised archetypal State, is not inconsistent with the notion of individual rights since the responsibility of the State to limit fear and be sympathetic, which are the source of such rights, remains the desire of the individual and so requires absolute obedience. Obedience is assured so long as the State satisfies its responsibility, although only conditionally since, despite the promises of absolutism, no State is seen as capable of realising its archetypal form.

It is also argued here that the consequence of the covenant is that the State is extended across, and therefore becomes widely intimate with, social space. By this is meant that, for the purpose of fulfilling its responsibility to attempt to eliminate fear, the practices preferred by the institutions and agencies of the State are extended towards, in fact into, the lives of individual subjects. This reinforces rather than weakens its fearsomeness, since weakening would induce the return of existential anxiety. By the intimacy which this extension or dispersal brings and by the reinforced obedience that results, it can also more easily fulfil its appointed concern for man's security, for example by dealing with fearsome individuals, and his welfare. This dispersal is the progressive extension of citizenship. Should the State not fulfil its responsibilities, the covenant would be further refined or its experts and functionaries replaced. We shall see below that the various governmental-disciplinary practices sponsored by and through the State exemplify the intimacy which comes from this dispersal.

Within the context of this progressive constitutionalism, the arrangements of the mythological State would be required to ensure that there are means by which the inevitable competition between interests, through which the dominant forms of claiming to deal with fear and sympathy are determined, can be resolved. Representation is one means of claiming that this is achieved. Provision is also typically made for the State to exclude itself from various spheres of activity, as a means of asserting that its fearsomeness is constrained. This absence is not to claim that the State forgoes the responsibility to resolve competitive disputes between those competing for that space left vacant by the State, for example between corporations, or that the State itself may not attempt to reoccupy that space *de facto* by alliance with other interests, such as theological interests for the purpose of promoting the civilising process or such as the market as our consideration of Hayek will make clear. It is a consequence of this that the archetypal State is originally conceived as neutral to man but that, given the immediate, persistent and elaborate engagement which has followed its creation, the State can no longer ever be neutral, since it is always required to intervene to limit fear and resolve the competition between the interests that compete for control of the State so that they may determine the preferred forms of fear and sympathy.

Such resolution cannot be too inequitable but, taking advantage of the common willingness to subjection, it is typically sectional and is established through the force of the State itself. The State, through its dominant interests, must exercise this responsibility with some care, attending to the range of competing interests while exercising its own fearsome powers, as the practices of the real State show. That is, the viability of particular governments of the State depends on the common belief that it acts through the covenant in the interests of every individual. Given that the limiting of fear converted from existential anxiety is the ultimate motivation for the referral of these responsibilities to the State, this is confirmation of justification of the forgoing of individual responsibility. That is, none of this is the mere development of rational, utilitarian arrangements of government. In this, the notion of dominant interests is not one which implies that individuals or groups exercise power as a quantitative capacity.[45] Instead, dominant interests are embedded in and reflective of a pattern of features which are the conditions of its existence and which form the conditions of the deployment of power. This pattern of features includes individual existential fear, including both its natural occurrence and its strategic creation by dominant interests; the created magnitude; the disposition to the forgoing of self-responsibility; the methods of dispersal and so on.

As a corollary, given the extent to which the mythological State has come to be engaged over time through progressive constitutionalism, the choice is presented to man to have the State converted into a means by which there may be a return to each individual of self-responsibility. This choice is presented through the process by which there is gaining control through 'becoming a part of' the State. By this constitutionalism and colonisation, the fate of the State comes into man's hands, even though the reality is that the competition for control to promote a preferred arrangement of fearfulness and sympathy largely favours sectional interests. This coming into man's hands is the next element, beyond submission, in the development of the modern notion of citizenship, as it signals the right to make judgements—albeit for the non-dominant in a largely formal manner only—regarding the extent to which dominant interests are in fact dealing with the problems of fear and sympathetic conditions. If the State were to be converted to a form that returned responsibility to individuals, this would need to be triggered by a perception of the seismic flaw at the heart of this mythological or transcendent metaphysical edifice. That is, due first to its own archetypal absolute fearsomeness and then its accommodation of sectional interest in its structural formation and in the establishment of sympathy for man, the State always has to convincingly claim that it satisfies the high risk of maintaining the balance between dominant and more widespread interests. Otherwise it becomes more the cause of fear and lack of universal sympathy than other causes, for example from those dominant interests or from other individuals.

What the State as a mythological magnitude has in its favour against any consideration of the need for such reform is, first, the typical willingness of individuals to forgo responsibility so that fear is eliminated and sympathetic conditions established; second, that the idea allows the option to conditionally appoint interests responsible for the realisation of the two primary responsibilities but their replacement if they fail to satisfy those expectations; third, the process of civilising, or persuasion in Plato's terms, which aligns individuals to mythological arrangements and expectations; and, fourth, a consequential preparedness to continue to refine the arrangements of State through amended prescriptions, or replace its incumbent officials, in the hope that the archetypal State is ever closer. These factors overwhelm any awareness that obedience to the mythological State has come at the high price of forgoing of one's self-responsibility. In the case of the archetypal mythological State, this forgoing of responsibility for oneself would be complete, but in return for this there would be full and effective attention given to the fear-sympathy nexus. It is at the heart of the relationship between the mythological State and the individual that this idealised or archetypal existence is seemingly attainable. That is the power of the illusion of the real mythology. This, the privilege of dominant interests and the consequential high price of forgoing responsibility that continues to be paid for pursuing it over the long historical period during which the modern State has been evolving, constitutes the denied flaw in the arrangement.

Transformation of the State from a conception based on a mythological premise to one which is non-mythological would require that the perception of this flaw would be followed by an acceptance rather than the denial of the existential fear which is the primary motive for the creation of the fearful magnitude. In this Enlightened context, where the idea and practice of the State would remain but not as a fearsome entity, there would therefore be a disposition against fearful obedience. Moreover, the constitutional practices of representation, litigation and the exercise of other rights could be radically different than under a mythological State. The self-responsible individual could be engaged at the centre of any such practice rather than be only peripherally present or even bracketed from such practices. In that context, responsibility to and for oneself does not preclude, in fact it requires as a condition of its existence, mutual respect. Yet none of this is in any sense inevitable Progress, a myth to which the Enlightenment fell victim. It is only the deconstruction of myth and its replacement with a new quality which depends upon the establishment of a revised State form, with non-mythological arrangements and practices.

The argument put by Blumenberg that there should not be an overreaction,[46] that is that the abolition of dominant metaphor or myth should not lead to the rejection of representation born of the desire 'espoused by those who want to decide everything,' since that would 'deprive the weaker person, who previously never had to be found out, of his protection,' is accepted but qualified here. The identification of the State as mythological should not lead to an abolition of the State. It should lead to its reconfiguration, one consequence of which would be that the 'weaker person' would be 'enabled' in a way that is prevented by the manner in which mythological arrangements respond with apparent but false neutrality to the strongest sectional representation.

However, due to the mythological premise of its existence and nature, the likely persistence of its form and nature overwhelmingly outweighs the likelihood of such transformation. It is likely that there will be persistence of mythological belief, practice and perception, which is the provision of answers to or the reoccupation of obsolete, that is pre-Enlightenment, questions for the primary purpose of having a more powerful entity than oneself be responsible for dealing with the fear-sympathy nexus. This outcome also includes, just as the compliant assume mythological modes of behaviour, attributing mythological status to those individuals or groups who through frustration or mere difference are perceived as threatening, either generally to the dominant world picture or directly in a physical manner due to discontent. Consequently, the tactic of the State in response is determined as mythological. In this context therefore, that is where there is the induced but typically willing forgoing of self-responsibility, citizenship itself in its present form would properly be seen as a realisation of mythological thought and practice.

In short, irrespective of the challenges of realising self-responsibility, the idea of the State may properly be considered as mythological, in the sense that Plato intended, and further as a mythological magnitude, in the sense that Blumenberg intended. It is an idea of an entity constructed as fearsome and which must remain so; it is empowered by the forgoing of individual self-responsibility; it has a constitutional form, incorporating separated powers; its constitutional form is colonised by dominant interests; it disperses across social space through the induced or enforced engagement of all individuals; all these features are conditional upon a claim that the fear-sympathy nexus is ultimately being addressed; and the idea of it appears to have been gradually refined over the long term. What is now required is an exploration of the conceptual, then material, emergence of the State to demonstrate whether it has been realised as a real, political magnitude, the subject of continuous work within the political tradition and beyond. That will commence with Hobbes and move to an examination of a series of thinkers in the tradition who followed, were deeply influenced by, varied and elaborated the paradigm of government he established.

Part II
Establishment and Refinement

It is the argument presented here that Hobbes can be seen as the creator of the idea of the State as a mythological magnitude, that he was the initiator of the modern political myth. This is not to say that he worked with a clean palette but that, using arguments familiar to his predecessors and contemporaries, he attempted to resolve the problems that came with the beginning of the violent disintegration of the unitary theological myth. It is to argue that he initiated the modern phase of the political tradition whose participants took the tenets of his argument and have continued to work on the implications of these tenets down to the present. This is not a claim that these individuals were conscious mythologists but, given that the Hobbesian tenets were mythological, that the effect of their work has been to sustain and rework the notion of the mythological State as participants in the mythological political tradition.

3 The Leviathan, the Calling and Their Separation

HOBBES

There are good reasons why a search for the establishment of the modern mythological State might find Hobbes.[1] Even at a first glance, essential elements of such an idea of the State seem to feature in his conception of the Leviathan.

To start with Hobbes is not to say that there was no mythology within the thought of political philosophy before him. Indeed the contrary. Neither is it to say that Hobbes himself was a conscious mythologist. As the owner of a 'highly Opiniative and Magisterial manner'[2] and belonging 'to that phase of the scientific revolution which had not yet relinquished the hope of taking all knowledge for its province,'[3] he would have bristled against such a description. It is incontestable that he regarded himself as a scientist and as one whose intention was to put politics on a scientific basis.

Blumenberg and Hobbes

The pointer to begin looking at Hobbes as a mythological political theorist comes from Blumenberg. The position held by Blumenberg is that, to the extent that philosophy is a process of dismantling things taken for granted, a philosophical anthropology cannot begin with the question whether man's physical existence is what results only from the accomplishments 'of his nature.' Instead, the first proposition of such an anthropology should be that 'It cannot be taken for granted that man is able to exist,'[4] that contingency is a primary condition of existence and that there is nothing inevitable concerning the existence of man. This principle applies not only to man as a species but also man as the product of his social self-construction: not only may his existence have ceased at any time but he may have turned out very differently than he has if contingent circumstances had intervened differently. It is in this context that Blumenberg makes a directly political statement relevant to the argument here. He refers to the Hobbesian State as an artifice constructed by social contract to establish a civil condition for man because his natural condition demonstrates that this ability to exist cannot be taken for granted.

For Blumenberg, what is significant about this is that it explains both the appearance of institutions such as those of the State and also explains the appearance of the absolutist State. The Hobbesian State is an artifact constructed to 'eliminate'[5] the lethal antagonism of the 'state of nature' or 'war of all against all' or the 'absolutism of reality,' all being realisations of absolute contingency and therefore 'contrary to reason.'[6] It is to avoid this absolute contingency, and the resulting existential anxiety that presented itself in the violent religious and political circumstances of the day, that Hobbesian man enters the civil condition through voluntary social contract and constructs a State which is argued here to be mythological in nature. Among these features is that the mythological magnitude performs the dual roles of a creation intended to limit existential anxiety by converting this into fear of itself and yet a creation, despite its absolute power, believed to be manageable by being engaged.[7] By direct implication, since the 'human relation to reality is indirect, circumstantial, delayed, selective, and above all "metaphorical"', mankind is not distinguished by any 'human nature' but by his symbolic forms, such as the State, which he constructs to solve the problem of his existential vulnerability and which are then claimed for and ascribed to his nature, for example as they are by Aristotle, as a political animal. So Blumenberg sees 'no other scientific course for an anthropology except . . . to destroy what is supposedly "natural" and convict it of its "artificiality" in the functional system of the elementary human accomplishment called "life"'.[8]

Hobbes himself emphasises the artificiality of the Leviathan as a construct necessary to solve the problem posed by the combination of man's nature and the hostility of his social predicament. The question that flows from this reference by Blumenberg to Hobbes is whether the Leviathan actually includes all of the essential characteristics of the mythological magnitude, including its absolute empowerment through full submission to it by individuals in return for the claim to deal with the fear-sympathy nexus, the emergence of dominant interests and the prospect of its coming into man's hands. If it does, then the foundation of the argument for the mythological nature of the modern State can begin to be argued. This question will be approached by first examining the Hobbesian enterprise in its own terms. The work of Skinner will inform some of this examination. Then a judgement will be able to be made about the extent of Hobbes' mythological disposition.

Hobbes and the Construction of the Modern State

Hobbes is best seen as a key thinker of the political theoretical tradition, not as a radical or renegade philosopher who wrote one influential work on politics. This 'traditional' perception of Hobbes is the one adopted by

Oakeshott. But Oakeshott does more than merely situate Hobbes in a tradition. He elaborates what a concept of a tradition is and also observes that 'the *Leviathan* is more than a *tour de force* . . . we may consider it in its tradition, and doing so will find fresh meaning in the world of ideas it opens to us.'[9]

Oakeshott speaks generally about the nature of tradition[10] and then identifies three particular traditions, respectively the master conceptions of Reason and Nature, of Will and Artifice and the Rational Will. The first two are for him at the root of European intellectual history, the third not appearing until the eighteenth century. *The Republic* represents the first, the *Leviathan* is the head and crown of the second and the *Philosophie des Rechts* represents the third. The notion of the political tradition argued for here is not that put by Oakeshott, since here it is argued that there is a significant cohering theme whose aspirations and internal inconsistencies are the source of the twists and turns that he separates out, but the broad comments he makes apply to the concept of tradition presented here as the context of the principal argument.

Hobbes' perception of himself might have been as a 'traditionalist' but this was as far as is imaginable from being a mythologist. He saw himself as a scientist and as more than that. Not only did he employ rational methods in the pursuit of his range of scientific interests but his work was also directly focused on addressing the real and urgent problems created by the political turmoil of his time.[11] In effect, he was attempting to justify an idea of the State with which those that want too much liberty and those that want too much authority[12] could be accommodated, that is between the Parliamentarians and the divine rightists defending the Crown, who between them had plunged England into civil turmoil during the seventeenth century. His primary aim was to argue for a political arrangement which would rationally establish a regime of peace and which would be sustained because it was accepted as legitimate. His method was scientific, his aim political.

This is the context of Skinner's account of the poor historical foundation of the influential Whig ideology of an immemorial parliamentary tradition, poor because there had been a deep institutional rupture created by the Norman conquest of 1066, on which much of the Parliamentary position was based.[13] Realising this allowed Hobbes to gather and reinforce the arguments of others against the position of the Parliamentarians, in favour of the *de facto* legitimacy of the royalist line, established by force and then absolutist in nature. This legitimacy was based on the demonstrated capacity of such *de facto* power to draw allegiance through the provision of protection to its subjects, that is, through an argument as to the 'mutual Relation between Protection and Obedience,'[14] to establish a regime of peace as the only rationally arguable alternative to anarchy. On this view, expressed first by such others as Ascham and Nedham, Hobbes established the basis for his analysis of political obligation generally[15] and thereby, along with a diverse company of Christians and secularists as well as royalists and parliamentarians, for his justification of engagement with the newly established Commonwealth in 1649.[16] Much of this thinking by Hobbes and others was based on the presumption of the inherently warlike behaviour to which mankind is disposed, generating a need for someone more potent than the rest that might restrain them by force.[17] So protection constitutes a sufficient title to allegiance, from which follows the validity of any conquering government that delivers protection.[18] It was in this way that Hobbes proudly boasted that he had 'framed the minds of a thousand gentlemen to a conscientious obedience to present government.'[19]

Hobbes' purpose was to eliminate the widespread fear caused by this political turmoil and to do so by claiming legitimacy for particular political arrangements. He felt this fear strongly at a personal level.[20] At the heart of this turmoil was, for Hobbes, 'a general inclination of all mankind, a perpetuall and restless desire for Power after power, that ceaseth only in Death' and that men 'naturally love Liberty, and dominion over others.'[21] In pursuing this purpose, his stated method was to put politics on a scientific basis,[22] that is, reason as the persuader. This is not to deny that he came back to the view, following an early rejection of the humanistic arts, that rational persuasion could be most effective when promoted through rhetoric.[23] The rhetorical devices he preferred included the use of irony and mockery against his opponents, especially the Catholic Church, although not beyond the point where it would lead to violence or offend civilised society, as all men 'ought to endeavour peace.'[24] It was this that generated his solution that clarity about moral virtue comes from seeing virtue as whatever conduces to peace. Then, since whether a given action will conduce to peace remains a matter of opinion, it is necessary to appoint some person or persons as Arbitrator or judge, conformity to whose decisions must be agreed in advance despite the necessarily arbitrary nature of those decisions. That is, this Arbitrator must be a sovereign power.[25] However, this power maintains the peace not merely by arbitration but also by punishment, power and strength and 'by terror thereof he is inabled to conforme the wills of them all.'[26] So the authority of the sovereign Arbitrator must be absolute.

Hobbes' way through to this position was not the simple move of fully empowering the person of the Sovereign or Parliament but to imagine the State as an artifice,[27] as the seat of sovereignty, to make laws, punish and do all else to provide for 'the safety of the people ... [by which] is not meant a bare Preservation, but also all other Contentments of life.'[28] This artifice could be occupied by such particular incumbents as a King or a Parliament. These operate by way of attributed actions, by which the State, as 'personator' or representative of the sole authority of individual citizens, can perform actions which are validly counted as having been performed by those voluntarily authorising citizens. These then are the actions of them all as united.

By such authorising, that is by converting oneself from a natural person acting for oneself into an artificial person being represented by an artificial entity, the citizen forgoes any right to interfere in the actions which he has authorised and which are performed on his behalf.[29] He gives up his right to govern himself and must not oppose the sovereign. Since it is he who authorises the sovereign, it would make no sense in the Hobbesian world to oppose the sovereign authority.[30] This is important, as it is a point on which Hobbes is sometimes misunderstood as a defender of individual rights.[31] It is true that the Hobbesian individual never forgoes the right of self protection. In fact Hobbes is clear that not all rights are alienable,[32] especially the right to protect one's life against forceful assault. However, should any political regime claim to satisfy that individual need, that regime cannot be resisted. Skinner emphasises the point.[33]

This is close to the heart of Hobbes' absolutism. Whereas he is commonly thought to have left a contradiction at the heart of his system and thus left open the door to liberal ideology, the inalienable right to protect oneself was only real in the scarce circumstance that government failed to claim responsibility for the safety of the people. Because of this, Hobbes was wrong within his own argument when he called this right inalienable. But the importance of his assertion about the fundamental nature of individual safety, and the justification for him making it, was that this 'right' was the limit case for government, rather than an inalienable claim by individuals.

Hobbes' approach to artificiality is demonstrated by his interest in the representation of individuals, certainly those who were natural persons and who voluntarily authorise others to represent them but also especially those who are not natural persons. The latter are those who can be represented but are incapable of authorising their own representatives.[34] Hobbes adds to these a final group who are artificial and can have words or actions attributed to them but who are either inanimate or, if persons, either 'Children, Fooles, and Mad-men,' that is those who are unable through incapacity to authorise their guardians.[35] Through this strategy, Hobbes has provided for the representation of every person or thing, whether they voluntarily enter such a relationship or do not. Complemented by his argument concerning the provision by government of the protection of each individual, this is the heart of his absolutism. Beyond that, he has thereby effected the process by which the sovereign State is created, by which each individual agrees 'to conferre all their power and strength upon one Man, or one Assembly of men, that may reduce all their wills, by plurality of voices, unto one Will.'[36] It was this artifice, whose actions we authorise and which fully represents us as individuals,[37] with which each individual has a personal political relationship and by which device alone are the people brought to a unity. There was no 'body of the people' which preceded or could intervene in that relationship.[38]

Hobbes' prescription, therefore, was that any incumbent of this artificial entity, that is the sovereign as person or council who bears the person of the

State, was due unreserved obedience,[39] in return for which protection must be provided by them.[40] Should they fail in this, obedience may properly be redirected to any new incumbent who could provide it, although the people themselves cannot instigate this change due to the nature of their authorisation of the sovereign and thereby the forgoing of the right to interfere in his actions and the responsibility to own the actions of the created sovereign power.[41]

As a consequence of all this, Hobbes has a particular notion of liberty. Argued within his scientific framework, liberty is comprised of an underlying ability to act, complemented by the absence of any impediment to this ability being exercised, whether by preventing or obliging action.[42] However, since for him covenants in the state of nature do not fall into either category, as they may always be broken, they do not compromise our liberty.[43] When we move into the Commonwealth we are bound by its laws and so our liberty is constrained, except for the theoretical right to protect oneself. However, although our liberty as subjects is constrained by such laws, our fundamental liberty is not, because we make the rational choice, for reasons of protection, to be obedient.[44] We are not constrained to act or not to act in making this choice. Hobbes relies on this argument to justify a rejection of the freedom of Classical Greek democratic thought on which he blamed the Civil War, any recurrence of which he was determined to prevent.[45]

He also relies on this argument in his claim that people were free to submit to the post-regicide Government in 1649 because that government claimed the right to protect and provide for all individuals.[46] The power and authority available to the incumbent of this artificial entity must be absolute, that is unlimited,[47] so that it could ensure compliance with the prescriptions, as laws, that would provide for the safety and contentment of the people.[48] Hobbes is clear about the absolute nature of the power of the incumbent.[49] Because the State represents every person and because its actions are voluntarily authorised by and attributed to each individual citizen, then *ipso facto* the citizen authorises the laws enacted by the State to enforce preferred behaviour on himself and others. The constraints provided by these laws constituted the coercion that was the condition of liberty for Hobbes.

However, one can see problems of both argument and emphasis in the theoretical work which forms the basis of the arguments in the *Leviathan*. The first is that Hobbes argues that fear of others in mere nature is insufficient to enforce compliance with covenants, because nature has created us all equal.[50] This contradicts his account of the widespread fear that exists in the state of nature due to the war of all against all. Despite the possibility of transitory alliances between individuals, this fear results in some making slaves of others and so is the motivation for the entry of each individual into the protective relationship with the absolute State. That is, on the one hand the state of nature[51] is where individuals exist in a state of such equality that there is no cause for fear and on the other it is a circumstance of intolerable fear. Skinner acknowledges the failure of Hobbes to deal with this important point,[52] but Skinner does not explore the significant implications of this failure. Is man profoundly afraid in the state of nature or not? More broadly, Hobbes acknowledges that, with the move to the Commonwealth, fear of the consequences of disobedience is the only means to ensure compliance. However, he denies that this constrains the fundamental freedom of the individual in any way since compliance is still the choice he makes, even though fear causes him to want to make this choice: we always remain free to break the laws.[53] He uses a similar argument regarding the move into civil society in the first place: we are always free not to enter.[54]

The problem for such an argument is of course that, constrained to comply with the laws by both the 'continuall feare, and danger of violent death'[55] in the state of nature and the fear of being punished by the 'terror'[56] of the State for not complying with laws that we not attack others, we are still free, that is in his terms unconstrained, to choose, according to Hobbes. There are problems here regarding fear. On the one hand, he regards it as the fundamental condition of social and political arrangements, arguing that the state of nature is so fearsome that it is the overwhelming cause of individual submission to the lawful State, and then describes the lawful State itself as a source of terror, necessary to ensure compliance with its laws.[57] On the other hand, to support the argument he is attempting to put regarding the legitimacy of political arrangements that he prefers, that is that a government can only be legitimate if allegiance to it is freely given, he is dismissive of the impact of fear and any claim that it affects the freedom of choice is a 'fraudulent pretence,'[58] insisting that it does not in any way constrain such freedom.

One could accept this latter argument if fear was an occasional factor in any such choice situation. But Hobbes has made it the condition of the decisions both to enter civil society and to submit to the laws. It is a condition of such overwhelming significance that any claim that the choices to leave the fearsome state of nature and then to comply with the prescriptions of a legitimate but terrorising sovereign power are free, can only be sustained as a nice point of argument. On Hobbes' own argument, fear must come before, and drive, reason. If one makes a choice to avoid terror and death, either in escaping the state of nature or in submitting to a terrifying sovereign power, it can hardly be claimed that this was a free choice in any real sense. It is better described as a primal reaction to a profound threat to one's very existence. A consequence is that one cannot credibly argue as Hobbes does that an individual has the inalienable right of self-protection, when the sovereign can claim at any time an irresistible responsibility for the protection of each individual and that such a claim requires complete concurrence on the part of the individual. Consequently, the claim for such an inalienable right is here regarded as merely a reflection of the limit case for government.

In fact, the point might be made against Hobbes, and by strictly applying his premises that fear is not a determinant and that lack of constraint is the criterion of freedom, that it would in fact be by choosing to remain outside any Commonwealth of the kind he prefers, that is to govern oneself, that we would demonstrate freedom. One might accept Hobbes' latter argument if he had not made the case for entry into civil society so compelling, that is if there was real choice in this. But that would have required him to make the state of nature a more accommodating place, in effect that man's nature is other than naturally warlike. His entire case for an absolutist state would then have been in serious difficulty.

From all this, it could be said that Hobbes was someone who experienced political turmoil even to the extent of strong personal fear. His determination was to construct an argument which would help prevent any recurrence of this fearsome circumstance. He did this by generalising the cause of the turmoil into a universal feature of human conduct which mankind would be strongly motivated to avoid. He then imagined an artifice, vacuous in itself but terrifying when 'personated' by an 'authorised' incumbent, which was the only means to bring peace to the compliant, through the establishment of a regime of law which operated through universal fear of punishment. He then made legitimate the allegiance to any ruling incumbent of that artifice that established this peace, through an argument that claimed this allegiance to be the result of free universal choice. Reason was engaged by Hobbes to establish the legitimacy of a fearsome personated artifice which was constructed to eliminate fear through the inducement and enforcement of compliance. The problem is that he made the desire for compliance so compelling that one should take the rational choice of compliance as a limit case for government rather than a demonstration of the use of reason or the exercise of liberty. This is reason in the service of a mythological disposition.

Hobbes and Archetypal Myth

Although he should be seen in the context of the thought of certain of his contemporary theorists, Hobbes was clearly also doing something new. What that was had significance in itself, but its further significance will be brought to life when we consider the later unfolding of the political myth, especially in the context of the discussion of Rousseau. What was new is seen by Gierke as Hobbes' substitution for the two original contracts of society and government a single contract through which each individual submits to a common ruler who himself plays no part in the making of the contract.[59]

In this, the features of the Hobbesian concept of the State can be seen to be virtually archetypal, at least prototypical, regarding the establishment of a mythological magnitude. Regarding the three stages of myth making outlined in the first chapter of this work, Hobbes comes close to establishing the credentials of his idea of the State as the archetypal myth. In doing so, he is also setting up the premises for its subsequent ongoing refinement.

We have seen that the features which any such archetypal idea would need to satisfy to qualify as mythological include the creation of an absolutely empowered artificial entity, a mythological magnitude, to which individuals forgo their individual self-responsibility typically willingly by inducement, otherwise by compulsion. In return for such submissiveness, in the form of an understanding or covenant between each individual and the magnitude, the entity claims responsibility to eliminate individual fear and create sympathetic conditions of existence. Such sympathy reinforces the requirement that the entity is brought to exercise its fearsomeness only in the realisation of compliance, that is in no arbitrary manner. Finally, the fate of the magnitude comes into man's hands. This assumption of the fate of the magnitude by man opens the door to its slow activation over time and results in the dispersal of the magnitude across social space, the purpose of which is to ensure at least that no individual can be a source of fear. The consequences are that, though incumbent authorised 'personators' of the magnitude may be replaced, the entity itself is never unmade, due to the continuing fearful concerns of individuals, and that individuals are incorporated into the dispersed magnitude. This allows competition between interests to colonise the entity as 'personators' to determine what constitutes fear and sympathy.

With one important exception, an exception that points only to the process of historical refinement of the political myth after Hobbes, these characteristics are all fundamental to the Hobbesian account of the State as Leviathan. The Leviathan satisfies the conditions to qualify as a mythological magnitude. Although Hobbes was concerned with the urgency of the political problems of his day, his disposition towards mythological concepts as the ground for his idea of a State that would solve those problems is clear. His definition of the nature of mankind as warlike led him to conceive the absolutist entity to which submission of each individual is induced or compelled, for the purposes of the elimination of fear and the creation of sympathetic conditions of existence. That is, for the 'safety of the people (and) also all other Contentments of life.'[60] Not only are these characteristics featured in the conceptual machinery of the Leviathan but they are also featured archetypally. Hobbes instituted the modern political myth.

The one mythological characteristic which is not a feature of the Leviathan is the coming of the magnitude into man's hands through its dispersal across social space. Beyond the effective creation of the concept of the mythological magnitude, Hobbes does not explore the full potential complexity of the nature of the magnitude and its relationship to man, although the seeds of that complexity are all present. Although his emphasis on both the preservation of individual will and attributed behaviour allows it, there is no exploration of the potential of individuals to engage with sovereign power and negotiate the elaborate dimensions of rights and governance, beyond stating that sovereign power may take a parliamentary form.[61] Although there is a cold presumption of sympathy towards the individual by the State built into Hobbes' notion of representation and there is provision for 'Contentments of life' for each individual, there is no full consideration given by him to the conversion of subjection, to guide the

State regarding the elimination of fear or to induce sympathy from the State towards the individual.

There is, in other words, no conversion of the testable covenant to one based on the matching of absolute power with absolute sympathy, and so there is no wide colonisation of the State by groups of interest or by individuals and so no dispersal of the magnitude across social space, except for the principle of universal submission. Hobbes does not provide for the active dispersal of the magnitude by its protection of elaborated individual rights, as Locke was to do. Further, he fails to provide for its active dispersal through any broadening of the base of governance. There is a good reason for this. It goes to the heart of Hobbes' status as mythologist and should be seen in the context of the analysis by Gierke of the importance of Hobbes' resolution of the issue of the two contracts, of society and of government. Hobbes was dealing with what in the long-term refinement of the myth of the State will become significant for Rousseau and then Kant. This is the issue of the general will. In denying any contract of society, that is of a general will, Hobbes was developing a rationale for a direct relationship between the individual and the sovereign power. This was an understandable approach for someone concerned to limit individual fear, which is argued by Hobbes to be at the heart of all government, through a relationship between the individual and the sovereign power. Fear is personal so is best dealt with through such a personal relationship.

The problem with such an arrangement, a problem to be seen by Rousseau and Kant, is that this leaves each individual with only his own concerns, that is uninterested in the interests of others and so of government. So, the individual must be brought to a concern for others as well as himself. At the heart of this problem is that for Hobbes any notion of community comes only through and therefore after the creation of the sovereign entity and so is itself artificial because it is derivative of that artifice. Rousseau's solution is to imagine a general will created between individuals without primary regard for any government. The government itself is secondary to that general will but carries out its imperatives. This shift is the realisation of the coming of the fate of the entity into man's hands and is the fulfilment of the Hobbesian political myth, to be refined in Kant.

This shift is what is meant by the dispersal of the mythological entity, which first requires its colonisation by man: the fate of the myth is to come into man's hands, as Blumenberg argued, and this is achieved by the authorised power of the sovereign magnitude generating an individual and a general will through processes of dispersal across social space. This colonisation and then dispersal can ensure that, through its functionaries and practices, each individual (the responsibility for whose fears has been transferred to the entity) is, counterintuitively, empowered through his submission. Thus he is prevented from being fearsome but he does share in the fearsomeness of the magnitude and so is not fearful: the purpose of the myth can claim to be fulfilled. This also places the artificial Hobbesian notion of membership, unlike the organic Rousseauean notion, in a new perspective. This is an issue the seeds of which therefore lie in Hobbes but which his successors, beginning with Locke then continuing with Rousseau and Kant, deal with as the ongoing refinement of the political myth.

What Hobbes did, in proposing a solution for the problem of existential fear, is to set the terms for such refinement. The exploration of colonisation and dispersal in this sense was not his primary purpose. He is concerned to claim the establishment of absolute power to eliminate absolute fear. For him, this absolute power has a single, central subject which is the source of all prescriptions regarding behaviour, that is in law. It is god-like in its nature. He established the centrepiece of the idea of the mythological arrangement of State which his successors in the political tradition were to refine by arguing for its dispersal across social space and by making the myth more sympathetic, without diluting the fearsomeness on which its elimination of fear depended. Theirs is the work on the idea of this myth.

The Mythological Significance of Hobbes

Hobbes crystallised and transferred to those that became his successors in the tradition a problem with which we continue to be concerned. In Blumenberg's terms, we remain unnecessarily consumed with answering pre-Enlightenment questions. This has resulted from the establishment and then ongoing work on the modern political myth, achieved through the creation, elaboration and then continuous refinement and engagement of the fully empowered State, by the forgoing of self-responsibility, to ensure its sympathy without diluting the fearsomeness needed to eliminate our existential and particular anxieties. Given that subsequent political theory and practice in the Western political tradition remains fundamentally concerned with addressing the implications of absolutism, Hobbes established the principal reference point for that concern. His argument concerning the features of the preferred form of the State not only fulfilled all the key criteria of mythology but also established the principal reference point for the idea of the modern State itself. As a consequence of the mythology of his analysis, he created the modern State as mythological and set the idea of it on a firm course. He did not bring the fate of myth into man's hands but he did set that issue up for ongoing refinement, in the manner that he addressed the issue of the elimination of fear.

It should be restated that the distinction between the idea of the State and the actual forms which it takes is important. Hobbes made the mark which became the primary, one might even say primal, reference point for subsequent elaboration of the idea of the State, this elaboration constituting one key aspect of the ongoing work on myth, the other being the material realisation of these ideas. This work continues, both conceptually and through its concretisation. This is not to deny a relationship between this idea as a work in progress and the structural and practical work on the real State, as we shall see.

Further, to the extent that political theorists had influence, and it can be argued that many of those being considered here had such influence, their mythological theoretical propositions in turn serially influenced the structural refinement and therefore the operation of the concrete State. It is in this latter context that practical political judgements are made within communities regarding the extent to which these refinements have moved political arrangements closer to the realisation of the archetype. It is also in this context that judgements are made regarding whether the performance of particular governments, that is incumbents, of State are satisfying the dual mythological expectations held of them or whether they should be replaced, or whether such performance reveals structural flaws that require critique and reprogramming.

LOCKE

Although there are clear differences in their key premises, the Hobbesian paradigm will be argued to be the context within which the Lockean analysis should be seen. This will be argued on grounds that Locke worked, within the political theoretical tradition, on problems posed by Hobbes' conception of the State rather than worked on the idea of the State as on a *tabula rasa*. Secondly, it will be argued that Locke not only worked within the Hobbesian paradigm but was surely aware he was doing so, even though his immediate protagonist was Filmer.[62]

As with Hobbes, before any judgement can be made about Locke's mythological disposition, it is necessary to examine the Lockean enterprise in its own terms. This examination will also be informed by the analysis of Locke's work by Dunn, and to a lesser extent by Waldron, Strauss, Macpherson and Manent. In effect, the textual examination of Locke will be more a test of the interpretation by Dunn and Waldron than that of Macpherson and Strauss. In establishing his critical position regarding Locke, Dunn distances himself from the analyses of Locke by Macpherson and Strauss. He regards the Marxist analysis of the former as penetrating but a distortion of the Lockean argument and he asserts that Strauss' claim of the strong connection between Locke and Hobbes[63] would have been unknowing on Locke's part.[64] Although the Straussian position would lend immediate and strong support for the position argued in this work,[65] that is that Locke was building directly on Hobbes' work, there are elements of the interpretation of Locke put by Dunn and Waldron that, if sustainable, better fill out the argument put here. This is no denial of the impact of Hobbes on Locke here. On the contrary, their connection is merely given a more circuitous but richer route by looking at Dunn. Further, although Dunn's argument may in the end be regarded as richer than that of Macpherson,[66] there is no denial here that one effect of the Lockean argument was to contribute to the exploitation of non-propertied workers and that this fact might well be argued to have a place in the mythology of the modern State.

The Fearsome State and the Move to Assume its Fate

The purpose of this examination of the text is to allow a judgement regarding the extent to which Locke can be seen as having amended and refined the idea of the Hobbesian mythological State. For this, we will now examine a range of key elements of his thought. These include the theological base of his argument against that of Filmer, the central role of the religious calling of the individual and the value of one's property broadly defined, as standing on that base; his position regarding political authority; the supremacy of the Parliament as a strategy to avoid the misuse of prerogative power; the way that his theological and jural conception of the state of nature complemented his argument for equality and freedom; the insensitive nature of his notion of legitimacy; his highly conservative conception of political participation and the obligation of tacit and express consent; and the conservative nature of his conception of political resistance. These elements are the means by which Locke begins the transfer of the magnitude's fate into man's hands without diluting its fearsomeness.

The Theological Premise, the Calling and the Right to Property

The first premise of the argument by Dunn and Waldron is that one must first see the thought of Locke in theological terms. Further, one can argue that it is the calling, connected to the right to property, that founds Locke's arguments against absolutism. The argument here is that the calling is where we begin to see Locke's delicate move to transfer the magnitude's fate into man's hands while sustaining its fearsome nature. Although Dunn firmly places Locke in historical, political time and acknowledges the impact of that on his thought, in the end it is the firmly held religious convictions, especially the Calvinism[67] in which he was raised, which are predominant in Locke's political theory. This is not to deny that beyond his Calvinism but complementing it, his own anxiety[68] made unlikely other interpretations of the world: he is clear that 'The great end of Mens entering into Society . . . [is] . . . the enjoyment of their Properties in Peace and Safety.'[69]

The primary reference of his theology provides the context of the central role of the 'calling' for Locke, which is the foundation of the lives of all men because it is the role determined for each person by God. Locke even accepts the oppressiveness of existing social structures, except where they contravene this foundation. So, the liberties that he champions are either those which allow the individual to meet his calling or allow him to oppose those structures when they claim religious endorsement for the corrupt practices of the powerful or when they seek to sanction the forcible appropriation of property from their legal possessors,[70] although Locke did regard unlimited appropriation as morally perilous, even if it did raise the standard of living.[71] His egalitarianism was Christian,[72] in that for him it was not the authority of any human minister which counted but each individual confronting his God in a social world which neither made.

This is the individualisation of the religious experience, although it is too much to claim, with Dunn, that this relegates social organisation to the minimal value of 'contingent convenience.'[73] The individual remains within an intractable hierarchy but his individual theological needs are for Locke of pre-eminent importance. This was not incompatible with the fact of social inequality, unless that interfered with the calling. The calling was sustained by labour but the purpose of this was the fulfilment of the will of God[74] and therefore the attainment by the individual of salvation, rather than the underpinning of the capitalist system of production. Terrestrial utility was to be allowed but men were owned by God and should act to satisfy his expectations. This was the law of reason.[75] For Locke, the calling gave each individual his place in a social structure which was, and would remain, unequal but in which the economic conditions that were associated with his religious responsibilities, the satisfaction of which were protected, could be pursued.

Locke's arguments were theological and they were patently directed against Filmer. This was largely because, besides Locke's own Calvinism, the absolutist arguments which threatened Locke's beliefs were argued by Filmer in theological terms. Locke's anti-absolutist position therefore concerns the extent to which, in such an unequal social structure as England had, a man—say a king—may have power over another man concerning both his beliefs and the property which those beliefs protected.

The centrepoint of Filmer's argument was that the contemporary, hierarchical social world embodied the providence of God. There was always continuity and homogeneity between man and God, who provided to man throughout his existence a set of rules for social behaviour embodied in institutions of social control.[76] For him, therefore, contractarian political theories implied anarchy, breaching the great chain of being from God. But the transfer of authority from God, which began with Adam, plays a double role in Filmer. The transfer of authority and of God's gift of property were a single act:[77] that is, all authority is property and all property depends on authority. The relationship between man and the natural world was only conceivable through property and no-one but those with authority have a *prima facie* legal and moral claim. It was this which forced Locke, in response, to argue that property right is not reducible only to positive law, that the king is not its only owner by any process of transfer and that holding it is a right against forceful seizure by anyone including the monarch.[78] But Locke's response set a new, broader context for these issues, wherein he gave an account of how humanity may have alienated their freedom to political institutions which left them substantially unfree. This response, the abstract arrangement of the state of nature, is the source of the startling misconceptions about his thought,[79] as we shall see.

Political Authority

This was the background to the issue of political authority, through which Locke addressed key elements of Filmer's position. Without challenging contemporary social structure, Locke's view was that no threat to the performance of the individual's calling or the enjoyment of his property could be tolerated. Hence his rejection of Filmer's absolutism. In effect, Locke's argument here instigated the transfer of the magnitude's fate into man's hands.

First, he rejected Filmer's argument that the Old Testament's revelation of God's bequest to Adam is a sample of divine positive law, that is where God has spoken mere men must be silent. Locke's state of nature, his alternative to Genesis, is not historical but it does specify the continuing moral order within which human beings themselves make history by their voluntary actions;[80] second, he responded to Filmer's challenge regarding the issue of the derivation of right from the people through his concept of conditional tacit consent; third, he accepted Filmer's charge that natural freedom implied the permanent right of individual secession from a polity. Filmer's position was that God's intentions in creating government, the grounds for obedience owed to the usurper and the duties of the latter are all directed to preserving life,[81] that is to make it secure. For him the contractarians denied the existence of this structure of authority, which went from the monarch through to the father of the family: all kings were fathers and all fathers ruled,[82] hence his invocation of the fifth commandment as a means of insisting on obedience. For Locke, however, many of these issues come down to who should judge the degree of oppression which justifies popular resistance to the government[83] and, by implication, how to deal with fear. In this context, it can be argued that the oppression and resistance are what the *Two Treatises* were about.

The Supremacy of Parliament

Locke dealt with this broad question of authority in terms that responded to Filmer's account of it. Far from being an anarchist, he argued for a supremely powerful parliament, even finding a place for prerogative power. The effect is that, in the transfer of authority from the absolute sovereign to parliament, the Lockean magnitude remains pre-eminently fearsome.

In dealing with this question, the problem which Locke faced, crystallised in *Patriarcha*, was how to deal with the factors that were generating the deep fear among the Whigs. These included the threat of popery and the menace of the arbitrary use of prerogative power, the perceived solution to which was to establish this supremacy of the parliament, thereby eliminating autonomous executive power. The Tories were intent on preserving the autonomy of the executive and the hereditary succession to the throne. But the Whigs were conscious of the subversive implications of their strategy, so they sustained a commitment to the 'true Prerogative,' one exercised in the interests of the people as interpreted by their representatives, that is themselves.[84] But they needed an ideological position that avoided Filmer's charge of anarchy and assimilated their position to the solid continuous historical order of the English polity.

This was Locke's enterprise in the *Two Treatises,* to provide a systematic refutation of absolutist theory in the form of Filmer's patriarchalism. His refutation was intended to set the limits to legitimate royal authority and to empower the community to judge whether they had been transgressed: it was the proclamation of the right to revolution even though he hardly encouraged exercising it. The background to this remained the desire for order and allegiance but the rights of the individual to resist the excessive use of absolute power within God's world were now in the foreground.[85] This is the context in which Locke asserts the superiority of the legislature over executive power. Indeed 'the legislature is not only the supreme power, but sacred and unalterable.'[86] Once the legislature is constituted, the people have no power to act so long as the Government stands,[87] that is except for revolution.[88] The legislature was important because it provided representatives chosen by their communities, thereby binding them to the laws they pass[89] and in so doing providing an institutional check on taxation and on the arbitrary appropriation of private property. Shaftesbury wanted greater representation of the landed gentry but Locke opted for a novel argument regarding the use of prerogative power.[90]

The State of Nature

It was against this background that Locke assembled his argument in the *Two Treatises*. Its premises came from the background he shared with Filmer, that God created the universe, and the relation of every part to the whole, for His purpose. The question that follows, given the lower ranks of creatures subserve the higher,[91] is whether this justifies the jural relations between men, how much political power one man can have over another, especially if a monarch uses this immorally. Locke's challenge was to unpack political relationships so that such immorality could be resisted but without undermining God's purpose for man.[92] This would reinforce the authority of Parliament but not threaten the freedom to serve God.

Locke's notion of the state of nature, with the embedded Law of Nature, reveals how he begins to meet this challenge, since in that state man belongs to the created order of nature but can make his own history. This state is ahistorical but not asocial.[93] It is the state in which men are placed by God, so the reading of God's purpose for man, especially through Christian revelation, is crucial. Locke rejects Filmer's reliance on the Old Testament in favour of a natural theology which emphasises the Christian normative creaturely equality of all men.[94] This is Locke's entrée into both the constitutional limits of political authority and bourgeois property rights: men make claims on, and have responsibilities towards, other men and nature. His state of nature is a criterion outside history, providing the terms by which to judge its moral notions. So not only is it not asocial but also not psychologically or logically prior to society. It was a response to the denial by Filmer of any government emerging from a state of nature and thereby Filmer's reference to Genesis.[95] Filmer's argument that the unitary authority devolved from Adam to the sovereign was despatched by Locke pointing to the plurality of legitimate sovereign authorities, including those in conflict. Filmer could not claim any law by which to judge sovereigns as there was no sovereign to validate it.[96]

So in Locke's ahistorical state of nature under the theological law of nature, men were, rather than constituted by the perilous status imposed by absolutism, equal and free and none had authority over another. Only if they breach the normative behaviour sanctioned by God or are enslaved following a just war should they be treated as beasts.[97] By definition the state of nature is a jural condition of equality and freedom, uncontaminated by history as the source of wickedness. Rather than an exhaustive set of rights and responsibilities, it is the jural context against which these should be set and understood, a jural template. It is logically prior to the state of war or the legitimate polity. It is any relationship between men without aggression and without the explicit reciprocal normative understandings that constitute a polity.[98]

Against this background, Locke makes a number of observations regarding the social and economic factors and circumstances which lead to the move from the *status naturalis* to civil society. He does not deny that men are born into families, biologically incapable of survival outside such units and requiring a long period of education to produce the habits of moral conduct, but he dealt with this at length only because of Filmer's patriarchal model. Locke's view was that men are forced into society by the enticements of the family but also, due to the Fall, the need to embrace labour and, because there is scarcity, private property. This is the cause of insecurity which men meet at the hands of other men. So in these pre-political conditions, they remain with the family and accept the authority of their father as their agent with the world.[99] Locke was baffled by the manner in which families became a society, except to explain it by accretion, cooperation and ultimately consent, converting this into a political community. This was supposed as the early golden age of government, where kings were fathers, and a condition disrupted by the acceptance of money as a means to exchange and wealth. It is the differentiation of wealth between men that creates social conflict and moral degradation. Further, for Locke, political organisation is not a precondition for an advanced commercial society but it is a precondition for its continuance over time. This was due, on the one hand, to external conflict caused by the hunger for land, the result of economic development and population growth, and, on the other, to internal conflict due to scarcity and acquisitiveness. These combine to make government essential as a protection both against external aggression and for internal order. But this does not make Locke blind to the fact that the extensive power consequently given to the good ruler is inevitably abused by the bad, leading to revolution and to the need for ways to fetter monarchical authority. For Locke, only Christian revelation and the restraining effect of constitutionalism could limit the disasters which then threatened social order.[100]

Locke's Insensitive Legitimacy

Locke was favourable to legitimate political authority but his account of this, against Filmer's absolutist notion of legitimacy, emphasised the dependence of authority on the wills of individuals in subjection to God. The Lockean argument regarding the logical preconditions for a legitimate polity derived from his move against Filmer's position that God provided moral education in eternal structures of social authority. Locke saw this as the manipulation of His order by a handful of rulers and he responded by arguing that God has imposed religious duties on each individual through their intellectual capacity to know moral truth: all men are equal because their jural situation is the set of duties they owe God, for which they logically rather than contingently require the particular kind of freedom that allows autonomous choice. The consequence is that the legitimacy of social arrangements is drawn from the will of its participants.[101]

Yet, consistent with the delicate balance of his broad argument, this is not a call for mass democracy[102] but a series of relationships necessary to accomplish God's assignment. Against Filmer, Locke argued that rulers had no indefeasible rights. It was the behavioural realisation of the duties of submission by subjects which only contingently realised those rights and only if rulers did not deploy these duties to adorn their private purposes. Locke never proposed an egalitarian political structure as an alternative to the repressive society of seventeenth century England. All society was required to do was enable individual religious duty in an environment of the innocent delights that came to some from economic progress. This was the insensitive basis of legitimacy. In this context, the rights of rulers derive from the wills of subjects because mutual obligation has been created and political obligation is inseparable from the structure of individual religious duty.[103] The problem for Locke was the authority to deal with those who encroach on others' jural space. His solution was to invoke the law of nature, which governs the relationships between men, allows punishments for infractions and which derives its legislative power from God. Its foundation is logical not historical and it applies only to the execution of His purposes.

This is also the backdrop for his specification of a political society, a key condition of which is that it has a binding decision procedure. Since this must recognise that no man has authority over another, the procedure must take account of each person. Hence his prescription of majority voting on legislative issues, although this is not majority voting by the whole population, which he would see as both dangerous and practically absurd. For Locke, tacit consent to the views of the majority, tightly defined, is obligatory for all citizens, generated by the hypothetical agreement of the individual to be a member of the society.[104] These obligations require that all individuals sit in formal structures of reciprocal rights and duties, none of which relate to any rights of rulers but only to each other as fellow subjects and based on the principle of prudence, that is the consequence to others of disobedience. Such obligations are logically dependent on the prior consent of those subject to them and this takes two forms. Tacit consent is incurred by anyone who voluntarily takes advantage of the resources of the country and simple voluntary territorial presence is sufficient for this.[105] It is this which in part forms the basis of sovereign executive power, for it 'is derived from the transferred power to execute the law of nature possessed by each member of (the society).' The other form is express consent, such as an oath of allegiance, which is the making of a sign of indefinite agreement to obey the rules.[106]

Locke's argument strikes some trouble at this point, for although he stresses the voluntary nature of the commitment which makes a man a full member of a society, he describes this as terms imposed on him by a society as a condition of his drawing benefits, such as the right to inherit property. In dismissing Macpherson's argument that this is the only motive in Locke for entering political society, for Dunn it is 'coming of age' that is the occasion of the giving of consent. This brings with it full political responsibility, not just the right to dispose of property.[107] Locke is trying to dismiss Filmer's claim that allegiance is a natural relationship, based on the paternal relationship with a territorial overtone, so that he can argue that legitimacy and therefore allegiance is contractual. The problem is the additional claim that society sets the terms under which an individual, landed gentry or not, will be given the status and therefore rights of a member of society and subject.[108] We shall see that this difference between voluntary and enforced allegiance, which is the trouble that Locke strikes, is located in the centre of the mythological analysis.

Participation, consent and prerogative

Locke's next challenge is to balance his desire for participation, constrained by the notion of tacit consent to avoid egalitarianism, with the empowerment of the parliament, which he reinforces with the use of prerogative. There are many challenges in sustaining this delicate balance. First, his notion of tacit consent is problematic in the context of the right to resist. The former convincingly occupies the superior position. Yet he is not forgoing the right to resist a government should it be guilty of immoral behaviour, since he is only arguing in principle why a government may be resisted.[109] But he is not specific about the creation of a legitimate political society. He clearly accepted the historical origins of the English constitution, despite the unsteadying hiatus of the Norman Conquest. He rejected absolute monarchy because the form of its claims to legitimacy is incompatible with the logical precondition for legitimacy, which is that absolute monarchy could be based on consent, but this would make its basis consensual and this is what the theory of absolute monarchy denies. This issue has mythological implications, as we shall see.

Against Hobbes' argument, Locke denies that conquest can ever be a basis of legitimacy, since legitimacy requires the voluntary and formal acceptance by its subjects and general submission is not a general consent.[110] Locke did not provide any criteria for free, mutual agreement but did consider agreement as being made on behalf of the subject by representatives.[111] But their selection would involve no egalitarian, or even formal, process: for Locke, social structure is such that hierarchy was unthinkingly accepted by most men and this was morally appropriate. It is the acceptance of the distribution of power and authority that constitutes legitimacy, so long as there is a framework of recognised institutions for articulating the will of the people.[112]

Legitimacy does not for Locke exclude the authoritative use of prerogative power, as we have seen. Certainly he elaborates the authority of the prescriptions of a consensually based legislature, wherein the legislative sovereign activates the right to execute the law of nature, and the consequential right to demand the obedience of subjects. These rights are determined by the constitutionally proper positive laws.[113] But a more extensive power of execution is the prerogative power, necessary because legislation is incapable of providing for the full complexity of social circumstance. Filmer argued that, although its proper exercise is located in the rule-bound tradition of constitutional practice, it is properly seen as logically prior to statute. Locke, acknowledging the fact that there are many cases to which rules do not apply and in which there is a demand for the deployment of force, faced the challenge of the control of this power.[114] The challenge derives from the fact that the constitution determines what the power may not do, not what it may do. In principle, therefore, it may be used against the law and there can be no terrestrial judge of the rights of the issue.

Locke realised that the prospect of the use of this power reverting to that imagined in the idealised paternalism of Filmer, with the tacit consent for socially good acts that this would draw, was impossible. Men made the social world, with all its manipulations in the interest of men's historically heterogeneous purposes, and could not transfer responsibility for this to God.[115] Equally, the social world is totally historical and so cannot furnish any abstract criterion with which to judge history, so there can be no complete resolution of social dilemmas. Here the issue of prerogative is felt hardest. One the one hand, individuals have the right to appeal against the misdeeds of the legislative to an eternal authority, thus reducing the polity to anarchy. On the other, despite his support for such action, Locke is wary of this power, given the likelihood of self-serving use by social and political interests. Men have consigned their social fate to be determined by a set of rules and its custodians. In so doing they have both conferred on their environment a greatly enhanced predictability and order and avoided the naked confrontation of self-righteous wills. But in some measure men could not escape entrusting their fate also to a power which cannot be regulated. For Locke, the formal legitimacy of this power lies in its use for the general good.[116]

But legitimacy is not for him socially located. The final criterion is the consent of the subjects, not as constitutionally mediated consent of a legislature but the continuing consciousness of each member of society. So prerogative power finally has, unlike for a royalist like Filmer, no authority over the individual, since obligations are only those recognised as such. This was not a denial by Locke of social authority but a recognition of the dilemmas and complexities of establishing such authority: his entire account of political change depends upon the dialectic between the urge to accept the authority of benign monarchs but reject those monarchs who abuse that authority.[117] One might be alert here to the spectre of the archetypally mythological conundrum, wherein one apparently has the final right to direct action against the oppressive use of centralised and delegated force but where in practice one is required to forgo one's right to do so to constitutional institutional processes, so that the prospect of anarchy and therefore fear may be avoided.

It might be noted that it is fair to reject any claim that Locke, following Hobbes, contributed to a deterioration in the moral responsibility of political acts because these are to be judged by what comes of an act and not in terms of a legal system enforced by divine sanctions. When Locke says that the normative status of an unconstitutional act may be changed by the end for which it is performed, say in the exercise of prerogative power, he does not imply that an immoral act can be sanctioned in the same way. The exercise of such power in this way is not a breach of promise and can only be undertaken to carry out the axiomatic purposes of society, that is in the interests of subjects.[118] Further, any claim that for Locke self-preservation is a right that is logically prior to any duty is rejected on the grounds that it overrides other moral considerations only when self-preservation was directly at stake.[119]

Right of Resistance

Consistent with the delicate balance of his broad argument, Locke argues for the right of resistence but applies firm caveats to this. Although his position was conservative, he based his argument on the conditions that apply to the state of war or conquest, as disruptions to the peace of the state of nature. Force reduces to beasts those who use it and they may be treated accordingly.[120] He proclaims this as the official theory of absolutism.[121] When force is used to breach this peace, men should take action to restore this peace and safety, but through the magistrate.[122] Locke expresses the view that absolutism, a claim to control human beings against their will, is a claim to make them slaves, since its purpose is to prise away from the individual his freedom and open him to unlimited and immediate exploitation. Whether in a state of nature or in political society, absolute power is the loss of legal rights and freedom. Hence the individual has in perpetuity against the aggressor the right of war, that is to either destroy him or re-establish the integrity of the legal order.[123]

Locke makes significant political observations in his related analysis of conquest, with its associated comments about the status of the slave. A war against an aggressor, a just war, may initiate the condition of slavery. But an unjust conqueror cannot acquire dominion by conquest. This is a direct rejection of a key argument of Hobbes. But no conqueror, even in a just war, can acquire title to property, especially to land, except in fair reparation. Equally, unlike for Filmer, legitimacy cannot for Locke derive from usurpation. Only the free consent of the subjects can bestow that, since the rules of succession are a constitutional matter.[124]

Nor can the unjust use of force by rightful authorities carry authority over the subjects. Because subjects are highly subservient, this is unlikely to lead to the dissolution of the government unless the ruler is persistent or unless he establishes acute anxiety in the minds of subjects. In such cases, they may resist his abusive actions. The preferred means of resistance by the individual for Locke is the making of an appeal to the people, preferably to the Parliament.[125] In an absolute monarchy, resistance is necessarily more individual and more physical. All this was ultimately drawn from the law of nature and the authority of that lay with God. In effect, for Locke the yearning which men feel for security creates a psychological dependence upon their rulers which gives their rulers enormous freedom of action. Errors which rulers may perpetrate will normally be accepted placidly by their subjects. But the destruction of the climate of trust will threaten their effective control and this destruction can only be caused by their gross misconduct. If it is destroyed, the people will eventually resist.[126] This resistance does not necessarily turn to anarchy, even if the people become a confused multitude, because the hierarchy would not disappear and there would therefore not be a descent into a general state of war.

Thus has Locke located resistance alongside his notions of property rights, the template of state of nature, political authority and legitimacy, consent and representation—all within the context of his theological individualism—as the elements of the argument by which he began to bring the fate of the absolute magnitude into the hands of man but without tempering it as fearsome. So was Leviathan transformed into the supreme Parliament.

The Coherence of Locke's Thought

The making sense of all this, which brought Locke to the full exposition of his theological framework, occurred in large part when he was in exile in Holland, where he repaired in fear from 1683 to avoid persecution for his political ideas.[127] These ideas were not merely the result of psychology and theology but were also motivated by concern for others, what Waldron would call his sense of egalitarianism. Whereas Hobbes accepted as true an interpretation of the lives of most men which made them simply unendurable, Locke did continue to take seriously the problem of preserving rationality for the lives of all men. It was because self-preservation was in Locke's eyes inadequate as a continuing human end that he could not abandon the majority of mankind to the careers of irrational, naturalistic deprivation which was all that the economy could make available to them. For him a state of licence was simply a destruction of security.[128]

For Locke, it was not the economic circumstance of man that gave him the perspective to question the moral legitimacy of seventeenth century England. Rather, it was his personal relationship with God, the 'Archimedian point outside the realm of human contingency from which the individual could judge the world and act upon it.'[129] Locke's religion, more than his politics or economics, would ease the pain.

This is the context in which the claim for both Locke's liberal and bourgeois credentials should be seen, that is, the claim that he was both the proponent of the creation of a predictable legal order, with the physical security and the central role of constitutionalist popular approval which goes with that, and the champion of the centrality of property rights and the spirit of capitalism.[130] For both Waldron and Dunn, the primary motivator was neither of these, but Locke's objection to the arguments of Filmer.[131] We have seen however that religion was not merely a theological exercise. It was bound to labour as the capacity to improve one's lot in God's world. Consequently, an important concern of Locke was to protect property against the arbitrary encroachments of political authorities. But this was not an interest in a redistributive social justice. His was more a strategy which dealt with the threat of non-Parliamentary taxation and the confiscation of freeholds.[132]

From this argument regarding property, therefore, it is not to be taken that Locke was the champion of private economic life, although he did not discourage it so long as the motive was founded in theology and the means of acquisition were consistent with one's calling. This was the compromise delivered best through one's labour. One's calling was as much to those assigned as the victims of social organisation as to its beneficiaries. But hard labour could serve as a guarantee of the authenticity of one's efforts, so long as one undertook this at God's calling.[133] Men are put into the world by God in particular social situations and with particular talents and their responsibility was to fulfil that role, especially by disciplining their entire lives to that fulfilment. Physical labour could serve as the concrete token of dutifulness. In all this, one may see Locke's sense of egalitarianism—not a secular one and so with no proposals for the destruction of the terrestrial hierarchy. Men were equal but as Christians, however unequal they may be as members of societies. They were born into trouble and called to labour.[134]

It is true that the seed of subversion may be seen in this egalitarianism, for in Locke's account of the calling there was no role for a leisure class. But there was also general dismay over those who failed to heed their calling to work.[135] Further, God provides the knowledge necessary to improve anyone's physical situation and thereby generate economic growth so that man may procure happiness, both here and in the next world. This knowledge is attained through systematic reflection by all men,[136] through hours of daily self-education. The discipline that results is not intended to control political rulers or improve civil order but is what ensures their own salvation.

For Locke, the social structures are social facts which constitute the context of individual lives: his central assumption is the ideological validity of hierarchy. He portrayed most men's consciousness as so firmly conventional that only the most cursory governmental attention was necessary to ensure that any social structure in which men lived over time was cemented together by profound expectations and emotional dispositions. But this excessive plausibility of existing social structures[137] could also be argued to have formed the real target of his most powerful works. The apparatus of moral indoctrination available to any society was crushing in its effectiveness and crude in its incidence. The *Two Treatises of Government* was then an attempt to develop criteria for restricting the range of legitimate claims which can be levied in terms of any society's conventional moral principles. The social duty of intellectuals like Locke is to create moral and social space for each individual against the compelling mass of the social structure. However, although Locke's concern was for human freedom, this concern did not extend into egalitarian political revolution. In fact, a fully egalitarian social democracy would have offended his deepest assumptions.[138] Again, his delicate balance.

Locke and Mythology

As a result of continuous civil strife, fear pervaded seventeenth century English society and it is hardly coincidental that Hobbes' conceptual framework largely mirrored political arrangements at the time, arrangements that might bring peace to what had been, and promised to continue to be, a society in turmoil.

Hobbes' framework has been argued to have been in effect an attempt to establish the proto-typical political myth in the Leviathan, a conceptual magnitude with absolute power created as an absolute limit to existential fear. It was itself to be held in absolute fear, with the claimed effect that it would eliminate fear. This fearsomeness requires the forgoing of self-responsibility to the magnitude so that the latter is absolutely empowered. This forgoing would typically be voluntary but if necessary induced or imposed and it is the basis of the understanding or covenant between the individual and the magnitude, a covenant elaborated into constitutional arrangements which reflect the undertakings of each party. Within this covenant is the responsibility of the magnitude to create sympathetic conditions of existence for its subjects or their 'contentment' as it was for Hobbes, as a strategic move to discourage the magnitude itself acting in an arbitrarily fearsome manner. As with the elimination of fear, however, the body of subjects have no purchase on what constitutes this 'contentment.' The Hobbesian magnitude should then be subject to ongoing work such that its fate comes into man's hands.

Now, if the mythological analysis of the State has validity, what should be apparent in the work of those that followed the conception of the Leviathan, itself with its roots deep in the English polity, are the beginnings of the work on this myth of the State the effect of which was to identify and resolve the implications of the Hobbesian mythology. This work should be seen to be motivated by a concern that the full empowerment of the absolute State has introduced, somewhat as a political Trojan horse, the real prospect of abuse of its power such that it becomes itself a primary source of arbitrary fear among its compliant subjects. Without diluting the fearsomeness of the magnitude, necessary always to give form to existential anxiety experienced by every individual, this work should refine the constituting arrangements that apply to the magnitude. This should take the form of attempts to bring the fate of the entity into man's hands by constitutional change and by its dispersal across social space, so there should be increased influence over 'fear' and 'contentment,' for example by the emergence of representative dominant interests, and a complement of which is the first extension of individual rights. There should be evidence of the creation of space within which these interests and rights can act without interference, a withdrawal of the magnitude from specified areas of activity but without denying its final responsibility in relation to 'fear' and 'contentment.' One manifestation of this is the conditional withdrawal of the magnitude from agreed spheres of activity, but in that through alliances between the dominant interests and the magnitude. Importantly, the notion of subjection can be fully consistent with the concept of individual rights, since rights are typically the representation of the expectations of the individual under the covenant. None of these changes are to be seen as a dilution of the fearsomeness of the magnitude but as its colonisation by and therefore the incorporation of 'corporate' and, less effectively, by individual interests. It is apparent from the analysis given here that all these features are in evidence in the work of Locke.

For the purpose of the argument put here then, it is not significant that Locke's primary target is Filmer rather than Hobbes, since Locke's real target is absolutism. What is significant regarding his opposition to Filmer is that the theological premises of Locke's argument provides Locke with the means to establish the primacy of individual rights against the interests of the State. These rights are not only that the State may not interfere with the individual's attempt to satisfy their religious calling but similarly regarding the individual's laborious appropriation, enjoyment or disposal of property. It should be remembered that Locke does not restrict property to physical goods or land but includes their lives, liberties and estates, all of which rights are held but in a manner that is very insecure in the State of Nature, which makes him willing to quit this and join society.[139] Locke's position against Filmer was that in none of this did those placed by God in a superior position in the social structure have power over other men. In particular, autonomous executive power would be eliminated by empowering the representative Parliament with majority voting. In such a manner would absolutism be given a more elaborate and less arbitrary constituted form.

For this, Locke needed a notion of the State of Nature in which men are placed as equal by God. This notion was a template, uncontaminated by history, against which any polity, along with its attendant rights and responsibilities, could be judged. It was also a state in which, despite the freedom to appropriate its goods, there was insecurity due not to warring but to scarcity and from which men were therefore induced to withdraw to the security of civil society and government where they could pursue through contemplation and hard work their duty to God. The fact that he felt obliged to solve this problem suggests that for Locke the state of nature was still constituted by existential anxiety, although in a form not so intimidating as it was for Hobbes. He proceeded to affirm the natural or inalienable property rights of individuals,[140] with this forming the basis of his justification of the legislature as a powerful arrangement by which anxiety could be transformed into fear and there could be dealt with by affirming these rights: anxiety and fear could thereby be argued by him, in a manner which Hobbes could not argue, to be able to be limited. In effect and although with different results, for their own particular political purposes, neither accepted the virulence or intractability of anxiety, that is irrespective of what political arrangements were constructed for its limitation. They each therefore could not contemplate any strategy based on a self-determination which accepted that intractability and seeking self-determining ways to address it, preferring instead to assert its limitation by the construction of what was in effect rational myth.

But for Locke, man needs the freedom of choice required to satisfy his duties to God. The consequence is that the legitimacy of social arrangements is drawn from the will of its participants. For those that breach the common responsibilities of the State of Nature, or following man's move to society, the law of nature allows for their punishment. More importantly, Locke allows for resistance against immoral acts of the State, in particular to restore the peace when absolutist force has been used to deprive individuals of their rights or freedoms. In this context, he emphasises the illegitimacy of any conqueror's claim to property, especially land. It needs to be added here that Locke did seem to justify the enlargement of one's possessions,[141] that is the accumulation of capital. Dunn rejects any claim that Locke intended to morally legitimate capitalist production[142] but it is not difficult to argue that capital accumulation was at least an intended effect, given Locke's statements.[143] It is virtually impossible to deny that, in addition to the political arrangements that he promoted, there was significant advantage from such arguments to dominant interests, especially the propertied class, over those without such interests.[144]

In all this, Locke's mythological efforts were arguably generated by a desire to eliminate the anxiety caused by what for him was real political crisis. From all this it can also be said that Locke clearly rejected the magnitude in the absolutist form in which Hobbes had proposed it. He did so by establishing and protecting the priority of individual right to theological freedom and property over that of the holders of sovereign power. In mythological terms, Locke began to move the fate of the magnitude of the State significantly into man's hands, which is to say that he began to incorporate man into the functioning of the magnitude. In establishing these rights in this way, Locke does not venture to abolish the concept of magnitude *per se*. On the contrary, we see that his notion of the Parliament is 'supreme' and, with any Government *in situ,* the people have 'no power.'[145] Generally, the calling gave each person a place in the social structure but Locke did not call that structure into question.[146] Neither did he argue in principle against the use of prerogative, only that it was used in a manner approved by the Parliament. Locke certainly wanted order and allegiance to limit civil strife and it was through the legislature, to which the executive must be subject, that this would be achieved. Dunn's claim that Locke was in difficulty regarding whether this allegiance was voluntary or obligatory can be explained within the mythological context as the difference between voluntary submission by the individual to the magnitude to eliminate fear and the enforcement of submission by others to ensure he is not fearsome.

Regarding the status of the legislature, Locke did not conceive it as a broadly representative body—he would have found any egalitarian political structure, especially mass democracy, unthinkable. Egalitarian social democracy as a moral ideal would have offended his deepest social and moral assumptions.[147] Majority consent was obligatory, and a tacit form of this was sufficient, with the presumption that sectional representation was sufficient to satisfy this feature. Hierarchy was unthinkingly accepted by most men and, for Locke, this was morally appropriate. He accepts the use by the custodians of social rules but also the use of power which cannot be regulated, so long as it is for the general good not as determined by their representatives but as judged within the consciousness of each individual. Therein lies the right to revolution, should the judgement be made of abuse of designated power in relation to the calling or property rights, although his hard preference is always that such protest be through appeal to the Parliament wherever possible. He denies that resistance should or would turn to anarchy. Locke sees that the overwhelming force consigned to rulers by the people has 'conferred such deadly power on' them but sees this as to be expected since their aspiration is the comfort of secure social arrangements. Further, he saw the ideological validity of hierarchy, though his aim was to set limits to the potential misuse of this power and this trust.

So Locke has sustained the political mythological magnitude but begun to work on it to begin to bring its fate into man's hands. He delicately balances two features of this entity. On the one hand, the magnitude must be fully empowered to eliminate fear, for example of popery, and create the conditions for contentment, especially to create a space in which each individual could exercise his right to pursue his calling and to accumulate the material product of his labour. On the other, he sustains an attempt to have it incorporate, and therefore be the agent of, dominant interests of the society. More, he initiated the incorporation of the common man more prominently into the field of the fearsome modern State, so that the individual began to acquire its power through his submission. He did this through the arguments he used against the absolutism of Filmer: property, consent, the jural conditions of the state of nature, what constitutes legitimacy, resistance and the theological individualist base of all these. Locke's arguments against Filmer were for this incorporation not for a radical egalitarianism.

It should not therefore be seen that he left the magnitude in a more timorous condition than Hobbes, in that rare resistance to it was justified only if it severely abused its trust, for Locke never contemplated that there be no 'supreme' magnitude.[148] Its incumbents were merely to be replaced through 'resistance' if they failed to satisfy their responsibilities regarding 'fear' and 'contentment' under the covenant. There must not be an abolition of magnitude *per se,* for that would necessarily be anarchy. As a consequence, it can be argued that Locke consolidated the mythology of the entity by accepting the necessity of the existence of the widely empowered entity and by beginning the work on that entity to bring it into man's hands, drawing all individuals into its field by affirming theological and property rights while making it especially sympathetic to dominant interests who would make claims about the satisfaction of fear and desire.

Broadly, Locke's analysis can be argued to be a correction of the two basic failures in Hobbesian theory and thereby the proper genesis of the markers of popular liberalism, that is, by establishing natural individual rights and then by protecting these against the incursions of an absolute power. However, these moves do not dislodge the Hobbesian fundamentals, that is, the edifice remains founded on the base of a presumed status of individuals as equal and rights-bearing but fearful of contingency in the state of nature, on the consequential presumption of a consensual move to political society and on the identification of arrangements claimed to ensure their protection and welfare. From the perspective of a rational mythology, it may be argued with equal conviction that Locke has only begun to correct the weakness in the Hobbesian myth which, despite the move to a political society from the vulnerability of the state of nature, left mankind fearful but now of the absolute monarch. The Lockean arrangements, centred on the establishment of a supremely powerful legislature, still require that individuals transfer 'all their natural power' to an entity subject to emerging constraint, that is they still forgo self-responsibility. The legislature is a means of converting anxiety to manageable fear but, despite Locke's prescriptive insistence, by the very empowerment of the legislature it cannot ensure its elimination. Locke has amended the Hobbesian arrangements but not solved the problem which Hobbes produced. Rather than constructing a 'final' myth by accepting that anxiety can only be managed through individual self-responsibility, they were each committed to its limitation but, grappling with the dynamics of Reformation society, searched only circumstantially for arrangements which would give effect to this.

Before proceeding to consider how Montesquieu worked on the Lockean form of the Hobbesian idea of the mythological State, there is one other element of Lockean thought which should be raised. We have to now been concerned with the elaboration of the idea of the mythological State, through Hobbes and Locke. It is the intention to defer consideration of how this idea has been embedded in individual practice to Part IV, in particular in the exploration of the social ontology of Wittgenstein and, in that context, the work of Elias and Foucault. However, as an indication that practice was also close to the mind of Locke, some things should be said here about that, principally by looking at some of the material we have just examined but in another light.

Locke was clear that individual rights were central to his thought, especially regarding property in terms of its broad definition. This included not only the right to physical property but also the right to resist the State if it should threaten property generally. In this regard, he could be said to be the initial contributor to the first trajectory of mythological liberalism, that is the idea that fear and desire for sympathetic conditions can be dealt with by establishing conditions of reason, freedom, autonomy and responsibility. However, Locke can also properly be seen as describing the embryonic conditions under which the second, interleaved liberal trajectory is established, its subversive element if you like. In this regard, except where there is contravention of the right to fulfil one's calling, he is at least tolerant of the oppression of the existing hierarchical social structures, of social inequality, of an inegalitarian political structure, of indifference to the absence of universal suffrage, the climate of trust and psychological dependence on rulers and of hard physical labour which he actively promotes. It is no inflation of these factors to see them as a tolerance or even promotion of docility and productivity. Thereby are both liberal trajectories installed in the mythology of the State almost from the beginning. We shall see more of this in Rousseau and Kant and then Hayek.

MONTESQUIEU

Although it was to wait for Montesquieu to be given its full elaboration, a key element of the Lockean framework was the separation of legislature and executive.[149] In this, the legislature remained supreme.[150] This notion of separation is problematic, despite arguments as to legislative superiority and despite arguments that each is based upon the dual capacities of individuals in the state of nature, because the deliberations of the legislature can produce law but not action and so are incomplete: only the executive can realise the necessary unity of law and action. The consequence is that there is a flaw in the Lockean argument as to the supreme power of the legislature. It was a flaw to be directly addressed by Montesquieu.

Locke's attempt to limit the fear produced by the Hobbesian political arrangements was extended by Montesquieu through the doctrines of the separation of powers[151] and the mixed form of the State, but still within the 'Hobbesian' framework. Montesquieu rejected the Lockean principle of legislative supremacy due to the danger it posed to individual liberty, thereby recognising in the Lockean legislature the very danger that Locke saw in the Hobbesian absolute monarch: the common desire for power[152] and in that a continuing source of anxiety due to the likelihood of its abuse.

But Montesquieu rejected the Hobbesian claim that this desire is constitutive of human nature. Only institutional arrangements, whether democratic or aristocratic, produce this in individuals.[153] Therefore the solution lay in reforming institutional arrangements, by neutralising these individually but not collectively through separation and contest.[154] The benefit of representation perceived by Montesquieu is not so much its continuity with those it represents but its capacity to prevent the represented from taking active resolutions.[155] Like Hobbes and Locke, he saw the danger and the fear which results from unrestrained popular discourse. He diminished the importance of the judiciary as being required only when the other powers are in dispute and specifically in relation to England where this activity is exercised by the people, referring to the jury. By this, he argues that the executive be separate from the legislature but for their effective equal strength, irrespective of the 'in principle' superiority of the latter, so that the tendency of the legislature to abuse its power with respect to those it represents is diminished. Thereby he further reformed the Hobbesian magnitude while addressing the flaw that Locke let slip into his own amendment of Hobbes.

This rearrangement to promote the balance of strength between legislature and executive is not a neutralisation of their respective power as claimed by Manent. Montesquieu saw the flaw in Locke's 'Hobbesian' arrangement and attempted to resolve this within its own terms by balancing the powers. However, balancing powers is not their neutralisation. That he saw the role of the independent judiciary engaged when these two powers were in dispute implies that he was not arguing for such neutralisation. Neither is the subsequent emergence of the colonisation of the executive and judiciary by the legislature an insurmountable problem for Montesquieu. He perceived the danger of that and argued for its prevention.

There are two important features of this arrangement. First, that the necessity for decisions will overcome the competition between legislature and executive; and second, that the decisions made will tend not to be what either power wants (due to the necessity of compromise), although for Montesquieu they are likely to promote the liberty of individual citizens. This likelihood derives from the tendency of each power or party (that is, the legislature and the monarchy as executive) to attract its own partisan support, which requires satisfaction. Dynamically, the balance between these which results will be sustained by the tendency for support to shift to the party of lesser influence, due to both the desire born of personal interest and the desire of citizens not to allow one party the oppressive power which accompanies ascendency. This also minimises any prospect of unilateral popular initiative.[156] The essence of this arrangement for Manent is originary popular powerlessness, which can also be seen as a commitment to the limiting of fear. This powerlessness which limits fear constitutes liberty for Montesquieu.[157]

Montesquieu and Mythology

The mythological implications of this are clear: liberty in such a constructed arrangement is constituted by that of which a citizen or her representative is incapable, due to the focus on the attempted elimination of anxiety or at least its radical limiting, rather than by what is able to be done (as responsibility for oneself) by accepting its inevitability and then constructing arrangements appropriate to that condition. Montesquieu argues that the tendency of his preferred arrangement to be both intrusive and oppressive, that is where law (which determines liberty in this context) becomes pervasive, is prevented by the denial of excessive rights or opportunities to any party, which constitutes the optimising of both liberty and independence. In a mirror image of the Hobbesian and Lockean strategy, Montesquieu may thereby be claimed in some sense to have headed back towards a state of nature, in the sense that we are governed more exclusively by a State that governs us less. Without pushing this point too far, insofar as we are governed less, we are approaching a state of nature. And because this state of nature is still not a state of war, but offers us acceptable security and prosperity, we have no motive for leaving this state. Some might argue controversially that this is the fulfilment the original program of liberalism, that is by reversing the order of the factors: the representative institutional regime initially was the ingenious device making it possible to leave a state of nature that was compellingly (for Hobbes) or at least strongly (for Locke) unbearable; but finally refined (for Montesquieu), it became the ingenious device making it possible to live in an essentially satisfying state of nature as individuals came to constrain themselves through the balance of its influence.[158] At least this is the claim.

To this extent, Montesquieu can be argued to have increasingly fulfilled the Hobbesian agenda by realising the potential of the modifications made by Locke to the Hobbesian framework. For Montesquieu, existential anxiety has largely been eliminated through the creation of balanced, separate powers. Manent does acknowledge that this reading of the effect of Montesquieuean arrangements, that is an artificial state of nature, is a contradiction in terms. His response is that we are each divided between the natural man and the citizen now within us. That is, we are both in the civil state and in the state of nature.[159]

This negative individualism is driven by the attempted elimination of anxiety converted to fear. It is at the heart of the Hobbesian paradigm through to Montesquieu and will be argued to continue beyond him. Its spirit is 'to separate the will from what it desires, or to prevent each person doing what he cannot prevent himself from desiring. The people cannot do what they want, they can only elect representatives in the hope that they will do what the electorate wants; the representatives in turn cannot do what they themselves want, but must be keenly aware of what the executive wants; and the executive cannot do what it wants since it must seriously take into account what the legislature wants. A mechanism of decision-making that makes sovereignty useless now replaces the absolute sovereignty of Hobbes' Leviathan and also that of Locke's legislative body.'[160] Effectively, while the concern of both Hobbes and Locke was to construct arrangements which would eliminate anxiety (from the war of all against all and from the fear of hunger), Montesquieu's concern was to eliminate the anxiety created by those Hobbesian and Lockean solutions, thereby further shoring up the legitimate mythology of the State. He achieved this by fully empowering all three powers but then fully balancing them, by each of which the individual is increasingly engaged.

But this negative individualism is the essence of the denial of the possibility of a non-mythological self-responsibility. This 'Hobbesian' arrangement can be contrasted with that available in the Aristotelian Greek city-state, wherein compromise is positively sought in a genuinely agonistic deliberative process rather than institutionally pre-factored as it is in the Montesquieuean working through of Hobbesianism. The liberty which is constructed by the Montesquieuean process, based as it is on the proscription of incursions of and on others, is negative in that freedom 'is less doing what I want than being able not to do what you want me to do.'[161] This claim that the growth of liberty was negative is mythologically significant, especially given the proliferation of individual rights subsequently generated by the Montesquieuean arrangements. 'Being able not to do what you want me to do' is the creation of spheres of activity from which the magnitude withdraws, except that it is expected to protect that state of being itself.

In Montesquieu we are therefore presented with the claim of an ultimate strengthening of the legitimate mythology of the Hobbesian-Lockean State as a device which carries the claim to radically limit anxiety, a strengthening brought about by elaborating the modifications that Locke made to the Hobbesian framework. In doing so, Montesquieu claims to have realised the mixed constitutional form of State as a state of nature devoid of war and hunger, that is, of anxiety born of social and natural causes.

It may be observed here that, following the radical contingency introduced by the turmoil that came with the factionalisation of the State following the emergence of Protestantism, it should not be surprising that a solution would be sought in which the State would come to assume an absolutist form: existential anxiety was generally increased, so it would be seen that a State form that provided absolute protection was needed. Neither should it be surprising that the absolutist form required modification in itself, as through Locke and then Montesquieu, to eliminate the factors in these absolutist and post-absolutist (respectively) solutions to the original problem, which themselves generated fear.

However, in such arrangements there is no individual sovereignty. What there is, due to the fear of others within and outside the State, is a set of institutional dynamics which construct individual liberty in a form which proscribes, and ultimately prescribes, certain behaviour and establishes a perpetual covenant of submission to those institutions, rather than in a manner which realises individual self-responsibility. The objective meaning of these institutions is argued here to have been such that they denied any sense of positive self-responsibility.

Consequently, Montesquieu can be claimed to have demonstrated a strong mythological disposition. He did this through having accepted the Hobbesian mythological archetype, as amended by Locke, and by having protected its determinative power or fearsomeness. He attempted to protect the notion of the fully empowered magnitude of the State and to enhance that by correcting what he saw as its principal flaw, that is the danger of its possible excess which Locke had not resolved. He correctly saw that the possibility of such excess posed the greatest risk to its own continuance. So, he recommended amendments to check its power, without neutralising it, through a theoretical mechanism of internally balanced forces to prevent the dominance of any single institutional interest. This idea included creating spheres of activity from which the State sympathetically withdrew but without forgoing its dual ultimate responsibilities. Competition between dominant, institutional interests was for him preferable to any single institutional dominance, as proposed by Locke for the legislature.

The institutions of the State as conceived by Montesquieu may not have been able to act unilaterally but they did not constitute a weak State. It was still a State to which obedience was due, so long as those who were obedient believed it acted sympathetically towards them. Appearing to constrain the fearsomeness of the State, the separation of powers promoted the dispersal of the fully empowered State across social space, even if this was still slowly being matched by the increasing sympathy, in that it encouraged competitive alliances between an increasingly wide range of interests and thereby promoted the colonisation of the State by such interests as the landed gentry, the emerging bourgeoisie and the Church. Competition, withdrawal and colonisation ensured the continuing existence of the magnitude.

However, Montesquieu's contribution to the mythologising of the State went beyond mere intellectual mechanics. Kriegel refers to the tracing by Emile Boutmy of the associative rather than the representative genesis of modern government.[162] This reveals that Montesquieu's emphasis on the separation of legislative, judicial and executive functions denied that there was in fact juridical unity that subordinated these other functions to its rule. That is, there was more unity than the separation that Montesquieu asserted. Rather than the myth of a founding parliament, Royal will functioned from above downward through these institutions. It is in this context that Halevy's identification of the amalgamation of judicial and legislative powers in England early in the nineteenth century should be seen. He revealed that British judges could exercise legislative functions and legislators the functions of the judiciary. As a consequence, 'once again we are compelled to correct Montesquieu's interpretation of the British Constitution. His two definitions of that Constitution—a constitution based on the separation of powers, a mixed Constitution—are not equivalent, and the latter is the more accurate.'[163] The point here is that Montesquieu's idea of the advantages of the embryonic separation of the British political institutions was a misreading of the actual cross-hatched institutional arrangements as they existed and operated. His was therefore a special contribution to the political mythology: it was imaginative as well as structural. But it came at an increasingly high price to the individual subject, since liberty was for him only the negative 'being able not to do what you want me to do' rather than the promotion of being able to become responsible to and for oneself.

But, despite Montesquieu's heroic attempt to eliminate the inherent problems and contradictions within the Hobbesian paradigm, what was perceived to be a further, fundamental problem still existed. It is this which was of concern to Rousseau. Its essence was that the 'Hobbesian' paradigm, especially as amended by Locke, was intended to constrain the institutions so that a space was created within which the rights of individuals could be exercised in security. The difficulty was that this created a selfish individual, the bourgeois, rather than an engaged person, a citizen who was interested in promoting the interests of the community. It was this which Rousseau took as central to his thought, and which would have a persistent influence on and then through Kant down to Rawls, as well as down through republican thought to Pettit: the right of the State to positively intervene into the lives of men to ensure their engagement. From a mythological perspective, this is the identification of a central weakness in the 'Hobbesian' conception of the mythological magnitude. If the purpose of mythological arrangements were merely to create a space to protect but not interfere with individual, selfish freedom, this would remain a weakness at the heart of the political myth. For the myth was sustained by not only forgoing one's responsibility for the elimination of fear and the creation of sympathetic conditions of existence to it but also incorporating oneself into its dispersed arrangements of government as an active forgoing of self-responsibility, a personal commitment to its sustenance. That is, being a citizen in the Rousseauean sense. In addressing this matter, Rousseau overlaid the mythology of republicanism on the liberal myth and thereby extended the liberal trajectory of the idea of the State through an act of critique and positive re-programming.

4 Imagining a General Will

ROUSSEAU

Hobbes was clearly an important foil for Rousseau, who both admired and attacked him on a range of such issues as the two swords;[1] the state of nature,[2] where he takes a contrary position;[3] and the nature of man.[4] Regarding the latter, he also comments on the 'dangerous reveries' which Hobbes has left among the 'extravagances of the human mind.'[5] These extravagances surely referred to the nature of man: 'Above all, let us not conclude with Hobbes that because he has no idea of goodness man is naturally wicked, that he is vicious because he does not know virtue, that he always refuses to those of his kind services which he does not believe he owes them.'[6] Of equal importance, he rejects Hobbes' analysis of sovereignty.[7]

Broadly, and in the context of these references by Rousseau to Hobbes, the position adopted here is that the political philosophy of the *Social Contract* may legitimately be interpreted as the search for a theoretical critique and reprogramming of the order propounded in *Leviathan*.[8] In this search, there is much that is not only uncontroversial but easily regarded also as admirable, even if unrealistic and unable finally to be realised. Rousseau sets out to argue for social arrangements the key feature of which is justice through order. He wants a society which is orderly in that men's passions are tempered by law and custom, where harmony and restraint take the place of generalised conflict, the justice of which is demonstrated by the highest places being occupied by the most virtuous, and where everyone can control his passions and act with moderation.

Rousseau sees this as possible only through an artifice the masters of which are the great lawgivers who found the harmonious community. That is, this is not a politics born of the natural state, since it relies on close community bonds not possible in the wild, given the isolation and therefore self-interest of individuals in that state.[9] Disorder is characterised by inequality, which is a reflection of the capriciousness which produces wrong opinions about individuals and leads to a flawed sense of personal identity. What must be emphasised is virtue, humanity, courage and moderation, not personal wealth. Wealth, especially in the form of personal property,[10] should not be disallowed but it must be a matter of moderation.

For Rousseau, the means to achieving all this is the establishment of a rational general will through social contract, which is manifest in universal laws and which grounds the authority of the Republican State.[11] Such laws will prevent the individual from being subject to the will of others, since all will obey the laws.

For him, political and moral philosophy are inextricably linked. Man is not just a natural and passive being. He is also active. The idea of relations and order are not merely imposed upon him, he constructs them himself. In fact, he has 'a natural love of order.'[12] But the problem of morality is only real for artificial or civilised man, who can compare and make judgements and so knows what order is. Established by God and therefore acquired through his conscience rather than his reason, man has 'a love of order in general,' a concept at the heart of Rousseauean moral and political theory.[13]

Rousseau's man moved from the natural state to the artifice of the social state not as the result of the activity of a conscious will but due to a chance combination of causes.[14] The natural state he has left evinces order and harmony, the product of an intelligent and beneficent Lawgiver and is a place where each part is assigned its own place. For Rousseau, order means the mutual harmony of parts, obedience to universal laws.[15] But this order does not extend to individuals, who must themselves establish order in their relations. And this is a problem, for man cannot find harmony in disorder but neither is order and peace easy to attain. In fact, Rousseau's language in describing this seems more like the descriptions by Hobbes of nature being in a state of warfare. This is due to the individual's desire for profit, often against the general interest.[16] Unlike primitive man, who is self-reliant but uncooperative as he strives for his own survival within the harmonious state of nature, civilised man within the artificial social order constantly strives to attain superiority over his fellow man and is therefore in continuous conflict. Man is therefore morally responsible for disorder.[17] Hence, the challenge posed by Rousseau is not the question of how to impose order upon the disorder of nature but a matter of creating order from artificial disorder.[18]

The new entity to be created is the just, ordered society, rational and consciously willed. Although this entity is an artifice, Rousseau borrows the image of the natural order in his description of it. In it, each individual finds himself a part of the whole on which he is dependent for his life and his very being. That is, individuals do not exist as separate entities but the State and individual exist for each other.[19] Even though the pursuit of the common good is weaker because it is artificial, a just social order demands that, through the promotion of the general rather than the individual will, this must be developed and prevail. So, the natural order with independent individuals needs to be replaced with an artificial order in which individuals have submitted themselves to the political state in accepting the supremacy of the general will. They are, therefore, no longer those same isolated and independent individuals that they were in the natural state. Mankind thus passes from the natural state to the enjoyment of civil liberty and subjection to the sovereign authority whose cornerstone is the social contract. This is not emergent society, the state into which men emerge from the natural state and in which long-term relationships begin to form and generate rivalries. This is a state which comprises civil, political society and its organising principle is the concept of order.[20]

The ordered society cannot come into being by relying on man's natural impulses and on natural law. His instincts for self-preservation, such as fear of pain and death, are moral and conscience is the arbiter.[21] In fact, it is the capacity for pity towards the weak, the guilty and humanity generally which suits man to live in society. However, this becomes a faint echo by the time recognisable social arrangements are established. So another power than nature is required if man is not to live in isolation or disorder, hence the creation of an artifice which will maintain order against man's natural instincts. Such an artifice is neither a continuation nor the restoration of natural order.[22]

It is disorder which Rousseau regards as the primary source of inequality. Disorder is not merely the absence of harmony but the lack of hierarchy, or the wrong assignment of individual elements within the whole. Seeking an unassigned rank is the result of pride or ambition and is the source of disorder. Such feelings begin in comparison with other species, to whom man is superior, and are then transferred into social experience in a manner that denies his conscience or sense of virtue.[23] Like Hobbes, Rousseau not only saw the differences between men but also saw that there was a distinction between natural and artificial inequalities. However, for Rousseau, natural inequalities should not be allowed to develop into inequalities of the moral or legal kind. Law should bring about equality. The differences in the natural state are just that, they are not inequalities because there is no basis of comparison there. But without a basis for comparison, that is outside society, neither is any sense of personal identity possible. Identity comes with the move into society but through the competition born of comparing oneself with others and the consequential ascription of value and utility. Thereby comes disorder.[24]

But comparison can also establish the tyranny of opinion and, with that, the gap between reality and appearance.[25] It establishes the basis of status hierarchy and creates the identity of the individual, especially of the moral individual, within the context of the whole. Through this is disorder generated: disorder as wrongful assignment of individuals within the social hierarchy, thus as inequality; disorder as ambition, thus as the conflict caused by seeking one's own ends and not the common good;

and disorder as immoderation or the expression of uncontrolled passion. Behind much of the various criteria of success, such as riches, honour, and command, stands the thirst for pre-eminence. This was an understanding Rousseau shared with Hobbes.[26] For Rousseau, wealth beyond moderate levels cannot be justified, as it is always at the expense of others.

So there must be a transformation of the customs and criteria used by the community to assess relative worth, for the fundamental cause of conflict is not the pursuit of real economic goods to satisfy physical needs, although that happens, but the tireless pursuit of status so men can command such prizes. With such status comes the desired personal identity.[27] It is in this context that Rousseau makes his important distinction between *amour de soi*, the self-love which is the basis of preservation of the individual and which is therefore in conformity with order, and *amour propre*, the ambitious egotism which produces enmity, hatred and jealousy and therefore disorder.[28]

In this context, Rousseau makes an important distinction between two sensibilities, physical and moral, the latter capable of both negative and positive effects. It is negative when it attempts to constrict the circle of the lived experience of others. It is positive when it leads us to expand and strengthen our innermost self, being a fruit of self-respect rather than egotism. A person with such sensibility looks simply to his own well-being without concerning himself with that of others. But the man ruled by egotism directs his attention exclusively to others and only judges himself in comparison with them. Further, he explores the results in his own life of reversing the usual degeneration from self-love to egotism, a process in which he leaves society and frees himself from the tyranny of opinion. When a man leaves society behind, it is possible to rediscover independence of mind and with this comes also the rediscovery of the natural order. Rousseau suggests it is possible to develop a personal identity which is independent of social interaction. If one places oneself outside the social order, inequality and disorder can cease to become a problem. Alternatively, a wise man, using only his own eyes and heart and recognising no authority other than reason, may lose the urge to dominate others or take pleasure from their misfortunes or be wealthy.[29] These are features which would not be out of place in the life of someone who has resumed self-responsibility.

From all this, Rousseau faces the challenge of how to go about transforming passionate disorder into virtuous order, to discover the order within him and make this a political order. This is the place of the social contract in his thinking. In the universal society of mankind, a condition distinct from the natural state but without political authority, Rousseau sees individual need that has grown to the point that it can't be fulfilled without the assistance of others. This circumstance produces the strong and the weak but it is unstable, regarding both survival and personal identity. There must be political authority.

Not any such authority will do, as some would be worse than anarchy.[30] Such polities would fail to protect all their citizens equally because they would favour special rather than the common interest, that is they would be tyrannous. Rousseau thus rejects what he sees as the Hobbesian argument that arbitrary power is better than no authority at all. Rousseau takes the view that tyranny is always unacceptable. The concord that is necessary to eliminate the anxiety of the natural state and the concern about the activities of a tyrant can only come from a sovereign authority that can create laws and who is guided in this by a social contract. This is the rule to inspire the just constitution. His challenge is to conceive a circumstance where independent, rational, fearful but ambitious individuals will opt for the common good, an arrangement that will eliminate fear and induce the majority of self-interested individuals to agree to it.[31] This is not simply the conversion of natural man to a civilised state, as the natural state itself is an artifice constructed by Rousseau and it is almost impossible to say with confidence what is artificial and what is natural in man. The very notion of the natural state is not something that can be thought of as having actually existed in the past, nor will it in the future. It is a hypothetical construction which has a role to play in the context of a study of what are in effect normative principles. The hypothesis of the natural state helps to form a clearer judgement concerning the present condition of mankind.[32]

In this process of construction, although excessive passion must be tempered, there must also be justice. Rousseau's solution is that each individual must subject himself to the authority of the general will, comprising every individual, and he will be received as an indivisible part of the whole, that is as a citizen, whose interest is the common good. This is a rational choice, as it ensures the interest of each. The sovereign, or general will, has the interest only of its members.

It is important for Rousseau that this contractual arrangement binding the individual to the sovereign general will is reciprocal. By this, each will accept the authority of this sovereign on the condition that the same is true of all others, making all equal before the law and ensuring that each must seek the common interest to advance his own. Further, the sovereign cannot impose any prescription that is useless to the community.[33] Because each is an equal member of the sovereign general will, all have equal expectations of each other. Further, it is the sovereignty and universality of the law that also delivers justice and liberty. It is the only means by which the sovereign can express itself and constitutes its legitimacy. Its universality rationally excludes sectional interest but promotes private interest in the sense that justice is equity.[34]

This notion of justice based on a conception of law is not available to natural man. His state has to do with natural feelings of self-respect and pity as a means of preserving the species.[35] This is a form of order but not one which established individuals as part of a social whole, so as order it is unstable. The other form of order would come from the social contract and a law based on reason in which it would be self-evident that harmony was more in the interests of the individual than the conflict that derives from the simple pursuit of individual interest. It can only be established, as civil law, by being grounded in the legitimate political authority which must, through the social compact, seek the greatest good for all. Men have a moral obligation towards the natural law while citizens have a juridical and political obligation towards the civil law. The natural law is the supreme authority but its jurisdiction does not reach beyond the inner life of man. Further, the social contract is the base for all individual rights for these liberties are born with the advent of the political constitution.[36]

The whole theory of the social contract is, ultimately, no more than a rational justification of a law-governed society. It is not in the true interest of men to live in a condition of complete independence or under a political constitution where the sovereign will resides in one person alone and where equality under the law is not respected. The sovereignty of law and equality under the law are central to Rousseau's response to the problem of the relation between justice and utility, so the principal point of his political doctrine is the relation between the sovereignty of law and liberty. As law is identified with the general will, liberty is possible only through obedience to the general will.[37] For Rousseau, liberty is not the same as being independent. The citizen who is subject to the general will is not independent since he is subject to the sovereign authority, but he is free because he is not forced to obey the will of any other individual. Liberty is the right to do everything which the law allows.'[38]

Here lies the difference with Hobbes. For Hobbes, the liberty of the subject is dependent on the obligation that each one accepted when he submitted to the sovereign authority. It consists of the right of self-defence and the right enjoyed by each citizen that he should not be forced to do anything that might be for his harm. But, above all, the liberty of the subject is expressed in those things not mentioned by the sovereign, that is, where the law is silent.[39] Rousseau is concerned that this leaves open the possibility of the imposition of one individual will on another. This is the difference between negative and positive freedom. The liberty of the citizen does not consist only in the exercise of the right of sovereignty. It also implies protection from all wrongs and injustices. The limits of the liberty of each individual also mark the point at which the liberty of his neighbour begins. The guarantee of these reciprocal limits is provided by the finality of law. The sovereignty of law provides encouragement for each citizen to respect his neighbour's rights because law ensures that no-one can enlarge the sphere of his freedom at the expense of others. When the liberty of one person is infringed by another, the latter imposes his will on the former. Consequently, the will of one has become subject to another, which is for Rousseau the very opposite of liberty.[40]

Rousseau's social contract has generalised the notion of sovereignty, as the direct source of final authority, from an elite institution to the entire society, thereby engaging all citizens in a regime of mutual constraint in a manner that Hobbes' political arrangement, or the amendments to it of Locke and Montesquieu, could not. For Rousseau, the legitimate State guarantees security, which is its superiority over the natural state. Moreover, men accept the social compact precisely because they prefer a more secure life over one which is precarious. Such an arrangement ensures the control of the individual's inner passions so that he lives in harmony with a law which he has imposed on himself, which is an inner law that reflects a love of justice and moderation.[41] From this comes order and the common good, for the purpose of law should be the well-being and security of each individual as well as the good and security of the republic.[42]

The principal threat to the success of Rousseau's arrangement is the constant threat of sectional interest, which may get the assembly to agree to their wishes and thus allow merely private interests to prevail. Then the State is despotic, an argument Rousseau appears to share with Montesquieu.[43] Rousseau prescribes only collective decisions. That all participate in defining and are equal before the law, that is are submissive to the general will, is another correction of Hobbes, for whom the sovereign cannot be restricted by the laws he has created.[44] In these arguments, Rousseau follows the republicanism of Machiavelli.[45] His republicanism means not only the pre-eminence of a constitution where law is sovereign over men and the common good takes precedence over individual self-interest, but a government by a small elite of wise and virtuous magistrates, that is an aristocracy, though sovereignty resides in the people. Force will be used when required by the general will to impose equality under the law. Rousseau emphasises that the republican concept of liberty is the freedom of men who have no desire to serve or dominate others.[46] It is typified by civic virtue, which is born of love of one's country and inspires courage, firmness of purpose and sometimes even heroism. It is not the moderation, fairness and tolerance called into the service of Christianity as the love of humanity: 'Christianity preaches nothing but servitude and dependence. Its spirit is too favourable to tyranny for tyranny not always to profit from it.'[47] This is not to say that Rousseau was offended by the human virtues as such. The supreme achievement in politics is working towards the elimination of the use of force.[48] For him, true politics was inseparably linked with the great legislators who knew how to transform a mass into a people by changing human nature.[49] Equally, there should not be excessive wealth, for this induces subjection to the will of the wealthy and the great and this is the death of liberty.[50] The people feels secure when it sees that no-one is allowed to flout the law and that even kings themselves cannot govern in a way which is contrary to law.[51]

To make all this work, the people must take the trouble to attend the public assemblies, to take up arms against all enemies, to keep watch over the activities of its magistrates. Then will the polity be secure against enemies within and without. Rousseau was specially hard on the institution of representatives as those who would sap civic virtues and make the loss of liberties more likely.

For Rousseau, the political arrangements he prescribes will bring order and justice. No-one will impose his will on another, there will not be a state of generalised hostility and individuals will be allocated status levels in a manner that would not be unjust. This is achieved through the construction of an order which is artificial,[52] a construct founded on the will of the sovereign authority. Where society exists without political authority there is disorder; where there is natural order there is no society. Moreover, the fact that political authority exists is not, in itself, enough to ensure that there will be order in human affairs. There must be a sovereign, but the sovereign should give the general will and the law the first place. It is the legislator who discovers which are the best laws for the different peoples and must be able to transform each individual, who is himself a perfect and separate entity, into a part of the greater whole. The legislator is compared by Rousseau to God because, in an analogous manner, he is the author of the political order and wise in that.[53] Republican order is an artificial order. It owes its inception to the artifice of the social compact and the art of the legislator, who, like a skilled engineer, is able to arrange all the parts of the machine so that they work in a harmonious way to achieve the purpose the machine was made for.[54]

All this does not translate into extreme democracy, where each is everything, that is debater, executive and judge. Although sovereignty resides with the people, there must be delegated roles. This is democracy modified with wisdom, residing in an aristocracy. As with Montesquieu,[55] equality comes only through the institution of law and the creation of citizens. It is an hierarchical arrangement from the sovereign, which is all individuals comprising the general will, down through magistrates as executive to the people as subjects. The magistrates, who are to be the most wise and virtuous and will pursue the common good, must be elected by all the people. They will enjoy no privilege, as the republic is generally to be a place of moderation. Since the primary and ineradicable motivator of men is admiration and preferment, they must be brought to better judgement.[56] Opinions which develop naturally as a product of social relationships must, in effect, be transformed artificially. It is, therefore, the same engineer who has constructed the political machine who must, through his art, modify social attitudes. To be able to transform men's tastes and values in this way is the greatest proof of the Lawgiver's skill. The wise Lawgiver can and should institute laws which convey the approval or disapproval of the public in the form of reward or punishment. In Rousseau's view, laws should not only have a negative function, discouraging wrong-doing through the threat of punishment, but should also exercise a positive influence, urging men to do good by holding out the possibility of a reward.

Rousseau's project is ostensibly to provide a theoretical definition of the most suitable ways in which men's views can be altered to make them moderate but without forsaking the principle that the individual acts only in accord with what he judges to be his interest. He does not say that men have forsaken the desire to obtain great wealth because they have become altruistic, but rather because it is not in their interest to pursue wealth, that is because wealth is no longer esteemed.[57]

A just Rousseauean political order would have rules which govern the way individuals are channelled to the various forms of employment available. Its aim should be to provide the conditions which make happiness possible and which encourage the individual to lead a moral life but it also has the responsibility to see that each person has the opportunity to gain personal fulfilment irrespective of the caprices of fortune, such as which family one is born into. People should be engaged in the work most suited to their talents. For Rousseau the ultimate effect of such arrangements is not the good of the whole but of the individuals, that is individual happiness, good customs and civic virtue. Idiosyncratically, for Rousseau the best social order is one which attaches men most closely to the land and is least vulnerable to change. There should be discouragement of social mobility: happiness does not come from change and the struggle to get on but from stability of character and inner balance between desires and qualities.[58] Further, the republic should be small so that, when all the citizens know each other and can closely observe each other's behaviour, those who resort to intrigue to get on have less chance of success.[59]

Rousseau's next move introduces uncertainty, even contradiction, into his wider argument. The problem emerges with a key statement, which follows from what has already been said, that is that unless law reigns in the hearts of men there can be no republic as he prescribes it. One may take an uncritical or even generous interpretation of this,[60] although there is a less generous interpretation that can be made from within Rousseau's own text which we will explore shortly. For the moment, taking generosity as the mark, the interpretation is that Rousseau was intending that a just republic can be preserved only if its customs are admirable—good laws themselves are not enough. Taking the lead from Montesquieu, who was cautious in this regard,[61] and Machiavelli, Rousseau argued that patterns of behaviour can be changed without recourse to the force of law. In fact, good customs are essential. The preservation of the order of the republic cannot be achieved unless the men are sober, hard-working and temperate, and the women chaste, demure and devoted to the running of household affairs. Even their private lives should be open to public scrutiny. In the latter regard, a special office should be created within the magistracy with the appointment of censors, whose task it would be to see that the general behaviour within society did not become too lax.[62] Further, Rousseau advocates the establishment of a civil religion as a tool for ensuring compliance with the law and the standards of behaviour it requires. For those who do not assume the beliefs of this religion, the consequences include banishment and even death.[63]

We shall return to this point. But it should at least be said here that what emerges from all this is a vast difference, even a fundamental contradiction, between, on the one hand, the establishment of a polity through the rational belief that it is in the interests of each individual to comply with the standards of behaviour on which it is founded and, on the other, social arrangements that require the use of surveillance, fear of banishment and death as means of ensuring compliance with those standards.

IMPLICATIONS OF ROUSSEAUEAN THOUGHT

Before commenting on the mythological significance of Rousseauean political thought, it will be helpful to make some observations concerning its more immediate implications. Behind Rousseau's aspirations for virtue, well-being and order stands a desire to construct a universal sense of the common good so that fear and material disadvantage among men in society will be eliminated, especially as that is caused by the unbounded pursuit of individual and sectional interests. If law is sovereign, then common interest governs and the sovereignty of the law guarantees liberty and equality under the law. This is the greatest good of all.[64] The purpose of law should be the well-being and security of each individual as well as the good and security of the republic. But this does not mean that, in a just State, the public good requires the full sacrifice of the individual's private interests. For Rousseau, in a State made just by just laws, the public good might be incompatible with the extravagant desire for wealth or power but it does not militate against the citizens' well-being and security.[65] That is, it is dealing with fear and sympathetic conditions which lies behind the social and political strategies that he elaborates and, ultimately, behind his desire to establish the just, ordered society. His aim is to find a way to allow men to fulfil their innermost desire, to live in harmony.[66]

His principal strategy to deliver justice and harmony is this conception of the general will, a fully empowered sovereign entity to which all individuals must make themselves totally subject. The first cleverness of Rousseau is that he seems to make such total subjection easy, since the general will is comprised of all individuals in the first place and they have equal influence on its deliberations. The next cleverness is that he makes this first membership apparently easy because the reasonableness of all individuals will have them understand that it is in their individual interests to comply with the prescriptions of the general will: the relationship between them all and with the general will is reciprocal.[67] This is therefore not only the law but, because of our compliance, it is the law we give ourselves.

But this is where the difficulties begin. Rousseau is forced to acknowledge that most men are more likely to use the reason that brought them to the social contract to justify the pursuit of what they see as their own interests, rather than those of others. This forces Rousseau to engage a series of tactics which ultimately undermine the premises of his argument. Men have to be brought to understand that their real nature is the pursuit of harmony and justice, that is a sense of the common good, the pursuit of which is the general will and which becomes this law we give ourselves. Each individual must forgo the range of characteristics and thereby the interests that make him an individual[68] and adopt those that are for the common good, not only those of justice and order, which he will come to appreciate are really in his interest. That is, in the republic instituted by the social contract, if one is a citizen all are. The compact moves every single person towards a common identity, which precedes all the other aspects of the personal identity of the individual. He may be strong or weak, rich or poor, be more or less intelligent, be of one class or another. In the republic all these qualities which go to make up the uniqueness of the individual recede into the background.

Even when he is exercising his equal rights as a member of the sovereign general will, his personal preferences must be put to one side.[69] Only by undergoing such a radical transformation at the hands of the general will is an individual not subject to the will of any other individual, the republican ideal. This forgoing of his own interests is crucial because it is at the heart of Rousseau's argument against groups of individuals as factions, whose presence is the source of disorder.[70]

This is the making of not just a change but of a fundamental change to human nature.[71] The republican individual may not be subject to any other individual will but he is completely subject to the general will. He must be transformed into the kind of being that would fit the expectations of the general will. Rousseau is clear on this.[72] The full force of the general will may be used to achieve this. Rousseau is clear about the awesome power of the general will, the creation of which is the justification for changing of human nature, the annihilation of the individual's natural resources, the complete absorption of the individual.[73] He emphasises this point.[74] It is this fully intrusive power of the sovereign general will which is the source of his proposal for the surveillance of private lives and for his institution of civil religion, with the extreme measures of banishment or death that it can impose for non-belief.[75]

This power led Berlin to observe that Rousseau does not mean by liberty the 'negative' freedom of the individual not to be interfered with, but the possession by all of the fully qualified members of society of a share in the public power which is entitled to interfere with every aspect of every citizen's life.[76] Rousseau was himself concerned about this level of power, as Constant indicated.[77] This is not a contradiction of Rousseau's statement that, although the people cannot be represented in its legislative power, it must be represented in its executive power, which is force applied to Law.[78]

For Rousseau, it is the whole that matters first. Despite his arguments that individual interest is important, he requires such a shift in individual interests to conform to the general will that any comprehensive sense of individuality is to be forgone. This means that individuals do not exist as separate entities. The individual may be sacrificed for the preservation and the good of the greater whole. The body politic should be able to exercise the same kind of absolute control over its subordinate parts as in the physical realm the individual is able to do with regard to his own limbs. Rousseau does attempt to qualify this by insisting that, as much as the individual exists for the State, the reverse is also true otherwise there would be tyranny.[79] A Rousseauean might simply argue that the two are equally important to each other but the problem with such an argument is that, as Rousseau himself acknowledges, the State may go to extraordinary lengths to change human nature, including annihilation of natural individual resources, so that an individual understands that his interests are best served by complying with the prescriptions of the general will.

Rousseau's argument allows a better understanding of his commitment to hierarchical social and political arrangements and to the need for each individual being happy with his place within it or being brought to such happy acceptance. The idea that order consists in everything being in its right place did not originate with Rousseau. The idea has a long history, going back at least to Cicero. Rousseau himself states that it is better for men to accept the place where they are rather than to seek to escape from it, this no doubt because personal ambition is a source of political disorder.[80]

This in turn explains Rousseau's approach to the division of labour. The problem of social order, which derives from the inability of individuals to preserve themselves against obstacles in the state of nature,[81] is connected with the definition of the rules which govern the way individuals are channelled to the forms of employment available. In the just society each person could be happy whatever his lot might be from the division of labour. If honest labour provides those who work with the same degree of dignity and respect and almost the same economic rewards, everyone will be content with his situation. From this, for Rousseau, the construction of individual identity requires society. Without society there is no such thing as the individual and individual identity emerges as a result of mutual comparison. Further, the price of individual identity is disorder. Each must find his place within this and be, or he will be brought to be, content.

It is a key reinforcement of Rousseau's artificial sovereign authority, that is the general will, that it cannot be represented. This may be because of Rousseau's concern that special interests may attain a dominance in the legislative process or it may be because, as Constant saw, this 'monstrous force' that Rousseau had created made him fearful of handing it to any representative to use. Only the entire body of the people can approve laws. Rousseau relied for the selection of the laws on the wisest of the wise, the elected legislator, who discovers which are the best and most suitable laws for all the different peoples and must be able to transform each individual, who is himself a perfect and separate entity, into a part of a greater whole. Rousseau specifically compares the legislator with the Deity regarding the characteristics necessary to properly carry out this role.[82] There are echoes of Montesquieu in this.[83]

The picture that is emerging is one of a 'monstrously empowered' entity, the role of which is to create a single social organism which individuals understand, or are brought to understand, represents their individual interests, that is their self-interest.[84] But to be clear about his interests, the individual must undergo radical change to his nature, 'annihilating' his natural resources and significantly devaluing, if not forgoing, any interest that does not promote what the social totality regards as the common good. The test for him in this is whether, in his voting on legislation, he is revealed to have the same view as the majority.

Even if Rousseau's premise were sustainable, that all this is an induction from the reason that causes man to leave the natural state and enter civil society, this political arrangement would be difficult enough to justify. But that very use of reason is unsustainable, and Rousseau himself is brought to acknowledge it. More fundamentally, there is the problem of where the general will comes from in the first instance, since there is not the level of reason in the natural state that is required to institute it and there is not sufficient reason in the civil state to sustain it. How can men who only obey the dictates of their egoistic nature conceive a political order in which sovereign authority is directed by the general will and seeks only the common good.[85]

This raises questions about the social contract and the morally valid rule on which it is based. For Rousseau, when each citizen pledges his loyalty to the sovereign authority formed by themselves, which in turn is pledged to work for the common good, they have made a completely rational choice.[86] The problem is that in a situation where there are no moral relations, and in which men follow their instincts or their feelings, it is a contradiction to suppose that a law exists, and even more so a law of reason.[87] In the absence of moral relationships and prior to the development of reason, it is impossible to conceive any rational principle which could direct men along the path of true morality. There is no reason in the state of nature which might be the basis of forming the social contract as a rational basis for entering civil society.

Regarding the 'enlightened' man living in society, he is equally unlikely to be guided by the natural law, since his own interests are still paramount. The passions, opposed to the prescriptions of natural law, have developed and act with greater force than reason itself.[88] For this man knows that his behaviour runs contrary to the precepts of natural law, but he still believes that he has more to gain from wrongdoing than he can hope for by plain dealing.[89]

It is this natural law which Rousseau aims to transcend in the social contract. While rational, that is natural, justice is grounded in reason and conscience, civil law is grounded in the legitimate political authority which must, through the fundamental social contract, seek the greatest good for all. In the just society instituted by the social contract, the supreme judge is the general will. The natural law is still the supreme authority, but its jurisdiction is primarily within the inner life of man.[90] Further, since it is on the social contract that all individual right is based, citizens do not enjoy these rights to liberty before the political society is instituted.

But the rational, universal, just civil law by itself won't do the trick, even for Rousseau. He says as much to Mirabeau.[91] That is, until that day when law is stamped in men's hearts, it will not be law but men who rule. The only just and sound constitution possible is that where law reigns in the hearts of the citizens. So long as the influence of the law is excluded from this sphere, the law will never be universally obeyed.

From this it can be read that for Rousseau a just republic can be preserved only if its customs are admirable. Good laws by themselves are not enough. He is clear about the difference between law and custom. Law operates only in an external way and its influence goes no further than men's actions; customs alone reach the inner man and direct men's wills.[92] This is the road that ultimately leads Rousseau into the difficulties that cause him to radically question the rational social contract as the basis of civil society. The foundation of his conceptual edifice fades away. Men don't enter a civil state because of the good reasons for doing so, but because they have absorbed 'lawful' practices from the cultural context into which they were embedded from childhood. Worse, why would those cultural practices have been disposed to the production of a general will devoted to the common good, which Rousseau's social contract requires? Given the acknowledged selfish nature of man, it is far more likely to have generated arrangements that recognise such a nature. Rousseau recognises this, for it is the justification for his requirement that a censor be appointed to scrutinize private lives and, more generally, for the importance of the civil religion in his political theory. This is the religion which would lead to banishment for failure to believe and being put to death for failing to act accordingly.[93]

All this is the creation of an ordered society but not through the enhancement of the honoured sense of the common good that is the *raison d'être* of a general will, realised through a social contract entered into rationally and willingly, and realised through just laws. On the contrary, it is the production of order through life-long training in civil religious belief and by the extensive intrusion by any member of the sovereign body, which in turn uses as much force as is required to ensure compliance. Should these foundations be in place, then civil law may have the desired effect. But Constant warned about the dangers of the impact of this combination of custom and law, in which each citizen's life was tightly controlled by the group, and any form of private life free from the interference of the society at large was out of the question.[94]

These are the features of Rousseau's republic. It is because of them that this republic is incompatible with a modern conception of freedom as respectful self-responsibility. But if Rousseau's own acknowledgement of the priority of custom over reason places a thunderous cloud over his efforts, it is the acknowledgement of the intractability of individual interest that brings the downpour. Rousseau acknowledges that each individual may have a particular will contrary or dissimilar to the general will which he has as a citizen. His particular interest may speak to him quite differently from the common interest and he may wish the rights of citizenship without being ready to fulfil the duties of a subject. The continuance of such an injustice could not but undo the body politic.[95]

So there is inevitable tension between the violent passions formed repeatedly within society and the artificial political order intended to eliminate it. The republic must be seen as a short-lived and unexpected victory over the forces of violent spontaneity at work within society, forces whose final triumph is assured. The republic can never free itself from the threat of dissolution since it represents what is for the common good and men are more concerned for what is to their immediate advantage. Rousseau himself says: 'If Sparta and Rome perished, what State can hope to last forever? If we want to form a lasting establishment, let us not therefore dream of making it eternal.' For Rousseau, this is the descent into despotism: 'Just as the particular will incessantly acts against the general will, so the Government makes a constant effort against Sovereignty. The greater this effort grows, the more adulterated does the constitution get, and since there is here no other corporate will to resist the will of the Prince and so to balance it, it must sooner or later come to pass that the Prince ends up oppressing the Sovereign and breaking the Social treaty.' As to the cause of this, he states that 'Dissolution of the State also comes about when the members of the Government severally usurp the power they ought to exercise only as a body; which is no less serious an infraction of the laws, and produces even greater disorder.' This is the opening of the door to universal self-seeking and the rule of dominant interests. It is the ruin of his idea of the republic, because it is always prey to injustice, inequality and disorder. But it is a sign of the idealism of the nature of his republic that there is no room for compromise in the nature of sovereignty. Rousseau's is a black and white view of its universal validity and viability, that it cannot be compromised by the intrusion of personal, irrespective of dominant, interests. As a consequence of this frailty, it is doomed to the dissolution he predicts for it.[96]

ROUSSEAU AND MYTHOLOGY

There is a delightful passage in the *Essay on the Origin of Languages* which points to the conception and construction of myth. It identifies the relationship between fear and the creation of mythological figure by which we deal with the experience.[97] Such may have well been said finally about Rousseau's own attitude towards the notion of the general will. He would not have seen it as such, let alone that his work was continuous with that of Hobbes, that is beside being a positive critique of it.

Rousseau was not only fully aware of the work of Hobbes, Locke and Montesquieu, the 'Hobbesians,' but his work can be seen in the context of a concern to address issues that for him were problematic in their work. The context for this concern was not only that the Hobbesians and Rousseau all shared a commitment to the presumptions of the political theoretical tradition but also that this tradition was, and has continued to be, infused with a concern to answer pre-Enlightenment questions. That is, its protagonists display a mythological disposition in addressing the theoretical questions within that tradition and that certain issues which are of primary concern within that tradition, such as how to construct the kind of State that assumes responsibility for individuals, are themselves mythological in nature.

It was in this context that Rousseau addressed the issue of the construction of an orderly society. Hobbes' solution to the problem of conflict between individuals, that is a society that was not ordered, was the establishment of an absolute sovereign, monarch or parliament, who would retain that status so long as it could claim to be protecting individuals from fear and creating sympathetic conditions. Locke addressed the dangers of the likely arbitrariness of that absolutism by replacing the absolute sovereign with a legislative arrangement that was supreme and effectively immune from challenge, with a constituency that was representative but of dominant interests, balanced by the sculpting out a space within which the individual had certain freedoms from interference by that legislature. This was at the same time an increased drawing of individuals into the field of the State by empowering them through their submission. Montesquieu's idea was to further constitute the fearsomeness of the supreme legislature by a separation and balancing of powers the effect of which was to constrain each arm from arbitrary interference in the lives of men, that is into the spaces in which individual freedoms could thrive but without weakening its fearsomeness. The effect of this balancing was the further enhancement of the inducement of individuals into that State field.

For Rousseau, none of these conceptions of the State went to the heart of the matter, for the sovereign authority of Prince or Parliament stood separate from the body of the people and so could not effectively prevent intrusion into the lives of ordinary men, both by Prince or Parliament and by other individuals. This was due to the lack of engagement of all individuals in the political process. So Rousseau created the body of the people as the sovereign authority, in the form of the general will which realised the common good by the establishment of just and universal law. This was not just an aggregate but a unified whole, an entity. By this total engagement, his Sovereign was an attempt to preclude arbitrary intrusion in one move.

The Rousseauean general will carries all the features of a mythological magnitude but one which, because his work addresses a flaw in the mythological features of the respective entities of the Hobbesians, claims to be a strengthening of the idea of that magnitude. It was the Hobbesian myth amended in a version of his own. None of this is to claim that Rousseau was a conscious myth maker, as I have said. Like the Hobbesians, he would have strongly rejected this accusation. However, working within the political theoretical tradition that continued to focus on pre-Enlightenment, mythological questions, the effect of his working on that of his predecessors is the apparently firmer establishment of the political myth.

The mythological features of the sovereign general will are clear. Rousseau's artificial polity is primarily concerned with the dual problems of individual fear and individual well-being.[98] It is for the purpose of eliminating fear and creating what the general will would regard as well-being that Rousseau embarked on the conception of an entity whose principal feature is order. Further, it sets out to eliminate that fear by itself being fearsome, as its powers of enforced change to human nature, including through such methods as universal surveillance, punishment and the putting to death of its unbelievers, show. Although Rousseau rightly points out that the necessary fundamental change to human nature will be accepted willingly by many who see advantages to them in doing so, others will no doubt become the new Rousseauean person only through the application of the force of the general will. This fearsomeness is emphasised by the absence of any balancing force. There is no separation of powers here as Montesquieu provides. Here it is the legislature, acting on behalf of the sovereign general will, and its fully compliant executive which is supreme, much more than with Locke. Through all this the individual is strongly empowered by his incorporation into the field of the sovereign will by his submission to it, where that submission occurs willingly.

The Rousseauean magnitude is certainly conceptually sympathetic to what it sees as the interests of its constituents, especially through the notions of equality and the common good. Further, unlike the 'Hobbesian' myth, Rousseau's magnitude is fully dispersed across the social space by its binding of all its subjects into an entity with a frame of common concern and cooperation. It is this binding which for Rousseau is the optimal means of creating order, by eliminating the fear between individuals. Rousseau claims that it achieves this without causing them to forgo some space for individual freedom and the protection of property rights, that is by retaining the essence of the Lockean liberal framework. But it goes beyond this through a 'positive' sense of freedom, realised through the general will and its manifestation, the law we give ourselves[99] and to which our sense of reason and justice causes and requires us to subject ourselves.

It is this general will, through which fear is claimed to be eliminated and well-being promoted, which constitutes the archetypal dispersal of the myth fully across social space. Since there is no external sovereign authority to cause the change of behaviour which will eliminate fear, this same result is achieved by Rousseau through this imposition on oneself of the 'generally' accepted prescriptions regarding acceptable behaviour. Man has created the artifice of the general will through the social contract between all the people and, in doing so, has created himself as an individual artifice, since every person will submit to the contract and so radically changes his nature for what is promoted as the common good and his own. Thus is there the claim of the elimination of fear and the creation of sympathetic conditions of existence. Further, by this binding and by the unrepresented nature of the Sovereign general will, it has come fully into man's hands. If it were not for its own internal flaws, this would be the realisation of the archetypal myth.

Finally, the mark of a true myth is that it assumes responsibility for individuals. That is, they are not responsible to or for themselves. The notion of the general will as Rousseau conceives it certainly makes that mark. In particular, one must not only submit oneself as subject to its prescription but must assume a mental perspective such that we adopt for ourselves what will be for the common good and must do so with every piece of legislation before the general assembly. That is, this is not a general agreement on some basic sensible arrangement such as that we should not injure or in other ways disadvantage each other. It is the prescription that we are required to adopt the position of the majority on every matter before the legislature and there is an argument that says we will be subject to surveillance, banishment and death if we do not. We must pledge obedience to all others.[100] That is, we have completely forgone self-responsibility, since the majority of others will determine what is in my interests, given that my reasoning cannot pass the test of being itself always in agreement with the reasoning of every other.

However, although Rousseau's work has dealt with the problems of dispersal of the myth and its ownership by man, both of which were severe shortcomings in the work of the Hobbesians, and claims to have done so without forgoing the individual space of individual freedom and property which they provided, the political myth of the Rousseauean State now has new problems due to his solutions to these shortcomings. In the end, these solutions make the Rousseauean republic unsustainable. They include that the sovereign authority has become itself a pre-eminent source of fear since not only is there no distance between the sovereign and each subject but each other person may act as its agent, and its powers are those of 'annihilation' of the personal resources of the individual. Unlike the absolutism of the Leviathan, let alone the constrained Lockean and Montesquieuean State, which is located at some distance from each individual, the Rousseauean prescriptive sovereign is one's neighbour, he watches everything one does and he can invoke the terrifying power of this annihilation. This is the point made by Berlin.

It can do this as there is no distance between Sovereign and the individual and no balancing power to constrain it. This flaw derives from the rejection by Rousseau of the general will being represented, whether this be because of his concern that there is no institution which could be trusted with its power or due to a concern that it would be overtaken by dominant interests and therefore inequality. Ironically, the general will is the most dominant interest conceivable. Strategically, Rousseau could have opted for representation, despite the inevitability of the emergence of dominant interest, since citizens are more likely to accept the presence of other interests, that is they would not expect only 'common interests,' so long as the 'fear and sympathy' nexus was satisfactorily provided for in regard to themselves. This would have been a compromise for Rousseau, for example the amending of the social contract to allow a competition of individual interests, but one which might have helped make his polity—his mythological magnitude—sustainable. In the form in which he conceived it, he acknowledged that it was not. Further, his arrangements consequently do not allow any real sense of personal freedom, as Constant pointed out. The intimacy of the threat of the empowered sovereign will allows insufficient personal space, despite his contrary assertions. This contradicts the rationale for the social contract and undermines his enterprise. This is a magnitude in which there is full forgoing of individual self-responsibility, justified by the claim of the elimination of fear and the delivery of sympathy which it itself determines.

Finally, even without this particular blow to the social contract, Rousseau's polity is a failure on its own terms because, by his own acknowledgement, personal interest will always intervene and irreparably tear the delicate fabric of the rationally constructed social contract. Neither the social contract, and therefore the general will for the common good, nor the republic itself as he conceives it can be sustained.

THE SIGNIFICANCE OF ROUSSEAU

So with Rousseau we have all the features of the Hobbesian myth but with the full dispersal across social space and therefore its complete coming into man's hands. The effect of his work is that we have an entity that can claim to be sufficiently fearsome to eliminate fear of others and to determine the sympathetic conditions of its subjects through the notion of the common good which stands behind his social contract, as the general will and 'law we give ourselves.' In this mix, individuals must forgo to the general will their responsibility to and for themselves. Rousseau would argue that the space of individual freedom imagined by Locke survives, although that claim is strongly contested by this analysis as precluded by Rousseau's determination to eliminate personal interest through radical, not minimal, change to man's nature, rather than to accommodate it.

The Rousseauean form of the political myth assumes responsibility for individuals, not because all have a concern for the common good, but because they may only devote themselves to and must answer only to others and must radically change their nature to do so. In this, their own interests in justice and equality will be promoted. This is the narrow sense in which individual freedom is conceived by Rousseau. There are those who willingly accept this to eliminate their fear by submission to the magnitude of the sovereign general will. These are the ones whom Rousseau would claim demonstrate the viability of his social contract. But there are likely to be many more whose nature will be unwillingly annihilated by this fearsome entity, if not by custom of civil religion then by surveillance, banishment and death. They demonstrate there is no universal, rationally chosen contract. Finally, Rousseau acknowledged that this is so.

Rousseau's premise is that the Hobbesian paradigm is flawed because it is the worst source of fear and because it fails to foster the engagement of the subjects of the entity with each other regarding those issues that go to its viability. In the terms of the argument of this work, for Rousseau, the failure in Hobbes and Locke of the sovereign entity to engage its citizens in governing themselves is the failure of the magnitude to thoroughly disperse itself across social space. Without this dispersal or mutual engagement of its subjects, there remains the risk of antagonism, and therefore fear, between them and thereby of continuing instability or even disintegration of the mythological political arrangements. In addressing this, Rousseau remains within the tradition of political mythology but continues to work on its substance in an attempt to make the political myth more robust.

In particular, his notion of the general will, or sovereign, is not only universal but its prescriptions are fully enforceable, even to the point of man's natural resources being 'annihilated' so that 'each citizen is nothing and can do nothing without the rest.' That is, it is a fearsome entity, even more so than the Leviathan. Further, the primary aspiration of this entity is to eliminate the fear of its constituents, achieved through the establishment of a fully ordered society in which no individual or group can dominate any other individual. To achieve this, he enforces the radical change to human nature such that all individuals act only through reason and not personal interest. Further again, the sovereign general will is sympathetic to the interests of its subjects in that it largely eliminates inequality and creates opportunity for the fulfilment of individual interests, but by requiring the realignment of those interests with the general will. Finally he sets out to maximise the dispersal of the magnitude across social space, strengthening it and bringing the myth fully into man's hands. Without its intractable flaws, the effect of Rousseauean theory would be the fulfilment of the concept of the political myth. Further, in bringing it fully into man's hands, the Rousseauean mythological model strains to disallow the magnitude being colonised by competing, dominant interests. In fact, when such dominance finally and inevitably occurs, it is for Rousseau the dissolution of the republic.

This does raise a question about the model of the political myth used here, which argues that the inevitability of the emergence of dominant interests is a typical feature of the mythological magnitude rather than a dissolution of it, as Rousseau argues regarding the republic. That is, how can the Rousseauean republic be mythological if it cannot share this typical feature? The answer from this examination of Rousseau is that, finally, it cannot. Rousseau attempted to create an alternative to what was in effect the mythological entity of Hobbes but failed. Personal interest is irrepressibly a part of human activity, this inseparable from the desire to eliminate fear and to enjoy sympathetic conditions of existence. There can be no credible, and therefore sustainable, political myth without it. No amount of effort to change human nature to deny this personal interest will be successful, that is no amount of reason, surveillance, civil religious belief, custom, banishment or threat of death will eliminate it. And attempting these tactics is self-defeating as it creates an absolutism far worse than that of the Leviathan. The Hobbesian myth cannot be improved by the Rousseauean route. His turns out to be a side-road in the progressive refinement of the Hobbesian political myth but one that identifies key flaws in the work on it up to that point and one that is suggestive of a way forward.

This is not to say that influencing human nature *per se* is wrong, only that linking it to the elimination of personal interest is doomed. 'The law we give ourselves' is a good notion if applied in a non-mythological manner, if it is not the instrument for assuming responsibility for the individual, as Rousseau does. The creation of an entity so fearsome as to eliminate fear of others but by empowering itself so fearsomely reveals the self-defeating notion of such dominant mythology. Rousseau has addressed the problem of the Hobbesian myth but with flaws that are far worse. He identified the Hobbesian flaw and his solution of the universal engagement of equal individuals, so bringing the myth's fate further into man's hands than the Lockean parliament, may have succeeded as myth had it not attempted to eliminate personal interest. Because it did that, it caused his work, and so his work on myth, to fail.

Putting Rousseau's failed attempt to eliminate domination to one side, we are left with a polity which has all the features of the mythological magnitude. Rousseau's republic is unrealisable because of his attempt to eliminate personal interest[101] but his political legacy retains all the essential features of the political myth, including ultimate dominance by others. This includes his notion of the general will, a legacy which flows from him to contemporary analysis through Kant to Rawls and through republican theory to Pettit. His failed attempt to solve the flaw in Hobbes and Locke left a legacy of a strengthened but still flawed myth, yet one suggestive of the road forward, as we have said.

Before we proceed to consider the impact of Rousseau's thought on Kant, there is call, as there was with Locke, to acknowledge that Rousseau promoted the idea of liberty through submission to the universal law of the State, a freedom which claimed to end fear and satisfy want, thereby satisfying the first trajectory of liberal mythology, as liberalism is understood here. Further than that, his thought provided for submission to the general will, for hard work which was undertaken in a context of low social mobility and where one had to be happy with one's place, which was typified by sobriety, in a social and political environment which forcefully reconstructed human nature, in which general behaviour was under constant surveillance and where the consequences of non-compliance included banishment and even death. There was, that is, as much of the second trajectory of the notion of liberalism adapted here, that is of the manufacture of docility and productivity, as there was of the first.

We now look at the impact of that legacy on Kant, who assumes all the apparent strengths of Rousseau's improvement of Hobbes and Locke, such as a fully empowered entity, the general will, the law we give ourselves, the universal application of reason, in effect the dispersal of the myth, and addresses himself to the residual weaknesses, including the issue of representation, special interests and a sovereign which is the State not the people. The effect of the work of Rousseau on the thought of Kant[102] will be seen to be a renewed attempt to strengthen the political myth but the further highlighting of its irremediable flaws. In effect, Kant's was the next attempt to extend the dual liberal trajectories through critique and positive re-programming.

5 The Reason of Protestant Politics

KANT

Kant is not an obvious protagonist in the consideration of the emergence of the State as a mythological entity. Long ignored as a political philosopher, but now firmly in the ranks, his credentials are seen to be his emphasis on principles of right, law, justice, freedom, equality, individual independence, social contract and a constitutional State which is to assure these principles.[1] Nonetheless, as with his predecessors in this account and irrespective of what might have been his intentions, the effect of his work is that he has an important place in the attempted reform and consolidation of the mythological State.

The political mythology in Kant comes at least, although not only, from the influence on him of Rousseau. What Rousseau had seen was that in the pursuit of individual interest, especially in relation to religious activity and the product of labour, there was no active commitment on the part of the majority to the persistence of the arrangements or to their strengthening by the active engagement of every individual. As Manent says, they were, for Rousseau, bourgeois.[2] The effect of this had been the revelation of a major flaw in the Hobbesian archetypal myth.

Rousseau did not appreciate that correcting this flaw would be a move to strengthen the political myth, a myth which had been developed into a form that protected the selfish individual through structural arrangements. As we have seen, however, this attempt to eliminate individual interest was doomed, as Rousseau acknowledged, due to its intractability. A flaw remained in the practical idea of the mythological State regarding how individual interest might have its way but so that all interests were addressed, rather than especially those which were dominant, and so sustainable government was possible. Ironically, the work of Kant addressed this issue. Although for his own metaphysical purposes, he took the Hobbesian and Rousseauean frameworks and amended them, dealing with this flaw, albeit in passing. In this, Kant's work would have the effect of using a Rousseauean tool to strengthen the political myth in a manner that Rousseau himself, because of his theoretical aspirations, could not.

The significance of the Rousseauean analysis therefore lies not only in the identification of the characteristic limitations of the emerging mythological form which Hobbes, Locke and Montesquieu had constructed but also in the influence it had on Kant and thereby on the development of the mythological political tradition. In this context, the next section of this chapter will raise a series of inter-related concepts. This will include looking at the scope of Kant's metaphysics of morals; considering the significance of Rousseauean anti-naturalism and the general will; how these relate to Kant's account of the social contract, his views about the necessary move from the state of nature; his account of the constitutional tri-partite State, the nature of freedom and citizenship; the issue of tacit consent and his rejection of resistance to the State; and the role of the State in distributing offices and in punishment. Broadly, what will be argued is that in developing his political philosophy, Kant drew on fundamental ideas of the Hobbesians and of Rousseau, from the latter his anti-naturalism, general will and the consequential notion of freedom. However, through his metaphysical morals, he converted these into institutional arrangements sometimes very different from those imagined by Rousseau.

KANTIAN METAPHYSICS, ROUSSEAU, GENERAL WILL AND THE KANTIAN STATE

To give context to the consideration of the Kantian State, it will be helpful to look at some of the key arguments of the *Groundwork of the Metaphysics of Morals*, a work which along with the *Metaphysics of Morals*, holds the central position not only in Kant's metaphysics but also in his account of the State.[3]

Kantian Metaphysics

Kant's purpose in his two principal moral works is to clarify how it is that the supreme principle of morality is found in ordinary consciousness.[4] He does this by presenting the argument that, first, metaphysical morality rests in common moral consciousness; second, that by understanding this requires that standard moral philosophy should be relegated in favour of the metaphysical; and, third, that the need for this principle comes from man's dualistic nature as both intelligent and sensing. Kant is arguing that there must be *a priori* knowledge of the grounds of morality by man, separate from the ethics derived from his empirical nature,[5] from which it might be said that metaphysical moral law is grounded not in man as such but in that part of his nature that belongs to the world of pure intelligence. For Hunter, Kant is in effect claiming that morality is grounded in the self-sufficiency of pure intelligences as a community of rational beings.

It follows that this morality is not only metaphysical but necessarily exists, as it is the only means by which human beings can think the notion of a moral law that necessitates the human will unconditionally, that is merely by the idea of it. The moral law is thereby an unconditional or categorical imperative.[6] In a complementary sense, to will a maxim as a universal law, that is as a categorical imperative, means to purify the intellect of its sensuous limitations so that it can will in accordance with the mere idea of the law.[7] Kant's crucial step towards showing the possibility of the categorical imperative and the necessity for metaphysics is by arguing that, by a mere thinking of its idea, that is independent of all empirical ends, he has immediate insight into its content. This content is the necessity that all subjective ends or wills are conformed to a universal law or general will.[8]

Through all this we see the inextricable link for Kant between the metaphysical status of morals, the categorical imperative and the general will, which together constitute the ground on which his notion of the State stands. For Kant, the State arises from a real unification of individual wills into a general will for the purpose of realising natural right or allowing intelligible beings to form a community through the moral use of things.[9] For Hunter, Kant's 'democratic' construction of the people, obeying only those laws they could prescribe for themselves, that is laws that are categorically imperative, is the transposition of the metaphysical image of the spiritual community into the political register. Through this, Kant unifies ruler and subject in the figure of the all-powerful self-legislating general will, thereby collapsing the distinction between State and society. Rather than seeing monarchy, aristocracy and democracy as optionally equivalent forms in which political sovereignty can be exercised, Kant treats them as physical correlates of the spiritual community, as the united will of the people. As such, they are required only as long as the will of the empirical people falls short of rational self-governance, being destined for subsumption by the only form of government that can realise this condition, the pure democratic republic.[10]

Kant, Hobbes and Rousseau

This background makes it clear how Kant's thought was consciously directed against Hobbes, in a number of respects. In fact, he addresses a significant section of his work specifically 'Against Hobbes.'[11] It is there that he elaborates his arguments concerning the nature of the social contract as the universal agreement that not only precedes but is a prerequisite to civil society. There he also outlines his concept of right as based in law, from which are derived his notions of freedom, equality and independence of individuals as citizens. He also outlines there the rational, not factual, nature of the social contract, and the necessary compliance with the laws that are inferred from that idea of reason, under sufferance of the use of force. From that flows his argument denying any right of resistance against the supreme legislative power, therefore coming ironically to the same conclusion along a route very different from that travelled by Hobbes.

In finding this, his position is that, unlike with Hobbes, a head of State has clear obligations to the people, so that he finds that Hobbes' 'proposition is appalling.'[12] Nonetheless, there are strong connections between the thought of these two figures and we will return to them.

It is equally clear from this brief background exposition how his work was subject to the influence of Rousseau.[13] For him, as for Rousseau, man has the capacity to make himself, a facility by which he may come to govern himself. But Rousseau's influence on Kant goes deep. On one view, Kant's 'main aim is to deepen and to justify Rousseau's idea that liberty is acting in accordance with a law we give to ourselves'[14] and Kant 'sought to give a philosophical foundation to Rousseau's idea of the general will,'[15] perceiving it as an anticipation of his account of the categorical imperative.[16] As we have seen, Kant draws this link between good volition by an individual, the universality of the categorical imperative and individual autonomy made through a self-imposed universal law.[17] Rational beings impose laws upon themselves because they are rational, that is without requiring another incentive. These laws are categorically imperative, that is of universal significance, and by this self-imposition they establish their autonomy.

These are key elements of the anti-naturalism which Kant saw in Rousseau, for whom human beings could be conceived either physically or from a metaphysical-moral perspective.[18] Mankind is capable of resisting the demands of nature[19] and it is this freedom which enables progress or perfectibility through the exercise of reason as autonomous in relation to nature. The Kantian elaboration of this separation of nature and reason, that is this freedom, is reflected in the distinction between phenomena and noumena, where the former were subject to Newtonian mechanics while the latter responded to moral considerations.[20] But despite the availability of this sense of individualistic freedom, there is a struggle within this division by which we are each constituted between our phenomenal and noumenal characters. Nonetheless, it is reason by which the individual will is influenced. Kant thereby rejects inclination in constituting the forms of freedom or autonomy. The key is that freedom for Kant is, as with Rousseau, to be seen in the context of the general will and the categorically universal laws which derive from that sovereign will.[21] He affirms this, in discussing property rights, when he asserts that 'the aforesaid will can justify an external acquisition only insofar as it is included in a will that is united *a priori* (i.e. only through the union of the choice of all who can come into practical relations with one another) and that commands absolutely.'[22]

These strong influences of Rousseau continue in Kant's examination of the connection between the general united will and legislation. Here he identifies the status of the members of society as citizens, the attributes of which are freedom, equality and independence.[23] Kant is thus using the Rousseauean notion of the universal, sovereign general will, the law we give ourselves, to establish the foundation of his moral polity through a series of rational connections between key notions: through his reason, man makes himself rather than being determined by the dictates of nature; this is the beginning of his freedom; from this reason also comes his duty and the consequential determination of law that must be moral and universally applicable; this leads to the establishment of the categorical imperative as the foundational principle of law imposed on the individual by himself and which thereby is the law of the State; this is the condition for the elaboration of individual, universal freedom since every individual is therefore acting in accordance with reason and the universal law he gives himself; it also constitutes his status as a citizen or member of the polity as free, equal and independent. This is not only his case for individual freedom but also for that as a prerequisite feature of the State.[24]

From his Rousseauean political fundamentals, Kant projects both backwards in time and forward to the grounds for the establishment of the legitimate State. Looking back in hypothetical time, he does allow a range of rights in his state of nature, albeit insecure ones. For example, property acquisition there is sanctioned by the community in expectation of the formation of the civil state.[25] This rational and necessary move to enter civil society and the constitutional State, which emerges as an obligation or duty to the State, draws its imperative force from the anxiety generated by the natural state.[26] Looking forward in hypothetical time, Kant draws from this Rousseauean foundation in constructing his account of the nature of the State, the primary elements of which are the uniting will of a constitution, the relation between individuals as a civil condition and the totality of individuals under law as a State.[27] He continues, in elaborating the institutional features of the State as comprising the sovereignty of the legislator, the executor as the ruler and the judicial authority.[28]

Consistent with Rousseau except for the priority of these institutional arrangements, the members of the Kantian State are citizens, who enjoy the conditions of freedom, equality and independence. Then he parts company with Rousseau, arguing that only active citizens are fit to vote. His examples of passive citizens, which are not reflective of Rousseauean universality, are employees and women, that is the majority of citizens, who are underlings because they are under direction or protection of others and so not independent. For Kant, this lack of independence does not deny them their freedom or equality. They simply cannot vote or manage the State, although such a person can work his way up from a passive to an active condition.[29] To do so requires features of both nature, which excludes women and children, and capacity, which is being one's own master and having the property to support him.[30]

Neither does his consideration of the tri-partite State and its superior relationship by contract to its citizens reflect Rousseau. He converts Rousseauean ideas to his own, in that for him the general will, drawn through a metaphysical morality from an original contract, not only supersedes the interests of individual citizens but becomes the politically dominant tripartite arrangements of the State, a step Rousseau did not take. For Kant, the legislature may indeed be the general will, but this means several things that are not Rousseauean: although this will comprises all citizens, only the judgement of minority, dominant interests as to what constitutes a universally applicable law will determine its prescriptions, since only they can vote, because women and most workers are excluded; the legislature, as part of the tri-partite State, is not only superior to all citizens as subjects until they have all realised their full moral-rational condition but is in a command position over them; and, reinforced by the application of the principle of tacit consent, it cannot be resisted. Rousseau's position had been that the general will comprises all citizens as voters, and not only can the general will not be represented by its legislative deputies but the jurisdiction of government ceases immediately upon the citizens merely assembling.[31] For Kant the three authorities of the State are superior over all as subjects, as a commander is to the obedient, and this condition is through the original contract as an idea of this act.[32] The general will has become the widely empowered State.

He explains that this circumstance comes about through the surrender by each of his wild, lawless freedom to find freedom again in dependence on laws from his own law-giving will.[33] That is, this superiority of the general will, which derives from the contract, determines both the nature of Kantian freedom, a notion he does share with Rousseau, and the commanding authority of the tri-partite State, a notion they do not share. In short, they share the idea of the origin and nature of freedom but part company in Kant's adaptation of that in establishing the status and nature of the institutional form of the State. The source of this difference is the Kantian metaphysics of morality.

This framework of ideas produced a further range of proscriptions and arguments which, although based on the notion of the general will, sees Kant part company further with Rousseau. These follow from the representation of the general will in the fully empowered legislative State, the move Rousseau doesn't make. First is that, because the State realises the moral general will, citizens cannot challenge its authority, necessarily remaining subject and submissive to the supreme authority of the State.[34] In a manner that has echoes of Hobbes, Kant then draws out that this is what 'All authority is from God' means. For him, this saying is not an assertion about the historical basis of the civil constitution but sets forth an idea as a practical principle of reason: the principle that the presently existing legislative authority must be obeyed, whatever its origin. He also makes clear that there can be no resistance against the State even if the sovereign breaches the law.[35] He only allows a questioning of State authority through complaint. Resistance would be a denial of right, due to the incontrovertible status of Kantian law, and would effectively abolish the constitution.[36] This view of the State is not Rousseau's, for whom all jurisdiction ceases the instant the People is legitimately assembled,[37] but it is his institutional elaboration of the Rousseauean idea of the nature of the general will.

Kant complements this hard line with other prescriptions, several of which have relevance for a mythological perspective. First, again putting his Rousseauean roots on display, he emphasises the rational rather than empirical basis of the social contract and how it binds the legislature to reflect the general will.[38] Second, the State has the right of taxation for the purpose of creating minimum conditions of existence for its citizens.[39] Here he is acknowledging the responsibility of the State to ensure that all of its subjects are provided conditions to the minimum extent sufficient to sustain the society as a coherent whole. This is certainly not a welfarist position but neither does it reflect a consistent attitude towards equality. It does display an integrative role for the State, thereby minimising forces of dissatisfaction and disorder, achieved by ensuring that all members enjoy at least minimum conditions of existence but without allowing poverty to become a means of acquisition for the lazy and so does not become an unjust burden on government.'[40] In this context, Kant refers to the complex relationship between Church and State, recognising the need of the Church by the State but stating that the Church cannot be allowed to challenge the State's authority and create civil disharmony. The accumulation of assets by the Church is potentially against the interests of citizens and the society generally. But he is clear about their separation.[41]

Further, he outlines the rights of the supreme commander of the State as the distribution of offices and dignities and the right to punish, the first two wherein the State has limits to its power but which indicates the strategy of its dispersal, the other whereby the offender is presumed complicit in his punishment by the State, but each of which has a consolidatory effect regarding the moral-rational State. Regarding civil offices, the commander may appoint but not freely dismiss.[42] Regarding punishment, there are significant principles inherent in the Kantian position. These include that punishment by a court can never be inflicted merely as a means to promote some other good for the criminal himself or for civil society but only because he has committed a crime.[43] More will be said about this issue.

We shall comment on the range of direct implications that follow from these Kantian elaborations and mutations of Rousseauean ideas, before examining their mythological significance.

THE IMPLICATIONS OF KANTIAN POLITICAL THOUGHT

What is clear from this exegesis is that there are many features of the Kantian system, some of them foundational, that are drawn from Rousseau, either directly or by implication. On the other hand, Kant has also amended or even rejected key elements of Rousseau's work. It will be for the final section of this chapter to argue why this is so, but first we will clarify the effect of these commonalities and differences.

There is fundamental common ground between Rousseau and Kant, especially in that the Rousseauean general will is the frame which Kant fills out as the metaphysical morality of the categorical imperative[44] and which becomes the basis of freedom and of the substance of the State. This ground is a compelling framework for action in that it defines the obligatory nature of all moral behaviour, obligation which for reasons of personal interest or the fulfilment of moral duty, respectively, has the full commitment of each initiated individual.[45] A prerequisite of such commitment is the emergence of a reconstructed human nature, which for Rousseau means the 'annihilation' of personal resources and the reconfiguration of personal interest as a concern for the common good as it takes the form of the general will. The means of this transformation is a law that each man gives himself. For Kant, it comprises a rational metaphysics of morals separate from man's anthropology except for its application and not as a concern for individual happiness.[46] The consequences of not acting in a manner consistent with the universal morality of the categorical imperative bring down on the individual all the force of retributive justice, Kant's own version of Rousseauean 'annihilation.' For both, elaborating human nature understood in this way is what constitutes freedom.[47]

However, Kant ignores what is in the end the serious warning by Rousseau regarding the nature of what he will make of this fundamental common ground. For Rousseau, a sense of the general will cannot emerge spontaneously within the individual but can only emerge if there is a long preparation for it in custom. Individuals are not independently and immediately rational in the Kantian sense. This is a point the communitarians will make in response to Rawls' early, Kantian work. The consequence is that the rational decisions and actions by individuals that Kant argues will materialise in a manner consistent with the categorical imperative will either be empty of content and so be unhelpful in determining principles of behaviour or will not likely be consistent with the categorical imperative, that is they will instead be relative to the customary presumptions of the particular community. As such they are unlikely to be decisions and actions which could be the basis of universal laws. Hegel[48] and Nietzsche[49] saw this. Hunter has a different kind of objection, that the search for the categorical imperative and therefore the realisation of the general will should be seen first as a process of initiation into a particular way of life rather than as the pursuit of a metaphysical reality.[50]

The point is that, as a principle to guide the development of standards of behaviour, the categorical imperative is devoid of content of its own, because the only available reference points are socially evolved standards, and so will be unhelpful in that development. But even if this were not so, beyond the obvious resonance that this notion of custom has with mythology, the much higher likelihood is that such standards are likely to emerge in a customary fashion within a community over time rather than be the subject of processes of independent, individual rational thought. Further, it is more likely that custom will have at its heart the protection of personal interest rather than a general will solely for the common good. Rousseau acknowledged that but Kant did not, except by qualification.

Saying this does not deny a debate about the viability of the postulates of Kantian practical reason. It is Kantian metaphysics which is at issue here, so there is still a proper debate available about the viability of the postulates, as Blumenberg sees.[51] But Kantian metaphysics is certainly challengeable, as we see from Hunter. His argument is that the proper status of the metaphysics is not, as is commonly held, an all-encompassing, universally integrative schema that is superior to other notions of morality because of the claim that it does subsume them. Hunter argues that this belief is part of the self-fulfilling myth of Kantian metaphysics. That is, it is no more valid than the prudential ethics of the civil philosophy of Pufendorf or Thomasius, but was developed at least in part to undermine the validity of that alternative morality, which gained a foothold in German universities in the eighteenth century as a ground for dealing with the social destruction caused by the religious conflicts of the Thirty Years War. Kantian metaphysics, for Hunter, developed in reaction to the non-theological political implications of that morality in an attempt to re-establish a transcendent morality in the German universities, that is to resacralise the university programme and re-establish the supremacy of Protestant theology in the State apparatus.[52] The mythological significance of Hunter's analysis will be drawn in the next section, but we can say here that Kant's claim of universality for his ethics cannot only be seen as a moral code with metaphysical status since it was also a strategy to resist civil philosophy.

So there is common ground between Rousseau and Kant but that ground is sometimes very unsteady as at a number of significant points Kant either departs from or actively rejects the arguments of Rousseau. Another such point is their separate views about the nature of the social contract and the conditions of the entry into civil society. They appear to have a similar view about the nature of the social contract. As Rousseau puts it, each individual puts his power under the supreme sovereign will, each becoming a member of the indivisible whole. This is necessary because the obstacles to survival in the state of nature prevail over the individual's capacity to maintain himself and because men can then only unite so that, by cooperation, they might prevail over such obstacles. This requires that each alienates his rights to the community, making everyone perfectly equal, with the same rights over others that they have over oneself.[53]

Kant's account of the original contract strongly echoes Rousseau.[54]. His is not the voluntary forming of association of Hobbes or Locke, for in Rousseau and more strongly in Kant, this move into civil society in the form of a State is a rational obligation.[55] But what follows is a significant variation by Kant of Rousseauean thought. For Rousseau everyone is included in the social contract[56] and is an equal part of the general will,[57] so that he is therefore a citizen with the right and responsibility to vote in a general popular assembly. For Kant there is inclusion but not universal equality. Certainly he includes equality as one of the three principles of the civil condition, but he heavily qualifies that in regard to material equality. Perhaps more profoundly, he introduces the distinction between active and passive citizens and only the active, one who is one's own master and has property, can vote.[58] The passive include employees not in public service and women, so are the majority.[59] He allows that anyone can work his way up from this passive condition to an active one,[60] although Mendus argues that this possibility is denied to women, so denying them equality.[61]

Now, we can make the easy argument that Kant was wrong about women and servants, that this undermined his basic principle of equality in the conception of the Constitution that realised the general will and therefore his conception of the republican State was flawed. We shall come to that argument. The more interesting question is what was the purpose of his distinction between active and passive citizens. Kant was undoubtedly prejudiced against those who had not acquired the reason and morality he proposed and he may also have been protecting his notion of individualism, but his purpose was at least to convert the essence of the Rousseauean concept of the general will into a sustainable idea of the State, formed by his absolute metaphysical standards, which in the end Rousseau could not do. To achieve this, he had to amend Rousseau. This involved him accepting what Rousseau saw as the flaws in the Hobbesian-Lockean idea of the State, in which individuals did not govern themselves. Separating active from passive citizens, that is those who he believed, if wrongly, were capable of independent rational behaviour from those who he believed were not, was a key part of doing this. Allowing only independently rational individuals to be active in civil society was a key part of realising his moral-rationalist conception of the State, which would thereby be comprised only of individuals who could govern themselves. As to the effect of this, I will argue that this has mythological significance.

There is another sense in which Kant allows inequality, in relation to material existence. This was something which Rousseau wanted to minimise.[62] However, for Kant, the equality of individuals in a State is consistent with great inequality in their possessions and rights generally.[63] Unlike Rousseau, Kant strongly reintroduces and sustains the notion of personal interest, another mutation of Rousseau necessary to ensure his idea of the State was sustainable.

The apparatus upon which Kant hung these concepts was the constitutional republic. There were similarities here with Rousseau, a solid republican, but Kant consolidated his ideas in a manner which distinguishes his idea from that of Montesquieu, also claimed as a republican.[64] This shows how he had effectively adopted the Hobbesian-Lockean-Montesquieuean apparatus of government but strengthened it, just as he had done with key ideas of practical government of Rousseau. For Kant the available options for the possession of the sovereign power were autocracy, aristocracy or democracy and the available options for the form of government are republican or despotic. For him, democracy is necessarily a despotism because it establishes an executive power in which all decide, if need be against one, so that all, who are nevertheless not all, decide. This is a contradiction of the general will with itself and with freedom. Against this, republicanism is the political principle of separation of the executive power (the government) from the legislative power.[65]

One need not be concerned just yet with Kant's ultimate aspiration for the pure republican form that follows the realisation of universal metaphysical moral rationality, at which time these three political forms become redundant. What is of interest are the intermediate political arrangements which Kant preferred. The apparatus he chose for his republicanism was the tripartite arrangement of powers imagined in Montesquieu's refinement of the Lockean schema. However, even though these are three separate powers, it is not quite Montesquieu's arrangement. Whereas Montesquieu's was an empirical wisdom of systemic checks and balances under the control of citizens and therefore in principle in contest, for Kant this arrangement had the necessity of Reason.[66] Montesquieu was a political thinker and therefore an empiric, interested in a cleverly thought-out system of checks and balances.[67] The core of Kant's metaphysics is not cunning but logic, though a logic still in the service of mythology.

Further, for metaphysically moral reasons, this was a State which could not be overthrown. This is not consistent with the Rousseauean position.[68] For Kant the conversion of the general will into right produces very different conclusions, since there can be no revolution.[69] The Kantian State is not only an irresistible object of reason but even the worst behaviour of its representatives and officials gives grounds for nothing more than gradual reform.[70] The important question is why he argues this. We shall see.

Complementing this rejection of political resistance are Kant's arguments regarding individual criminality and punishment, wherein metaphysical reason is the basis on which he imputes unmitigated intention in the criminal act.[71] He then applies the test of the categorical imperative as the means by which this all works. But the all-pervasive rationality of his concept of right leads him down a path which is alien to the real world of criminal activity, as his attitude towards the criminal act and its punishment shows. His position is one which sees the crime and the response to it as a display of wickedness, criminal will and retribution: equality requires retribution,[72] wickedness justifies retribution[73] and the criminal has willed a punishable action, thereby placing himself outside reason, although the punishment is rational.[74] But the key is his argument that whoever steals makes the property of everyone *insecure*[75] and 'therefore deprives himself (by the principle of retribution) of security in any possible property. He has nothing and can acquire nothing.'[76] The concern to ensure order and security, in defence against fear, is a matter of primary concern here, not the promotion of respectful self-responsibility of the individual offender.

Broadly, however, his account of crime and punishment faces insurmountable difficulties. It requires him to argue the impossible, that is to split the criminal into two incommensurable parts, one a co-legislator and the other who decides to offend. For him this avoids the contamination of his law but at the price of arguing that the real practice of legislation takes place out of the real world. Second, the judge can only consider the rationality of the criminal act, that is whether it complies with the standard of a universal law. In determining punishment in this retributive world, there can be no consideration of personal motive or maxim.[77] Again, Kant makes rational what is empirical but thereby strengthens the concept of the State and its laws, although at the cost of what it is to be human. It is a disembodied justice. It is also administered by a State which by nature of its retributive approach to justice is a fearsome entity. It would appear in no way to threaten Kant's foremost aspiration, that is the desire that all individuals rationally acquire a metaphysical standard of morality, for there to be constructive engagement with the offender rather than retributive punishment.

What we are beginning to be left with in the Kantian idea of the State is an entity founded on the absorption of the Rousseauean idea of the general will but converted as the metaphysically moral categorical imperative and fully elaborated. To this common foundation there are added key differences between them, constituted by those arguments in which Kant varies or rejects secondary arguments of Rousseau or by which Kant amends Rousseau. These amendments include a rejection of the ground that rational behaviour must find in custom. Even if one accepted that Kant was not claiming that individuals had access to pure objective Reason, there is still an argument against his claim that each individual can imagine laws that should apply universally. If his argument is that not every individual can do so, then it at least undermines his argument for only retributive punishment. This challenge to the categorical imperative as a meta-ethical position is reinforced by the arguments about behaviour that affect only the actor, regarding which there is no case for that behaviour to be a universal law. Further, his amendment of Rousseau introduces a strong strain of unnecessary structural inequality and thereby injustice into the conditions of citizenship, both in relation to their status and regarding the accumulation of material possessions.

These flaws are reinforced by Kant's statements regarding the institutional arrangements of State, where he accepts the framework of the tripartite separation of powers but, again, amends this so that it reflects his meta-ethical Reason rather than the empirical and pragmatic approach of Locke and Montesquieu, the principal advocates of such an arrangement. The compelling rationality which grounds this arrangement for Kant, and the sense of right that it reflects, makes the State unchallengeable in any direct sense, even where there is injustice, and the individual who breaches that right will be punished retributively, without any credit for genuinely mitigating circumstances. When these elaborations are added to his own strong arguments regarding the necessary exit from the state of nature into civil society and the constitutional state, and the notion of non-popular tacit consent to legislation, we get a strong sense of an involuntarism that is the condition of existence of all individuals and of the creation of the irresistible power of the Kantian law and State.

Kant would claim that such self-coercive laws and such a fearsome State are needed to pass the test of being able to prevent the invasions of freedom of which the state of nature is constituted, that is to surely protect individual freedom as he conceives it. Kantian freedom is not the private, State-limiting individual rights of Locke, but a public, community-constituting engagement of individuals whose interests are realised in the right of the State. But such a claim would be wrong. The flaws in the categorical imperative show this. Essentially, Kant goes too far. That is, in the wake of his hard expectation for absolute morality and reason, we find inequality, injustice and inhumanity. Individuals, having surrendered all their natural freedom in entering civil society do not receive it all back, as he claims.[78] They do not receive back the right to choose what only affects them as individuals, only those behavioural choices that every other person agrees to make, nor do they receive equality of benefit as a citizen.

Kant was undoubtedly optimistic regarding the progress that was likely in human society,[79] in particular regarding the establishment of political arrangements which would eliminate violence within and between nations, and relied upon the virtues of reason as the foundation of his prescription for the promotion of such arrangements. However, these arrangements and this progress are achieved only at the price of significant proscription, exclusion and coercion. There is no room here for the principle of insufficient reason, in which there may be justification for a decision based on the benefit derived from the balance of probabilities rather than on a requirement for an indefinitely exhaustive and compelling basis in reason,[80] and the reliance on the respectful intentions of self-reliant individuals which that allows. Kant, like his predecessors in the mythological tradition, does not trust the individual unhobbled from the rigours of his moral and practical reason because of the indeterminacy of his intention. Here we are starting to get to the heart of the flaw in the Kantian moral-rational system. For Kant the prescriptions of the categorical imperative, the involuntary move to civil society, the obligatory nature of the original contract, the moral formality of the operation of the institutions of the constitutional State and the Rule of Law, the retributive conception of punishment for breaches of law which need not have immediate popular assent, the rejection of any form of political revolution or resistance, the 'greatest inequality' in possessions and rights, the intolerance of lying, the denial of equal rights to women because of their submission to inclination and the highly restrictive concept of individual freedom—all these are misguidedly prescribed to ensure the establishment of a fully ordered society without the threats of the state of nature, through the metaphysically rational-moral construction of fully obligatory, coercive and constructive political arrangements.

The interesting question is the value of all this. Why reject Rousseau's warnings about the necessity of custom and practice, which are unlikely to produce a community that will conceive universal laws to act in a manner consistent with such custom and practice? Why ignore Rousseau's warnings about the necessity for equality, both regarding civil status and material possessions, given that the absence of equality is destructive of the civil state that realises the general will? Why go so far as to deny the choice of individuals to behave in any manner they choose so long as that does not affect others, even if others may not wish to behave in that manner themselves? Why deny any right to overthrow the ruler, even if there is serious abuse of the authority? In determining punishment, why refuse to acknowledge in any way the personal circumstances motivating an offender?

One could say that this is the kind of political theory one gets within Kantian metaphysical philosophy, where reason and morality are uniform and compelling. Another answer would be that Kant was working through the implications of the Rousseauean concept of the general will into a set of political arrangements that were sustainable and to do so required amendments to Rousseau's arguments. Yet another answer, that preferred here, would be that Kant was working within a mythological political tradition and that this is the foundation of his development and variation of Rousseau's thought. The presumption of this tradition having been that mankind needs a fully-empowered tri-partite State, that is one which must by its nature be fearsome, as the preferred means of eliminating 'envy, addiction to power, avarice, and the malignant inclinations associated with these,'[81] that is fear and desire, and one in which power comes from the transfer of sovereignty from each individual, each of whom thereby loses responsibility to and for himself in compliance with a metaphysical general will realised in that State. This is the context within which the political application of Kant's moral-rational metaphysics should be seen. We shall elaborate this argument.

A Kantian would probably object that Kant of all people was committed to the notion of individual responsibility, whereby each person is responsible for ruling himself. In response it can be said that Kantian responsibility is still responsibility to an *a priori* metaphysical morality in the form of the general will, not to and for oneself. Because of the dictates of the categorical imperative, the behaviour of each person is completely determined in the end by what all others agree is acceptable behaviour, without exception, given that my reasoning will never always agree with the reasoning of others. Further, in establishing his grounds for his sense of responsibility, Kant, following Rousseau, denies the large part of what is human nature and so denies any opportunity for the individual to incorporate that nature in his responsibility for himself. That is, their anti-naturalism causes them to reject any argument that reason and nature can together be an integrated basis for moral judgements. It was a fundamental argument of Rousseau that it was only by the separability in man of his physical or natural features from his metaphysical or moral nature, and by the exercise of the latter, that he was free.[82] Kant deepened this argument of Rousseau, proposing his distinction of phenomena and noumena[83] and arguing that the rational moral law came only from the latter.[84] The point is that the responsible individual Kantian self, unlike that proposed by the philosophical naturalists like Hobbes and Nietzsche, is one which asserts that an independent faculty of reason can serve as a cause for action. For the naturalists, reason is dependent upon certain desires, drives or impulses of a more fundamental kind.[85] The individual that Kant wants to claim is responsible for himself is not the full individual with all his human features, only that part which reasons and which claims to reason in universal moral terms. It is not the individual driven in part by his desires and impulses and therefore an individual wrestling with his own fearsomeness as he tries to act respectfully. Kant is bracketing that part of human nature. So, not only does the Kantian political individual forgo responsibility to a metaphysical general will but, in doing so, loses all the features, other than a form of rationality, that make him human. We are to be ruled by disembodied Reason, not guided by the Principle of Insufficient Reason.

KANT AND MYTHOLOGY

Kant should be seen as having worked within and contributed significantly to the dominant political theoretical tradition, with its mythological presumptions, and in interesting ways. Like each of the theorists examined here, he grappled with both political circumstances of his time and with theoretical problems presented to him by his predecessors within the tradition. Like them, he was unaware of the mythological significance of their or his own work, but because the premises of the tradition are identifiably mythological, it can be argued that Kant's work, like theirs, has mythological significance. His non-mythological significance, the extent to which his thought could contribute to the development of a coherent sense of self-responsibility, might lie in both the content and method of his approach, should its metaphysical foundation be withdrawn.

Kant's mythology rests at two levels, one in which he worked with but corrected the political thought of Rousseau, the other in which, on that base, he goes well past Rousseau and conceives what may be called a pure mythology of the State.

At the first level, Kant took hold of Rousseau's theory and argued that, appropriately amended, it could form the basis of a form of government which drew on key Rousseauean ideas but was sustainable. Men were capable of governing themselves, individually and thereby collectively. By retaining but logically reworking the concept of empowered, complementary tri-partite institutions developed through Locke and Montesquieu and by complementing these with a Rousseauean reason that as the general will could constitute the foundation of the State, he appeared to have captured the key elements of both the Hobbesian and Rousseauean contributions to the tradition. He had effectively worked on myth to strengthen it, accepting Rousseau's arguments where they aided this but rejecting or amending those arguments where they did not do so. For him the former included the commitment of all citizens to its sustenance, the latter regarding such elements as the right of dissent and resistance, the nature of women and the dependent status of most workers. The effect was that he appeared closer than any of his predecessors to realising the aspiration of the creation of the fearsome mythological magnitude that can effectively eliminate existential fear through the forgoing of individual self-responsibility and the consequentially increased dispersal of the myth across social space. Not only that, he provided for the essential alliance between the State and the Church and outlined the means by which the State is also dispersed through the appointment of office holders as its agents. This is the myth of the magnitude in apparently full bloom. That is, supported by a rational reconception of human nature, the Kantian State epitomised the forgoing of individual self-responsibility in the service of the fear-sympathy nexus. Having said that, this bloom was not so full that it could not be reworked by Rawls, who has brought Kant into the contemporary world, and reconceived by Pettit, who sees the contemporary State in republican terms. Rawls' ongoing work was inspired in part by the flaws that remained within Kantian political thought.

But this mythological thought is not merely metaphysical. It is also political. For Hunter, the Kantian political model was constructed as a direct, strategic competitor of that of Pufendorf and Thomasius. The latter intended the desacralisation of the State and the Kantian model was intended to reverse that so that Protestant theology could again find a dominant place in social and political affairs in eighteenth century Germany. The aim of Pufendorf's civil philosophy was to find an arrangement that would eliminate the social turmoil and consequential fear that had come from generations of religious conflict in Germany. Although Hunter rightly sees vast differences between the thought of Pufendorf and Hobbes, one can at least detect a common argument regarding desire for the emergence from a turbulent condition into a secure civil state under a fully empowered artificial authority for the purpose of the elimination of fear. It was the strategic template employed for the resolution of the problem experienced respectively in eighteenth century Germany and seventeenth century England as a consequence of their respective religious conflicts.[86] In effect, Kant's attempt to deny Pufendorf was a reaffirmation of his denial of Hobbes, that his own politics had rejected Hobbes and the strategy which Hobbes and Pufendorf shared.

This is emphasised by the strategy which Kant adopted to do this, also revealed by Hunter. Kant's terrestrial intention was to firmly establish his resacralising pedagogy in the universities for the 'delineation and grooming of a certain kind of cultural deportment' of pastors, teachers and academics[87] and 'With this transformation, German university metaphysics was able to reassert its claim to moral oversight of civil ethics, law, and politics.'[88] This was a training of prospective dominant interests, to optimise the chances of his post-Hobbesian, anti-Pufendorfian mythological metaphysics.

But there is a second, related level of mythological significance in Kant. His metaphysical moral and rational aspirations require that the individual enters a process of ethical self-formation, by which he becomes one with the general will through observance of the moral law, which is the categorical imperative. The only form of State which conforms with this rational moral community is the pure republic. But this republic is ultimately unnecessary, since Kant envisages the emergence of an ethico-civil society coextensive with the political State and destined to displace it from within. So Kant's political metaphysics ultimately resiles from the ideological neutrality of the desacralised state not by giving this state moral ends, but by envisioning its progressive withering in favour of the moral state hidden within it.[89] Here we have an obligatory condition to which each individual must submit himself, that is to forgo responsibility for his full self and the consequential determination of a differential morality suited to himself and his social circumstances. Such a regime would require this individual to renounces all 'envy, addiction to power, avarice, and the malignant inclinations associated these.' This is to say that Kant has constructed, standing within the mythological magnitude of the State as a means to its realisation, a non-political moral-rational mythological condition, submission to which by self-transformation would eliminate fear and uncontrolled desire and which would ultimately subsume that State.

The means by which individuals gain access to the community of rational-moral beings is by their induction into a particular way of life, into new existential relations to themselves and their world, as *paideia*.[90] Kant teaches his readers to relate to themselves as beings whose higher intellectual selves are in danger of corruption by their lower sensible inclinations, thereby inducing the desire for pure practical philosophy for their self-purification and self-completion. Kant founds the metaphysics of morals as theory in a desire for pure knowledge that has been induced by the metaphysics of morals as *paideia*.[91] Kant's readers are his students at the university, the prospective elite of dominant interests. These institutions were the battleground between his metaphysical philosophy and the civil philosophy of Pufendorf and others. The battle was for the minds of students who, as pastors, teachers and academics would rise to pre-eminent theological, social and political status and deliver to German university metaphysics the moral oversight of civil ethics, law and politics that it sought. Through this different understanding, Kant's politically astute aspiration to train this elite is an attempt to establish the high moral regime which would eliminate the envy, addiction to power, avarice, and the malignant inclinations associated with these, since, given human beings' predisposition to satisfy their sensuous inclinations, they will corrupt each other's moral disposition and make one another evil.[92] However, through their self-purification and consequent realisation of the categorical imperative and general will, this elite would deal with these moral problems. They would do so by assuming dominant positions within the tri-partite constitutional republican political arrangements of the State and transform the practices of those institutions and the citizens they manage accordingly.

So it can be argued that the Kantian response is a more highly refined solution to this problem than that of Pufendorf, because where the latter relies, like the Hobbesians, on a set of institutional controls external to the fearsome and desiring individual, problematic as that is, the former intends that there is no need for controls as such, since the prospect of fearsome and desiring behaviour is swept away by the rise of the individual into the metaphysical world of reason and morality, represented at this level by the general will that had founded the tri-partite constitutional State, but which ultimately would shed that skin. This is metaphysics better seen as mythology.

However, despite the extent and depth of Kant's thought on his political arrangements and on his metaphysical moral, there are problems. Taking Hunter's analysis as a lead, we can say that, beyond the first level mythology of consolidating the Hobbesian and Rousseauean political arrangements, Kant sought to create a pure, rational, Protestant State, a pure democratic republic in fact. As a key strategy to realise this, he sought to train an intellectual and moral elite, a dominant elite. Doing so would see off the threat of Pufendorf's civil philosophy. Kant's was a more highly refined solution to the Hobbesian-Pufendorfian problem of persistent and widespread religious unrest. But Kant's republic, even before it emerged from the chrysalis into its pure state, could bear no resistance, required no universal suffrage, allowed wide inequality and operated by presumed consent. Once it did emerge, however, it became a State to which one would rationally be required to forgo responsibility for one's full self, that is one's temporal self, and enter a condition in which there was no envy or power or avarice. There was thereby no source of fear or desire for always-better conditions of existence. This was a pure mythological State. Its citizens do not require to be made docile and productive because they make themselves so as they enter this pure rational, moral condition. This is the reason that Kant excludes the majority from participation in the affairs of this State, since they have demonstrated that they are not rational or moral in the sense that he requires and have not joined the general will through the use of those qualities.

A principle flaw in all this is that Kant can't decide between, on the one hand, individuals reaching this condition only through their own rational and moral efforts, which is his key premise, and, on the other, whether they require extensive training to do so, his political strategy making this preference clear. As a consequence, it is deeply unfair to exclude the majority of individuals, those who have not denied their temporal selves, from both training and from participation. Worse, it is unfair, even immoral, to then make them subject to the imposition of his rational, moral, Protestant regime. Such subjection is clearly a cause of fear, since State injustice must be tolerated and breaching its rules draws harsh retributive punishment, and clearly denies sympathetic conditions beyond the minimum, since one must tolerate great inequality in rights and material comfort.

Mythologically, this is the attempt to establish a regime which, in eliminating envy, power and avarice, directly confronts the deep problems of fear and sympathetic conditions of existence for the rationally and morally compliant in a time of social turmoil. But this confrontation requires a State that, to maintain the pure moral and rational standards that this metaphysics requires, will deny empirical experience, and any system of morality drawn from that, as inferior and corrupting. It will be ruthless in its retribution for any offending behaviour.[93] In fact, it is likely to be intolerant of a broad range of features of what it is to be a human being, as opposed to those that characterise Kantian humanity.[94] In its attempt to eliminate fearsome behaviour, the Kantian State itself becomes a source of existential fear.

One background mythological issue that should be kept in focus in the evolution of the mythological tradition, despite the refinements that Kant ultimately made to Hobbesian thought, is that what they held in common was more profound than their differences. This distance between Hobbes and Kant was constituted only by the fact of the application of a rigorous rational-moral discipline to the conceptual tools of the former, as modified by Locke and Montesquieu to ensure that it persisted and taking account of the further criticisms and innovations of Rousseau. Hobbesian and Kantian political arrangements are similarly grounded in fearsome State power; their respective and differing notions of the state of nature presume it to comprise the violence which results from the absence of effective systematic law; the Hobbesian view that the pre-civil sovereignty of the individual as the ultimate authority of any civil group was a precursor to the Kantian view that the right of civil society over its citizens was merely the sum of the rights transferred to it by individuals through contract and consent, and that the resultant State was mechanical rather than organic in nature; their sharing of the argument that those conditions of the operation of the natural state required exit into civil society, although they constituted this requirement differently; their rejection of the validity of political resistance; that they would both have found any notion of universal representation alien; and their common view that even the illegitimate inception of a State, including by revolution, will not exempt citizens from obedience to that new authority.

In effect, Kant critiqued and reprogrammed the political myth by transforming the institutional arrangements developed sequentially by Hobbes,

Locke and Montesquieu and embedding these into his enhancement of the general will as conceived by Rousseau. It was the mythological State in its most robust form yet. Here was certainly the fearsome magnitude of the State created to stand over and against man as a human being. This is the State of the united general will, by which its fate has come fully into the hands of the moral-rational man but which no individual could deny since it is the inevitable product of a necessary moral reason that must eschew the anxiety and desire born of the violence in the hypothetical state of nature. Because the move to civil society emerges as an obligation to the State, this directly implies not only complete obedience to the hypothetically-consented prescriptions of the State and the complementary proscription of political participation for the majority, of dissent and revolution but it also empowers the State to inflict severe corrective retribution on those who breach these prescriptions. It is a fearsome magnitude indeed. But this obedience, produced by the forgoing of self-responsibility to a universal categorical imperative and to dominant interests that Kant himself strove to train, comes with the claim for the sympathy of the State, at least in that the rights it claimed from individuals were returned to the individual 'undiminished.' This 'undiminishment' of course cannot be so, given not only the initial forgoing of responsibility for oneself but also that this forgoing is obligatory and that the categorical imperative precludes individual choice about matters that don't concern others. More fundamentally, this condition ultimately denies all the faulty but inspiring characteristics of being human and that are thereby the fabric of human being: he eliminated existential anxiety but at the cost of, or even for the purpose of, eliminating both the repeating disappointments and the fine aspirations that are at the heart of humanity. This denial was too high a price to pay for promises regarding fear and sympathetic conditions, even if those promises were made in the context of a supremely moral and rational existence. Further, this is the political myth taken then to an even higher level of refinement, motivated by his own political aspirations to trump the civil philosophy of Pufendorf through the creation of elite or dominant interests whose influence would promote the forgoing of empirical self-responsibility and so eliminate fear and desire in the creation of the pure democracy, the pure myth of the State, as a precursor to a pure condition of moral rationality. This truly was reason in the service of myth. It was a myth reflected in both the trajectory of a disembodied sense of freedom and autonomy born of the idea of the moral and rational Kantian State, especially for his active citizen, and in the trajectory of the assumed practices of docility and productivity, especially for the passive. Nonetheless, its own flaws were to provide the opportunity for successors, especially Rawls, to work further on its refinement. One might observe, however, that the inspiration for this continuing work on myth smacks of the ever optimistic but misplaced energy of Sisyphus.

Part III

Modernisation

The political mythological tradition that was initiated by Hobbes and refined by his successors from Locke to Kant was brought into the contemporary era by Rawls, who engaged Kant in his own attempts to reinvigorate political theory. Pettit took a different approach, in addressing these issues from a republican perspective, but his approach was no less mythological and has therefore broadened the appeal of political mythology. We shall consider Rawls and Pettit in turn as exemplars of the modernisation of the dominant political mythology.

6 Reason and the Myth of Justice

RAWLS

Rawls' Broad Argument

A Theory of Justice has been characterised as an attempt to resuscitate political theory by bringing back together an elaborated appreciation of what is both feasible and desirable in politics.[1] It is argued that Rawls has produced a considered notion of justice with which we are intuitively in tune, being based on an uncontroversial moral individualism,[2] that it will be good for every person. The same work has also been seen differently, as an attempt to promote a view about the universality of liberal concepts generally, about a particular concept of the person, including an asocial and autonomous nature, whether such individuals can be objective about the concept of the good they are claimed to pursue and whether the State can be neutral regarding notions of the good.[3] This Chapter will explore these perspectives in this and his subsequent work, looking to identify any mythological implications. A principal reference point for this exploration is the influence of the moral, political thought of Kant, whose political philosophy Rawls sought to revive and whose thought permeates Rawls' theoretical work.

Rawls' early work is an abstracted contractarian approach wherein individuals in an Original Position choose preferred political arrangements to minimise the effect of a malevolent opponent when self-knowledge, but not knowledge of general facts about human society, is bracketed,[4] that is when the balancing of competing interests is the primary concern.[5] They define public rules to identify activities that lead men to act together to produce greater benefits and assign fair claims over the proceeds. For an intergenerational flavour, Rawls says these are individuals with continuing lines of claims,[6] such as through families. They are not an assembly of all those alive at one time, Rawls making the Kantian assertion that this is immaterial since everyone will choose the same option, being equally rational.[7] From the first principles, the basic structure of society is developed, including institutions, rights, property and the economic arrangements.[8] These are arrangements in which all reasonable expectations can be met and claims can be reasonably resolved, that is through a notion of the rule of law[9] which has wide support.[10] The aspirations that drive the choice of the basic structure are not personal but general desires for such primary goods as rights, opportunities, wealth and self-respect[11] and they are ranked and pursued within an individual's rational life plan.[12] In prescribing this personal strategy, Rawls' Kantianism disallows any personal envy.

The outcome he says will be a fair arrangement, justice as fairness.[13] The two principles of justice chosen are the guarantee of fundamental individual liberties and of the distribution of resources that favours the disadvantaged while sustaining equality of opportunity.[14] Again from Kant, he constructs this thought experiment by presuming that these two are chosen,[15] claiming universal concurrence. He requires choice on the basis that a malevolent opponent may choose the place of the principal in the society.[16] In doing so, he utilises the principle of insufficient reason, the gambler's option wherein risk is taken about the possible outcome, but only as an accounting technique.[17] One reason he claims the two principles would be chosen is the universality of their benefits and therefore the sustainability of the consequential arrangements.[18]

For Rawls, such principles can only be delivered through the establishment of a liberal, constitutional democracy which adopts welfarist economic and social policies.[19] The institutions are those of a bicameral legislature, separation of powers and a bill of rights, all under the rule of law, that is, an elaboration of the 'Hobbesian' institutional model.[20] He does not prefer a capitalist or a socialist economy,[21] so long as there is equalising distribution of wealth, the equal promotion of opportunity through education, corporate competition and a minimum income[22] and saving for future generations.[23] The State can give no preference to any majority moral or religious creed but must underwrite equal liberty in such matters.[24] In a Kantian vein, he generally denies the right to resist an unjust law passed within the context of a just constitution,[25] on the basis that such laws can be worked on. If this doesn't produce a fair outcome, there can be justified civil disobedience.[26]

Rawls' ultimate justification for endorsing justice as fairness is that it is rooted in our customs[27] insofar as they have embedded in them our fundamental notion of goodness. He argues this by separating Right from Good: his two principles are to be respected because they are right, that is they represent accepted public rules, before and therefore independent of whether they produce good results. What is Right is what 'fits into ways of life consistent with principles of right already on hand,'[28] that is accepted custom, and, true to his Kantian constructivism,[29] it is prior to the Good[30] while being consistent with it.[31] The Good includes such ideas as rationality, primary goods, comprehensive conceptions, political virtues and a well-ordered political society.[32] Primary goods are those things people want and they include rights, liberties, opportunities, income, wealth and self-respect.[33] Further, a political society with these features will be stable.[34] For Rawls, people will understand that acting justly, in a manner consistent with the principles of justice, will promote their individual interests.[35] This brings him back to Rousseau and so to Kant. Further, the desire to act upon these principles is satisfied only to the extent that it is regulative of other desires. Importantly, 'It is acting from this precedence that expresses our freedom from contingency and happenstance.'[36] As a context for the basic individual liberties, freedom at least includes freedom from contingency and happenstance.

There have been two main camps of criticism of Rawls, one from the more extreme end of the liberal spectrum within which he has positioned himself and the other from communitarians. *A Theory of Justice* was criticised by libertarians like Nozick for conceiving a State that interferes too much in the lives of individuals and therefore for breaching the fundamental Lockean rights of liberty and property.[37] Nozick's claim is for a minimal State, the role of which is only to offer protection to all through the monopoly of force, and thereby required only so much taxation as necessary to sustain itself, with only minimal interference in citizens' lives. He sees two problems with Rawlsian theory, that Rawls fails to account for pre-existing ownership of property, which would change the agreement about the two principles,[38] and that it requires an unacceptable level of intrusion into the people's lives.[39] The first objection seems to misrepresent Rawls' enterprise, which is an hypothetical thought experiment about the application of agreed moral standards rather than the basis for a programme for actual social reform. Pre-existing property ownership can be accommodated within the two principles in an actual programme, since ignoring such ownership would breach the first principle. The second appears to misrepresent him by asserting that Rawls' taxation law allows capricious intervention, which is not his intent.

The other critique has come from communitarians, from those whose primary concern is for the common good and for whom morality can only be seen in traditional practice rather than derived in abstraction as a tool to redesign communities. This is the shadow of the admission Rousseau was ultimately forced to make concerning the rootedness of preferred principles and practice in custom but which Kant did not acknowledge. Communitarians reject notions of justice realised in institutions that profess to tolerate and protect the rights of a wide variety of conceptions of the good life, because they say we cannot detach ourselves from the kind of persons we are in identifying such notions and choosing them rather than others.[40] In essence, this is a rejection of the kind of enterprise which Rawls undertakes in *A Theory of Justice,* that it could be of any interest to those in the real world what political philosophers like Rawls do in imagining a hypothetical Original Position and trying to extract principles of justice from it. Best to examine our immanent traditions and develop principles by addressing the problems inherent in them. Any claim for an individual's rights should never have priority over the common good because individuals are never self-sufficient, independently rational and autonomous, asocial atoms.

Individual choice can only be enhanced in the context of institutions that sustain a social context for that enhancement.[41]

For Sandel in particular, Rawls' disembodied concept of the self forces him to acknowledge that the self must at least be conceived intersubjectively, otherwise there is no basis for agreement under the veil of ignorance about principles of justice and because of Rawls' own statement that it is a community that owns the asset of individuality that we claim as individuals.[42] Sandel also argues that we cannot determine the right before we allow for the good, because our choices about what is right are fully informed by our individual natures and therefore our changing aspirations[43] and this requires first understanding the community which constitutes our identity. The latter claim is probably too strong, since we are not fully bound by the influence of the community. In any case, Rawls does accept the broader point concerning the primary impact of society on the individual,[44] although he did argue that such common notions should not be mistaken for a conception of the good. Accepting the broad point does bring Rawls close to Sandel's position.

But Rawls could defend himself regarding this issue of the impact of culture on other grounds. In the Original Position the protagonists have available to them a wide range of general information sufficient to secure social cooperation and in a manner that would generate support for the concept of justice. It is true that the parties do not know the particular circumstances of their own society but 'they know the general facts about human society.'[45] That is, they are aware of the traditional foundations of every society and the value of building political institutions which will respect foundations which protect them against the malevolent opponent, which deliver fairness. As a consequence, their endorsement of the two principles will be on that understanding. Further, from stage two of the four stage process where the constitution is being chosen, 'the general facts about their society are made available to them.'[46] Here are the intersections between the two principles and the customary practice of any community. Rawls gives greater emphasis to this when in 1980 he states that he is grappling with parochial problems specifically within the United States, so cannot be easily accused of arguing for abstract theoretical solutions generated by asocial individuals.[47] Further, given that the communitarians themselves acknowledge that custom is not the only determinant of behaviour and that the individual can himself participate in that,[48] Rawls and they are closer than they each claim.

But despite this defence of himself, there is a change in emphasis in Rawls, although he remains a Kantian. The approach he outlines in his Dewey Lectures (or *Kantian Constructivism in Moral Theory*) in 1980 is to discover deeper bases of agreement and understanding,[49] that is, as he had outlined in *A Theory of Justice* (1971), of consensus.[50] That hadn't changed but what had changed was that his focus was now on his own national community rather than on the discovery of universal principles of justice.

Although now mitigated somewhat by a cultural relativism, a key reference point in this remains his Kantian, albeit culturally relative, concept of the moral person. In the Lectures, he links (a) the notion of a well-ordered society to (b) the concept of the moral person through (c) the Original Position. The first is a society of cooperating, free and equal persons regulated by a public concept of justice and therefore stable; the second is the power to pursue a concept of the good in the context of a sense of justice; and the third is the means of the modelling how moral persons, as citizens of a well-ordered society, select principles of justice.[51] Actualised in the American context of reason and cooperation, justice as fairness remains the selected concept of justice. However, what is Reasonable, that is the detailed principles of justice agreed in the context of fair terms of cooperation, presupposes the Rational, that is the application of these principles to a view about one's relations to others and the world: right has priority over the good.[52] Put another way, what is feasible subordinates what is desirable. Given that this process is undertaken by autonomous individuals, this is all a refinement of Kantian thought.

But Rawls did find the communitarian critique of his Kantian concept of universal truth and of the autonomous person compelling. In *Justice as Fairness: Political not Metaphysical* (1985), he admits faults of exposition in *A Theory of Justice* and further that his views had changed.[53] He now wants to emphasise the political rather than the moral or metaphysical nature of his concept of justice.[54] Increasing cultural diversity requires a concept of justice that provides an agreed justification for institutions and promotes stability.[55] This will encourage a tolerant overlapping consensus of opinion. This cannot be based on any single, dominant comprehensive concept of justice.[56]

Such a shared basis for a political conception of justice in a democratic society cannot be achieved by philosophy in a search for truth about an independent metaphysical and moral order.[57] So Rawls has to reject the Kantian comprehensive moral doctrine, resting as it does on ideals and values that are not generally shared in a democratic society.[58] He does not abandon Kant or liberalism, just any comprehensive notion of them. His political liberalism does forgo any moral ideal and any notion of individual autonomy, but it promotes tolerance of a wide range of views about the good, including comprehensive doctrines. He has agreed with the communitarians that the conception and imposition of any notion of the Good, from Kantian metaphysics or any which is not implicit in the beliefs and practices of the community in question, cannot be justified. By 1988, he is still seeking some sense of a transcendental Kantian truth but now by trying to identify the reasonable ideas of fairness within the particular, American culture.[59]

Preliminary Comments

Despite the apparent shift in Rawls' position, this is still the presumption of a pre-existing idea of fairness which all ideas of the good, including those that are comprehensive, have in common and which allows them to be seen as mutually compatible. In his search for peace and stability, he takes the key issue of competing ideas of the Good off the agenda.[60] Unlike Hobbes, who saw man as so cantankerous that it required an all-powerful sovereign to enforce peace, Rawls presumes that the capacity for peaceful resolution has been created by the customs of a democratic society and he can just get on with justifying American democratic institutions, which will accommodate wide views about the Good. For the sake of establishing peace, he is here denying the very arguments that political philosophy is all about. He has presumed the mid point in his beginning. That is, he doesn't indicate the cultural processes that have already created this idea of fairness, which he then uses to justify democratic institutions, except to say that they are cultural and democratic. He is presuming key elements (that is, the processes of agonistic civilising) of what he says he is trying to create (that is, peace) by bracketing what needs to be addressed to achieve this (that is, wide differences of view resolved by imposition rather than cooperation based on a sense of fairness). More importantly, he thereby camoflages the historical prejudices, injustices and mistaken beliefs that lie embedded in what he calls Good and Right.

Consequently, his notion of overlapping consensus looks pale. What he should have acknowledged is that there is a 'first order' Good, the product of some kind of agonistic, even violent, customary processes which have embedded a particular notion of justice, so that these processes may be chosen in his Original Position and with which the democratic constitution and institutions developed, implicit in which are 'second order' goods such as his version of liberties and so on. What we have argued up to this point is that what Rawls claims as the rational principles of justice of a democratic society are themselves a comprehensive Good because, emerging through political thought at least from Hobbes, they are replete with moral and other presumptions about the fearful nature of the individual, rights, representation, institutional arrangements, consent, resistance and fair distribution: Good does precede the principles upon which Right is founded, which in turn precede particular goods. These principles present themselves as superior to other conceptions of what is Good (and therefore Right), such as theological autocracy or a system which, unlike the dominant form of democracy, promotes self-responsibility and therefore genuine, continuous and widespread participation in the deliberation and implementation of the representative political process. The dominant form of the democratic, constitutional State doesn't do this. Rawls has not explained that it was this gradual emergence of democratic institutions, with all their inherent notions of what is Good, which slowly produced his notion of fairness in the first place. He has turned a blind eye.

The communitarians focused on aspects of Rawls' theory that highlighted its moral universalist aspirations, the autonomous and asocial character of his individualism and the theory of the Good that is implicit in the State claiming to adopt a position of neutrality between concepts of the good. The bulk of the present work, although coming from a different theoretical base, supports that criticism. In the face of their criticism, Rawls seems to have withdrawn from his early, metaphysical Kantianism into a political rather than moral account of justice but one in which he presumes rather than explains much of what he should be arguing, that is the processes which produced the customary sense of reasonableness and cooperation which he uses to justify his two principles and on which he founds the basic, democratic structure which allows varying concepts of the good. Specifically, he regards Right as prior to the Good[61] or the Reasonable as prior to the Rational.[62] For him, the basic structure that finds itself through such a public conception of justice as the institutional arrangements of a constitutional democratic State, or Right, is prior to any comprehensive religious, philosophical or moral doctrine, or Good.[63] However, it is the argument of this work that his concept of Right, emerging as it does in the form of the tripartite constitutional democracy, is itself founded on a range of historical conceptions which taken together have come to constitute a comprehensive moral conception. This comprehensive conception is mythological. That is, the mythological precedes Right and the mythological is a comprehensive, albeit questionable, Good.

RAWLS AND MYTHOLOGY

We will now examine in more detail Rawls' thesis, the changes to which it has been subject and the mythological significance of these. There are three aspects on which I wish to make particular comment: his Kantian mythology; his work on the Kantian myth; his stepping back from Kantian metaphysics, the effect of which is an ultimately failed attempt to strengthen what is his contribution to the mythological tradition.

Rawls' Early Kantianism

It is not hard to see why Rawls set himself in a Kantian context in trying to revitalize the political theoretical tradition. Kant's political theory can be argued to have consolidated the significant features of both the 'Hobbesian' and 'Rousseauean' contributions to that tradition. Rawls was attracted by the universality of the moral imperatives of Kantianism and by the kind of rationality that came with the autonomous Kantian individual, whose reason could be relied upon to critique and reprogramme those elements of Kant's own work which in the late twentieth century were anachronistic. These elements included the limitations to political participation, particularly based on class and gender, the proscription of any resistance to the State, the lack of interest in the fair distribution of resources, a retributive concept of justice and, beneath it all, the oppressiveness of the notion of a general will. Unaware of the mythological presumptions of the tradition within which he worked, Rawls was presented by that tradition with a morally robust theoretical arrangement and the opportunity to make his own contribution to it by addressing what he saw as its shortcomings.

Early Rawlsian theory, up to and including *A Theory of Justice*, can be seen as driven by deep, that is tectonic, ideas that have mythological significance traceable through Kant back to Hobbes. These elements do not reappear in Rawls in the same variations as in Hobbes, since the Hobbesian framework underwent enough amendment by other thinkers to apparently improve its functionality as myth. But it has been the peculiar dynamics of Hobbesian mythology within and against which his successors, including Rawls, continued to operate.

Rawls' Original Position and the arrangements that flow from it contain the voluntary contractarianism that Hobbes employs to relieve fear. They do this by effectively denying the wide application of the principle of insufficient reason,[64] demonstrating Rawls' preference for the elimination of the fearsome influence of the ever-present malevolent opponent rather than the risk that accompanies self-responsibility. The Two Principles emphasise this point, given that they are chosen to optimise individual rights and equal distribution of resources and opportunities to ensure that elimination. The structural arrangements that Rawls chooses to deliver on those principles are the standard Western democratic institutions championed by the very thinkers that we have considered, including Kant.[65] We have examined at length the genealogy of that institutional mythology and in that their creation of a constituted but fearsome entity the claims of which, as in Rawls, are to eliminate fear (his First Principle) and create sympathetic conditions of existence (his Second Principle), by forgoing self-responsibility to the Kantian political institutional arrangements, with their dominant interests. The optimised inclusiveness of these principles is their full dispersal across social space. What is interesting is that, by the time we get to Rawls, these ideas about the preferred institutional arrangements have become so embedded in the political tradition that he does not even raise the question of their origin, genealogy and status.[66] This is despite the fact that they have been gradually and even violently established over a long time and on the basis of particular notions of the Good, the cost of which has been the forgoing of self-responsibility and especially for the benefit of dominant interests.

Organic Implications and Contingency as a Condition of Fear

Setting the context for the problems Rawls will have with this metaphysics and genealogy is that his structural arrangement and inclusiveness resonate with the medieval, one might say mythological, notion of the organic conception of society.[67] It is true that Rawls states that his idea of social union does not invoke 'a perfectionist or organic conception of society.'[68] However, although he does not claim organic perfection as a goal of his preferred arrangements, the network of core attributes of organic systems are core elements in his arrangements.[69] From these attributes a range of other organic ideas is derived.[70] This is an arrangement which is premised on co-ordinated, unified and hierarchically integrated activity. It is the myth of the fully harmonised political society. It hardly allows for the self-determining edginess of individual self-responsibility promoted by a different kind of State.

In this context of harmonious tranquillity, Rawls raises the issue of contingency and its necessary elimination. For him, contingency is a condition of fear and not of hope, as it might be.[71] He accepts that the contingency of human existence is both natural and social in form and that it is multiplicitous and personal in nature, but his response to this contingency, crucial as it is to his analysis of justice, is open to challenge. Social contingency, as the sense that we are not only conceived but continue to be significantly determined by factors outside ourselves, invites one of two principal responses. One may adopt the view that it is possible to construct arrangements which will eliminate or neutralise it and that this will be the basis of a certain kind of individual freedom. Alternatively, one may adopt the view that nothing can effect such an elimination, that being encouraged to do so is a seduction into submission, and attempt instead to construct arrangements which might moderate its effect, although without preventing its continuing recurrence, by promoting the responsible capacity of the individual in contingent circumstances. In this response to contingency, the promotion of individual capacity would constitute a different sense of freedom. The first view would be seen to be based on a denial of the intractability of contingency and therefore as unable to constitute freedom in this sense. The alternative view produces a stronger sense of freedom but one which requires constant individual attention to the management of contingency.

Rawls does not conceive that freedom might consist in the recurrent situational and differentially successful attempt to manage contingency. For him, a full sense of justice (as 'fairness,' in the form of the two principles) will realise our nature as beings that are both free and rational in the Kantian sense and such 'freedom (is) from contingency and happenstance.'[72] He claims that we cannot express our nature by following a plan that views the sense of justice as but one desire to be weighed against others:[73] for 'this sentiment [of justice]) reveals what the person is, and to compromise it is not to achieve for the self free reign but to give way to the contingencies and accidents of the world.'[74] By being just in the Kantian sense he conceives, one eliminates or neutralises the effects of social contingency and so is free. Free, effectively, from fear.

Rawls' choice is that adopting principles of justice will provide a guarantee against the incursions of contingency, while the alternative position presented here acknowledges the inevitability of this contingency and that it is better to recognise this than pursue a quest for the unattainable and at the very high price of forgoing self-responsibility. For Blumenberg and by our amendments and extensions the position proposed here, the choice is clear.[75] That is, the most appropriate primary response to contingency is to enable responsible, respectful situational assertion by individuals rather than rely first on a search for the establishment, elaboration and administration of principles, goods (for Rawls these are rights, opportunities, powers, wealth and self-respect)[76] and arrangements, the aspiration of which is to eliminate contingency.

Rawls' early Kantian approach to this problem is revealed in the highly conservative nature of his preferred maximin strategy by which he claims the two principles of Justice as Fairness would be chosen.[77] His view is that the parties deciding the principles of the Original Position behind the veil of ignorance would choose principles as if to protect themselves against the possibility that their place in society would be decided by a malevolent opponent.[78] This assertion intentionally excludes alternative strategies whose adoption would have a different impact on notions of justice and citizenship. He excludes the wide application of the principle of insufficient reason. Under this principle, parties would not forego reason in their deliberations in the Original Position, but they would recognise that in any consideration of practical matters it is reasonable to propose something on insufficient grounds,[79] given that such consideration will always proceed without definitive evidence, that is based on provisional rhetoric.[80] In the context of such a principle, rational decision rules may therefore include those based on the argument of the considered wager.[81] Parties to the experiment Rawls constructs might wager that their position is likely to be decided by their own capacity to secure any position, that is, rather than that it may be determined by a malevolent person:[82] they may fully trust themselves without disrespecting others. Under such conditions, the inevitability of the proposal of the two principles as necessarily optimising justice as fairness disappears. Rawls cannot reject this claim on the basis that there may be some individuals in the Original Position who would wish to adopt this approach of the wager but that most would not, since it is clear that for him there must be unanimity and that 'Therefore, we can view the choice in the original position from the standpoint of one person selected at random.'[83] The effect of this claim is the demise of Rawls' unanimity, allowing the introduction of the individually self-responsible, respectful negotiative process which the acknowledgement of the virulence of contingency encourages.

This position regarding the elimination of contingency, especially as a source of fear, was not a position held by Rawls only in his early work. Throughout his theoretical work, even in his amendment of and eventual departure from Kantian metaphysics, Rawls was concerned to imagine political arrangements in which fear is first eliminated. This is apparent from *A Theory of Justice,* where he constructs the thought experiment in which the conservative maximin strategy will ensure that every malevolent opponent is thwarted,[84] to *Political Liberalism* and beyond, where his primary aspiration is still the construction of the fully ordered society.[85]

Rawls' commitment to the Kantian framework has other implications. Its Hobbesian-Lockean and Rousseauean roots begin with the social contract, which he claims to generalise and to carry 'to a higher level of abstraction.'[86]

This passes into his notion of 'justice as fairness' which he relates to 'the high point of the contractarian tradition in Kant and Rousseau.'[87] He adopts the Kantian notion of autonomy as the source of his rational-moral law, that is from the choices which result from the freedom and equality of all individuals as rational beings, and the Rousseauean notion that freedom is acting in accordance with a law which we give to ourselves.[88] For him, these are the conditions which found the establishment of the Original Position and the two principles of justice. He denies that the principles which determine action could be based on social or inherited characteristics, that is rather than through the exercise of rational autonomy, due to the heterynomous implications of that claim.[89] As we have seen, Rawls' establishment of the Original Position is such that this heteronomy is consciously excluded by the veil of ignorance which constitutes the conditions of choice. Heteronomy, determination by a law external to oneself, is a profound source of contingency and therefore fear. Rawls also views the necessary adoption of the two principles as categorically imperative in the Kantian sense, that is as necessarily the product of free and equal rational beings and irrespective of particular aims, since such aims are necessarily contingent.[90] The strong implication is that for all this Rawls requires a Kantian notion of the self, one which emphasises its unity by the rationality and planned coherence of the individual's life[91] and which 'is prior to the ends which are affirmed by it.' For Rawls, there is no way to get beyond deliberative rationality: 'We should therefore reverse the relation between the right and the good proposed by teleological doctrines and view the right as prior.'[92] This position is also drawn from the notion of Kantian autonomy, since the latter accords with the assumption of mutual disinterest.[93] We have seen the problem in this assertion, since one cannot get beyond Good.

In short, in his search to found a re-invigorated political philosophy, which was in effect a quasi-organic mythology, Rawls relied first on such Rousseauean-Kantian notions as the moral imperative and rational autonomy as the basis of his notion of fairness and then on the 'Hobbesian' institutional arrangements needed to give these effect. Each of these has strong mythological credentials, as we have seen. As it had been with Kant, this was reason in the service of myth, all the key characteristics of which survive in his work: the fearsome magnitude of the State, its engagement through forgoing self-responsibility, its fate coming into man's hands and its wide dispersal through the engagement of all individuals in the belief that fear as contingency can effectively be eliminated and sympathetic conditions of existence created.

Rawls' Work on the Kantian Myth

The challenge for Rawls in his revival of the political tradition was to show 'what can be is what should be' about the way that the magnitude, as it is called here, operates. That is, to show that what is feasible is what is desirable about it. In effect, he had to justify afresh the magnitude, comprised of the customarily established political arrangements, by showing that it could 'deliver' for every individual and engage him. This is the basis for his construction of an argument that started with outflanking the fearsome malevolent opponent. He chose a Kantian framework for this.[94] However, having taken on Kantianism, he was aware of its shortcomings and set out to rectify them. He proceeds to critique Kant to eliminate the flaws, the effect of which is to make the idea of the magnitude still fearsome but sympathetic, while remaining within a Kantian framework.

We have seen that there were flaws in Kant's scheme. Rawls' principal strategy for its revision is his Two Principles, the first optimising individual rights and liberties and the second optimising redistribution of resources and individual opportunity, all of which he produces out of a Kantian sense of universal morality and the autonomy of the rational individual. The magnitude is thereby made more sympathetic without limiting the power it requires to give effect to these aspirations, a power still derived from the forgoing by individuals of their self-responsibility.

However, this revision is not always done in a manner which is consistent with Kant's arguments. He acknowledges that he uses the Kantian arguments regarding the autonomy of the individual to establish the basic structure of society,[95] which is 'the way in which the major social institutions fit together into one system, and how they assign fundamental rights and duties and shape the division of advantages that arise through social co-operation. Thus the political constitution, the legally recognised forms of property, and the organisation of the economy, all belong to the basic structure.'[96] Rawls claims that 'this and other additions are natural enough and remain fairly close to Kant's doctrine.'[97] However, Kantian equality is strictly confined to the legal interrelations of citizens. It does not go beyond legal equality.[98] In his desire to make the State fairer than Kant, Rawls has gone well beyond Kant so that he may shore up the mythological imperative that the State is the creator of sympathetic conditions of existence.

Further, Rawls claims that the two principles assume that the parties to the Original Position 'desire certain primary goods. These are things that it is rational to want whatever else one wants.'[99] For Rawls, such goods include 'rights and liberties, powers and opportunities, income and wealth.'[100] Although he states that they are required as parts of rational plans of life,[101] thereby avoiding the prospect that each such end has value for its own sake, for Rawls the rationality of the life plans involves the application of morality in the distribution of essentially non-moral goods such as wealth. He acknowledges that this is 'a prospect that would ... have filled Kant with horror.'[102] The Kantian State was indeed less sympathetic than that of Rawls, and, for that, was less robust as myth, even though it was an advance on the conception of it by Hobbes and Locke. Rawls is stretching Kant in working on the myth he inherited from him.

Rawls acknowledges that he has 'departed from Kant's views in several respects,'[103] specifically in assuming that the choice of the noumenal self is a collective one, that is that the force of the self's being equal to all others is that the principles chosen must be acceptable to other selves and each must have an equal say in adopting the public principles of the ethical commonwealth. This collectivity of the self would be against the grain of Kant. It would also be inconsistent with the principle of self-responsibility, even though that must be informed by respect for others.

What these amendments clarify is that the intention of the early Rawls is to correct the flaws in Kantian political theory, the effect of which is to strengthen the dominant political mythology. Its strengthening is by claiming there is a way to pre-emptively eliminate contingency, thereby fear, and to promote the creation of sympathetic conditions of existence, through the assumption of self-responsibility from individuals. His amendments to Kant's effective strengthening of the tradition of political mythology are evidence that Rawls' principal concern was such an elimination: his conception of the rationally obligatory nature of the Original Position, as a neo-Hobbesian, neo-Kantian device; the organic disposition of his all-inclusive conception of society; his endorsement of the negative libertarianism of the constraints of the Montesquieuean State form;[104] his amendment of the Lockean notion of rights through the difference principle; and his support for the Rousseauean sense of 'the social system [which] shapes the wants and aspirations that its citizens come to have.'[105] His position is the then-latest in a line of theorists who progressively critiqued and re-programmed the Hobbesian paradigm for the purpose of extending its trajectory rather than seeing its inherent flaws and radically criticising it. His mythology, like the variations of his predecessors, effectively assumed responsibility for an entire society, that is for others rather than oneself, and in that sense at least it was flawed. Rawls assumed too many of the priorities of the Kantian Idealist mythology, designed to overcome the malevolent demon of Cartesian doubt, and in doing so ignored the potential benefits of a non-metaphysical application of the categorical imperative and the Kantian postulate, along with the potential of the principle of insufficient reason. But doing so would have produced a different theory of justice.

Rawls Forgoes Kantian Metaphysics but the Myth Remains

Rawls' Communitarian Credentials

The communitarians criticised the metaphysical Kantianism of Rawls' approach. Although he could defend himself against some of these criticisms, he came to accept that one must look within a culture for moral principles upon which to build political arrangements and not attempt to construct such principles on an abstract, universal basis. He did this unaware that there is as much mythology in community moral principles as there is in the rational arguments of apparently autonomous individuals. Rawls did look within and saw his principles of fairness embedded in his own American culture, acknowledging by implication that one cannot rely on any concept of an autonomous rational individual as the means to get to such principles, as the individual is fully embedded in culture. This shift by Rawls was from a comprehensive doctrine to a political one, leading to his emphasising the priority of the Reasonable over the Rational or of Right over Good.

Rawls could defend himself against the charge that he ignores the primacy of culture, in fact he accepts that fairness is embedded in our culture and emphasises it more in later work. But the real point is that the communitarian criticism was telling, and Rawls accepts that justice is a notion embedded in, he comes to argue in American, culture. Rawls' reformulation and re-emphasis allows him to respond effectively to key communitarian criticisms. In particular, he claims, against the Kantian concept of the self attributed to him by Sandel,[106] that although the individual as a citizen must be separate from his conception of the good within the political realm, he can acknowledge that they may regard it as simply unthinkable to view themselves apart from certain religious, philosophical and moral convictions in non-political matters. He claims, against those who like MacIntyre assert that his concept of the self is detached from society,[107] that even in his earlier work he acknowledged 'a social setting as well as a system of belief and thought that is the outcome of the collective efforts of a long tradition'[108] and that this is reinforced by his later argument regarding the public nature of the articulative process.[109] He also responds to claims like that by Sandel that communal goods cannot be limited to the non-political arrangements.[110]

Equally, he responds to those such as Walzer who assert that he ignored cultural differences by intending that his theory can be applied universally[111] and that he assumed some universal vantage point from which to determine his principles and to determine the distribution of goods.[112] Rawls distinguishes between political and other goods[113] and he makes clear that he is referring only to democratic societies in his delineation of public political culture.[114] This in turn allows him to reject the assertion that his account of conceptions of the good is arbitrary or subjectivist: one can still be committed to the truth of a moral doctrine without it having to be included in political matters and one may not be committed to the truth of a political judgement without forgoing its objectivity as based on reasonableness. Finally, he acknowledges that the priority he gives to right over good is compatible with various senses of good (for example the rational as a good; the permissibility of comprehensive conceptions of the good; the well-ordered society as a good), so although the liberal State is not to promote any particular comprehensive notion of the good, there is a compatibility between Right and Good and a political conception must draw upon various ideas of the good.[115] On all this may be based a claim that there are reasons to regard Rawls as himself significantly communitarian.[116]

For Rawls, the fairness of these arrangements is to be achieved by a process of systematic articulation of ideas which are implicitly shared due to their being embedded in the communal culture and practice. The Original Position models the conditions of fairness through which the representatives of these free and equal citizens articulate the terms of the social co-operation through that basic structure, while it also excludes matters of the good through the veil of ignorance. In this sense, justice as fairness is purely political. It claims to imply no conception of the good or of the nature of the self: it is the rational articulation of arrangements drawn from shared ideas of fairness.[117] It is because these ideas, unlike those relating to matters of the good, are implicitly shared and articulated in a publicly rational manner that they are justifiable.[118] For Rawls, the paradigm cases of such public rationality are the speeches of the legislature and the decisions of the Supreme Court in a constitutional democracy,[119] which constitute politics as having a high formal status rather than through the cut and thrust of respectful self-responsible individuals grappling agonistically with the fearsomeness and aspirations of themselves and others. He appears to apply the practice of rationality to his own political constructivist theorising, although this is somewhat misleading since the purely political principles it generates can be regarded as if they were the outcome of rational construction.[120]

Justice as fairness is now a political and not a metaphysical concept on which is based the argument of Right before Good. The problem is that the rejection of metaphysics and the embracing of cultural embeddedness do not lead to an acknowledgement of the full cultural embeddedness of the idea of the State or of the mythology therein.

Kantianism and Mythology

Yet Rawls remains too much a Kantian. That is, he has rejected Kantian metaphysics but retained enough Kantianism to sustain what is claimed here to be mythology. Far from recognising the long emergence of the democratic concept of the State and justice since Hobbes, with all the questionable cultural and moral presumptions embedded in that concept, Rawls denies any coherence in the emergence of that idea, taking the view that there was an incoherence which could only be sorted out by the application of Kantian reason.[121] For him 'The course of democratic thought over the last two centuries, say, shows that there is no agreement on the way basic social institutions should be arranged if they are to conform to the freedom and equality of citizens as moral persons.'[122] He goes on by claiming only a conflict between the Lockean and Rousseauean traditions, seeking a fundamental rendering of freedom and equality in justice as fairness.[123] Rawls has not seen the mythology in both Locke and Rousseau and so still sees these as different political traditions. He therefore doesn't see that his attempt to resolve that 'impasse' is further work within the mythological tradition.

Rawls' post-metaphysical mythology also emerges clearly in is his distinction between right and good. He asserts that the right is prior to the good and has priority over it.[124] He states his reason for this,[125] having pointed out that primary goods are 'rights and liberties, opportunities and powers, income and wealth.'[126] What Rawls is effectively doing here is elaborating the mythological importance of the sympathy of the magnitude, necessary to balance its fearsome power, whereby it is also constrained so that spheres of activity are established from which the magnitude withdraws. That is, the magnitude remains empowered to enforce right in the form of primary goods but is constrained to withdraw from matters which relate to what is Good, as determined by a person's own interests and aims. Necessarily for Rawls, these comprise the elements of a successfully executed rational plan of life and will prominently feature such human goods as 'the familiar values of personal affection and friendship, meaningful work and social cooperation, the pursuit of knowledge and the fashioning and contemplation of beautiful objects.'[127] There is little wrong with such personal aspirations, if the individual chooses to pursue those, but to specify such a list as a model for all presumes a coherence that is as ideally Kantian as it is, protected by the 'Hobbesian' institutions of State, mythological.

Rawls' Amended Kantian Mythology Remains Flawed

As with his predecessors, the content and effect of Rawls' work is not comprehensively mythological. There are elements of his thought that would survive mythological deconstruction. Examples would include his promotion of the principle of just economic arrangements, enforced by law,[128] and his insistence on the preservation of wealth for following generations.[129] Further he would not contest that there is some injustice in the laws, since the parties in the Original Position sign up not only to the laws that sustain the two principles but generally to enter into a state of affairs which carries with it 'political duty and obligation':[130] they accept that a society can never be completely just but they will abide by just constitutional arrangements so long as the inevitable imperfections of a constitutional system are shared equitably.[131] Further, there is nothing distasteful about the attempt to establish the optimally extensive system of individual rights. Looked at in one light, this can be construed as optimal self-responsibility. The problem is that in Rawls these rights come at the cost of the forgoing of that responsibility and colours the nature of those rights. If he were to acknowledge the full embeddedness of his notion of justice as fairness in the genealogy of the State, argued here to be mythological in nature, he might well be dissatisfied with the constitutional democracy that he so wholeheartedly embraces, and argue his justice as fairness on a non-mythological foundation.

Nonetheless, despite Rawls' attempts to correct the flaws in the Kantian political mythology and realise an idea of the State that achieves its two primary purposes, serious flaws remain. First, within the context of his own premises, Rawls' argument fails. His argument that, despite the foundation of his concept of justice in custom, reason alone will produce a notion of Right in the form of the basic structure and that this has priority over Good,[132] is wrong. As we have argued, there is a comprehensive Good which precedes Right and the constitutional democratic structure that it forms. This is the mythological condition by which the State claims to deal with individual fear and desire for sympathetic conditions. This is a Good because it satisfies Rawls' own definition of what constitutes a comprehensive Good. His error is shown when he says that a political concept of justice involves no prior commitment to a wider doctrine but looks to the basic structure and elaborates a reasonable conception for that structure alone.[133] It has been argued in this work that the basic structure itself is the product of a long-refined mythological, and in Rawlsian terms comprehensive, idea since Hobbes and that reason has been employed, not just since Kant but since Hobbes, in the service of that mythological thought.

The implication is that, in direct contradiction to Rawls, the mythological State cannot be neutral: Right is founded on Good and so has no priority over it. Further, this State must reject concepts of the Good that contradict its mythological premises, such as those based, at one extreme, on religious fundamentalism or, on the other, on individual self-responsibility. Mythology makes his claim to State neutrality unsustainable: even when it operates through alliance and agency, say through Church or market, the State is always interested in and responsible for the practices of individuals, given its assumption of ultimate responsibility for the relief of fear and the creation of sympathetic conditions of existence. This allows for both the State forming relationships of alliance and agency to ensure these are carried out but, more significantly, it allows for the artificial construction of what constitutes both fear and the desire that sympathetic conditions are to satisfy.

More generally regarding the unavailability of State neutrality, the notion of liberalism which Rawls is promoting here is one in which State coercive power, constituted by the corporate power of free and equal citizens, is exercised only in ways to which all citizens would agree as rational beings.[134] It is this rationality which constitutes, he claims, rather than is constituted by, political stability.[135] Stability is therefore for him coincident with the rational legitimacy of the regime: he denies that his theory is pragmatic in that it simply seeks to avoid conflict. Nor does he accept that the competition between conceptions of the good may destabilise, since reason will ensure the tolerance necessary to sustain the overlapping consensus of such conceptions.

This reveals something more about the nature of the mythological relationship between right and good. The elimination of fear requires the elimination of forms of life which challenge the dominant form. The justification for such elimination is that any form of life which challenges the dominant form is a source of fear. Consequently, the concept of right must at least be complemented by a determination of good. The result is that, in any mythological political system, there is not only promotion of rights and liberties but also of how those rights and liberties will be exercised through forms of individual life. Rawls developed this latter notion to such a level of refinement that he conceived the good as an individual life plan,[136] and that, as rational, such an individual plan will inevitably form part of a coherent mega-plan for the entire community. For him, this mega-plan comprises a well-ordered society, the integrated coherence of which eliminates the uncertainty and competition which is the source of fear.

Beside these arguments is that put by Rawls that political stability is a result of, not a justification for, this exercise of public reason. His preference is clearly for political institutional arrangements and practices which assure stability and unity in the face of pluralism: he does not assert that different comprehensive doctrines should stand alone politically but that they should be accommodated in a single State form. This is the attempt to ensure the elimination of the potentially destabilising and therefore fear-producing effects of pluralism. His argument is that these political arrangements are the result of the exercise of public reason and that their stability is secondary: it is not a matter of 'bringing others who reject a conception to share it ... by workable sanctions if necessary. ... Rather, justice as fairness is not reasonable in the first place unless in a suitable way it can win its support by addressing each citizen's reason.'[137]

The problem here is that reason is so defined, derived as it is from his conception of culturally shared intuitive ideas, as to presume stability as the outcome. The political arrangements could not be other than stable, given the manner in which he conceives reasonableness. There is no undertaking the riskiness of working towards provisional stability by agonistic, respectful self-responsibility. For Rawls it must be categorically assured from the start, by eliminating any element that might introduce risk, including such self-responsibility. He was clear about his post-Kantian aspirations well before *Political Liberalism*, stating that it is necessary to adopt 'the method of avoidance' such that 'differences between contending political views can at least be moderated ... [and] ... social cooperation on the basis of mutual respect can be maintained.'[138] Although without the comprehensive moral imperative of Kant, his theory remains true to the Hobbesian-Lockean presumptive, pre-emptively establishing conditions of peace, order, stability and unity. This mythology has caused him to deny that, alongside the centripetal force of shared ideas, stands both the centrifugal force of contrary views concerning the preferred basic structure, which may derive from various rational but ideological comprehensive doctrines, and the position of those who might wish to exercise the principle of insufficient reason through the construction of nothing more than provisional arrangements. He does not conceive that there may be no universality or unanimity regarding preferred arrangements and that stability as he defines it is not a necessary or, depending upon its price, a necessarily desirable outcome. His argument, again, is circular. Even his insistence that the pervasive influence of the basic structure be realised by being made fully public[139] does not lead him to consider that this form of the constitutional democratic basic structure might not be preferred.

The attempt to eliminate contingency is shown by Rawls' bracketing of any reasonable, pluralist comprehensive doctrines from the basic structure by the veil of ignorance, the intention of this anti-perfectionist neutrality being to avoid the coercion of individuals by the State on behalf of any preferred doctrine.[140] Although Rawls does not emphasise the point, this proscription would appear to have the added benefit of eliminating the general contingency which may result from conflict between such comprehensive doctrines. However, rather than having this eliminative effect, such proscription could have the opposite effect, that is it would have a destabilising impact due to the frustration of unresolved views. This is because Rawls' attempt to sustain the classical liberal protection of the individual from the State as a principal source of contingency may well increase destabilisation. In that circumstance, it would be counter-intuitive, at least on Rawlsian liberal grounds, to exclude comprehensive doctrines from the public political process that determines the basic structure, as he does[141]: it would be their agonistic engagement, for example by encouraging respectful debate within a context of redesigned institutions, which would be a more fruitful strategy against contingency and its associated fear.[142]

Further, his latest conception of the liberal State as a corporate body of free and equal citizens is problematic. Qualified by the cultural imperatives which Rawls claims as implicit from his earlier work, this corporatism is to be seen within a contractarian frame which is characterised by a common human reason with stout parallels to the Kantian general will[143]: for him the liberal ideal is that, since political power is the coercive power of citizens as a corporate body, this should be exercised, regarding constitutional or justice questions, only in ways a reasonable person would endorse.[144] This denial of the strong possibility of difference regarding such questions suggests an unreasonableness on the part of those with a different view which, in the face of the engagement of coercive power of the State, amounts to the elimination of dissent on political issues as destabilising. There is presumed consent to or forceful imposition of political liberalism on those who dissent on political issues because of the adoption of comprehensive doctrines, or because of their preference for an agonistic search for accommodation, or especially due to the rejection of rational life planning, or on grounds of deep cultural difference. This would be the context of a punitive, rather than a restorative, approach to matters of criminal justice. On such grounds, Rawls' argument for an anti-perfectionist State neutrality on both political and politically driven comprehensive doctrines would not be available.[145]

There is also another possible reading of this agument. That is, that it does not seem to recognise that Rawls has bracketed any comprehensive concept from the determination of the basic constitutional structure, so any interest apart from those supporting the Two Principles to eliminate the malevolent opponent, which I have argued is one comprehensive Good, will be excluded and suffer the exercise of the coercive power of the State.

Rawls comes to acknowledge that he is vulnerable in this regard. He states 'it is usually desirable to settle political questions by invoking the values of public reason. Yet this may not always be so.'[146] Further, he states that being reasonable is not primarily an epistemological idea, rather 'it is part of a political ideal of democratic citizenship that includes the idea of public reason,' the content of which includes 'what free and equal citizens can require of each other with respect to their reasonable comprehensive views.'[147] This is the constitution of the reasonable, that is including political matters, by moral constraint.[148] The consequences of these acknowledgments are various. Since there is no final bracketing of such comprehensive doctrines from political reason available, Rawls cannot sustain an argument regarding the priority of the political, nor that the State can be neutral in an anti-perfectionist manner, nor that political liberalism can claim priority over alternative conceptions of constitutional justice driven by comprehensive doctrine. This provides some comfort to the claim here that his political liberalism is a rational mythological strategy designed as a political form which is constructed as the locus of forgone individual responsibility. This is so even though that form is constrained to the extent of constitutional democratic arrangements, the intention of which is to eliminate contingency as a source of fear, for example through bracketing or through the exercise of State coercion. Such contingency would be characterised in a Rawlsian pluralist society by the competition between comprehensive doctrines and its elimination would deliver a well-ordered Hobbesian-Kantian polity. Rawls has finally to acknowledge what is inherent in any mythological political paradigm, that is that the elimination of fear draws concepts of the Good into the determination of right and that coercion is adopted early rather than late in this arrangement.

We may therefore now argue not only that Rawls' enterprise is mythological but that, as all political mythology is doomed to be, it remains a failure in that. The version of justice as fairness presented in *Political Liberalism* shows the failure of the touted aim of myth to create an entity which is fearsome but fairly so. Rawls' argument that comprehensive doctrines should not trump but be subject to political values and arrangements may seem attractive, that political arrangements should be value free, but there are two problems with this. First, it cannot be argued that the political should have exclusive priority over the comprehensive since there are cases in which the principles of justice should be bracketed. That is, there are cases where the categorical imperative, on which Rawls' principles of justice are founded,[149] should not apply: gay marriage, choosing the moment of one's death, quiet drug use and so on should be a matter only for the individual, even though they may feature negatively in some comprehensive moral doctrine, and so the political should have no priority. Irrespective of this normative circumstance, because the institutional arrangements of the mythological State are a vacuous framework created to be colonised by dominant interests who make the best claim to deal with fear and sympathy, comprehensive doctrines colonise the political process to prescribe and proscribe practices which are properly the province only of the principal. That is, against Rawls' argument for the priority of Right, his mythological arrangements are actually established to allow the promotion of comprehensive interests. The State is always unfairly fearsome because it is merely the institutional structure, its idea gradually assembled from Hobbes to Montesquieu and reinforced by the engagement of every individual through Rousseau and Kant, the latent power of which is used by the dominant to promote their own interests while delivering differentially on fear and sympathy across the community. It is more than ironic that competition delivers into the hands of the dominant the very fearsomeness that is required, along with passing the fear-sympathy test, to create submission to its interests. As a result, Rawls' argument therefore fails because, despite his Kantian arguments to the contrary, he has assumed the flawed premises of the political mythological tradition. The result is that, far from the conception of justice and the State being the consequence of the exercise of each individual's reason concerning equality, it is the consequence of the primal desire for the elimination of fear and the desire for sympathetic conditions of existence. Dressed up in the palliative of the exercise of reason, submission is, again in Rawls as with his predecessors, the heavy price of not being responsible for dealing respectfully with one's fear and creating one's own sympathetic conditions. Reason in the service of myth.

SUMMARY

In all this, Rawls is sustaining and strengthening what has been essential to the mythological political tradition since Hobbes. Because its first premise is fear of conflict, Rawlsian liberalism, eventually divesting itself of the strong metaphysics of Kantianism, retreats into a sterile process of presumed co-operation, parliamentary debate, judicial decision and pre-emptive State coercion, even when the communitarians force recognition of the virulence of competition between comprehensive goods, but without forgoing the mythological practices of the unfairly coercive State. Rather than accept this competition in an agonistic process sponsored by a reformed State right down to the level of individual disputes, Rawlsian liberalism restricts itself to the formalised safety of such debate, decisionism and pre-emptive coercion, concealing the mythological features of the State. Its principal effect in doing so is the continued protection and strengthening of the mythological political paradigm, persistently in the form of liberal ideology, whose unrealisable *raison d'être* is the claim of eliminating fear, on behalf especially of dominant interests, rather than the empowerment of self-responsibility.

Put simply, Rawls in effect denied the mythological implications of his position, that is that the State ultimately cannot be neutral, that it is in fact the forum in which competition for dominance regarding notions of the right and the good, as the means to achieve that combination, are resolved. Rawls' notion of liberalism not only protects that competition but is itself also a competitor in the sense that it established pre-emptive control over the determination of the nature of structural arrangements, sustaining those that had been created and refined since Hobbes.

Unaware of the mythological presumptions of the political tradition within which he operates, he attempts to argue that Right can and should always precede Good. Those from Hobbes who constructed what were to become Rawls' principles and arrangements were motivated first by a comprehensive Good not Right. What Rawls calls Right is just an amended way of organising the fundamental ('first order') Good, which is the claimed elimination of fear and the creation of sympathetic conditions of existence by which self-responsibility is forgone. It is argued here that primary goods or rights as the 'second order' Good, on the other hand, are ways of ensuring the realisation of the intentions especially of dominant interests, which come to control the arrangements of Right but who must make popular concessions to sustain the arrangements they dominate. The breadth of those rights is a reflection of the vast extent of the dispersal of those interests in a way that deals with the primary concerns of individuals—notions of the Good are therefore at the foundations of the sectional benefits of civilising.

In this context, Rawlsian liberalism becomes a reworked option among competing non-neutral mythological political arrangements. This in turn requires an acknowledgement that Rawlsian liberalism is a non-neutral doctrine which, like those of his progenitors, is incapable of eliminating contingency and therefore fear. Like other comprehensive doctrines, Rawlsian liberalism is in itself a source of such contingency by its very tactics of attempting to assert its superiority and to bracket compelling issues and other comprehensive doctrines. This is also to say that there is no safe ground which may not be either the source of or subject to fear.

In the end, then, what kind of political arrangements are we left with by Rawls? He relies on arguments which are either flawed or circular. These arguments are unsuccessful attempts to ignore the implications of the mythological premises inherited from the tradition. His flawed arguments include that social co-operation can be presumed in a democratic community because of the existence of certain ideas shared in the community; that the exercise of reason will produce agreement on matters fundamental to the basic structure; that the exclusion of notions of the good from the jurisdiction of the State will lead to stability rather than undermine it; that stability is a product of, rather than a justification of, the process of public reason; and that the liberal State can be neutral, when it is founded on a comprehensive notion of the good which justifies the exercise of coercion by the State.

Rawls took the Kantian political myth, identified what he saw as its significant weaknesses and critiqued and re-programmed these through his two principles, the effect of which is an attempt to strengthen the myth, within the context of the trajectories of the political mythological tradition, but without addressing its fundamental flaws. He at no time forgoes the core elements of the Hobbesian-Lockean-Kantian mythology. That mythology especially includes constituted absolustist liberal democratic institutions and rights which are intended to be colonised by dominant interests and which have been used to affirm their own interests through the promotion of strategies of normalisation based on the forgoing of individual self-responsibility while claiming to deal with the nexus of fear and desire. Rawls retreats from Kantian constructivism but then presumes reason as the foundation of communal political ideals, themselves steeped in mythological presumptions, and so is blind to the mythology upon which that reason rests.

In short, Rawlsian theory is in effect a sustained critique and reprogramming of the Kantian political myth, correcting its weaknesses then camouflaging its mythological roots and attempting to protect it from challenge. Initially, he employs a constructivists strategy in devising a rational-moral political order without the flaws of the Kantian myth regarding fear and sympathetic conditions. Then, moving away from Kantian constructivism with the charges of the communitarians, he adopts a political framework, emphasising that Right precedes Good, based on the claim that reason and fairness are embedded in his American culture. This claim denies the mythological genealogy of the institutions and proclamations of the constitutional, parliamentary State he defends and camouflages that his reason and fairness are founded on mythological premises, that in fact they constitute a comprehensive Good. So Right cannot precede Good. Second, his claim for a political framework is used by him as a strategy to protect his neo-Kantian theory against other comprehensive Goods. However, this defence is unsustainable, given its own status as a comprehensive Good. The Rawlsian scaffolding is merely one among a range of competing comprehensive Goods, this one based on mythological principles, to which Rawls has in effect attempted, unsuccessfully, to give a pre-eminent status. He remains firmly in the ranks of the political mythologists.

7 The Liberalism of the Market

HAYEK

Hayek is thought to be the outstanding twentieth century representative of the classical liberal tradition of Locke and Adam Smith.[1] His defence of this tradition came first with *The Constitution of Liberty* and culminated in *Law, Legislation and Liberty*, which is the principal subject of the following analysis. His contribution to epistemology was significant, particularly in the social sciences, where his position was that, in the context of the severe limits of human knowledge, only abstract and negative rules of just conduct were enforceable by government. This gave advantage to his use of Smith's invisible hand, although, as we shall see, this is not unproblematic in the context of his championing of the market.

A more difficult proposition is that for him there is no alternative to the choice between living a tribal existence or that of full capitalist individualism. This individualism is won at the cost of any real sense of respect and so of sympathy for the disadvantaged. It can be argued to have been the product of his sustained attack on socialism and totalitarianism, although he had set out on his intellectual journey as a Fabian socialist.[2] A related consequence of his anti-totalitarian position is that Hayek spends much of his time arguing against socialism but hardly any time exploring the reason why people are drawn, typically willingly, into supporting it. Scruton raises this point[3] but it is at the heart of the wide arguments presented here.

Hayek and Rawls

By the time he wrote *Law, Legislation and Liberty*, Hayek was not only fully aware of Rawls' account of justice but admired it.[4] This admiration finds form in certain elements of his own analysis, though not without his own stamp. These elements include the idea of a hypothetical initial position in a desirable order of society, although this position would be chosen by Hayek on the basis of chance where for Rawls it is a matter of ministering to the effect of a malevolent opponent.[5] More significantly, he agrees with Rawls that preferred principles of justice don't select specific distributions of desired things as just, given the wants of particular persons, but define the constraints which institutions and joint activities must satisfy if persons engaging in them are to have no complaints against them, irrespective of distribution.[6] This latter point is important to Hayek's broad argument and is central to his political philosophy.

The Rules of Just Conduct

An apparently firm footing for Hayek's broad argument is found by many in his account of the rules of just conduct, on which his concept of a spontaneous order is based, which in turn strongly favours the market over such organisations as government, except for a selection of key responsibilities of the latter. The argument to be put here against this is that, not only are these rules an unsteady base for such a mountainous scaffold but, on his own argument, the State cannot be corralled to the limited functions he proposes but permeates his entire social and political arrangement. Thereby he reveals strong mythological credentials.

For Hayek, rules of just conduct have emerged over the long term and are the means and product of social evolution, the mark of evolutionary success.[7] They are universal markers of both culture and custom,[8] in which context their function is to 'say under what conditions this or that action will be within the range of the permissible.'[9] They do so by clearly indicating what someone must not do, rather than what they must do.[10] Each rule is therefore end-independent.[11] However, it is also set in a fully dispersed network of rules,[12] the aim of which is an abstract order distinct from the order of actions,[13] but which, because of the impossibility of setting a rule for every action, contributes to that order by allowing for innumerable outcomes. Rules can and should be amended but only to be consistent with the wider system of rules. They labels *kinds* of actions, not in terms of their largely unknown effects in particular instances, but in terms of their probable effects, which need not be foreseeable by the individuals.[14] Because they are abstract, rules are typically followed as non-articulated practices.[15] They are a foundation of the general expectations of individuals in a community, a satisfaction that confers legitimacy on a government.[16] They are to be obeyed irrespective of the known effects of particular action.[17] Rules thereby comprise the inherited values guiding a society[18] and are accepted as not requiring justification.[19] So here we have a universal, non-articulated, abstract, customary network of rules for conduct but for which the result of compliance is unpredictable.

Compliance with these rules not only justifies but will require government coercion so that there may not be the intrusion of arbitrary power and so freedom may be assured.[20] Rules of conduct thereby protect domains of freedom but do so negatively,[21] identifying in a process of generalisation what may not be done and leaving it up to the individual to create the positive content of his own domain.[22] Law, which takes these rules for granted,[23] enforces them and thereby ensures this peaceful existence of individuals in society.[24] Law does this not by specifying ends.[25] It may restrain an individual only as his conduct may encroach upon the protected domain of others.[26] Its goal is the abstract order of rules, the particular manifestation of which no one could predict but which provides for countless different purposes of different individuals.[27] Thus does law serve the general welfare.[28]

Hayek makes some telling comments about the emergence and status of political and other institutions as they relate to these rules. He argues that early representative bodies were not first concerned with rules of just conduct, coming to that role in time.[29] However, in the modern era, he sees two distinct tasks of government, the enforcement of the universal rules of just conduct and the direction of the organisation built up to provide various services for citizens at large. For him, the latter carries misleading connotations because the provision of services by government does not mean that it has to do so: government has assumed the right, often exclusive, to provide them.[30] In fact, marked by command and the pursuit of particular ends, the rules governing the apparatus of government necessarily possess a different character from the universal rules of conduct. Law, strongly but not exclusively connected with rules of conduct, is similarly to be distinguished from the 'laws,' the free invention of the legislator[31]. He states that this is often misunderstood, causing law to be seen only as an instrument of organisation for particular purposes.[32] This leads him to separate rules of just conduct from rules of organisation, reflecting his distinction between the private law, concerned with freedom and so incorporating the criminal law, and public law[33] respectively. Further, although the enforcement of law is assured by the superstructure of a Constitution,[34] the function of which is to prevent the legislature from arbitrary coercion,[35] the rules remain of pre-eminent importance. More generally, he throws a shadow over democracy, in the sense that the early claim of Parliament to sovereignty meant only that it recognised no other will above it; that belief in democracy presupposes belief in things higher than democracy; and that, wherever democratic institutions ceased to be restrained by the tradition of the Rule of Law, they led to totalitarian democracy and then to plebiscitory dictatorship.[36]

All this has significance for the individual, as 'The fact is, of course, that this mind (of man) is an adaption to the natural and social surroundings in which man lives and that it has developed in constant interaction with the institutions which determine the structure of society. Mind is as much the product of the social environment in which it has grown up and which it has not made as something that has in turn acted upon and altered these institutions.'[37] So, Hayek begins to question common notions of both law and political arrangement, hiving off what should be their lasting concerns with principles of justice from the merely pragmatic, the latter adopted due to persistent selfish demand of the majority. Complementing this is that the individual mind is significantly a product of the socio-political environment rather than a driver of it.

The broader significance of rules of just conduct is emphasised by the link Hayek makes between those rules and the spontaneous order, the next stage in his ultimate justification of the market and the apparent depreciation of government. Referring to various features of these rules, such as their provision for an unknown number of future instances, their negative character, their protection of the individual domains of freedom and by their passing the test of universalisation, he states 'these are all necessary characteristics of those rules of just conduct which form the foundation of a spontaneous order, but do not apply to those rules of organisation which make up the public law';[38] and 'We have chosen the term "rules of just conduct" to describe those end-independent rules which serve the formation of a spontaneous order, in contrast to the end-dependent rules of organisation. The former are the *nomos* which is at the basis of a "private law society" and makes an Open Society possible; the latter, so far as they are law, are the public law which determines the organisation of government.'[39]

Although he would strongly deny it, we can see signs of his mythological thinking emerging in his account of the relationship between private and public law. His claim, and it is fundamental to his entire argument including as it relates to the respective separations of 'made' order and 'spontaneous' order and thereby between State and market, is that private law as the rules for just conduct is separable in kind from public law as organisational law. There are two arguments against this claim. The first founds an example relating to the status of criminal law and taxation law. Despite his assertion, criminal law is a clear case of a jurisdiction that cannot be neatly categorised as private, even though it relates to the enforcement of just rules of conduct on the private citizen, since such enforcement is realised almost exclusively in public law.[40] Taxation law, as it relates to the provision of services which the market cannot provide, is another example of the public enforcement of rules that accrue to the private individual on moral or other grounds.[41] Hayek himself acknowledges that the distinction between the two has been blurred, but attributes much of this to an inappropriate strategy regarding 'social' aims and the associated provision of services that the State has assumed beyond its mandate.[42]

More strongly, the provisions of public law regarding crime and the provision of services are properly seen as a disguise for deeper mythological presumptions that have located themselves in private law. That is, Hayek makes no comment about the influences to which these rules of just conduct have been exposed during their long evolutionary journey, and the prejudices that they thereby inevitably carry, preferring an account in which they are internally robust or either self-correct or can be corrected by occasional conscious amendment. The fundamental notion of concern about the absolutism of reality and its embedding in the rules and in consequential practices of spontaneous orders regarding subjection, fear and desire, is given no consideration by him. Further, Hayek does not indicate the material strategies that should be used by government to ensure the compliance of every individual with these rules. There is nothing he proposes in this that is inconsistent with the mythological aspirations regarding subjection, fear and sympathetic conditions. In fact, we shall see that he wants the 'spontaneous' market to take the lead in addressing this mesh of functions, thereby affirming his mythological credentials. The question will then be that concerning the relationship between his liberal ideology and his mythology, a question that will be answered by an argument that, as with his eminent predecessors, the former disguises the latter.

Spontaneous and Made Orders

Hayek defines order as a state of affairs in which a multiplicity of varying elements are so related to each other that we may, from our acquaintance with some part, form correct expectations concerning the rest.[43] In society, we depend on the matching of our intentions with the expectations we have of the actions of others and this matching determines the actions of individuals and is the form in which order manifests itself.[44] Within this systematic approach, he distinguishes two kinds of order, made and grown.[45] A made order is a construction, an artificial order, 'an organisation' with specified purposes, simple, concrete and serving the purpose of the maker. The grown order is self-generating, thereby spontaneous;[46] it is abstract in that it may persist while its elements change and, other than being preserved by its own elements, it has no purpose because it is not created by any outside agency. A government agency is typical of a made order, society itself and the market being typical of a spontaneous order.[47]

He fills in this outline by explaining how the two orders work. Following on from his consideration of the rules of just conduct, Hayek sees the status and operation of rules as the key to understanding both orders. He first examines the nature of the rules required to produce overall order and suggests three categories: those rules followed due to the consistency with which the environment is presented to individuals; those followed for customary reasons; and those requiring coercion to assure the overall order. One example is that, in an exchange society, individuals will always desire a larger return for their efforts than a smaller one and this rule will require a certain kind of order.[48] In general, however, rules are followed because they have normative status, irrespective of individual desires.[49]

In the broad context of rules, his main interest is in those by which we can affect the resulting order, rules of law. Although an order originally formed itself spontaneously because the individuals followed rules which were not deliberately made but had arisen spontaneously, people learned to improve those rules, and it is conceivable that the formation of a spontaneous order can rely entirely on rules that were deliberately made. He adds that usually only some of the rules, those of law, will be deliberately designed, while the remainder as rules of morals and custom are of spontaneous origin.[50] Consequently, even where we can alter some rules of conduct which individuals obey, we can only influence the general character and not the detail of the order.[51] We shall return to the implications of this, that is that the potential base of a spontaneous order is only made rules, for his broader argument that the spontaneous order must *ipso facto* be self-generating and so have no design or specified purpose.

For Hayek, a typical example of spontaneous order is society itself. It can exist only if, through selection, improvement and enforcement, rules have evolved which lead to behaviour that makes social life possible. This includes that they are end-independent and the same for all. Even a limited similarity in the behaviour of individuals may be sufficient if the rules which they all obey are such as to produce an order.[52] Here we see his link between spontaneity, rules and abstraction. Further, society as the spontaneous overall order features a series of spontaneous overlapping sub-orders, often with common core members who will sometimes obey conventional rules without the necessity of commands and at others will act as an organisation under the will of a chief.[53] Presumably, at still others, they will act under rules which began as commands and became customs or vice versa. Broadly, however, the development of society into a complex order was due to its spontaneity and so its independence of any organisation.[54]

An organisation or made order, on the other hand, is ruled by specific commands which serve particular results.[55] It relies on rules as well as commands but these rules must be for performing assigned tasks, which presupposes a place for each individual who must obey these rules.[56] It is sensible to supplement the commands of an organisation with rules and then to use organisations as elements of a spontaneous order but not the reverse.[57] This is Hayek's defence against interference in the market and we shall return to this. Complementing this thought, Hayek states that when we pass beyond the biggest organisation, government, to society, we find an order that relies solely on rules and is entirely spontaneous in character.[58]

Regarding the compatibility of the two orders, Hayek makes several points. These include that, because the collaboration of any group will rest on both kinds of orders, for example both society and government, he does not deny they can coexist, although not in any way we like.[59] This is the context of his statement that society, as a spontaneous order, will generally need government to ensure its rules are obeyed and, importantly, to ensure the order of the mechanism that regulates the production of services.[60] Further, he acknowledges that, beyond this assurance role, government can properly provide services that the market is unable or unwilling to provide, that is they share a service-provision function.[61]

There are problems with these arguments and claims by Hayek. Regarding the separate natures of his grown and made orders and the rules of conduct on which they rest, rules are indeed followed because they are normative. However, in our examination of Wittgenstein we will see that this means that rules are the subject of training, often finally acquiring the status of certainty. These certain rules, or norms, in their turn take their place in a plurality of interconnected language games, both as customs or commands in a world-picture or form of life. Wittgenstein sees such world-pictures as a kind of myth, argued here to be consistent with the notion of mythology presented by Blumenberg and amended in the present work. Thereby, rules and commands not only evolve from norms, and vice versa, but carry all the mythological characteristics, including the provision of a place within the customs and traditions of a community for political structures and, in that regard, such features as willing subjection in return for claims regarding the elimination of fear and the creation of sympathetic conditions of existence.[62] They are not straightforwardly rules regarding conduct but part of a network of ideas and practices which criss-cross, as connections, what Hayek calls grown and made orders. Grown and made orders are not separable, in kind or in fact.

Two things follow from this. First, it is strongly arguable that a spontaneous order, although not made, can have purpose, even particular purposes. Further, such purposes can have mythological content. It is a condition of society as the overall spontaneous order that there must be general subjection of each individual through the observance of customs and laws that may be against his own interests. This is also Hayek's position. However, there are specific markers for subjection, such as compliance with individualised programmes of rehabilitation for criminal activity. It is also a condition of society that fear and sympathetic conditions will be addressed, for which there are such specific markers as the acquisition of docile patterns of behaviour and the support for the less capable, both taken by government down to the level of the individual and made specific. This connection between abstract, customary rule and concrete, specific purpose is inseparable. Secondly, when we alter the rules of conduct, we influence both the general character of the prevailing spontaneous order (in its concern for subjection, fear and sympathy) and the specific behaviour of particular individuals through their relations with the organisation. The manner in which government undertakes change of individual conduct, a matter that Hayek does not address, needs to be in a manner consistent with these abstract mythological norms, as we shall see with Foucault. Finally, against Hayek's position, Wittgenstein allows for the possibility of following one's own rule, insisting that whether someone follows rules depends on what he is capable of doing not how he acquired that capability,[63] and not just the general rules of just conduct which act for Hayek as the boundaries of individual behaviour. Although he does not say so, it seems to follow from Wittgenstein's point that if one followed a rule of one's own, doing so would be following both an abstract, general rule and a specific, concrete rule.

There are other indicators that point to the inseparability of grown and made orders. As Hayek acknowledges, a particular organisation (i.e. government) is required to enforce compliance with the rules on which society as a spontaneous order rests, that is the spontaneous order will likely not exist without enforcement by a made order; more significantly, that organisation (i.e., government) must set and sustain the structure (i.e., the conditions of existence) of spontaneous orders.[64] Further again, as we just saw, Hayek states that spontaneous orders rely on rules made by organisations, possibly entirely, so it cannot be claimed that society is preserved only by improving rules conducive to spontaneous (e.g. social) order. Society does not only exist on the basis of evolved rules that enable social behaviour, since rules can be selected by organisations (e.g. Parliament and government agencies) and applied purposefully as commands and in detail. Also, organisations rely on general, customary (not only specific) rules as well as on commands, so are a hybrid of the grown and the made. Further again, when we pass from government (as the largest of organisations) to the overall order of the whole society (the largest spontaneous order), the latter cannot be an order relying solely on rules or be entirely spontaneous in character, simply because society encompasses both grown and made elements and these mutate. Finally, the organisation that sustains the structure of spontaneous orders joins those orders as a service provider, incorporating its services into the network which includes services provided by the market. From all this it can be argued that the separation Hayek attempts to make between grown and made orders, a separation upon which his crucial subsequent argument regarding the difference in kind of market order and government, is not sustainable.

However, behind these shortcomings lies a deeper issue, one that explains why he denies this inseparability. On the surface, there are attractive elements in his systematic proposal. He apparently prefers individual autonomy to having the individual dependent on intrusive organisations. This lies behind his conception of separate spontaneous orders and organisations, whereby the latter is prevented from intrusion onto the operational field of the former, while retaining its roles of structural assurance and enforcement of compliance with rules of just conduct. But his analysis reveals no full understanding of the instinctual, and subsequently strategic, nature of the relationship between society and government. He does not recognise that fear and desire are significant drivers of both social and political life and arrangements. Therefore he does not acknowledge that the evolved rules of just conduct which he wants to protect from organisational intrusion are soaked in such instincts and strategy. Nor does he recognise why there is therefore a common demand for organisational intrusion not merely to respond to those in breach by coercion but, much more systematically, to generate strategies to prevent these, both generally and in concrete detail, and to provide fully sympathetic services. In this regard, Hayek does not recognise the argument that the State is burdened with social responsibilities for the understandable reason that, in return for subjection, its institutions can, unlike the market, be brought to account regarding prescriptions necessary to deal with fear and the desire for sympathetic conditions. As a consequence, his promotion of the autonomy of spontaneous orders is contrary to the understandable concerns of the vast majority of citizens. We shall see that these concerns would be made worse by his comfort with monopoly and his general denial of any individual right to organisationally supported programmes of voluntary individual development. In essence, his conception of preferred arrangements appear logical but politically selective and likely to produce greater levels of fear and desire than already exist in his rules of just conduct. Understanding these issues puts the criticisms outlined just above into a wider context and shows why spontaneous orders can and do have specific purposes and why spontaneous and organisational orders are not properly seen as conceptually or practically separable.

We have taken forward the argument regarding rules of just conduct and argued for the inseparability of spontaneous and organisational orders, in fact their symbiosis and integrated evolution. It will next be argued that, beyond that symbiosis and supporting it, stands the long shadow of mythology, a shadow which is properly seen as a base common to both orders, thereby permeating his account of the nature of the market order and his claim for the necessary separability of market and government, which in turn is the basis of his liberal ideology. The argument here is that, in critiquing the 'Hobbesian' myth, Hayek programmed his own strain of the genus of mythology. His defence of the independence of spontaneous orders will be seen to be an attempt to disguise the real mythology of the market, inextricably operating in concert with government 'at a distance,' in a combined strategy for producing docile and productive individuals in return for the forgoing of self-responsibility in the sense intended here.

Government and the Market

Hayek argues that grown and made orders are separate both in kind and in fact, which allows him to argue that the market and government should be understood as separate and any attempt to justify the intrusion by government leads inexorably to totalitarianism. The argument here is that grown and made orders are inseparable in kind and in fact, which will allow the argument that the market and government are inseparable; further, their lack of separation is a feature of their common mythological foundation. Hayek's position of separability is better understood not as separability but as distance, where the market acts as an agent and disguise for the mythological aspirations of government. His positive proposal does appear to carry certain elements of the notion of non-mythological self-responsibility as it is promoted in this work, that is the deconstruction of Hobbesianism, but his lack of acknowledgement of the instinctual and therefore strategic relationship between government and society leads him to propose arrangements which would not only defeat the notion of self-responsibility but worsen the effects of the fear and desire that he claims to eradicate from the totalitarian implications of government intrusion.

There is a good reason why Hayek does not acknowledge the strategic connections between organisation and spontaneous order, between society and organisation and between market and government. The first part of the reason is this rejection by Hayek of mythological politics in the Hobbesian form, although that only in part. The second is that he is in effect proposing a mythology of his own, with two parts, one being the classical liberal myth of individual autonomy, the other being the Hobbesian myth in reconfigured form, but which is disguised by his classical, 'spontaneous' liberalism. By reconfiguration is meant only that, although he shies away from the State because of its mythological baggage and so appears to separate government from market, the latter remains founded on claims regarding the satisfaction of the issues of fear and sympathetic conditions of existence in return for a subjection which is the forgoing of self-responsibility in the sense intended here. Rather than only the State, the market becomes the field for many of these issues, in that it is the agent of government: government retains the function of coercing compliance with preferred behaviour and assuring the conditions of existence of the market, while the market complements government in its claims to reduce fear and assumes much of the claim to satisfy desire for sympathetic conditions. Reinforcing this interpretation is that Hayek's strategy satisfies the account here of our preferred reading of the nature of liberalism, that is, that it is not an ideology but part of the phase-shifted trajectories of critique and positive proposal or reform, trajectories that sustains the political myth.

Government

The essential theme of Hayek's view of government is that it should be constrained[65] but clearly not emasculated. The function that best displays these two elements is the responsibility of government to sustain the rules of just conduct by its exclusive proprietary use of coercion[66] and thereby to deliver peace, freedom and justice.[67] The latter include the notion of the general welfare, at which governments should aim, although this comprises the securing of conditions in which individuals can provide for their needs, and is not the sum of individual satisfactions.[68] The principal means of the use of coercion is the law, which can only be abstract and negative, and the two products of which are a private order, in which a domain of freedom is created for each individual and the content of which only he can determine, and a public market order, the result of the free use by individuals of their own knowledge.[69] In this context, although they coexist, government is for Hayek separate from the market and should not intervene in its operation.[70]

Government therefore does have positive responsibilities in such a scheme. Apart from coercing compliance with rules of conduct, these include provision for the needs of those unable to survive in the market;[71] defence against external enemies;[72] provision of those services which the market cannot or will not provide,[73] a responsibility for which it can engage the coercive function of taxation;[74] and, more significantly, the responsibility for maintaining the structure of the market, its conditions of existence.[75] However, this coercive role should not be confused with the assumed role of conducting government business, in fact these are generally incompatible.[76] In that, law is not the same as legislation,[77] the focus of the latter being the management of government business rather than the definition of abstract, negative provisions for individual freedom. These provisions should not even be in the hands of the same body as the business of the development of legislation.[78]

Unfortunately, in the opinion of Hayek, this is exactly what has happened. The key feature of this is that, under the guise of its coercive powers, government has been entrusted with the supply of collective goods to various groups.[79] This serves particular interests,[80] denying both the general interest[81] and the possibility that all individuals can pursue their own interests.[82] Far more than corporations, typical of such groups are trade unions, which attract the weak.[83] Such groups also pressure governments, who need to attract votes, to intervene in the market in their favour.[84] Further, when the legislature assumes responsibility for directing the government apparatus, generates administrative legislation rather than law as the rules of just conduct and attempts to satisfy particular wishes, the resulting plan transforms society from a spontaneous order into an organisation.[85]

Hayek is therefore critical of the belief that the consent of the majority is the proof of the justice of a measure.[86] For him, this says much about the sad state of democracy, which, rather than being still the means of protecting individual freedom, has been converted into a bidding war the purpose of which is to buy the votes of special interests.[87] Worse, not only does this convert the spontaneous order of a free society into an organisation but it converts democracy into socialism and totalitarianism.[88] He is similarly critical of the degradation of the notion of individual rights, the proper status of which is to reinforce the necessary absence of arbitrary coercion through the universal rules of just conduct.[89] Instead, they are used as a talisman to ensure the delivery of particular things to particular individuals.[90] He is also disenchanted with the consequential notion of social justice, which he sees as illusory but which leads to support for government intrusion for the unrealisable purpose of distributive justice, to the socialisation of law and finally to socialism and its threat to individual freedom.[91]

Market

For Hayek, spontaneous orders are best left alone to evolve in their own manner, so they should be separate from government.[92] In this independent state, they have created a new and better life for all.[93] They have also created civilisation through forcing individuals against their wishes to submit to the discipline of freedom.[94] The market order, which does not only comprise the economy,[95] is a pre-eminent form of a spontaneous order. Like all such orders, it is run by rules of conduct, freely engages the knowledge of each participant[96] and through it is provided any service considered of value.[97] Its competitive nature effectively informs each individual, while pursuing his individual aims, how to best serve others whose existence they might not know.[98] Equally importantly for Hayek, over the last two centuries it has deprived everyone of power which can be used only in an arbitrary fashion.[99]

The properly functioning market is fair, in that all are protected by the rules of just conduct and are free to use their knowledge as they see fit, but it neither assures success[100] nor distributes equally[101] or in a balanced way.[102] Individual shares are the result of skill and luck[103] not desert.[104] Nonetheless, none of these latter characteristics justifies public supervision.[105] Complementing this is his view that private monopolies are not inherently harmful,[106] as they can be the optimum of efficiency, except when they use their position to exploit pricing,[107] to prevent competition[108] or for political influence.[109] Some monopolies are advantageous in providing services that would not otherwise be provided.[110] Government monopolies, on the other hand, do not receive Hayek's imprimatur.[111] The accumulation of wealth is fine, especially since its investment has benefitted more people than by giving it to the poor.[112] Wealth goes hand in hand with the market, which is a wealth-creating game that leads to an increase in the stream of goods and the prospects of all participants to satisfy their needs: a game of skill, strength and good fortune.[113] In this context, Hayek questions the whole issue of inherent value, espousing the market as the rightful way of settling on that, and separates value from merit.[114] From this, he denies that any particular services have value to the community and that value differs from remuneration,[115] which must be seen as in part dependent on pure accident.[116]

For Hayek the main threat to the market is the selfishness of organised groups, which comprise organised labour far more than corporations. Labour has gained its power through the assistance government has given to it to suppress those manifestations of individual selfishness which would have kept their action in check.[117] But the most important measure in defence of the market is its own competitive dynamic, which coordinates individual actions, constructs a high degree of coincidence of expectations and is thereby the result of a few individuals forcing a larger number to work hard and change their habits. It works 'only at the price of a constant disappointment of some expectations.'[118] Key features of the market mechanism therefore include that it works through a strategy of coordination through subjection that in turn creates productivity. It is thereby also a mechanism for increasing efficiency,[119] and therefore the productivity, of labour.[120] We cannot claim any moral right to the benefits we derive from the market, except to the extent that we have submitted ourselves to the rules that make the market possible. We have no right to a particular income, except through contract. Neither can we make a claim for the distribution of 'unearned benefits' on grounds that these benefits are owed to society, which would claim to distribute these to the deserving. For Hayek, society cannot do this as it is not an acting person but merely an orderly structure of actions resulting from the observation of certain abstract rules by its members.[121]

This denial of claim extends to education, except for minors and occasionally for adults in the first educational stage,[122] as this will not create equality of opportunity due to the multiplicity of factors at play[123] or correct unjust acts unless these are recent. If they are not recent, they should be accepted *de facto* and put down to accident. The more fundamental reason is that 'social and economic' individual rights require replacing the spontaneous order of society with a deliberately directed organisation, destroying the liberal order and individual responsibility.[124] It is far better to rely on the creation of wealth to improve the position of the lowest income groups, than introduce legislation in an attempt to do so.[125] Generally, however, 'nothing we can do, short of establishing absolute equality of all incomes, can alter the fact that a certain percentage of the population must find itself in the bottom of the scale.'[126]

The final credentials of the market, drawn from all this, are freedom and responsibility. For him, the only moral principle that helped an advanced civilisation grow was individual freedom, that the individual is guided in his decisions by rules of conduct and not by specific commands.[127] The reverse side of this is that social and economic rights are based on society as a deliberately made organisation by which everybody is employed. They could not be made universal within a system of rules of just conduct based on the conception of individual responsibility.[128] The individual must be allowed to be free and, being so, will demonstrate his responsibility.

The Mythology of Hayek

There is evidence that Hayek appears to reject the Hobbesian myth of the State. As a broad point, he denies that the word 'State' should have any status, due to it being metaphysically charged, preferring the term 'government.'[129] With that, he is critical of the mythical origins of society in social contract.[130] In discussing his alternative institutional arrangements, he states that there is no place where sovereignty rests in the general structure of authority, mainly because the belief that there needs to be an unlimited ultimate power is a superstition.[131] He adds that it is equally erroneous to believe that anything laid down by the supreme legislator is law and that only that which expresses his will is law.[132] He attributes this belief in an unlimited source of power to constructivist-positivist superstition[133] and points out that since Hobbes this has been the justification of absolute power, whether through monarchs or later democratic assemblies.[134] Legislation gives into man's hands great power by which great good can be done but the control of which he has yet to learn so it is open to produce great evil,[135] including the enforced obedience of private individuals.[136] As a corrective, he recommends a range of reforms to democratic arrangements.

In his apparent move away from the fully empowered State, we can see two elements. The first is the adoption of a reworked classical liberalism of negative principles and the second is, behind that, a positive programme which seeks to form individuals so they will comply with the standard range of mythological prescriptions, that is subjection in return for accepting claims that fear and sympathetic conditions are being addressed.

Regarding his classical liberal position, he presents himself as a strong advocate of individual freedom, within a personal domain protected by the enforcement of the abstract, negative rules of just conduct,[137] and of a properly operating democracy as one of its key safeguards.[138] These rules also establish the public domain as a field where each individual knows what he can count on, what objects and services he can use for his purposes and what range of actions is open to him.[139] Referring to Locke as an advocate of fair competition,[140] he argues that the market order not only serves everybody,[141] but eliminates what he sees as dominant interests[142] and, in a large claim, that it eradicates arbitrary power.[143] Further, although it is unclear that he appreciates the role of human instinct in democracy, given its long historical disposition to produce continuous claims about the resolution of fear and sympathy,[144] including by Locke, he sees enough flaws in it to want it significantly reformed.[145] He would effectively clean out the elements of democracy that he sees restrict individual freedom.

Yet behind this elaborate plan for freedom stands a different strategy which would have quite the opposite effect. The connection of these two strategies is the key to understanding the relationship between the idea and the embodiment of the mythological State. The former is a guise for the latter but they are each based on a foundation whereby each individual enjoys only the strain of freedom which the forgoing of self-responsibility allows.

We have already seen some of the key elements of this second strategy. The first set of these refers to the powers of government under Hayek's model, regarding its coercive powers,[146] ensuring the conditions of existence of the market;[147] provision of a minimum income for those that cannot compete successfully in the market;[148] and provision of services the market cannot or will not provide.[149] There are important implications that should be drawn from this set of government or State responsibilities. The first is that the State is still widely empowered and responsible, both regarding the use of force on and the provision of sustenance and services to individual citizens. More importantly, the State is responsible for ensuring the conditions under which the market operates, so must be seen not only as fundamentally inseparable from it but, and one must say it against the grain of Hayek's argument, implicated in its operation.

In fact, the proper way to see the market is as an agent of the State, carrying out activities which the State cannot carry out effectively or efficiently but the existence of which is assured by the State, although this is not a claim that the market is only an agent of the state. The market tells us about the nature of the State and its unrealised and unrealisable political and economic aspirations. The Hayekean State has transferred to the market both a responsibility to deliver peace and the creation of what comes to be regarded as wants as the preferred conditions of existence, although it retains elements of both for itself. This should be complemented by an understanding that, fulfilling a key underlying mythological aspiration, the market is a field, beyond the establishment and operation of the democratic arrangements of power, by which the fate of the magnitude of the State comes into the hands of man. They are not separate and, behind appearance, the State is to be judged by what the market does.

Further than this, the market is an arrangement of both subjection and subjectivication, as the creation of subjectivity. The subjection comes in the form of Hayek's form of competition, which also features the dominance of interest, since competition is for him always a process in which a small number makes it necessary for larger numbers to do what they do not like, be it to work harder or to change habits.[150] Regarding income, he states that the range of the chances open to someone attempting to attain a previous level of income are not of his making but the result of others submitting to the same rules of the game.[151] Or regarding the terms and conditions of contracts between individuals, the norm is such that it pays the individual to adhere to an established practice which will bring about his conformity.[152] Or that this manner of co-ordinating individual actions through the market will secure a high degree of coincidence of expectations and an effective utilisation of the knowledge and skills of the several members only at the price of a constant disappointment of some expectations.[153] Or that it is the market order which makes peaceful reconciliation of the divergent purposes possible, and by a process which benefits all, bringing interdependence of all men and so making all mankind One World.[154] This market is thereby a means and mechanism to realise subjection to dominant others, universal submission to its universal rules, coincidence of expectations across social space, conformity and interdependent membership in One World which at the same times achieves peace, that is the elimination of fear.

Contrary to the claims by Hayek, the market is a field of dominant interests. His criticism of the modern democratic process is that it is dominated by sectional interest, trade unions[155] far more so than corporations. He does not acknowledge that these unions were established in part to protect workers' rights and conditions against the exploitation of persistent dominant corporate interests.[156] The arguments of Hayek are in support of one side of this debate, encouraging uncontested opportunities for the corporate interests, including for certain monopolies.[157] The second effect of Hayek's strategy is that promoting the market as the field for this contest

The Liberalism of the Market 161

has the added advantage, over the parliament, that those forced to acquiesce have restricted recourse to processes of redress. Closely connected to this is the pursuit by dominant corporate interests of ever-increasing productivity of workers, as we have just seen.[158]

The market also takes on responsibility for the creation and satisfaction of individual wants, thereby addressing the issue of sympathetic conditions of existence, not only for each individual himself but for unknown others. For Hayek, more important than the market's sharing of information about wants that may be satisfied and for whose satisfaction an attractive price is offered, is the information about the possibility of doing so by a smaller outlay; also that such a market order relies on the fact that working brings the satisfaction of the wants of people of whom they do not know.[159] This satisfaction does not extend to the weak, however, who largely comprise the membership of trade unions[160] and minimum income for the weak is significantly a strategy to avoid social unrest.[161] The strong or competitive can have satisfactory conditions of existence but not the weak.

Consistently, Hayek argues that social justice is an illusion, and dangerous in that it leads to the command economy that is socialist and ultimately totalitarian,[162] so unequal distribution is in no way unfair.[163] The market, instead, is a game of skill and chance which is to be played fairly but in which we cannot demand results based on fairness or merit: the market determines value. He adds to these claims the weak argument that there can be no distribution because there is no agent to do so, when government can adopt such a function without straying into socialist territory, and the telling argument that it is unfortunate that free enterprise is defended on the grounds that it regularly rewards the deserving.[164] Further, although the market order accepts the classic civil rights as a defence of individual liberty, it precludes any socio-economic rights as enforcing these would destroy the liberal order at which civil rights aim.[165] In this context he allows for the education of children but, subject to one small concession, not to adults, despite his acknowledgement that market success thrives on information and that the market is consistently unfair in the outcomes it delivers to individuals. Finally in this regard, Hayek claims that the provision of socio-economic rights cannot be made universal within a system of rules of just conduct based on individual responsibility.[166] But his is surely a notion of responsibility based on a distorted notion of obligation, wherein the visibly suffering should be denied help because all are to be treated equally and our reason must dominate our tribal instincts.[167] This is a notion of individual responsibility and an attitude towards social justice which replaces respect for all with cold reason. There are echoes of Kant here.

The point is made in all this that, in his apparent move away from the mythical, fully empowered State, we see the apparent adoption of a reworked classical liberalism of negative principles of freedom but behind it a positive programme which seeks to form individuals to comply with the standard range of mythological prescriptions. These include a scheme of subjection in return for claims that fear and sympathetic conditions are addressed, but devoid of common notions of social justice or socio-economic rights and in the context of a distorted sense of personal responsibility. The field of this strategy is the combined force of the still widely-empowered, service-delivering government, or State, and the powerful dynamics of the market biased to dominant, even monopolistic, interests. It is the argument here that the reworked liberalism is a guise for Hayek's version of the mythology of the State, the freedom of the former constituted by a subjectivication in which enforced docility and productivity appear as the elimination of fear and the creation of sympathetic conditions of existence respectively.

The account of liberalism preferred in the present work gives some comfort to this interpretation of Hayek. That is, that Hayek has adopted a broad strategy of critique and positive proposal to sustain the trajectory of the increasingly unsteady mythology of the State,[168] latterly in its Welfare form. His critique consists in the rejection of the sovereign State, of a fully empowered State the range of which extends across social space, of the contemporary condition of democratic institutions, of notions of social justice and prevalent individual rights. His positive proposal includes a reconfigured notion of government and its institutions, complemented by a widely empowered market order but still being governed at a distance, biased towards dominant interests and against organised labour and those made weak, and a sense of individual responsibility based on cold reason rather than engaged respect.

Hayek's political philosophy is, like that of his predecessors in the political tradition, mythological. He does state that he rejects any mythological arrangement of government, so pares Hobbesian features to leave arrangements without sovereignty, claims a remnant democracy cleansed of dominant interests and which purports to protect individual freedom against the intrusion of the State and other individuals. His strategy in this is to claim separation of the private law of rules of just conduct from public laws and, therefrom, spontaneous order from made organisations in order to argue that the market order of individual freedom is separate from the mythological State, 'government' for him. However, these elements are not separable because Hayek does not recognise the mythology inevitably built into his rules: the social evolution through which rules of just conduct has passed has not simply delivered them functional superiority[169] but has left them saturated in the mythology of subjection, fear and the search for sympathy, as we see from man's early recognition of and continuing response to the absolutism of reality. But beyond the nascent mythology in his premises, the positive programme that he constructs on these premises also rests heavily on mythological thinking. His preferred form of government is blindly coercive rather than a set of institutions which work with those who break the rules in a constructive, cooperative manner. His government is fearsome, a feature reinforced by his Constitution,[170] but it also constructs sympathetic conditions through delivery of a range of services unavailable from the market. It is also responsible for sustaining the market, with its functions of enforcing cooperative practices that require peace and defining what constitutes sympathetic conditions. Realising these functions as general expectations in turn brings legitimacy to government.[171] In turn, his market is replete with mythological features, addressing fear and the delivery of services that create sympathetic conditions in return for subjection of all individuals to its rules and fortuitous outcomes. Its service delivery is also complemented by government. But it is the market, validated by government, which addresses fear and sympathy by the creation of docile, productive individuals, respectively. Thus does the fate of the magnitude come further into the hands of man.

So he has failed to reject mythology, instead, in fact if not by intention, creating a new version of the dominant mythology. Yet his is a flawed and failed mythology. It is flawed in that he does not recognise the mythology in the grounds of his creation. It is failed in that his attempt to create docile and productive individuals through a market order validated by government, a strategy which is presented under the guise of his 'spontaneous' liberalism but which is actually concerned with addressing fear and sympathetic conditions through subjection, creates a new fear. That is, in addition to the fear of the State, there is now the inevitable fear that individuals feel from exposure to the forces of Hayek's form of the market and the creation by others of forms of desire rather the creation of satisfying individually sympathetic conditions of existence. Despite the apparent distance between government and the market, Hayek's model retains all the key elements of mythological institutional arrangements. In short, having claimed to have divested himself of the Hobbesian political world view, he replaces it with an alternative, failed mythology rather than adopting a non-mythological approach, even though his preferred model flirts with certain non-mythological features. It thereby also fails as a non-mythological proposal. His notion of responsibility forgoes engaged respect, preferring the harsh logic of his reason, and his notion of freedom, and thereby autonomy, is heavily laden with prescriptions regarding subjection, fear and sympathetic conditions.

HAYEK AND THE TRAJECTORY OF LIBERALISM

It is accepted practice, and with good reason, to consider Hayek as a critic of the contemporary State and as the proposer of social and political arrangements which emphasise individual freedom. What is argued here is that he should be considered as part of a much wider canvas. That is, as the latest contributor to a political tradition which is founded on liberal principles, both as an ideology and, less overtly, as a trajectory of criticism and positive programming to sustain mythological politics.

164   The Mythological State and its Empire

This is a tradition which comes from Hobbes and his attempt to justify the idea of the State as an entity which, through universal subjection to it, could eliminate the fear that comes from social and political anarchy and satisfy the desire for sympathetic conditions of existence. It is a tradition which saw Locke, aware of the dangers of such pervasive power, promote the idea that the State should be more carefully constituted, without loss of its supreme authority, and brought more closely into the hands of man to create a space of freedom within which each could pursue his calling and enjoy his property. Montesquieu imagined a consolidation of this constitution through the protection and rewards available through the separation and balance of its fearsome constituent powers. Rousseau, in turn, saw the weakness of not engaging individuals as citizens in these arrangements and proposed an alternative idea to that of the Hobbesian State. But in failing to resolve the intractability of personal interest or the fear generated by the establishment of his general will, his idea and its attendant practices were doomed, as he came to acknowledge himself. Kant consolidated these two lines of thought, bringing Rousseauean general will together with the institutional arrangements and freedoms of Hobbesianism, for reasons that turn out to have had their own flaws of lack of participation and fairness and excessive expectations of subjection, and to have been a metaphysics heavily guided by the religious politics of his time. Kant's aspiration to train a moral-intellectual elite to lead this republic was a step towards a pure mythology, but in that he unjustifiably imposed regime of fear and inequality on the majority whom he saw lacked these qualities. In this, his scheme was a failure in mythological terms.

The shortcomings in the Kantian assembly were taken up by Rawls, whose two principles attempted to address the flaws in his concept of the State and its political arrangements by assuring individual liberties and a fair distribution of resources. He came to reject Kantian metaphysics and attempted to defend his scheme on non-foundational grounds, but we have argued his lack of success in this, unaware as he was of the mythological foundations of his thought and of the rational communitarian approach for which he opts. Admiring Rawls but closer to Popper's Open Society, Hayek comes to the position that the modern State has not only finally failed to deliver personal freedom from fear and want, despite the individual forgoing of self-responsibility but cannot do so because it is in fact a threat to that. Claiming to see the State as a mythological magnitude, he is correct at least in saying so. But his apparent denial that the core functions of social arrangements should rest only with government disguises a strategy to deliver peace and prosperity, that is resolving the problems of fear and the desire for sympathetic conditions, increasingly through the agency of a Darwinian market in which dominant interests are only constrained by the mythological presumptions of the rules of just conduct. More telling, the State remains widely empowered in this arrangement, to the effect that it still governs at a distance and positions the market as its agent, although this is not to say that the market is only a State agent. In this, Hayek shares with his predecessors in the political tradition the flaw and therefore the effect of unexamined mythological foundations. Given the emergence of the dual liberal strategies of critique and re-programming into our field of vision, his free and autonomous responsible individual is better seen as one subject to regimes that make him docile and productive, whereby fear and desire have in fact been respectively addressed.

This is therefore a tradition which has since Hobbes promoted two bound ideas and sought to give these ideas consistency: first, that it is possible to be free of fear and satisfy desires for sympathetic conditions; second, disguised by the first, that not only was the price of these freedoms the forgoing of self-responsibility to the mythological magnitude of the State and the dominant interests which will claim to assure these freedoms, but freedom from fear and want will be realised, subversively, by the manufacture of universal docility and productivity. Hayek takes his place within the company as an active contributor to the trajectories of this long liberal tradition as part of its latest phase of critique and positive programming, the ultimate purpose of which is to sustain mythological thought and arrangements, at the epicenter of which is the idea and practices of the mythological magnitude of the State. The place he occupies is therefore the third of the three pre-eminent initiators of a phase shift in the trajectory of this idea, a place previously occupied by Locke and Rousseau, as they had attempted to deal with the legacy of Hobbes. Like those predecessors, the thought of Hayek was also to have as much impact on the trajectory of mythological practice as on that mythological idea.

8 Freedom is the State

PETTIT

The Attractions of Republicanism

Of those whose thought we have explored as contributors to the political theoretical tradition, several might be regarded as carrying the ideology of liberalism. Others are seen as republicans. However, these lines of selection are not uncontroversial and are often blurred. This is the context within which we now turn to the work of Pettit.

While acknowledging that there may be objections to the claim that a single tradition can be seen to span the concern about the power of the State which emerged in the seventeenth century,[1] Pettit attempts to put a coherent but different conception of the tradition presented here. He argues that Locke, Montesquieu and Rousseau are best seen within a republican tradition stretching back to Cicero through Machiavelli and forward to Skinner, rather than merely as implied defenders or critics of a paradigm inspired by Hobbes. Consequently, liberalism and republicanism represent for him distinct strands of this debate and liberalism is better presented as a rationale against interference in the lives of citizens and therefore as distinct from the non-domination which he defends.[2]

For Pettit, the principal attraction of republicanism is that it offers a concept of individual freedom which is separate from and superior to both elements of the dominant prevailing analysis, that is from negative and positive freedom, which he characterises respectively as the absence of obstacles to individual choice and as the exercise of the facilities which foster self-mastery and self-fulfilment.[3] This preference flows from two arguments. On the one hand, he argues that republicanism prevents the domination which is allowed by liberalism's prevention of interference.[4] On the other, he argues that the realisation of republican non-domination will create the conditions for the subsequent individual pursuit of autonomy or self-mastery,[5] which he does not deny as a proper political ideal.[6] Non-domination is not freedom from interference, which is the basis of the imposition of a suitable system of law, but from intentional, arbitrary interference.[7] It is freedom even from the uncertainty that accompanies the prospect of arbitrary interference.[8]

Pettit has a clear picture of the role of the State in creating such conditions. Rejecting the liberal insistence that the State is the pre-eminent source of interference, Pettit argues that the State, effectively constrained, is the pre-eminent defence against arbitrary interference. Not only may the State interfere in the lives of its citizens but it must do so if freedom from arbitrary interference is to be realised. The role of the State is not merely to contribute to the reduction of domination but effectively to be responsible for its elimination.[9] One profound effect of this fully empowered legitimacy is that the constitutional and institutional arrangements of the State are not merely responsible for allowing or causing individual freedom. They, and only they, are that freedom.[10]

To protect his position against arguments that this wide empowerment of the State is itself a potential threat to freedom, Pettit emphasises the advantages of the corporatisation of individual interests,[11] but he also sees the very nature of the republican State as being crucial for the exercise by the individual of dominion over his own life. For him, it is a fundamental feature of the republican State that it tracks the interests of its citizens,[12] thereby establishing the conditions of individual freedom.

Pettit and Mythology

The work of Pettit can properly be seen as constructing a mythological account of the State. Despite the claimed difference between his characterisations of liberal and republican positions, they share fundamental features. In particular, they are each profoundly informed by the reality of existential anxiety[13] and are each conditioned by strategies that deal with that reality. The aim of both non-interference and non-domination is the elimination of such fear: that is, the interference which is of primary concern to liberals is the fearfulness generated by an intrusive State and the domination which is of concern to republicans is the fearfulness generated by the intrusive social practices to which a wide range of citizens are subjected.[14]

So, when Pettit states that non-domination is concerned with protecting the interests of a citizen, the proper test for his account of how republicanism avoids constraint of these interests is whether his preferred institutional arrangements do minimise fear in pursuing interests without the forgoing of self-responsibility. To justify the mythological criticism of Pettit's republicanism, it need only be demonstrated that non-domination is realised by such forgoing.

If this forgoing can be demonstrated, his republicanism is as much mythology as the other contributions to the political tradition we have looked at. It is not mythology merely because it is concerned with the elimination of fear, although that is an important feature. It is mythological because it claims that, by constructing political arrangements founded on the forgoing of self-responsibility, individual existential fear can in fact be effectively eliminated and sympathetic conditions of existence can be constructed. A non-mythological arrangement would accept that fear cannot be eliminated but, by the full and continuing acceptance of individual responsibility for oneself through respectful self-reliance and ongoing engagement in political affairs, it can be recognised and accommodated.

The Strong Republican State

Rejecting the liberal insistence that the State is the pre-eminent source of interference, Pettit argues that the State, effectively constrained, is the pre-eminent defence against arbitrary interference: not only may the State interfere in the lives of its citizens but it must do so if freedom from arbitrary interference is to be realised. Thereby he makes what is for him an important distinction between arbitrary interference (domination), the elimination of which establishes freedom, and systematic interference by the State, which not only is not necessarily dominating but which is necessary to promote freedom as non-domination. He begins with the empowerment of the State, wherein lies his distance from how he characterises the liberal position. He is also clear that the role of the State is not merely to contribute to the reduction of domination but effectively to be responsible for its elimination.[15] Thus, empowering the State is an advanced rather than a preliminary move for Pettit. We shall see that it may well be regarded as his endgame. Consequently, empowerment is to take a fully elaborated form.

To reinforce this pre-eminence of the State, Pettit makes it clear that it is only the State and not the individual privately which may pursue the establishment of liberty because such individual pursuit would end in the domination of the Hobbesian war of all against all: 'freedom . . . is not something that individuals can satisfactorily pursue by private, decentralised means and it is something that the state is able to pursue fairly effectively'[16] and 'The decentralised arrangement . . . has all the disadvantages canvassed in the state of nature that is demonised . . . by Hobbes.'[17] He does not consider the possibility of an arrangement whereby individuals remain responsible for themselves and, with the support of a different form of State, which promotes respect without promising the elimination of fear.

The full extent to which Pettit empowers the State is also clear from his insistence that it is the State alone which carries the responsibility for the establishment of republican non-domination.[18] The form which this State responsibility takes may be constituted only by the mythological, coercive constitutional-legislative-institutional framework.[19] It is the State as refined from Hobbes through Montesquieu to Rousseau to Kant. For Pettit, the only acceptable strategy for achieving non-domination is that of constitutional provision[20] and this is coercive.[21] This leap to resolution by coercion rather than by a search for means by which resolution is agreed is symptomatic of the requirement that individuals forgo self-responsibility, and thereby of the establishment of mythological arrangements. The fullness of the empowerment of the State is also made clear by the role given to the laws promulgated under these constitutional arrangements in the elimination of domination.[22] In this, Pettit rejects the Hobbesian claim that law is necessarily an invasion of freedom and endorses Harrington's claim that liberty in the proper sense is liberty by the laws.[23] By itself, this would satisfy a non-mythological arrangement, within which law would play a crucial role. But the means by which Pettit's republican law is generated and operates alienates rather than engages individuals, thus assuming responsibility for them, and so encourages coercion. This empowerment is also made clear by Pettit's assertion that it is proper for the jurisdiction of the State to be widely dispersed.[24] Specific areas of responsibility which Pettit urges on the State include external defence, internal protection, personal independence, economic prosperity and public life.[25] This is an elaborately intrusive State.

Beyond this wide responsibility, there is a further, open-ended concession to the intrusive State: 'Suppose that another person or agency is allowed to interfere with me but only on condition that the interference promises to further my interests, and promises to do so according to opinions of a kind that I share.'[26] That the agency he has in mind is an agency of the State is subsequently made clear by his reference to Paine's complaint against monarchy.[27] It is not yet clear whether Pettit has shifted ground between these two senses of what constitutes shared interests, that is whether the emphasis is on interests that are mine or only on those I have in common with others, but it is clear that this allows the State to assume wide responsibility for individuals on the grounds of tracking their perceived interests.

The effect of this optimised responsibility of the State, and of the coercive and universal arrangements which give it form, is that the legitimacy of republican State authority *per se* is not challengeable. For Pettit, the authority of the State to exist and promulgate laws and establish institutions for their execution, as distinct from a particular government or a particular law or a particular institutional practice, is not questionable if freedom is a primary goal. For him, freedom as the elimination of domination is not able to be realised except by the activity of, and only of, a State fully empowered in such a form.

The Republican State is Freedom

Pettit then outlines a profound effect of this fully empowered legitimacy. For him, such constitutional and institutional arrangements are not just responsible for allowing or causing individual freedom. They, and only they, are that freedom.[28] He emphasises this through a medical analogy, whereby the State should be seen as the antibodies that constitute rather than cause immunity.[29] This is a mythological State that is not only fully dispersed but one also in which liberty is constituted by the political absorption of the individual.

The Republican State Assumes Responsibility for its Citizens

What this claims, through the full empowerment of the Republican institutions, is that freedom and citizenship are given effect only by the direct and immediate realisation of institutional prescription in the legitimate practices of individuals. It is in this sense that constitutional-democratic republican institutions constitute freedom and citizenship for Pettit. It is a proper conclusion that the unchallengeable legitimacy of the republican State requires the assumption by the State of responsibility[30] for its citizens, who thus cannot themselves be empowered in this regard: only by individual citizens becoming immediate manifestations of State-prescribed practice can freedom and citizenship be realised. This is the full dispersal of the mythological State across social space, irrespective of any particular challenge that might be mounted against a particular government, law or institutional practice.

Pettit presents this in his 'power of attorney' analogy, whereby a person may interfere with me if it is in my interests,[31] but such an analogy does not capture the full force of the arrangements he is proposing, given that a power of attorney can be withdrawn but the State cannot. The institutions and practices of the State, beyond merely allowing or causing individual freedom, actually constitute that freedom and the institutions of State and citizenship are ontologically coextensive. There is no citizenship or freedom separate from the institutions of State, so any recovery by the individual of the State's authority to act as citizen could not be achieved without loss of that status or the freedom and citizenship which it constitutes. It is the State in its prescribed role of eliminating fear as domination, and not individuals, which determines, pursues, realises and constitutes freedom and citizenship: it is not just that there is no freedom without the State, but that it is only the State which determines, pursues and realises what freedom is and it does so through the practices of the individual citizen. The State has to this considerable extent assumed responsibility for individuals. Given the role prescribed for the State in eliminating the fear caused by arbitrary interference, the effect regarding citizenship and freedom could not be otherwise. Pettit fulfils the implications of the Hobbesian State's assumption of responsibility for individuals.

There are significant implications which follow from this assumption of responsibility by the republican State for its citizens, beyond the unchallengeable legitimacy of law-making institutions and coercive institutional practice. The first is that the pre-eminence attributed to the State by its full empowerment and its assumption of responsibility actually creates conditions of arbitrariness regarding State interference, given that fearful individuals may not wish to see a place for such empowerment or such a constitutive role. That is, Pettit appears to presume that there is no position available other than the extremes of individual private pursuit, which he rejects, and complete State responsibility in the establishment of freedom and citizenship.

If I do not regard it as in my interest for the State to assume responsibility for a coercive programme intended to eliminate what I regard as fearful circumstances by constituting through my practices what it regards as freedom and citizenship, my loss of responsibility puts me at the complete disposal of the State which allegedly 'furthers my interests . . . according to opinions that I share.' The State would itself be an irresistible source of fear as domination, irrespective of any claim of mitigation by constraint. That is, it cannot track my own interests and there will be no possibility of challenge by me.

This would be particularly so if I do not wish the State to assume responsibility for me in a prescribed role of eliminating fear but wish to accept fear and, with other citizens, deal respectfully[32] with attempts by either other citizens or agents of the State to interfere arbitrarily in my life by ignoring my interests, although I would wish a State whose functions are redesigned to play a well-defined secondary role in such a process. This wish would defeat the interests of the republican project in that, having claimed its justification as the only legitimate means of the elimination of arbitrary interference, it has established this elimination in a manner which is against what I regard my interests, even if it is not against what agents of the State regard as in my interests. Pettit appears to move between these two senses of what is in my interest. This is so irrespective of what constraints might be applied to State activity, since it refers to the conditions of the existence of the republican State, as opposed to other State forms, rather than to its actual practice. By assuming responsibility for me, the republican State is a condition of primary arbitrariness.

Further, if I regard it as against my interest for the State to be responsible for pursuing a programme to eliminate fear as domination, my capacity to contest specific, as opposed to the conditions of, coercive laws and institutions to that end will fully depend on the existence of effective arrangements for such contest. Should such effective arrangements not exist, this will create a secondary condition of arbitrariness, since I will be at the disposal of the State in regard to those specific arrangements. This would be a source of fear as possible or actual arbitrary interference, despite the claim of constraint. It would not track what I regard as my interests.

Finally, if the State assumes responsibility for me by the establishment of fully empowered coercive institutions of which my legitimate practices are mere manifestations and if there are apparent rather than effective arrangements for constraining the specific practices of the republican State, that is if there is both primary and secondary arbitrariness, then republicanism is attempting to give effect not only to a profound arbitrary interference by the State but is in this a regime that cannot be challenged.

Constraining the Republican State

In fact, the republican claim for the effectiveness of recommended constraints on the State turns out to be difficult to sustain. To deal with the problem paradigmatically generated by Hobbes, that is how to control the necessarily fully empowered State, the republican State must track or 'further my interests, and promises to do so according to opinions of a kind that I share . . . but otherwise they are blocked from interfering or are subject to a deterrent penalty for attempting interference. . . . In such a case it is not possible to see the interference as an exercise of domination; the person interferes with me but not on an arbitrary basis.'[33] Pettit elaborates this point.[34]

This variation begins to emphasise the communal nature of opinions rather than the individual nature of the interests apparently indicated in the first reference. This communal emphasis is extended further in a subsequent reference: 'the legal authorities will be entitled and enabled to interfere only when pursuing the common interests of citizens and only when pursuing these in a manner that conforms to the opinions received among the citizenry.'[35] In a subsequent reference, this communality becomes universality.[36] The shadow of Rousseau and Kant is clear. What is first presented as a constraint constituted by my individual interests has progressively evolved into a matter of the common good. This is an important—indeed fatal—shift, particularly in the context of the strategies recommended by Pettit for contesting State interference.

For the present it need only be noted again that Pettit's presumption regarding the available alternatives for the pursuit of freedom, that is the unaccepted private pursuit by individuals or the preferred pursuit by the fully empowered republican State, eliminates other alternatives which I may prefer. I may argue that it may not be in my interest to have the State assume responsibility for eliminating my fear, since it may be my position that fear is inevitable and my preference is that I will myself deal respectfully with attempts by the State or other individuals arbitrarily to interfere in my life, although I would want to do so with the support of redesigned institutions of State. Since this claimed elimination is against my interest, Pettit has invalidated his own primary constraint, with the consequence that he makes the coercive republican State[37] an arbitrary force. Pettit seems to be attempting to protect himself against this criticism by the evolution of the position that has been outlined, that is that the State is only required to track the interests which comprise the common good. However, it does not protect him from the argument that shared interests have no right to priority over the interests of respectful self-responsible individuals, especially in the context of what are his own presumably counter-majoritarian arguments, such as his preference for a bill of rights.[38]

This casts new light on the claim by Pettit that an 'empire of laws, and not of men'[39] is one in which the State not only thereby creates freedom but is also thereby necessarily constrained. For Pettit, if the laws are not subject to such constraints as being general, intelligible, consistent, stable and promulgated in advance 'then those who make, execute or apply the law may easily be given arbitrary power over others.'[40] However, given the primary arbitrariness of the republican position, no argument about the 'rule of law' *per se* will do as an argument for effective constraint of the State, even if such laws have the benefit of eliminating the incidence of situational violence by agents of the State. A rule of law which is intended to eliminate fear, even if it satisfies those particular constraints, would be an effective empowerment of the State to act arbitrarily, i.e. against my interests, rather than a constraint on that State.[41] Similar arguments apply to constitutional arrangements,[42] separation of powers[43] and such countermajoritarian arrangements as a bicameral legislature and a bill of rights.[44] Only a coercive rule of law which recognised my interest not to assume my responsibility for dealing with my fear and which allowed me to deal respectfully with those who interfered arbitrarily with me, with the support of a non-republican State,[45] would be effectively constrained. Such a rule of law would then not be a source of coercive and arbitrary systematic interference, the more intrusive for being not just coercive but also arbitrary. Given his position regarding the necessary full empowerment of the State and the justification for that, such a qualification is unavailable to Pettit.[46]

Given these arguments regarding the primary arbitrariness of the republican State and the implication of that for the republican rule of law and other structural arrangements, it is already impossible to sustain the claim that the republican State form can be constrained. However, this impossibility is further confirmed when the question of possible secondary arbitrariness, that is that it is possible to effectively constrain the State in its actual activity as opposed to the conditions of its existence, is considered.

Pettit recommends a range of methods of constraint. In the context of presenting republicanism as having communitarian credentials, he argues that domination is best seen as experienced through membership of a vulnerability class.[47] For him, 'Freedom is not the atomistic good associated with non-interference. It can be enjoyed by individuals . . . only so far as it can be enjoyed by the salient groups to which those individuals belong.'[48] There is no difficulty posed by an assertion that freedom can be achieved by groups of cooperating individuals but there is real difficulty when this expectation is used as the basis of an argument that the preferred process of contesting legislative, executive or judicial decisions through debate[49] is through, and only through, social movements.[50]

Constraint through Corporatisation

Corporatisation of interest may optimise the accommodation of individuals' interests by the institutions of State[51] but it is indicative of the extent to which statism rather than the interests held by individuals dominates the republican analysis. For Pettit, individual interest is best sifted and converted to incorporated interest since it is the latter which optimises the chances of interest being accommodated by the institutions of State as a condition of freedom.

This rationale has various consequences. The first is revealed by the republican position regarding the social movements recommended as paradigmatic for this corporate strategy. For example, the republican representation converts the environmental movement to one which is primarily concerned with a fear which is best addressed by empowering the operational State.[52] His position is that it requires those who are committed to various political causes to articulate the concerns they want the State to take up rather than by arrangements by which all individual citizens are either engaged to (in the case of environmental predators) or enabled to (in the case of environmental victims) accept respectful responsibility for their conditions of existence. Such pressure and such enabling need not be restricted to a primary responsibility of the State, that is there is no justification for the State to assume responsibility for individuals in this regard. A non-mythological State may play a secondary role in such processes.

Similar problems result from the manner in which republicanism presents a range of other arguments, particular regarding feminism,[53] socialism[54] or multiculturalism.[55] Each of these is presented as an argument which further empowers the fear-eliminating State rather than allows it to act as a catalyst to allow citizens who are women, employees or from ethnic minorities to assume self-responsibility and to actively engage men, employers and those from ethnic majorities also to do so, a process in which a redesignated State would play a facilitative rather than prescriptive role. Pettit may be 'constraining' the republican State to track what its agents see as in the interests of members of such social movements but such republican 'constraint' only confirms the assumption by the State of responsibility for its citizens.

Interest corporatisation is also the context within which Pettit's comments on inclusiveness should also be seen, especially through stakeholder representation in the legislature, executive and judiciary.[56] It is an extra dimension to the problem, that is beyond the meaning of inclusiveness as 'constraining' the republican State by its further empowerment, that the Statist-corporatist notion of interest does not allow Pettit to apply inclusiveness comprehensively, that is without exemption. It extends only to those interests which are filtered and brought together as a group interest. Inclusiveness thus excludes rather than includes any individual interest that is not shared.

At a more general level, interest corporatisation is a good example of the argument presented here in Chapter 2, and referred to since that point, regarding the disposition of the mythological magnitude to be colonised by dominant interests.

Republican Inclusiveness

There are a number of applications by which Pettit reveals the extent to which republicanism qualifies inclusiveness. In fact, qualification is so extensive as to make his notion of inclusiveness at least selective or at worst actually equivalent to exclusion. The qualifications or exclusions endorsed by the republican position include screening out categories of agents and other social groups, including through the gagging of debate and disenfranchisement through selective internal and external referral. The net effect of these qualifications to inclusiveness is the reinforced empowerment of the fear-eliminating republican State and its assumption of responsibility for individual citizens.

Pettit employs the tactic of screening both positively and negatively. Suitable institutional agents and options are to be screened in and the unsuitable out, the aim, beyond the attempt to predetermine a socially valued outcome, being that it will have 'the virtuous—"the choicest persons of the nation"—come to the top'.[57] He would apply this tactic at least in the selection of legislative and administrative agents.[58] Apart from a presumption about what generally constitutes virtue, the dubiousness of such a tactic comes from its attempt to pre-select individuals (or options) to ensure specific outcomes that are likely to receive wide assent. However, not only can this involve a presumption about what is socially valued but it denies that an alternative combination of refusing to make such presumptions and a more transparent process is at least equally likely to produce outcomes which reflect the full variety of social values. That is, screening runs the danger not only of getting the outcome wrong but also of reaching that outcome in a way that which will encourage suspicion and even fearsome dissent.

More significantly, such a tactic performs the function of eliminating the challenge posed by respectful, non-compliant individuals pursuing their own legitimate interests. It thereby reinforces the arbitrary-systematic interference of the fear-eliminating State which assumes responsibility for individuals. Pettit seeks to eliminate corruptibility, to which one cannot object, but it has the broader added characteristic of generally fostering compliance, which carries the danger of suppression. Ironically, this is a characteristic of which Pettit is aware in relation to the application of the parallel strategy of sanctioning.[59] In this circumstance, an alternative strategy of transparency which discourages corruptibility but which does not attempt to predetermine compliant outcomes would be preferred.

Another form of exclusion recommended by the republican position is the gagging of debate in selected circumstances.[60] Apart from a presumption about what is the desired result, such a process by which the State arbitrarily interferes with the interests of the constituents is likely to raise suspicion and dissent, especially given the wide democratic concern about weighting and pressuring of committees for such purposes. Such a strategy denies that, if politicians are subject to such pressure, it may well be for identifiable reason and a preferred strategy might be to relentlessly confront such reasons rather than attempt to subvert these reasons by mitigating the responsibility of the politicians. Similar comments might be made about equivalent republican strategies in relation to the use of committees generally[61] and in relation to the exporting of local control to extra-national bodies.[62]

Questioning such proposals is not to reject the content of arguments in these areas nor is it to doubt the strategic value of reference to committees or external bodies. However, the prospect of such bodies responding to such references with a more conservative position than already applies (unless the committee is fully manipulated) indicates the difficulty with gagging debate in the State and allowing disenfranchisement by seeing such bodies assume dominant positions in that State. This might lead to it being observed that it carries risks of the kind which result from allowing the State to assume responsibility for its individual citizens.

A further form of republican exclusion is that of secession or conscientious objection, recommended in selected cases where accommodation within the jurisdiction of the mainstream State is not achievable. In these circumstances, Pettit recommends that, at the limit, the ideal of non-domination may require that the group is allowed to secede from the state[63] but that where secession is not possible, it may still be possible to boost the freedom as non-domination of radical dissenters by conscientious, procedural objection.[64] Like other examples of republican exclusion, such measures are more likely to have the effect of creating a threshold difficult to cross rather than of easing the voluntary passage to separate jurisdiction. In doing so they would be effectively protecting the integrity of the fear-eliminating State. However, it might also be noted that these measures demonstrate the possibility of a legitimate alternative to that State which if allowed more generally would be transformative of the republican State from within.

What is being asserted is that each of these forms of exclusion, far from being constraints on the republican State, the purpose of which is to prevent arbitrary interference by its agents, is to affirm the pre-eminence of the State, resistant to challenge or disagreement and able to pursue its promise of eliminating fear by arbitrary-systematic interference in the choices of individual or even groups of citizens. This republican strategy is extended by Pettit's position regarding consent, where for him what is required for non-arbitrariness is not actual consent but the permanent possibility of effectively contesting it.[65] The first part of this is pretty much straight from Locke and Kant. Regarding the second, given what has been argued about the impracticability of individuals successfully contesting more than situational features of the vast array of State practices unless one's interests coincide with other members of dominant interests, this absence of the necessity of the State to seek consent would reinforce State pre-eminence, both regarding the conditions of its existence and its practices.

This provision seems to sit oddly with a republican State whose express responsibility is to track the interests of those affected by its actions, even in its corporate form. Such a State would be expected, more likely than other forms, to actively seek consent on a wide range of policies and practices rather than to act presumptively. It is true that if 'explicit individual consent is required for non-arbitrariness . . . then non-arbitrariness in public decisions becomes an inaccessible ideal.'[66] But not requiring explicit instantiated consent, that is on every key action taken by the State, is the absolute opposite position from presuming consent unless such actions are successfully contested. Pettit acknowledges the range of methods which a State determined to track the interests of its citizens might take.[67] However, applying to such methods the condition of presumed consent leaves the strong impression of not only presumptive statism but, when seen in the context of interest corporatism, of protecting the State against the legitimate claims by individual citizens. There appears to be far more of Pettit's 'automatic pilot' than of individuals who 'contest decisions at will.'[68] More profoundly, constricting the framework to the pre-eminence of a State form which presumes consent but which may be effectively challenged only by interests in a corporate form reaffirms Pettit's elimination of any other arrangement by which the conditions of the existence of the republican State might be challenged.

The Republic, Rousseau, Kant and Hobbes

Due to the influence of Rousseau on republican thought, this statism carries an apparent further Kantian theme. Pettit places considerable emphasis on the importance to republicans of notions of the common good, of the public good, of standard ideas and of overall levels of non-domination. His use of these is best understood in the context of the Rousseauean notion of the general will.[69] The real significance of this is elaborated by Rousseau himself, as he emphasises the need to change human nature, if necessary through the annihilation of man's natural resources[70] and through surveillance, banishment and death.

In Rousseau, there is no 'welcome form of constraint' here. Instead, there is, for the respectful but non-compliant, forceful imposition, even 'annihilation,' in which each citizen is institutionally reconstructed and then 'is nothing and can do nothing without the rest': the role of Rousseauean institutions is to interfere against even respectful individual interests, therefore arbitrarily, for the purpose of constructing common interests.[71] This not only informs Pettit's assertion that institutions do not cause but constitute both freedom and citizenship, but also explicates in what sense 'interests' and their 'tracking' is to be understood. Rather than supporting the respectful aspirations of individual citizens, the State, adopting through its exclusionary practices the corporate or dominant interests, becomes the active constructor and entrepreneurial sponsor of not only those 'interests' but of the status of citizen which is to carry them. It is only in this context that Pettit can state that what 'is required for non-arbitrary state power . . . is that the power is exercised in a way that tracks, not the power-holder's personal welfare or world-view, but rather the welfare and world-view of the public'.[72] That is, if Pettit's claim for Rousseau as a reference point is taken seriously, the republican State, far from being constrained by institutional and other arrangements, is formally and fully empowered as an arbitrary constructive and determinative force regarding both an individual's status as citizen and his interests.

Recognising the Rousseauean-Kantian influence on republicanism explains two further issues. First, it explains the republican emphasis on the preferred corporatist arrangements of interests, since interests that are corporatist in form are more likely than those that are individuated to promote what might regarded by the majority as the general will; and second, that giving priority to the general will promotes institutional stability.[73] It thereby protects the constitutional arrangements from which fear has been institutionally eliminated by constructive strategies.[74] It is also not to challenge the primacy of stability, in fact it is to reinforce it, for Pettit to enlist the Lockean argument that any particular government which has breached its trust by failing to do its job may be resisted and overthrown,[75] which is to say contested, but without challenging the conditions of its existence. As we saw in Chapter 2, overthrowing a government is not overthrowing government *per se*, but is in fact reinforcing it as an institutional arrangement. Further, the promotion of this sense of stability identifies the Hobbesianism implicit in Pettit's republicanism. In fact, one is reminded of Pettit's own assessment of later Rawlsian analysis.[76]

Therefore, beyond the necessarily arbitrary-systematic interference which the republican State performs, in that it can assume responsibility for its citizens against their individual interests in its pursuit of freedom defined as non-domination, it is intentionally constructive rather than passive in nature. In these terms, not only can it not be seen as constrained but it must be seen as unconstrainable and a source of arbitrary interference. This view is reinforced by other manifestations of this constructivity or intended absence of constraint, in particular regarding the determinative priority given to law over civility; the republican institutionalisation of trust; the republican reluctance to take seriously the equitable distribution of resources; the republican failure to recognise the determinative effect of concealment; the promotion of the intangible hand in the absence of a reliable criterion for its application; and the reluctance to make the institutions of the republican State operationally accountable to its citizens. These will be examined in turn.

The Republic and Civility

Pettit's analysis of the relationship between civility and law is at least ambiguous. At certain points he regards them as mutually indicative.[77] However, his position is clearest when he argues that law is determinative of such norms.[78] The implication is that, although effective law cannot be separate from civil norms, what constitutes civility is determined by the arbitrary-systematic republican State. This is a manifestation of the empowerment, not of the constraint, of the State which 'constitutes' both freedom and citizenship. It is Pettit's attempt to solve the Rousseauean riddle, that is that a regime of law cannot be successful without there first being a culture of civility. Unlike Rousseau, for whom law is based on cultural practice, he appears to reverse the priority, arguing that law can create civility. This is truly a powerful State.

The Republic and Trust

Pettit argues for extensive levels of personal trust, not merely by citizens in other citizens but also by citizens in agents of the republican State, whereby people confidently put themselves in the hands of public officials even when that reliance is not supported by the existence of effective constraints on those officials.[79] To reach this position, he has to accommodate Ferguson's warning of the need for constant and active vigilance.[80] To do so, he separates 'having trust' from 'expressing trust.'[81] The practical effect of such demands directed towards such empowered authorities is of course negligible. In effect, although this is a highly conditioned form of trust, this accommodation is clearly generated by an attempt to make the republican State such that citizens are effectively at the mercy of its arrangements and agents, which is the manner of personal trust. This appears to be an extravagant strategy, the only benefit of which, should it be valid, is to establish the republican State as the equivalent of a lover or friend.[82] This appears to be taking statism to an extreme position, emphasising the extent to which republicanism represents the assumption by the State of responsibility for individual citizens rather than the promotion of their self-responsibility. In this context again, republican notions of trust cannot be argued to be a constraint on the State, rather they appear to be a justification of its full empowerment.

The Republic and Material Inequality

A further demonstration of the absence of constraint on the republican State, that is the failure of the republican State to track the reasonable interests of its individual citizens, concerns the issue of material equality. Without adopting any socialist ideal, criticism of the republican position can be mounted on the grounds of equal access to the material resources needed to establish self-responsibility.[83]

Self-responsibility does not require that every person have access to the same resources, only that, within the capacity of the community to provide, they have access to sufficient resources to establish a self-reliant life free from exploitation, that is one that is respectfully self-responsible. This is an egalitarian position but only regarding opportunity, not resources. This is not a libertarian position, since, although it argues for freedom against State meddling, it does not rely solely on market mechanisms: the State has a crucial role promoting self-responsibility but nothing beyond that.

Pettit's arguments against equal resource distribution are different. He justifies his position by the dubious argument that 'for the state to provide one person with extra resources, and thereby to extend their undominated choices, it must deprive another person of those resources.'[84] This argument ignores the fact that, even if there is discounting for the cost of State administration, the impact on the choices of the receiving individual surviving on resources at a subsistence level would far outweigh the sense of loss experienced by a resource-laden individual forced to forgo those same resources. There would be a quantum gain in terms of the impact of resources on the choices of the former. Pettit can only argue as he has because his method is one of accountancy, that is that every unit of resource has equal value, no matter to whom it is allocated. There is no sense of value as it relates differentially to individuals in his analysis.[85]

This kind of thinking is a consequence of his principal focus on the overall level of societal non-domination.[86] This is a rationale which has as its primary benefit the effective protection of the interests of resource-laden individuals and the absolution of the State from responsibility, apart from at the extremes,[87] for establishing fair life choices for all citizens. It is not a State which is required to track what the majority of its individual citizens would regard as in their individual interests. This argument against Pettit is reinforced by his favourable comments regarding the free market.[88] He doesn't offer an opinion about the prevalence of great differences of bargaining power nor how he would address this. The interests of those that dominate the mythological arrangements of the State are well served in Pettit's republic. Sympathetic conditions are spare for the non-aligned.

The Republic and the Intangible Hand

The republican position also places significant reliance upon the effect of the intangible hand, that is on the effect of shame and glory, as a way to constrain agents of the State so that non-dominating behaviour is realised. These negative and positive sanctions are ranked alongside screening in this regard. Pettit thus establishes the central importance of social approval and the avoidance of disapproval to the republican position, especially in preference to the effects of the invisible and iron hands over market forces and management control respectively.[89]

There are a number of difficulties presented by the manner in which republicanism enlists the invisible hand to check institutional agents. First, it is clear that this use of shame and glory will have little effect without the intervention of the Republican State as sponsor.[90] Second, he acknowledges the difficulty in applying such a regime even within the legislature.[91] This is clearly a problem since it is the legislature which is required not only to determine screening methods but which is also responsible for establishing and guiding the 'forums for the discussion of the ethics of public life.'[92] Yet the difficulty establishing it within this primary agency of the State is acknowledged. Perhaps because of this difficulty, Pettit is forced back to self-interest as the reliable way to constrain bureaucrats and judges.[93]

Beyond although related to these difficulties associated with the invisible hand, there is a more fundamental problem. It is identified by Rousseau but relates to Pettit's republicanism and it relates to the power of opinion.[94] The regime of opinion was for Rousseau the problem rather than the solution. Manent draws out some of the implications of this, concerning both its self-referentiality and the over-value of wealth.[95] To this self-referentiality of opinion, Rousseau adds that the role of the institutions of State is specifically to construct tractable individuals, that is to 'make mild' those that are made discontented by the process which produces the glory and shame on which republicanism relies so heavily. Republican opinion promotes the interests of the wealthy and constrains the dissident.

So, when seen in the context of a radically screening State whose institutional arrangements arguably promote the perversion of standards which should apply to its own processes and cause a reversion to self-interest, there is a vacuous self-referentiality about opinion as the source of shame and glory. Further, it is a method which requires a further level of intervention by the State to deal with its inevitably fear-inducing effects. At two levels, the invisible hand is founded on intervention by the fear-eliminating arbitrary State: it empowers rather than constrains the State. In none of this is there a place for the fear-accepting, respectful and self-responsible individual supported by a redesigned State to stand against community disapproval.

For Pettit, although the republican State is urged to avoid introducing heavy-handed patterns of control that are likely to undermine the influence of this more or less autonomous mode of regulation, that is civility, it should be remembered that, given that this civility is built on an institutional infrastructure of republican law and regulation, any apparently autonomous status and influence it subsequently attains does not deny its source in republican law.

The Republic and Concealment

There is still another difficulty for the republican strategy in constraining the State. It concerns the determinative effect of concealment. Pettit is clear that, in the absence of effective challenge, the self-ruling demos may often run on automatic pilot.[96] We have seen that the republican position is that effective challenge is only possible in the context of a vulnerability class and through membership of social movements, the effect of which is to operationally strengthen the State by the accommodation and representation of such interests. The consequences are that, at least so far as the non-aligned individual is concerned, there is no effective challenge available and that consequentially the automatic pilot or tranquilisation will occur on the basis of unexamined practices. Under these circumstances, the republican provision that domination 'will be a matter of common knowledge among the people involved'[97] will not apply. This in turn allows that, contrary to the republican position, it would not be the exception that 'one person or group is in a position to exercise backroom manipulation,'[98] nor that 'a dominating party will always be an agent': that is, it may indeed 'be a system or network or whatever.'[99] Further, given the republican promotion of only minimal equality of socio-economic resources, the 'unscrupulous' would be 'in a position to make free with me.'[100] That is, in such circumstances, the differential practices and standards of not only 'backroom manipulators' but also of the empowered, determinative and fear-eliminating State and its dominant interests would remain concealed. The Machiavellian antics of agents of the widely empowered State would not be on view.

SOME OBSERVATIONS

Not one of the methods nominated by Pettit to ensure that the republican State will be constrained from arbitrary interference in the choices of individuals has the effect claimed for it. Although promoted as part of establishing or maintaining a structural and practical regime to eliminate fear through arbitrary-systematic interference, all are either direct or indirect sources of such interference. Generally, it appears that the primary republican aspiration to eliminate arbitrary interference, which is to eliminate fear, combined with a view of the incapacity of individuals to privately pursue freedom without generating a Hobbesian war, has led Pettit into a republicanism that relies on the establishment of fully elaborated institutional arrangements as the only means to realise freedom conceived as non-domination. It is for Pettit only the widely empowered State which can, by systematic interference, eliminate the arbitrary interference that individuals experience at the hands of others and can do so, allegedly due to a regime of constraint, without itself becoming a source of arbitrary interference.

However, because the republican aim is not the reduction but the elimination of arbitrary interference between citizens, not only is it the State and not citizens which must be so empowered but this State must be fully empowered. The form of this empowerment comes first in a coercive and universal constitutional-institutional framework whereby law is conceived, against liberalism as an ideology, as the source rather than an invasion of liberty. But beyond these structural arrangements, this empowerment also results, again in contrast to certain forms of liberalism, in a profound extension of State jurisdiction, not only in specific areas but generally in relation to the determination and promotion of the interests that citizens will share, although the operational effects of such determination is claimed to be in contest.

Pettit's first mistake is to believe that the ideology of liberalism is intended to avoid interference by the State. As the mythological analysis has shown, liberalism, by its very institutional arrangements, cannot be other than a source of such interference. His second mistake is, in attempting to deal with

Freedom is the State   183

the issue of domination on which he sees liberalism as failing, that he adopts for republicanism the institutional arrangements adopted by liberalism. These are the arrangements that emerged from Hobbes through Locke and Montesquieu, that is the constitutional, tri-partite, separated structural arrangements that assume responsibility for typically willing individuals and which take advantage of the typical willingness of fearful individuals to forgo their self-responsibility by promoting especially the interests of the dominant. In doing so, he reverses the rhetoric of liberalism and fully empowers the State as a source of interference.

The first effect of this full empowerment is that the republican State legitimacy is unchallengeable, since only the State and only the fully empowered State can apparently eliminate arbitrary interference to establish republican freedom and citizenship. Further, the republican claim is that citizenship and freedom are conceivable only as manifestations of the practices of the institutions of the republican State: such a State has thereby assumed responsibility for individuals and this is so irrespective of any legitimate contesting of any particular government, law or institutional practice.

Restricted by its own narrow presumption regarding the alternative choices, that is either a Hobbesian war or the fully empowered State which assumes responsibility for citizens by constituting their freedom, there is primary arbitrariness in the practices of the republican institutions. State activity, having assumed responsibility for the individual and thus determining (that is, 'tracking') what it regards as in his interest, will operate against what is in his individual interest. This, for the individual, may lie in the third alternative, self-responsibility. Because the republican State both fully empowers itself and assumes responsibility for him, it is a primarily arbitrary arrangement. This applies equally to the activity of all such constitutional arrangements of the republican State as the rule of law, the separation of powers, bicameral legislature and a bill of rights, unless provision is made to subvert such primary arbitrariness.

However, I have argued that there is a secondary arbitrariness on the part of the State, beyond the nature of the republican State *per se*. This is due to the fact that the constraints foreshadowed by Pettit are ineffective because the capacity of individual citizens to contest particular governments, laws or institutional practices is ineffectual. The features of republican interest corporatism, exclusiveness as inclusiveness, screening, debate constriction, effective jurisdictional disenfranchisement, absent consent, the priority of law over civility, the institutionalisation of trust, the tolerance of wide material inegalitarianism and the promotion of the intangible hand all show that not only is the State not constrained to respond to the legitimate interests of individual citizens but that it is in fact intended to be fully and arbitrarily empowered as a constitutive force, given the nature of the systematic interference invested in it by its function in eliminating fear as domination. These are problems identified by Rousseau and by Montesquieu.[101] Further, given that the systematic interference of the State is shown to be arbitrary because it assumes responsibility for citizens and is unable to be effectively contested and does not track what the individual might regard as his interests, the overall effect of the republican State is compounded by the inevitable realisation of the institutional practices within the form of life of citizens. Such an outcome is anathema to notions of respectful self-responsibility.

CONCLUSIONS – THE MYTHOLOGY OF PETTIT'S REPUBLICANISM

The rationale of his republican State is unsustainable. Established on the grounds of eliminating arbitrary interference, it is premised on arbitrary interference which is systematic in nature. This arbitrariness derives from the conditions of its existence, which require the full empowerment which allows it to assume responsibility for, even worse to 'constitute,' its citizens. It is due to this that what are recommended as constraints on the republican State fail to constrain it from arbitrarily interfering in this systematic manner. Further, they do so by affirming that interference, for example by presumptions concerning the alternative methods for the pursuit of freedom or the meanings which should be attributed to 'tracking' and 'interests' or the conditions under which the constitutional provisions apply. Further, they do so by assuring the circumstances which sustain that interference, for example by the corporatisation of interest, the constrictions that apply to debate or inclusion or consent and so on. The republican State necessarily breaches the conditions of its own existence by engaging systematically in the arbitrary interference which it claims to eliminate.

None of this is to indicate a preference for any liberal position over that argued by republicans. Although republicanism does profoundly assume the responsibility for individuals which necessarily denies respectful freedom, the assertion it makes against liberalism stands, that is that it allows, in fact establishes the fear which domination brings. Because republican interference is constituted by the assumption of responsibility for its citizens which is required by the claim to eliminate fear as domination, only a State form which establishes self-responsibility, that is which realises that fear must be accepted and addressed by individual citizens respectfully and strategically supported by a redesignated State, can honour an undertaking not to interfere arbitrarily. By this explanation, this cannot be a republican State.

The implications for the primary distinction claimed by republicans are of interest because, although non-interference and non-domination differ in regard to certain characteristics, they share others. The difference comes from the fact that non-interference, more concerned about the intrusions of the State, claims to minimise this, whereas non-domination, more concerned about interference by other individuals, aspires to optimise 'constrained' State interference[102] so that these forms of intrusions can be eliminated.

However, they share a characteristic more profound than those by which they differ. Each is motivated by fear, although each asserts that fear is sourced differently, and a promise of its elimination, one by optimising the allegedly constrained State and the other by its minimisation. They share reliance on interference by the State to eliminate sources of interference and to create sympathetic conditions but each assumes responsibility for individuals. By this, they each demonstrate their mythological credentials.

These mythological credentials are masked by Pettit's arguments regarding interference and domination, issues which are for him at the heart of the difference between liberalism and republicanism. He criticizes the liberal notion of freedom on the grounds that actual non-interference still allows domination, that is potential arbitrary interference. He gives the example of the slave of a benign master, who is not actually interfered with but always can be.[103] He argues that republican freedom is viable because by allowing non-arbitrary interference, that is which tracks the interests I hold in common, there will not be domination. Pettit is wrong on both sides of his argument. On one side, the slave to a benign master will develop a regime intended to ensure the absence of interference, and so structurally embeds the fear of arbitrary interference in his practice. On the other side, a prisoner subjected to a regime which tracks his common interests through punishment will be constantly subjected to arbitrary interference regarding location, consequential family access, choices of work and training, and levels of in-cell hours and property. This is so because, where it is used, the act of imprisonment alone constitutes punishment. Again, the prisoner is forced to adopt a regime of practice in an attempt to subvert decisions that will degrade these conditions of his existence and the fear associated with that.

From this it can be said that, contrary to the republican assertions,[104] there can be no domination distinguished from systematic interference and no systematic interference distinguished from domination, despite the variation between them. Further, in both circumstances it will be clear to the subject that, despite the self-imposition of a defensive, systematic form of life, there is no assurance that such arbitrary interference can be eliminated. Fear will persist irrespective of whether one is the subject of domination or systematic interference. Slavery and imprisonment both comprise a pervasive fear. If there is such core common ground between non-interference and non-domination, then, beyond those features which make them different, there is core common ground between liberalism and republicanism.

There are two broad comments that may be drawn from all this. The first is that it reveals that mythology strongly informs republicanism. This fear-eliminating theory promotes an arrangement that is founded on the full, and therefore fearsome, empowerment of the magnitude of the State: only a fully empowered State can claim to eliminate domination and such a State can only be, consistent with its refinement since the Lockean and Montesquieuean response to Hobbes, coercive constitutional-legislative-institutional in form. This is an arrangement which is fully dispersed across social space in its form and influence. This is an empowered and arbitrarily interfering, not a constrained, State and one in which the law is its instrument rather than its constraint. It is an empowerment founded on the assumption of responsibility for individuals, revealed by its position regarding the nature of freedom, that is that these constitutional and institutional arrangements do not deliver freedom but are that freedom; and that this State effectively determines, through its concepts of the common good, corporatisation, screening, gagging, disenfranchisement and constructivism, what it will regard as my interest.

In this, republicanism reveals again the apparent structural flaw in mythological political theory, that is that when the State is so fully empowered as is the republican State and is colonised by corporatised interests, it severely constrains the freedom of non-corporatised interests, which can be gagged, screened, disenfranchised and constructed so that the common good is realised in terms of corporatised interests, which not only colonise the institutions of State but become those institutions. This is the real effect of Pettit's claim that these institutions do not merely deliver but are freedom and are fully extended in their jurisdiction to give effect to this. The republican State is itself intended to remain a source of profound fear to non-corporatised interests. Such an arrangement is inevitable, given the mythological desire of interests to compete in colonising the magnitude to achieve dominance. The consequential emergence of a dominant interest and the effective elimination of fear for that interest effectively institutionalises fear for non-aligned interests, through its processes of interference. Even more than the Kantian State, this republicanism is therefore the form of government of fully realised mythology. Intended to institutionalise fear for unincorporated interest, which although respectful of others does not conform to the common good, mythological politics is therefore revealed as inevitably self-defeating as a means of eliminating existential fear. It is merely an instrument for the elimination of fear, and therefore a source of full sympathy, for those who successfully compete to colonise its fearsome institutions.

The second broad comment is that republicanism reveals that what is common to political theory in the Western mythological political tradition is more significant than the various *personae* that it has assumed, for example as liberalism or republicanism. This is not to claim that liberalism and republicanism are the same, though they have common ground, but that the mythology that informs each of them is the context in which they should both be understood. It is a mythological analysis which is more richly informative, shaping as it does both political creeds, than one which relies on applying the ideological features of liberalism or republicanism as interpretive tools. This includes consideration of constitutional structure and reform, individual rights and normalisation. In short, Pettit's republicanism displays strong mythological credentials, like the liberalism it critiques.

9 Defending the State against Scepticism

LOADER AND WALKER

Because it draws strongly on the work of Pettit, we will now look at an account in which the State is trusted to both make a society free of existential anxiety, rather than just that a claim can be made about its elimination, and to neutralise dominant interests. These are qualities which the account presented here rejects. The account of the State which we have presented might be seen by some as a form of State scepticism. Certainly, it is an account against those who argue that the State can and should be trusted to minimise fear. In this context, we will consider the principal arguments of Loader and Walker. This consideration is given in the context of the significance of their work on the highly topical issue of security and given that it is a direct challenge to the account of the State being put forward here.

Loader and Walker challenge those who are sceptical of the State on the grounds that claims about the dangers inherent in the State are either an unjustified criticism or concern characteristics of the State regarding security that can be neutralised or even reformed. The argument that will be put here in response is that the State in its present form not only should not but finally cannot be trusted in this regard. On the one hand, this is not an argument that security is not a social good, only that the democratic State as we know it fails the test of being able to deliver it. Nor is it an argument that those initiatives taken to limit the excesses of police and to develop constructive relationships between police and communities are without value. But these initiatives are argued here to be contrary to the fundamental disposition of the relationship between individual and State and the attempt to claim sustainable success for them disguises that disposition. This disguise not only limits the potential of the initiatives but leaves unattended the socially and personally distempered disposition. Consequently, the security function cannot finally be civilised or be a civilising force in the present context, especially by precautions taken by contemporary democratic institutions. On the other hand, it is an argument that a reconfigured State, one without mythological presumptions, could address these

The Meddling State

Loader and Walker consider various forms of State scepticism, although not one with the features presented in the present work. Working from the notion that the State forms part of our foundational social imaginary or frame of reference for the world,[1] the first form of scepticism for them is of the State as a meddler, in particular as it appears in the liberal and neo-liberal perception that the State curtails fundamental liberties[2] and interferes with the exploitation of negative freedoms.[3] They see this criticism of the State as drawing on three perspectives. The first is the historical, where they identify the Classical connection between *polis* and *police*[4] and the origin of the latter in patriarchal order;[5] and, from its secular and artificial origins in Hobbes and Locke,[6] the need for the State to justify political rule in the context of the professionalisation of police, especially given its supposed responsibility to protect the interests of individuals. This need is the context of the constitutionalism on which Montesquieu and his successors focused.[7] The second is the sociological, where the fear is that the State will overreach itself and, while concerned for the moral status of the individual, will nonetheless develop forms of policing[8] that threaten this individual-centredness.[9] The third is the conceptual, whereby the other forms of scepticism follow from the metaphor of meddling.[10]

Recognising that the implication of this form of scepticism is that there is a threat to individual liberty, Loader and Walker offer three responses. The first is to emphasise the trust-building functions of political community upon which the liberty and security of citizens depend; the second is a warning against the atomistic and unrelational nature of neo-liberal politics;[11] and the third is the need to address the fragmentation and weakness of public political authority, due in part to market-induced disparities in the security resources available to citizens.[12]

On the grounds of the mythological argument, these responses are problematic. Given the structural disposition of contemporary, non-participatory, post-Hobbesian mythological democratic arrangements to induce or demand subjection in return for assurances regarding the elimination of fear, we cannot merely emphasise trust-building functions or rely on increasing constitutional constraints while expanding the State-security nexus, as Loader and Walker recommend,[13] or on the modern, technological transformation and the professionalisation of policing.[14] Such an approach must persistently and finally be confounded by that structural disposition of the arrangements, which in fact constitute the 'single underlying moral order' with which the modern State remains compatible[15] and which significantly constitute the real social imaginary. In any event, the

The Partisan State

The second form of scepticism is that the State is partisan, essentially that the State acts either on behalf of itself or for such of its dominant interests[16] as the propertied[17] or the ideological[18] and against such potentially threatening marginal groups[19] as the poor,[20] minorities[21] or those suspected of terrorism,[22] thereby acting as agents to reproduce these dominant interests and the social order they dominate. This is a claim that the activity of these agents of the State is based on systematic inequality.

In acknowledging the validity of much of this critique of the State, although pointing to problems which for them can be rectified, the authors refer respectively to Thatcherite[23] Britain and the analyses of Benjamin and Schmitt,[24] concluding with an examination of the 'war on terror.'[25] In these considerations, they recognise the erosion, even demise of democratic government and the rule of law,[26] but they argue for the potential for social reconstruction.[27] They accuse those who claim State partisanship of denying the openness of political systems[28] and of clinging onto the belief that security is opposed to liberty.[29] However, regarding the latter they are only ironically correct: the lesson of the mythological analysis is that liberty is defined in terms of security: those individuals who subject themselves on the assurance that their fear and desire will be addressed have experienced normalisation not security and so enjoy liberty but only the kind that this nexus allows. Those who do not comply are made subject to the provisions of security and enjoy little liberty at all. Regarding their claim that the 'partisans' underplay the openness of political systems, one must agree, except to say that the capacity of policing to be shaped by common interest, including by disadvantaged groups and communities, is heavily conditioned by the level of subjection and compliance. The non-compliant of course remain exposed to enforced, potentially brutal, subjection, with no capacity to shape security strategies.

However, the wider position against Loader and Walker here is that, like their response to claims about the meddling State, their response to the accusation of partisanship fails to recognise that individuals only make themselves subject to arrangements of State because these arrangements materialise their general existential fear, so that they can come to terms with this and come to have influence over it. Therefore, the State must be fearsome and civilising is therefore based on fear. In this context, security is the endpoint of civilising as normalisation, so the use of excessive force on the unwilling is not only a means of enforcing their subjection but is the clear message to the compliant to affirm their continued subjection. In this sense, Loader and Walker not only misconstrue the basic relationship between individual and State but wrongly perceive that, in the exercise of security, the 'daily life of the majority of citizens remains in large measure unaffected.'[30] But these are the very conditions of the mythological State. Attempting to civilise the security precautions of the mythological State, with its constituted and separated powers, by claiming to use the present form of its democratic arrangements is directly against its interest and function.[31] This will not do the trick for long. The cyclic descent into institutionalized violence and inquiry will continue.

Following from this, the mythological institutions require the Darwinian emergence of dominant, that is partisan, interests, who acquire the function of giving assurances regarding these fears and desires. Such interests are also in the position to create fears, pandering to the vulnerability of the subject and emphasising the role and function of security forces, so that their own interests are artificially strengthened as a result. In that sense, Loader and Walker are incorrect in denying the necessity for such interests. Again, given their central function in this arrangement, only the generation of non-mythological arrangements may see the genuine constraint of such interests. In short, the argument I am putting here regarding dominant interests is not an argument in particular against democratising security, since dominant interests and democracy, as it is, are symptoms of a much more profound problem. This problem goes well beyond these symptoms into the fabric of the mythological nature of the State and the consequential expectations of the willingly subject regarding their fears and desire for sympathetic conditions. The mythological core is the necessary target before civilised arrangements will be possible.

The Culturally Monolithic State

The third form of State scepticism concerns the assertion that the State itself, as opposed to the various interests that associate themselves with and manoeuvre it, is a cultural monolith. That is, as a site of cultural production in its own right, it generates meanings and promotes orthodoxies and that frequently this is in close synergy with its repressive function, if not inseparable from it.[32] For the authors, policing in this context is about the production of a general order of security, as an end in itself rather than as connected to the assurance of some other good.[33] However, although it does not in that discriminate in principle between individuals or groups,[34] this uniformity is compromised by the realities of police decision-making *in situ*.[35] Rather than act as innovating champions of the disadvantaged, police typically discriminate on a restorative, therefore, conservative basis,[36] a circumstance reinforced by the fact that they do act *in situ* rather than universally: order is in the final analysis local. This produces a partial sense of order, although one still embedded in the State as primarily concerned both with general order[37] and the often subtle production of a monolithic 'one nation, one culture' from the intersections of meanings and interests.[38]

This conservatism in turn tends to generate intolerance of minority groups, an intolerance into which police inevitably intervene in their conservative pursuit of order.[39] In doing so, they become associated with the continuity of national social order.[40] This cements the State as the ultimate source of security and therefore police as users of violence against targeted individuals and groups.[41] This is also the means by which the vulnerable tend to 'overinvest' in the State as a means of overcoming their own vulnerabilities and seeking the fantasy of total security, especially by identifying with police as its source of assurance but overlooking their excesses. This, however, leads to an increased sense of vulnerability of 'unorthodox' elements,[42] including indigenous groups in a colonial setting, as a result of the attempted penetration of techniques of normalisation and order.[43]

Acknowledging the lessons that are presented by this form of State scepticism, Loader and Walker see two flaws: first, that State policing is not the source of social tensions and that there is no substantive connection between security, State and nation and so it can be reconfigured to realise a sense of pluralist belonging; second, that it overlooks that security is a social good. However, the argument presented here is that there is in fact a substantive connection between security and the mythological State: the elimination of fear is the first condition for the creation and sustenance of the State as a mythological magnitude and so security is the first condition of individual subjection to its prescriptions. That security is also a source of fear is merely a demonstration of the non-viability of the mythological model, a model in which contemporary democracy and its manifestation in security are inextricably implicated. As has already been argued, conversion to a non-mythological model may eliminate these problems.

The Idiot State

This form of scepticism is typified, for Loader and Walker, by the remoteness of the State and so its lack of locally situated knowledge and so, in turn, its incapacity to deliver security locally in an effective way. Further, since it is wilful in disregarding its own ignorance, we must not invest confidence in State planning.[44] This is the view of Hayek but also, against his market individualist position, of leftist communitarian and democratic experimentalist positions.[45]

Examples of the forms of policing which fall into this category include 'remote' sponsoring and active engagement in community and problem-oriented policing but each of which is conceived as a top-down model of producing local order.[46] They are also an attempt to have police re-establish themselves as the hub of civic renewal in the face of a proliferation of market-based and local government initiatives.[47] One consequence of all these variations is the production and distribution of new forms of knowledge, for example regarding the minimisation of risk generated by crime 'hot spots'[48] and which is used 'top down' by the State to judge police performance standards.[49] The principal problem acknowledged here by Loader and Walker is that multi-agency partnerships are notoriously difficult to steer and so the State is not only deficient in the sophisticated understanding required for this but, unaware of this and deficient in the flexibility needed to bring coherence to multi-level security, ploughs on regardless.[50] In the end, their position on this form of scepticism resolves into their previous point that it denies the value of security as a common good and that the State can play an active, virtuous role in its promotion.

From their consideration of all these forms of State scepticism, Loader and Walker then begin to assemble their positive response, built around the enhanced regulation of security forces under the watch of democratic institutions. Against this, the position of the mythological interpretation of the State is that the present form of democratic institutions is a symptom of the problem rather than the basis of a solution. This is not a claim against the authors that security is not a social good nor that the State is a key to its realisation. It is a claim that, unless the mythology is unpacked, the State is ultimately prevented from playing such a role. Except for that indefeasible caveat, their arguments in this regard are coherent, especially regarding the 'thickness' and constitutive nature of its social benefit,[51] although a non-mythological account would not make this by itself the most important benefit. That is, a level of honest, existential fear should be accepted as one base of respectful social arrangements: it is the illusion of the eliminability of fear that has created the problems with which Loader and Walker are grappling.

The Good of Security

For the reasons they give, security is a public good but one that suffers both fragility[52] and potential for unequal distribution.[53] For them, these flaws can be addressed by seeing security as a social more than an individual benefit,[54] that is the quality of security is enhanced for an individual 'when the security of those with whom that individual shares a social environment is also reasonably attended to.'[55] Again, this makes sense, although there is a tendency on the part of the authors to deny any value to anxiety and so to disregard the value of a sustained but moderate level of fear as one element of respect: from a proper response to the awareness of our existential vulnerability, rather than its denial, may come a sustainable kind of social cooperation. They then argue that security is implicated in the very process of constituting the social, as a means for us to develop identity and be aspirational.[56] They finish their consideration of the good of security by arguing that security, which should be significantly publicly funded, is not only constitutive of but axiomatic for social living, for example by being an education in what it is to be social.[57] That is, for them it is not pervasive of social fields, but deep and narrow: security not as a striving but as a way of being, living securely with risk. This might seem not too far wide of the mark, except for the point already made, that it is not risk but existential anxiety with which one must live. Not to do so, to attempt its elimination, is the cause of the creation and continuous recreation of the mythological State.

The Virtue of the State

Loader and Walker then argue that this public provision should be through the State and that the State can overcome the sceptical flaws they have just considered. Their proposition is that the degree of interconnectedness of the cultural and ordering work requires a single entity to undertake the provision of security; and that only the State has the virtue to do this, should its vices be able to be eliminated. This can be done through anchored pluralism.[58]

They argue the priority of the State from the fact that the tasks to be performed are a composite and, given the level of responsibility, capacity and co-ordination required, the State is pre-eminently qualified to deliver them. This is not a claim for State monopoly, since it could work effectively at a distance.[59] These tasks are five, three cultural and two that are ordering: first, identification, which is the State's role in the imaginative construction of identity and which contributes to collective security; second, mobilisation and allocation of resources, which is the extraction of taxes necessary for external and internal defence, as public goods;[60] third, deliberation, which includes the encouragement of careful consideration and discussion through the use of good reason; fourth, regulation as the overall system of normative order, which can no longer be straightforwardly attributed exclusively to the State, since other jurisdictional levels have equal claim[61] but the State can claim the function of harmonising these diverse regulatory initiatives; and fifth, commitment, which is the process by which the State will keep its promises regarding the positive and negative incentives at its disposal and will ensure that it sustains legitimate use of force, rather than descend into a police State[62], and so allow individuals to invest in its processes with confidence.

Anchored Pluralism

For Loader and Walker, the State avoids consolidating its pathologies in the undertaking of this cultural and ordering work by optimal openness to concerned interests and optimised checks and balances against meddling, bias and so on, and by recognising other sites of collective security, which altogether constitutes anchored pluralism.[63] This should operate positively and negatively, positively to engage the widest community consistent with the infrastructure of a single security space, negatively to ensure protected individual private domains and the constructive limitation of other ordering and cultural sites. They see the challenge of achieving all this as possible only if we abandon scepticism towards the State and emphasise its virtue.

Unfortunately, these noble aspirations leave untouched the inherent problems of the mythological State. Attempting to restrain the State and invest trust in the resulting arrangements does nothing to address the causal dynamic of an existential fear converted, by creation, into the artifice of the mythological magnitude, to which one makes oneself subject in return for assurances concerning the elimination of that fear and the creation of sympathetic conditions, outcomes apparently to be confirmed by gradually bringing its fate into the hands of man. This point is emphasised by the final attempt by Loader and Walker to establish the democratic governance of security.

Democratic Governance of Security

The challenges the authors set themselves are to explain why the virtues of the State are less apparent than its vices and how to loosen the grip of these vices to allow a virtue-laden arrangement of security.[64] Regarding the vices, they consider four pathologies of modern security: paternalism; consumerism; authoritarianism; and fragmentation, the manifestations of which are not necessarily mutually consistent. Paternalism is the elevation of the professional bureaucratic expertise and authority, not popular sovereignty, to pride of place in determining security practice. A growing scepticism about this has elevated community policing, mandatory sentencing and other initiatives, in parallel with neo-liberal arguments, to prominence as an alternative trend.[65] Despite liberal protective responses to paternalism, the war on terror in turn has generated a resurgent confidence in the security bureaucracy. The prospects of meddling, partisanship and the other vices therefore remain, without an adequate brake.

Consumerism is the insertion of market logic into the State rather than the replacement of the State by the market, in the delivery of security services to the community. There is an alliance between communities and, derivatively, politicians and expertise to define and plot this trend of community protection, usually through harsh measures.[66] However, the authors state that consumerism is still driven by such emotions as fear or fantasies of absolute security;[67] that it expresses confidence in the benefits of security without examining its vices; and, by supporting a shallow but wide presence of police, it makes security pervasive rather than axiomatic.

Authoritarianism is a typical manifestation of these vices, perpetuating insecurity by responding impatiently, rather than deliberatively, to social problems and so initiating the continuous 'ratcheting-up' of reactive strategies. An anti-democratic spiral results[68] in that the fearful demands of citizens are reactively met by politicians concerned primarily with re-election. Authoritarianism is thereby increasingly coercive and increasingly under-constrained, promising security but delivering the opposite.[69]

Fragmentation is close to consumerism, in that the latter tends to produce a rejection of State provision of services and have citizens seek to eliminate their own security risks.[70] This leads to a reduction of commitment to general policing and so to social fragmentation rather than participation in a collective project with security being seen as an enterprise in common. We are left with markets, tribes and individuals proliferating security measures that emphasise the 'sovereign agency,' thereby downplaying the importance of recognising the vulnerability and dependency of living with others, rather than realising security as a public good.[71]

Civilising Security

Loader and Walker then propose their solution to these problems through a consideration of what institutional matrix could deal with these State vices and promote its virtues. They use Pettit's notion of false negatives and positives, the attempt to specify political authority that will promote non-dominating social relations and so individual freedom by tracking common avowable interests. To track such interests requires, through institutional processes, the identification of false negatives (the unheard but legitimate claims of citizens) by a widely inclusive process and positives (claims that cannot be encompassed in any negotiated notion of common interest, for example those that are partisan).[72] Their view is that paternalism (because it merely imputes interests but allows for biased professional priorities), consumerism (because it still excludes groups that are hard to reach and lacks means to scrutinise the preferences of participatory processes), authoritarianism (because it presumes that executive will is the only legitimate security consideration and so ignores both false negatives and false positives) and fragmentation (because it responds only to those with capital and so it has no means to eliminate false positives) all fail this test.[73]

The authors then apply Pettit's test to their anchored pluralism as a means of enhancing the capacity of the democratic State to genuinely engage with citizens, so that it protects them from domination without itself dominating. That is, to identify the institutional matrix that security requires, to democratically govern the demands and expectations that govern security demands; and subject the coercive power to the scrutiny that security entails so that it is still seen as thick public good. The elements of this quest are resources, recognition, rights and reasons.[74]

Resources, Recognition, Rights and Reasons

Resources go to the issue of the choices to be made regarding which demands for order will be met and by which constituencies. In this the State as an anchor has three roles: explaining the limits of resources in a way that will generate debate and understanding about priorities that benefit all; allocating these resources so that they track only the common interests and ideas of citizens affected by this rather than following the unchecked advice of experts or being partisan or market driven and so on; and regulating in a way that is equitable, that favours the common good and anchors the plethora of market and communal practices. Recognition registers the value of the State fostering routine democratic deliberation, the benefits of which are that it addresses the problem of false negatives and so of domination by the State and others for which it is partisan and it reduces the State's tendency towards idiocy.[75] The mechanisms for this include electoral processes to display policies and processes for public consultation. The point is that inclusive deliberation contributes to confident membership concerning security. In this, the authors acknowledge they are embarking on an analysis of democratic theory and institutional design.[76]

They then consider rights as a vital ingredient of a civilising security practice, not therefore in conflict with security, situating them within their four-pronged heuristic for reconfiguring security. Through rights, a check is placed on State coercion, including for counter-majoritarian interests and in respect of service provision by actors other than the State, market or community.[77] Thereby rights facilitate democratic processes and help to bring security into that process because rights are directed to security. Finally they consider reasons, or the idea of public reason, as the importance of bringing sustained social contestation to the practice of security, to identify all claims of constituencies regarding security. So it deals with false negatives and, in a manner that recognition does not, deals also with false positives.[78]

Loader and Walker, then, are employing Habermas' constructivist universalism and Pettit's common avowable interests to deal with both false negatives and false positives to generate the development of cooperatively admissible outcomes.[79] Despite this, they acknowledge that there will still be compromise and aggregative decision-making but only after a full airing of widely diverse positions.

Civilising Security and Myth

Broadly, it might be said that the strategy that Loader and Walker propose, despite elements that could find a place in non-mythological arrangements, is fated to sustain the cycle of institutional violence and inquiry, as it is contradicted by the foundational ideas and the strong dynamics of the entire nexus of which the real social imaginary is comprised politically: individual existential fear; a constitutionally designed fearsome State; the demand for sympathetic dominant interests; individual subjection; widely and deeply applied methods of normalisation to direct instincts to comply with the prescriptions of these mythological institutional arrangements; individual rights as the reflection of this compliance; and persistent desire which searches for the most sympathetic conditions of existence attainable. Against Loader and Walker, the argument here is that the contemporary democratic State is central to the problem and it is not reason but instinct which is the primary driver in this arrangement. The appeal to reason and regulation does not confront the fundamental human and structural problems by which the mythological nexus has become the fundamental social imagining. The architecture and experience of that imagining is set firm against any strategy such as that which they propose: the deep disposition of the individual due to instinct and the crafting of him through normalisation; the institutional structure refined over centuries since Hobbes to fit in that normalised, instinctual individual; and the wide array of practices that have grown up to connect the two.

In this context, arrangements which set out to make debate inclusive and to protect it through regulatory self-constraint by and on the State and other individuals are being set a challenge they cannot meet for long. The interests of groups and individuals are firmly in the other direction. In the end, mythological arrangements are established on the basis of the claimed elimination of fear and the satisfaction of desire for sympathetic conditions and dominant interests are expected to deliver on these, even while giving priority to their own. This is the mythological social contract.

More narrowly, as we saw in the chapter on Pettit's republicanism, their reliance on his work comes not without a range of problems. Apart from the mythological foundations of his idea of the State, which constitutes freedom rather than delivers it, his notion of the tracking of interests is problematic because the interests being tracked are common interests rather than those the respectful individual identifies as his own. This is affirmed by Pettit's insistence on the corporatisation of interest and, thereto, the conditions he applies to debate, inclusion and consent. This is the proper context of their comments about common interests[81] and aggregative decision-making.[82]

The proper response to problems of security is to commence what would in time be seen to have been a gestalt shift, moving gradually to the wide promotion of non-mythological respectful self-responsibility by instituting redesign of political institutions and government practices to make these work in a manner that does provide the opportunity for the State to be trusted. This is not the market-driven responsibility of neo-liberalism, which has been argued to share mythological presumptions with liberal and republican notions of the State. It is a non-mythological condition in which citizens come to terms with their existential circumstance and are encouraged to bring themselves to adopt the characteristic personal code outlined in Chapter 1. In the end, although there are elements here that would be sympathetic to a non-mythological approach, the proposals by Loader and Walker appear to be another attempt within the liberal paradigm to critique the outer layers of foundationally problematic political aspirations and arrangements and to propose a repetitive positive programme to help sustain them, that is that the solution to the problems of security in the democratic State in its present form is more of the democratic State in its present form. In this context, a sceptical attitude towards the State, based on a mythological reading of it, remains justified.

Part IV
Embodiment

10 The State as Civilisation

INTRODUCTION

To this point, this work has been principally an examination of the evolution of the modern State as an idea. It has been concerned with how this idea was conceived and then worked on by a series of key political thinkers from Hobbes to Rawls, Hayek and Pettit, as they sought to work through the implications of the Hobbesian and Republican conceptual frameworks. Given that this idea is mythological, their work has had mythological presumptions and effects. Against that background, one emphasis has been on the conception of the structural arrangements of the State and the repeated claim that, through individual subjection to the entity these comprise, fear can be eliminated and sympathetic conditions of existence constructed. We have also reflected on how this has variously created conditions of a political status for the individual, in particular how the forceful presence of these structural arrangements affirms the claim that these two primary aspirations can be fully addressed, reflected through a suite of rights. But the continuing implication has been that this claim, and so the idea, is highly problematic because the State itself is a source of fear and ultimately works by trading on this fearsomeness and through the dominance of interests that determine the nature of fear and what constitutes sympathetic conditions.

In essence, there has been the repeated claim, on the one hand, that the State can be brought to eliminate fear, create sympathetic conditions of existence and, variously, deliver freedom; on the other, that to assure these benefits, we must accept that one must forgo respectful responsibility to and for oneself and be subject to the behavioural prescriptions endorsed and sponsored through the institutions of State. To the considerable extent that there is awareness of the requirement to adopt such behavioural prescriptions so that the claimed benefits of peace, fulfilled desire and freedom may be realised, there is therefore widespread complicity in this. The mythology of the State is founded on the promise of those claimed benefits but at the cost of that forgoing and of the adoption of those practices. We create the entities that we expect will create us as we wish ourselves and others to be created. The question is whether, in embracing this informal but real contract, there is an awareness of the profoundly pervasive nature of the behavioural prescriptions that are loaded into it.

We will now look again at that relationship between mythological State and individual but with the emphasis on a strategic and tactical, rather than on the conceptual and structural, perspective. It will be a visceral as distinct from the epidermal examination undertaken so far. Through the work on Wittgenstein, Elias and Foucault, we will examine how it is that these concerns for fear and sympathetic conditions bring the individual to an accommodation with the State, although this is not to say that their work is taken simply on their own terms. In particular with Foucault, and to a lesser extent with Elias, the reading here will be somewhat against the grain, as it has been for some of the principal theorists considered so far. But this reconfiguring of their work will provide an understanding of the materiality of the mythological State, how mythology is embodied in the hard lives of individuals. It will fill out the idea that the fate of the State comes into man's hands, with this idea taking on an ironic sense for the majority. Thereby it will explore the genesis of liberalism in absolutism and, through that, reflect on the notion of citizenship as a negative image of these mythological arrangements.

BROAD ARGUMENT

Broadly, this work argues that existential anxiety has driven the long and continuing imagination by mankind of fearsome mythological magnitudes which are always absolutist in nature but are then structurally constituted and engaged, through subjection and other tactics, in an attempt to ensure the elimination of fear experienced by individuals, both of themselves and of other individuals, and the sympathy of the magnitudes towards man. These imagined magnitudes then become the objects which man attempts continuously to realise in his social relations. That is, there is a disposition in man first to imagine and then to realise such magnitudes. The imagined magnitude then remains as the archetypal reference point against which actual instances are realised and judged, so that although man appears unreservedly disposed to imagine and be willingly subject to such entities, his subjection to any actual model is conditional because he always remains to be satisfied that any such model is a realisation of the archetypal myth and his preferred relationship with it. Mankind engages these created magnitudes, first by submission and then by giving them constitutional form, by which the fate of the entity is ultimately brought into man's hands. This provides privileged status to the interests that come to dominate such entities, although a formal status also comes incrementally across social space to all compliant individuals as citizens. Privileged status allows some influence over what constitutes fear and sympathetic conditions and how these are addressed.

Historically, with the irrecoverable breakdown from the sixteenth century of the absolutist theological myth brought about by the Reformation, Hobbes was one who demonstrated the continuing disposition to mythologise by conceiving that the resulting void could be filled by an absolutist political idea. The other theorists we have considered may then be seen as those who have undertaken the reworking of the imagined arrangements, that is the idea of engagement of the absolutist political myth in Hobbesian or republican form, in a manner that seeks to assure man that the empowered, fearsome political mythological magnitude to which he forgoes his self-responsibility is sympathetic to his desires. Finally, although there has been continuous gradual work on this myth within the theoretical tradition to achieve this outcome, absolutism remains the foundation of its principal form, democracy, irrespective of its liberal or republican forms.

However, it is one thing to put an argument, an ambitious argument stretching across time from Hobbes through to Hayek and Pettit, that the history of the idea of the State reveals a disposition to imagine, create and refine a mythological magnitude. It is another thing to show how this has been a real factor, not just in the ideas of the political philosophers, but in the sweated lives of men and women. That is, to show how existential anxiety becomes fear and how this is the key factor in the generation of the actual embodied practices of individuals and how such practices are inextricably linked to the formation, historical refinement and maintenance of the widely empowered but sympathetic idea of the State. What is needed is a psychology and sociology of political mythology. We don't have one but perhaps the nearest we have is the respective work of Elias and Foucault. Neither were mythologists but, read in an appropriate way, the social techniques and practices they uncovered contribute to an understanding of the emergence and refinement of the mythological State and of its varied but inextricable relationships with its citizens.

The principal focus of this chapter is an analysis of Elias' work on civilising. The following chapter will provide an examination of the work of Foucault, whose analysis of both governmentality and the modern disciplinary techniques are suggested here to indicate the refinement that civilising processes underwent in the modern era, beyond Elias' focus on the Middle Ages and the early modern era and, in that, to reveal the elaborating, material consolidation of the political mythology. However, to provide context against which the work of these two analysts is to be considered, this section will commence with an outline of the social ontology of Wittgenstein, specifically as his work relates to norms, rules and normalisation. Wittgenstein thereby provides a setting within which we can see how civilising, governmentality and discipline work to embed the idea of the political mythology in the lives of individuals.

NORMALISATION AND CERTAINTY

Wittgenstein cannot be brought into this argument as a political thinker in the sense that Hobbes, Hayek, Elias and Foucault may be seen. He does not appear interested in the nature of political institutions or in their relationship with individual citizens. His work, especially as it relates to the argument presented here, is more a sociological ontology, how ways of thinking and acting get anchored both across a community and in an individual. His analysis of normalisation and certainty, therefore, are equally applicable to both mythological and non-mythological ways of thinking. However, where his work is useful is that, given the argument that there are mythological presumptions at the heart of the political tradition from Hobbes to Hayek and Pettit, he helps an understanding of the process of the embedding of those ideas in institutional form and in individual practice. Thereby, he helps an understanding not only of the fact of that embedding but also how disassembling it would allow non-mythological ways of thinking and doing to flourish.

Wittgenstein's thought is directly relevant to a consideration of the mythology of the State. As it has gradually emerged through long-term work from Hobbes, this Western mythology has, in the context of the testable covenant between each individual and the magnitude, assumed the claimed responsibility to eliminate fear, guided by dominant interest but gathering the concession of each individual. The principal method for doing so is its gradual dispersal across social and geographical space by its elaboration and proliferation through the regimes and practices promoted by its institutions, officials, agents and allies, so that individuals develop a measured assurance that fear is, with the ultimate goal of its elimination, being substantially reduced and that active sympathy is also forthcoming. As the engagement increasingly includes constitutional democratic concessions, there is increased confidence that the claims regarding the fear-sympathy nexus can be delivered.

This desire for assurance is a search for ultimately unattainable certainty. There are two elements that comprise this quest for certainty, first the matter of the archetypal myth and second the separate but related matter of the realisation of that in the political myth. That is, there is an inherent disposition to absolutely forgo self-responsibility to the absolute, archetypal myth, given the strength of existential fear, but there then is strong inducement for this disposition to be realised by the actual forgoing of self-responsibility to a political magnitude *in situ*. This is the expectation that individuals' archetypal disposition will be satisfied in instances of the magnitude, that is particular sovereigns or governments, and thereby forgo their self-responsibility in return for the institutional promises regarding fear and sympathy. That is, dominant interests seek certainty that all individuals are forgoing responsibility to the institutional structures and prescriptions of the articulated magnitude. For their part, individuals seek to be certain that the magnitude is dealing with their fear and creating sympathetic conditions. This does not preclude, in fact it allows, that these are artificially created. Balancing these desires might be seen as a sign of the art of government.

There are therefore two levels of certainty here. The first, existential certainty, is readily realised as it is founded on the reality of existential fear and the desire for its elimination by the creation of a sufficiently fearsome mythological entity which is sympathetic. Such an entity might as well be theological as political or something else. As we shall see in looking at Wittgenstein, this certainty can occur unconsciously. The second level of certainty is more difficult to realise, as it requires that individuals be convinced that the political mythological magnitude, and within that the instance of it as a particular government, will deal effectively with fear and sympathy. This difficulty is caused by the reality of politics, given the prominent position adopted by dominant interests, the result of which always makes such forgoing to that instance highly uncertain and therefore typically conditional, despite the disposition.

The argument put here is that, taking advantage of the disposition to archetypal certainty, there are formative strategies engaged in the search to establish this second, political level of certainty. These strategies are best understood simply as training, in some sense of the kind that we shall see as involved in producing Elias' civilising and Foucault's governmental and disciplinary practices. Such training typically starts at infancy, as Elias will be seen to explain. The style of training can be formal or informal, that is by instruction or absorption. It is training in this sense that produces practices that convert the archetypal disposition to forgo responsibility into practices that reliably sustain mythological arrangements of State and, in turn, ensure that both others and oneself are not fearsome and contribute to the production of sympathetic conditions. This certainty is best thought of as behaviour and not as a mental state. Wittgenstein makes the point.[1]

For Wittgenstein, the ability to first recognise regularities in the world and then to recognise linguistic behaviour is innate, that is pre-linguistic.[2] In considering Wittgenstein, Kober sees that children in such a process 'are brought to act as other normal, competent members of their community do.'[3] This is being trained to act in a particular, customary way.[4] Practice precedes explanation.

It is not only that children learn, that is, are trained, by copying particular behaviours and language but that there is no point giving justifications for this. Civilising children seeks to work in this way and then subjecting them to practices of governmentality and discipline also aims to do so. Children have no immediate choice but to copy[5] and 'The basic form of our game must be one in which there is no such thing as doubt.'[6] But this should not be read to mean that such learning is merely mechanical. A child may learn that there are unreliable informants later than it learns facts that are told it but there is still an element of preference in their initial learning.

This is not choice as such, since there is strong disposition for children to be trained by parents and other individuals significant for them. But the element of inducement inherent in this process should not be discounted. Inducement may not need to be especially strong for a very young child to be trained, given the bonds that usually exist with a parent, but there is still inducement by the parent for the child to be trained, in the form of either love or punishment, and to this extent the child is induced. Elias emphasises that fear is socially instilled from early childhood. For its part, as much as it is disposed to, the child is further induced by such love or fear of punishment to want to be trained. It seeks certainty.

Although increasingly affected by doubt as a child grows, this inducement to adopt understandings and practices as certainties remains as an essential element of growth. For Kober, certainties do not compel you to follow them unconditionally but induce you to follow them, if you want to participate in certain practices of one community or another. They determine your acting only if you want to communicate with others. He also argues that certainties determine, that is are not dependent upon, other sources of truth.[7] In support of these statements, he draws further on Wittgenstein.[8]

Kober points out that children are born into a community and simply acquire the community's language and the community's world picture. Again, to the extent that Elias and Foucault can be read as describing what it is to be human, rather than merely describing a particular historical development, civilising, governing and disciplining are part of this. And the certainties of the acquired language-games are for the time being 'certain beyond all reasonable doubt.'[9] Although not simply, the same applies to more complex language-games since these grow from primitive ones. There is no strict distinction between language-games that are elaborate and those that are primitive, which themselves grow from pre-linguistic action.[10] Further, although more complicated language-games are not so obvious, almost all adults in a community would assent to them, since they become rationality standards of individuals belonging to a community,[11] to which one can add political arrangements and the practices associated with each of these.[12]

What is being argued here is that children, already disposed by the universal experience of existential anxiety to embrace archetypal mythological magnitudes, are trained in the behaviours and language-games of institutional arrangements, as they learn both fear and a dominant world picture, from an early age through strong inducement by adults and with their willing participation, initially at a primitive level. It is important that this willingness is properly understood. At an age where there is no sense of responsibility and no distinction made between their archetypal dispositions and what they might be induced to prefer, they desire the elimination of anxiety and the expression of sympathy in their reliance on parents or other significant adults. Early training takes advantage of this lack of distinction. Rather than provide for these needs while encouraging children to learn the means by which they can assume responsibility for themselves, parents and significant others typically satisfy these needs by assuming responsibility for children or allow, for example, educational or denominational institutions to do so. That they do so is usually the result of their own experience, reproducing their own lack of training in the self-responsible. Mythological practices are typically reproduced.

This is not an argument that such practices are universal or invariably deep, but that they are typical. Thereby, a child's disposition to the existence of mythological magnitudes and its desire that fear be eliminated and that sympathy is demonstrated induces training in the forgoing of self-responsibility. This general disposition readies children to then accept, as they mature, the assumption of responsibility for them by the political magnitude, through the strategic practices promoted by parliaments, courts, the plethora of executive agencies and their agents, as well as by such allies of these institutions as corporations and churches, by looking to these for the satisfaction of their concerns about fear and sympathy. Among this plethora, the State, typically seen as government, is argued here to play a pivotal, exemplary role. Children then become progressively sophisticated in such behaviour and language and these behaviours and languages can become certainties in the sense intended by Wittgenstein, that is as unquestioned references for truth statements.

Further, training is ultimately intended to produce practices in a largely unconscious manner. Beyond the universal lack of awareness of the disposition to archetypal mythological magnitudes, there is, in the case of such early training, a typical lack of awareness of the effect of this. Kober argues that it is not necessary that certainties, as opposed to things that are known by justification and reason, 'be known explicitly or be potentially enumerated, for certainties can also be mastered unconsciously.'[13] In saying so, he refers again to Wittgenstein.[14] Similarly, the effect of such training, where it works effectively and from an early age, reinforces the inherent disposition to create archetypal mythological magnitudes. While this disposition to create certainty about such magnitudes is pre-conscious, the beliefs and practices regarding the political myth are usually acquired pre-consciously but are then manifest as conscious dispositions: the child is unaware he is being trained to accept the reality of the mythological State but the man is typically aware of his disposition without at all necessarily questioning this. Indeed, given the continuous profile of political matters and the prevalent discourse of fear and desire encouraged by dominant interests, this awareness is a matter of constantly reaffirmed consent by non-autonomous individuals.

The world picture that an individual adopts within a community is comprised of an overlapping plurality of such language-games, of varying complexity but in which those that are more complex are built on those that are more primitive. The political language game is gradually acquired by the individual, founded on participation in a range of less sophisticated language games. Against this background, a world picture for Wittgenstein is a kind of myth, which 'exhibits the views and convictions of a cultural community or form of life. It may contain traditions, tales, or legends concerning the origin of the world, the world's shape and processes (the seasons . . . the behaviour of plants and animals . . . reproduction of the species, etc.) as well as *political structures* . . . and religious beliefs—in brief, all those matters which may be of interest in a community's life.'[15] Although this argument does not depend on it, it is interesting that for Wittgenstein a world picture is a kind of myth.[16] Wittgenstein does not provide a definition of the sense that 'mythology' has for him but there is nothing in his argument which is inconsistent with the notion of mythology used here.

Beyond the unconscious archetypal disposition but taking advantage of it, the language-game of institutional structures of the State, itself a part of a dominant mythological world-picture, is intended to be learned by individuals from childhood as a certainty through increasing levels of complexity and to a considerable extent pre-consciously. Further, this is to be part of the manner in which an individual, young or old, understands the institutionalised ways in which he comes to believe he can have fear eliminated and to experience sympathetic conditions. Where this training is effective, this language-game comprises the way we understand, talk about and behave in relation to the institutions of the State, as well therefore as the expectations we have of those institutions, that is, engaged through the forgoing of responsibility, that they exist to deal conclusively with fear and sympathy. The effect of this training, where it is experienced early and is effective, may be pre-conscious but the attitudes and practices which result from it are not.

This is not to say that there is no doubt in the form of questioning of the efficacy of such an outcome. But doubt, which follows learned certainty, almost always concerns the particularity or instance of the State (e.g., a particular sovereign or elected government or decision), rather than the concept of the State which itself is typically embedded as a certainty. This certainty is of the archetypal mythological magnitude, the disposition to which is rarely questioned. That is, the question is almost never seriously asked whether there should not be government by State of the kind described here as mythological, only whether a more satisfactory particular, or occasionally type of, government can be identified to realise this archetypal notion. Doubt typically applies only about such particularity. Most political scientists would merely recognise this as institutionalisation, the condition of a stable polity, but in the argument presented here this very stability is the sign of the effectiveness of the training in dominant mythological practices. This is not to say that other conceivable political arrangements, including those possible in a non-mythological form, may not also demonstrate stability.

This search for, this teaching of and the acquisition of certainty is normalisation. The search for certainty concerns the establishment of a political entity which will be accepted as fearsome but fear-eliminating

The State as Civilisation 209

and sympathetic. Further, it is argued that, in the context of the dominant mythology, normalisation itself, by its very nature, is mythological. Norms are best understood as preferred rules to be followed and it is the dominant mythology which heavily influences which rules are preferred.

This claim concerning rules can begin with Wittgenstein's statement that a finite array of incidents may be compatible with any number of rules[17] and continues with his analysis of the nature of rule-following, about which he expresses two views. The distinction between them is controversial but in the mythological context both views are fully compatible. One position is that rule-following is a customary, not private, practice.[18] 'Private' is used in the context of his denial of the argument that there can be a private language, so should not be read to deny the other position, that is that an individual can follow a rule of his own making. He does strongly imply that rule following is typically social and that certain activities that are guided by rules can only take place in the context of a community.[19] However, he makes it clear that rule-following depends on a person's capability and not on how that capability was acquired.[20]

Rule-following is therefore both a social and an individual practice. One reason it is social is that mythology can make it so but rule-following can be individual because individuals are capable of developing and following an individual rule, for example one which is not mythological. This does not mean that the social is necessarily mythological, only that wherever the social comprises the forgoing of self-responsibility, and this is commonly the case, then the social is mythological. A non-mythological rule would be one which is not normative in the sense of enforcing a dominant mythology. It would still be normative in that there can be agreement between self-responsible individuals as to what are to be the rules, adopted without forgoing self-responsibility. Practically, this is not to deny that there needs to be sensible run-of-the-mill rules that make things work, that is that are not the subject of continuous reassessment and agreement. These would be produced by a representative body not dominated by sectional interests and could be introduced without long consultation across the social body down to the individual level. Otherwise, any society, including a non-mythological society, would grind to a halt. But the concern here is that the tacit consent provisions of a Locke or a Kant or a Pettit can hide the introduction of rules that assume responsibility for others and favour dominant interests. Hence the need for thorough processes which allow that important rules are actually widely scrutinized both beforehand and after a cooling down period and changed, without requiring civil disobedience. Awareness of such scrutiny would constrain interests that might be dominant in the legislative or executive process.

The assumption of self-responsibility by individuals, which is the basis for non-mythological rule development, and the development of redesigned institutional arrangements, would not be instantaneous but progressively generated by individuals working together through different

State-promoted practices of participation. As explained in the Introduction, self-responsibility has to be learned, just as its forgoing is now learned, beyond the disposition. All this strengthens the argument here that although an individual may typically follow socially constructed mythological rules, he is able to determine his own non-mythological rules and work these into non-mythological individual and social practices.

Generally, the mythological significance of Wittgenstein is that he lays out some of the ontological ground which Elias and Foucault materialise. The function of Elias' civilising and of Foucault's rationalities is not merely to change human practice through training but to do this so that government, and the institutional arrangements which promote it, is seen as ontologically certain and effective in dealing with the fear-sympathy nexus. Wittgenstein was no mythologist but his account of certainty and of rule-following as normalisation identify the conditions to which political mythology aspires in attempting to realise the archetypal myth.

ELIAS

Although he was not a State builder, the question may still arise whether Elias was a mythologist. He was not and this is crucial for the significance of his work as a social analyst. The question for him, as it will be for Foucault, is whether he has anything to say that throws light on the construction of the State as a mythological entity. Certainly he did not place fear and desire alone at the heart of his sociological explanation. Nonetheless, a case can properly be made that these imperatives are among the range of core elements of his theses.

Before we examine the place in his sociological explanation of fear and the desire for sympathetic conditions and their role in State formation, a few things should be said about his broad argument. Building on his new sociological epistemology and the development of a conceptual architecture for his processual, figurational sociology, Elias undertook a range of substantive, historical studies. First among the latter is *The Civilising Process* and it is the lessons from that which are employed here for their mythological significance. However, one should acknowledge that it is in the programmatic *What is Sociology?* that he identifies three key interdependent markers for the development of a society, that is, the extent of control over natural events; the extent of control over social connections; and the extent to which individuals have learned, from childhood, self-control. The first two are argued here to be the sources of fear, triggers of existential anxiety, and the third is a key strategy for the elimination of fear emanating from social connections.[21] These are principal reference points for his historical studies.

The principal insight of *The Civilising Process* is the link between sociogenesis, which is the transformation in the division of labour, demography, social pacification, urbanisation and the growth of trade of a society, and psychogenesis, which is the internalisation of restraint and the resulting change in behavioural codes. Through this he reveals the dynamic of the emergence of the European State and its relationship with its citizens. In brief, the growth of the late medieval urban economy generated and depended on the monopoly of violence by the central State authority relative to the landed warlord nobility. Over time, this shift saw the warrior class converted into a dependent class of courtiers. This pacification facilitated trade, which underwrote the economic and military power of the central authority. So, restrained behaviour was rewarded by the emerging State so that, in the long term, these external restraints became internalised as self-constraints, thereby changing individual habitus and personality structure.[22] The mythological implications are clear, especially regarding the elimination of fear emanating from the warrior class by the induced and enforced forgoing of their self-responsibility to the magnitude of the State and the creation by that entity of sympathetic conditions. What Elias has thereby identified is a key early mechanism through which these mythological conditions are embedded at a practical level in the real world, in practices of both government and the individual.

However, there is another plane of Elias' thought which may not obviously affirm the mythological account of the State, even providing an apparent contradiction. These features include that human beings are born into relationships of interdependency and that these shape growth and development; that these figurations are constantly in flux; that over the long term they are unplanned and unforeseen; and that they are the context for the development of human knowledge. These features thus discount the importance of individuals in favour of groups; they emphasise the evolutionary nature of human development, the transformations that have taken place in processes of individual socialisation, and that habitus, the mould of the personality, changes over historical time as a result; also that such concepts as power are best seen as relational rather than as possessions; and that as people variously attempt to position themselves within social figurations, the level of insight and power over the operations of these figurations are fairly low.[23]

These key features of his figurational approach might appear to mitigate fear as a primary experience, in that interdependence could suggest a reassuring social environment with no need for a fearsome State; that constant flux might be seen to disallow the strategic nature of fear elimination; and that limited power implies limitations to fearful experience. However, interdependence will be argued to be both the social consequence of and the ground for training in forgoing one's self-responsibility, as Wittgenstein allows, so that its arrangements are therefore typically mythological; the flux which ensures unforeseen transformations of social configurations allows for forms to be gradually found in which external controls are internalised as self-control and these are reflected in the long term evolution in the character of habitus, which will be argued to become the personalised marker of mythology. In short, understood from the appropriate perspective, his analysis of social configuration reinforces the mythological lessons from the historical sociology presented in *The Civilising Process*.

Fear, Civilisation and Habitus

There are a number of features of Elias' thought which enrich the notion of a political mythology that is being presented here. He appreciates the powerful influence of fear in the lives of men and women and argues that this fear has been a driving force in the emergence and refinement of civilising practices and that this, in turn, significantly explains the formation of the State. He does not talk about mythology, except to claim that like all good sociology his work is a means of its elimination, but his demonstration of the relationship between the inextricable elements of fear, civilisation and State formation in fact suggests a way of explaining why and how the concept of the mythological State that is presented here is created, sustained and embodied. In effect, given that fear of others is the trigger of existential anxiety and is the form into which that anxiety is commonly converted, we create an empowered magnitude, the State and its company of interests, agents and allies, to which we forgo responsibility in order that it creates us through civilising us such that we are not fearsome but are increasingly productive. In fact, so that we are not fearful of others but of the State and its agents and allies. It is the attempted working through of this idea that has, along with the related desire for sympathetic conditions, inspired political theorists from Hobbes to Hayek and Pettit. Elias makes repeated reference to fear as a core factor in so-called primitive and in medieval life.[24] He also describes the fearsome medieval warrior society and other societies where there was not a complex and stable monopoly of physical violence.[25] Fear of external powers in the form of other people is for Elias a pervasive feature of human life before the civilising regimes were established. Substantially, for Elias it is for the purpose of eliminating such fears that the process of civilising emerges. To link mythology with civilising in this way is not an uncontroversial assertion, given Elias' emphasis on increasing interdependence and regarding the advantages which for him accrue to the internalisation of control. For reasons that are explained below, however, this is argued to be a justified claim.

Elias provides a range of examples of these processes regarding fear. A number of these seem unrelated to the control of fear as such, for example those that relate to various bodily functions and I shall come back to these. But there are examples which relate directly to fear, such as the use of the knife when eating[26]. More generally, Elias examines changes in aggressiveness. He describes the aggressive and therefore fearsome life in the Middle Ages as typified by 'Rapine, battle, hunting of people and animals.'[27] For

Elias, this was not only a condition for the knighted but was a common condition.[28] He relates the general excess of this behaviour simultaneously to the structuring of emotional control and to the structuring of society.[29] For him, it was the emergence of regimes of civilising that brought about moderation through self-restraint, thereby structuring the emotional world. Yet, in a sense with which Blumenberg would have agreed, primal fear is never extinguished, since it becomes a continuum with internalised fear. In the course of this civilising, he argues, inner fears grow in proportion to the decrease of outer ones.[30] Despite this self-restraint, fear never disappears.[31] Fear, especially of others, is both continuous and pervasive.

One key outcome of the civilising he describes is the development of a personal habitus, which for him is the 'durable and generalised disposition that suffuses a person's actions throughout an entire domain of life or, in the extreme instance, throughout all of life--in which case the term comes to mean the whole manner, turn, cast, or mould of the personality.'[32] The concept of habitus is prominent in *The Civilising Process,* the starting point for which is the nature of court society, where Elias sees both continuity and difference between that and subsequent bourgeois capitalist society. The differences, generated by the bourgeois in opposition to the practices at court, are interesting enough. They include the distinction between public and private life, the development of an economic rationality as a core of life and the dedication to work, which is that productivity increases. The continuities are even more instructive. Court society was based on a habitus, comprising a particular mode of conduct and psychic structure, which formed the basis of bourgeois life. Courtly rationality, as a form of the balance between short term desires and long term consequences, ironically became bourgeois legal rationality. This was not because of the former's organisation of power around economic capital—court society was rather organised around the display of such symbolic capital as status and prestige—but because court society identified itself through the practice of manners, an essential element of which was the management of emotion. It is the habitus which results from the adoption of acceptable practices as manners that becomes the 'second nature' of men and women.[33] This habitus or second nature is the outcome of civilising, which thereby produces us in a manner so that we are not fearsome to each other. This is not to say that, despite this durability, habitus does not continue to evolve in response to the shifts in relationships with others during one's life: 'the structures of personality and of society evolve in an indissoluble interrelationship.'[34] But it is the form that human material practice takes. Civilised behaviour, intended as not fearsome but as docile and productive, becomes 'second nature.'

The bourgeoisie solved the problem of the tension between the authentic expression of one's feelings and rationally controlling them in pursuit of long term goals by constraining the former within the bounds of a private life.[35] But it was court society that had adopted a regime of self-observation to promote a self-discipline that complemented the observation of others in the search for competitive advantage. In this context, the display of emotions, especially if produced by fear, became a sign of weakness on the grounds that it offered advantage to others. For Elias, this regime played the important role of sustaining the relational nature of power: the sovereign and the nobility needed each other equally, the former because of his need of the nobility as a weight in the equilibrium of the classes he ruled and the latter because only life at court gave them the economic opportunity and prestige they needed to retain their position. For him, the nobility do not exercise their potential collective power and overthrow the sovereign because of the competition between them for the advantage he can bestow.[36] This connection between fear, the adoption of emotional restraint, the creation of opportunity and the sustenance of the relational nature of power is for Elias fundamental to the emergence of the State.

The emergence of this connection can be seen in his description of the process of rationalisation, which is for Elias the progress of human reason and is synonymous with the civilisation of men.[37] Further, in a manner that is significant in the examination we have just made of Wittgenstein, he argues that the fears which grown-ups consciously or unconsciously induce in the child are precipitated in him or her and henceforth reproduce themselves more or less automatically.[38]

Even though he makes no reference here to existential anxiety and therefore moves a little too quickly to collapse primal fears into those that are socially and intentionally produced, for Elias fear is at the heart of the existence of every individual and from the earliest age. There is also no doubt that for him fear is a primary, perhaps the most fundamental, generator of social practice and, as we shall see, through the process of civilising that is intended to minimise it (albeit by replacing it with internalised fears), of the formation of the State as the monopoliser of violence.

Elias does not claim that the elimination of fear from threat of aggression is the only purpose of the civilising process. On the contrary, he is at pains to argue that there is a range of behaviours that civilising is intended to eliminate or transform. He describes at length the manners and display of bodily functions which, through the influence of the practices of court society, are suppressed or transformed.[39] But through that the process has a wide socially consolidating effect. When one acts in like manner, when one identifies with others, the prospect of threat diminishes.

Civilising, Monopolies and the Formation of the State

Elias connects the process of civilising, as the imposition first of external restraint and then of self-restraint over both one's emotions and pleasure drives, to the presence of a central authority sufficiently empowered to produce that result. This civilising is not to be understood as the production of uniformity, since self-restraint allows the proliferation of social function, even if within a framework of accepted patterns of behaviour.[40] But although there is diversity, Elias states that there is direction, not mere process, in this interweaved evolution of individual and community, although in a multilinear rather than a unilinear sense.[41] This directionality led him to see progress in human affairs, in respect of control over the natural world, the reduced level of brutality and the equality that comes from more widely established democratic arrangements. It is in this sense that society had become increasingly civilised. This view of progress attracted criticism, even though Elias later argued the continuing presence of disintegrative processes, which could overtake civilisation.[42] It will be argued that his way of looking at social processes is problematic and that, if he had understood civilising differently and had argued that civilising and decivilising were parts of exactly the same process, he might have avoided such criticism.

For Elias therefore, this diversity of social function existed increasingly in a world being given direction through the connection between civilising and the centralising of power into the monopoly that would assume the form of the modern State. Further, whether one lived a worldly life or went to a monastery, it was the structure of society that required and generated a specific standard of emotional control.[43]

Civilising therefore reveals an underlying dynamic towards the monopolisation of physical force and violence and, as a result, the development of a 'second nature' of self-restraint.[44] This 'second nature' exists in the form of a personal habitus, as we have seen. The field in which this nexus between self-restrained habitus and differentiated social functions develops is therefore one characterised by a monopolisation which forms the basis of the formation of the State.[45]

For Elias, this monopoly emerged not only in the exercise of violence but simultaneously through the emerging monopoly of taxation. He sees in this a financial trend of centralisation made possible by the competition between such social groupings as the nobility and the bourgeoisie but sustained because the sovereign maintained that competition in balance.[46] Troubled though this process was over time, it was often justified by the need to defend against external threat and it was allowed by the manner in which it was distributed to the benefit of royal favourites. The consequence was the gradual emergence of a central administration to support the centralised exercise of monopolised violence. There are a number of references that Elias makes to these developments.[47] The consequence was the emergence of the State as a recognisable entity.[48]

Here, on the one hand in the defence against external and internal threat and on the other in the distribution of largesse to favoured groups, was the embryo of the inextricable link between the absolutist State empowered through submission to eliminate the fear caused by threat and the complementary condition that its nature be sympathetic. The entity which shows a fearsome face to those who are threatening equally shows a sympathetic face towards those who are fearful but are prepared to become compliant, to say it again, to forgo their respectful self-responsibility.

Interdependence and Shame

There are two notions in Elias' proposal of civilising that, seen in a particular way, would challenge the mythological account of the State presented here. They are interdependence and shame, subjects that receive his extensive consideration.

The argument put by Elias that the monopolisation of violence is crucial to the process of State formation is the ground for his further argument that this is but one element in an increasing web of interdependence bonding people across a community, others including the division of labour, the growth of towns and trade, the use of money and increasing population.[49] Elias makes clear in *The Civilising Process* that this monopolisation was the first step in the internalisation of restraint, which continued to grow with increasing interdependence, especially with the rise of the bourgeoisie. With this, courtesy evolved into etiquette and so the range of behaviours subject to self-regulation expanded. As this has continued to grow and the rules of interpersonal engagement have become more subtle, the second nature of self-restraint is seen by some as evolving into a third nature, whereby the automatic nature of the self-restraint is now applied more flexibly in an increasingly interdependent world.[50]

There could be a line of argument that this challenges the argument of this work. That is, interdependency builds fields of interaction which, whether the subject of automatic self-restraint or of flexible but controlled response, no longer requires a fearsome State to eliminate fear: fear, including of the State, is dealt with through the techniques of such interdependency. Such an argument would be in error. Interdependence needs to be seen against a background in which the middle classes were ascending to the position of dominant interests, increasingly empowered by colonising the arrangements of State through submission. As a consequence, these elaborating interdependencies were not generated by the assumption of self-responsibility but by its having been forgone to the magnitude, a submissiveness undertaken to ensure at least growing economic dominance. Further, the skills upon which these interdependencies rely are the result of life-time training of individuals, in the sense intended by Wittgenstein. So, these second and third order interdependencies are properly seen as reinforcements of tectonic arrangements of the mythological State rather than as an alternative that dispenses with it. Interdependency is better seen as affirming rather than a challenge to the idea and practice of the mythological State.

A further possible argument against the mythological interpretation presented here is that posed by an assertion that for Elias fear might be significant but shame is the principal emotion.[51] This assertion would continue by saying that *The Civilising Process* gives pre-eminent attention to shame, more in fact than to fear.[52] Fear then would take its place alongside love, anger, grief and guilt as an important but secondary emotion. The implication for the argument presented here is that, as a second order emotion, fear could not convincingly be argued to be the foundation of the conceptualisations that realise broad political arrangements and our generally willing submission to them.

However, such an argument does not recognise fear, rather than merely as an emotion in itself, as the materialisation of existential anxiety.[53] The argument here is that fear is triggered by and takes its form in response to threatening physical and social incidents certainly, but is itself a manifestation of existential anxiety as a condition of humanity. Existential anxiety or *angst* lies outside any particular social, or natural, experience and so is argued here to be the deepest of emotions. Its inextricable connection is with the absolutism of reality and so it is a profound feature of being human for every individual. In this context, it is not appropriate to see shame as the master emotion, important though it is. The nexus between existential anxiety and fear occupies that space.

Elias and Mythology

In all this we have Elias' argument for the inextricable connection between personal fear and the creation of the empowered State as the wielder of monopolised violence. We have such consequential elements as the typically willing but also unwilling subjection of individuals to that entity, here in a systematic manner through the process of civilising as the embedding of non-threatening behaviour, and the emergence of the State as not only fearsome but as sympathetic to those who are regarded as its truest subjects. We have the elaborating web of functionaries, a characteristic of the increasing monopolisation of power, that constitutes the initial dispersal of the increasingly fearsome entity across social space. We have the creation of spheres of activity from which the entity conditionally withdraws, in particular the economic and theological, although this occurs without the entity forgoing its responsibility to strategically maintain the balance of power between social groupings, thereby sustaining itself as an entity and limiting the fear which emerges from competition between them over the nature of who should be fearful, and why, and who should experience sympathy. This is always on the basis of membership of or alliance with the empowered entity. Thereby we also have the effective incremental gaining of control of the entity by alliance. Thus we have the bourgeoisie joining the aristocracy as a dominant interest. We have all this in the context of the slow refinement of these arrangements, extended long over time. These elements are the foundation of a covenant between sovereign and subject, the basis of which is a balance of power held in place by the covenant of mutual dependence which founds it as relational in nature.

These elements are also the fundamentals of political mythology. These are the moves that are made in the attempt to establish the archetypal magnitude. While it certainly could not be argued that there was any conscious determination by Elias to acknowledge, let alone to explain the realisation of, such a political mythological archetype, it can be argued that the evidence that he collects and even the manner in which he patterns the connections across this evidence reinforces the argument that existential anxiety disposes mankind to creating a mythological magnitude in the form of the State. To that extent at least, Elias is beginning to show how it is that the disposition to mythologise is played out across social space. That is, how existential anxiety, commonly made material as fear of other individuals, is dealt with by creating an entity, through the forgoing of self-responsibility, that claims to be both fearsome and sympathetic. In Elias, these elements are also brought together in the act of civilising from the child's earliest age so that fear and aggression can be internalised. Fearsome individuals are dealt with by training them in practices that are no longer threatening. An entity that monopolises violence, even though it may act through agents and allies, can ensure the sustenance of the regime of training that does so. The same dynamic applies to the increase in sympathy through taxation and enhanced bourgeois productivity. Elias can be seen to contribute, no doubt unwittingly, to a psychology and a sociology of mythology.[54]

But Elias is not one who understands this process as one of the elaboration of myth. For him, civilising is a sign of the progress in human existence which is the elimination of myth. Consequently, we do not get from him any sense of deep existential anxiety as the foundation of fear, either in the early history of man or even in the life of every individual, except perhaps in the early history of primitive man, since for him fear typically appears to be socially induced. As a consequence, there is no strong sense that civilisation can be visited on or even embraced by the individual who forgoes self-responsibility. It might be noted, as an aside, that the argument here does not claim that subjection is always willing, since competition will always produce dominant forms of civilisation that are then imposed on the unwilling, both within and outside a particular social field. But there is not in Elias the complementary strong sense that social groups, despite being prepared to do so, willingly forgo their sovereignty to the king or State, since for him the emphasis is on an opportunistic intervention by the sovereign to push his interests between the competing groups who are merely seeking favour. He does not, but he might have taken the short step from what he does argue by concluding that it was the fear drawn from that competition which led to a ready subjection to sovereign power so long as the sovereign displayed sympathy towards them.

Consequently, Elias does not see the mythological nature of the State. On the contrary, he sees it as emerging through the natural processes of competition and consolidation, but significantly traceable to the fear that existed in uncivilized life. But it is arguable that these processes of competition and consolidation are attempts to establish political arrangements the effect of which was to eliminate fear through the construction of an empowered entity and the subjection of individuals to it through civilising. It is therefore open to refer this process to a disposition in man to create an archetypal arrangement which is mythological in nature. Further, that the many trials experienced in establishing this were characteristic of the caution that inevitably results from contributing to an arrangement to which, in this mythological referral, one must forgo one's self-responsibility.

Neither is there connection in his work between State formation and the notion of individual rights, which are mythological wherever they come at the cost of self-responsibility. This absence is hardly surprising given the historical period of his analysis and the purpose for which he undertook this analysis. Nonetheless, he does identify the emergence of the elements of individuation generated by the civilising process, which is strongly influenced in its construction by the process of monopolisation of violence and fiscal management which was for him the foundation of the State.[55] Without drawing too long a bow, Elias can be seen to allow for an interpretation that the status of the compliant and therefore sympathised individual would emerge from and was therefore inextricably bound up with both the nature of the empowered State and its behavioural prescriptions. The manner of its emergence is through the monopolisation and exercise of violence and fiscal management. Each of these is arguably a prerequisite for an account of common individual rights.

What Elias does argue for, and which is not provided for in the mythological model so far, is the notion of habitus as a 'second nature.' Such a concept can be used to explain why it is that individuals do not strain to extricate themselves from such subjection, that is beyond the acquired belief that they can live an existence free of fear: there is no highly conscious realisation by individuals of the mythological condition in which they exist so long as such subjection allows the sense of peace and sympathy adequate to the acquired expectation of the covenant.

Implications

What all this first points to is that, in relation to the emergence of the modern State, there are not two parallel processes going on, one in ideas and one in social practice, but two aspects or trajectories of the same process. Just as the violent competition between knights and the emergence of the bourgeoisie in the early modern period induced the civilising process and drove European society towards the establishment of absolutist nation States, with a monopolisation of violence intended to eliminate other fearsome behaviour and create sympathetic conditions of existence, political theorists like Hobbes, operating in the violent political wake of the Reformation, came to reconcile the disparity between various theoretical positions to come to a compatible conclusion, that is that an absolutist State was the solution to potentially anarchic political circumstances. That there have been these two aspects of the same process, two trajectories of liberalism in the terms we have been using to consider the political mythology of the State, supports the view that there has been a disposition in man, revealed as much in his practical politics as in his theoretical analysis of conceptual politics, for the creation of mythological magnitudes. It is immaterial to the argument presented here that the consolidation of the court and civilising processes had been underway before the Reformation of the sixteenth century, that is before the absolutism of the State began to fill the vacuum created by the disintegration of the absolutist theological myth. In fact, these are best seen as the prologue for the emergence of the two absolutist/liberal trajectories we are considering. For without the effect of the already-ongoing consolidation of the courts,[56] the absolutist State would have been less easily realised as an idea to fill this vacuum. Further, those processes certainly continued, overlapping and mutually informing, well after the emergence of such States.[57]

What can be said is that Elias uncovered the link in practice between absolutism, the forgoing of individual self-responsibility, at least for the warrior caste and the bourgeoisie, in return for the progressive elimination of fear and the creation of sympathetic conditions of existence. This was the early modern embodiment of myth in individual practice and set the ground for ultimately delivering the fate of the magnitude into the hands of man. It will now also be argued that, in its emphasis on the manufacture of docility and productivity, it pre-figured liberal practice, as understood here.

Elias uncovered a range of elements of the social and personal dynamic of the early modern period which, when welded together by his argument, affirms the mythological account of the emergence, consolidation and dispersal of the State. This is so despite the denial that should be made of him that his own thought held any mythological credentials. But his thought contributes strongly to an understanding of how it is that the mythological account of the relationship between the State and the individual works, that is how the individual is brought into the myth through fear and desire, how mythology is embedded, how absolutism is a key to this and what it means to say that the fate of the magnitude comes into man's hands.

We shall now examine the processes of governmentality and discipline and their link to liberalism and neo-liberalism, which Foucault begins to expose, as means by which this dispersal of the political mythology into the lives of men and women became wider and increasingly refined, especially from the seventeenth century but up to the present.

11 Governmentality, the Market and Liberalism

FOUCAULT

Elias demonstrates how individuals within certain social groupings were brought into the myth through fear and desire, how mythology is embedded in practice, how absolutism is a key to this, what it means to say that the fate of the magnitude comes into man's hands and how this all relates to the formation of the State.

To complete the argument regarding the thoroughly mythological nature of the State, two further points need to be established: first, that the embedding of the idea of it in practice has been spread out widely from court society; second, that this embedding has been, rather than a mere adjunct, the direct and intended strategic outcome of that idea. Regarding the content of embedding, those who would reject the idea of the State as mythological would claim that dealing with fear and sympathetic conditions are shored up through rational and just government reinforced by the practice of individual rights. Against this, the mythological argument is that fear and sympathetic conditions are actually dealt with by the manufacture of docility and productivity, respectively, and that this relies on the forgoing of self-responsibility. Foucault points the way to this manufacture through his notion of governmentality, a key feature of which is pastoralism, itself manifest in the notions of police, discipline and bio-power. These key points will be explored through two arguments.

The first argument has two steps. The first shows how this embedding has spread across social space and historical time and into individual lives. The second shows that, as with the attempts to critique and reprogramme the idea of the State from Hobbes to Hayek, seen as phase shifts in the mythological trajectory of the idea of the State, there have been similar phase shifts in the embedding of the practices by which the mythological State has been embodied, a practical trajectory. The second argument, also with two steps, reveals the fully integrated nature of the mythological State by showing the inextricable connection of these phase-shifted trajectories. The first step argues that liberalism is a lens through which this connection can be seen, that the trajectory of the idea and the trajectory of practice are the key elements of the liberal *persona* of the myth of the State. The second shows how these trajectories are already integrated within the thought of key political theorists of the tradition. We saw this in Locke, Rousseau and Kant but Hayek will be revisited as a paradigm case.

Preliminary Remarks

Foucault provides the best insight into how embedding has occurred widely and deeply across space and time. This is a matter of both how, in Blumenberg's terms, there has been a dispersal of myth and how Wittgenstein's notion of normalisation works. So, we might say that this is a matter of how the ontologies of Blumenberg and Wittgenstein are complementary and how both are materialised in the rationalities that Foucault unmasks. Foucault also makes important remarks regarding the nature of liberalism, which will assist in developing a framework by which the union of the trajectories can be seen.

We saw in Parts I–III that the function of the idea of the mythological State is to claim that it is the means by which fear and sympathetic conditions of existence are dealt with, a claim conditioned by the forgoing of one's self-responsibility. Yet we also saw that, in the latest iteration of this idea in neo-liberalism, this claim was disguised as the creation of free, autonomous and responsible individuals through the mechanism of the market and in terms of its values.

The first question of Foucault then is how this dispersal across social space occurs. Secondary but derivative questions will include how the liberal and neo-liberal ideas of the State are connected to the embedding of docility and productivity and how this happens in a manner that sustains the idea of the mythological State. This chapter proposes that there is a reading of the work of Foucault which helps us answer these questions. The argument here is that Foucault's notions of governmentality and liberalism suggest a framework we can develop to understand how the idea of the mythological State is embedded across social space from early modernity to the emergence of the neo-liberal State. However, as with other aspects of the broad thesis put in this work, this argument goes against the grain of common readings of Foucault and even against the grain of Foucault's own account of governmentality.

In exploring this argument, what we will find is that, from early modernity, there has been an evolution in governmentality that reflects the evolution of the idea of the mythological State from Hobbes to Hayek but not by easy and direct match. Parallel to the evolution of the idea of the State, there has been an evolution of practices which are justified by that evolving idea and have a confirming but, contrary to the claims of the proponents of the idea, a debilitating effect. As this idea has evolved through a rational trajectory from an absolutist to a Constitutional democratic and then neo-liberal democratic form, the latter imagining the 'free, responsible, autonomous individual,' governmentality has evolved from the fearsome practices of sixteenth century sovereignty through governmental practices to the self-creating, docile and productive individual of neo-liberal democracies. In effect, this is a claim that, finally, 'free, autonomous and responsible' equates with 'docile and productive.' The argument here will be that there is a strong link between these parallel but contrapuntal trajectories, idea and practice, and that this link is liberalism. This is in effect an argument that liberalism is a face and force of mythology and that it operates at two levels, one a high minded idea of individual freedom and the other the means for the disposition of individuals to be manufactured through subjection and thereby enfeebled. This contrary dynamic is the story of the mythology of the State, a story now become wider than that of the idea we looked at in Part I.

Given this emphasis on the long evolution of idea and practice, an examination of the most recent stages in the history of governmentality should reveal strong evidence of the embedding of these practices promoted in the guise of the idea of the mythological State. It will be argued that the neo-liberal emphasis on the self-creating 'free, autonomous, responsible' individual is this strong embedding but that it disguises an individuality for which the standards are the imperatives and vicissitudes of the market. Thereby, any notion of 'free, autonomous and responsible' is so contrarily established as to lose its claimed meaning, except in terms of the values of the market. Behind the evolution towards this idea of free and autonomous individuality, we shall see significant phase shifts from the period during which the practice of the modern mythological State began to be realised in the seventeenth century, when the embedding relied on early editions of pastoralism through police and discipline often dispensed by the State, to the contemporary attempt to have individuals 'take responsibility' for creating themselves as 'free, autonomous and responsible' but which should be understood as 'docile and productive.'

To claim that the idea of the State as mythological could have a role in this argument concerning the contemporary condition of political individuality sounds counter-intuitive, since the function of the State in contemporary political arrangements has been significantly devalued, particularly as neo-liberalism has spread through liberal democracies demonising it and championing the market. It is the market which is typically argued among neo-liberals to be the optimal forum for encouraging the emergence of the self-creating free, autonomous and responsible individual. However, beyond the fact that Hayek argued for an important role for the State, the argument here is that, although the State has increasingly withdrawn from the active delivery of programmes, even becoming itself a market environment, three other important propositions should be noted as deserving higher relief. These propositions remind us that, even in neo-liberal thought, the State is not vacating the political stage. Rather, it remains vibrantly alive and in its mythological raiment.

First, although Foucault gives priority to governmentality over sovereignty, seen here as still close to the heart of the idea of the mythological State, this priority should be reversed. Here it is proposed that, although there is a myriad of governmental technologies and devices that exist beside and outside it, sometimes loosely, the real idea of the State is of pre-eminent importance in giving these technologies validity and a sense of ultimate coherence.

Second, the increasing withdrawal of the State from active administration of programmes is not the fading of its mythological significance. The State operates increasingly through endorsed agents and allies, whether through a community of interest, contractual arrangements or by devolving operational responsibility to market forces over which it retains significant influence through its corporate regulatory, fiscal and other functions. The State governs increasingly at a distance but it still governs. More significantly, because of the persistent power of the myth, the State is perceived to retain its ultimate responsibility to dispense the mythological obligations upon which social stability, that is the balance between subjection, fear and sympathetic conditions, rests. It is the guarantor of this, the final court of appeal regarding this balance.

Third, this argument opens out into a wider connection between the State and liberalism, from which the conclusion is drawn, as it was for the evolution of the idea of the mythological State, that liberalism is an important face and force of mythology. Republicanism is another, as we have seen in Part III. Liberalism is both a critique of developments that threaten the balance between subjection and claims regarding the resolution of fear and sympathetic conditions, and a proposer of positive programmes serially attempting to insure against further imbalance. We have seen how this critique and reprogramming occurs regarding the evolution of the idea of the State from Hobbes to Rawls and Hayek. Liberalism as the *persona* of political mythology will correct itself in its neo-liberal or any other form, either as idea or practice, if imbalance emerges in the combination of subjection, fear and sympathetic conditions, that is, when the foundations of the mythology of the State are under threat. The strategies and tactics of liberalism will try to ensure that the State is kept in a vibrant condition.

These are the issues we will now examine, beginning with a brief account of Foucault's notion of governmentality. We shall then explore in greater depth a range of the specific but overlapping elements canvassed in that account to reveal how changes in governing over time came to be embedded across social space and deep in the lives of individuals. This embedding will be argued to be the idea of the embodiment of the mythological State in human practice, albeit subversively. Further, this embodiment is shown to point to the notion of liberalism preferred here, as the means of its implementation. We shall therefore then bring together various strands presented in the several Parts of this work to distil the argument that liberalism is a face and force of the mythological State, a means of displaying the two

Governmentality, the Market and Liberalism 225

principal trajectories of which it is composed. Then, to indicate how wide is the ground which this notion occupies, that is rather than being principally an ideological notion, two of its elaborations are then considered, one at the micro level of the nature of individual freedom and autonomy, the other at the macro level of alternative State forms. This chapter, and this work, will be brought to a close by arguing how the work of the liberal Hayek exemplifies the elaborated interpretation of Foucault presented here, not only at the level of ideas but also of practice. Thereby we draw a summary position regarding the complementary phase-shifted nature of the dual liberal trajectories, that is of the repeatedly reinvented idea of freedom and autonomy that disguises evolved practices that make docile and productive, by which the induced but willing participation in the continuous recreation of the mythological State is sustained.

Given that Foucault's sometimes schematic work on both governmentality and liberalism has been extended by his intellectual successors, the approach adopted up to this point of working principally through the major texts of the key thinkers needs to be varied. Consequently, where Foucault's work has been elaborated and amended in this emerging field, I shall refer to the work of some others in the following discussion but refer back wherever this is possible to Foucault.

The Wide Embodiment of the Mythological State

The sources and nature of governmentality

In his 1978 lecture *Governmentality*, Foucault presents a range of fresh and freshly combined ideas regarding the nature and history of government. For him, the problem of government seemed 'to explode in the sixteenth century'[1] as a result of discussion concerning 'How to govern oneself, how to be governed, how to govern others, by whom the people will accept being governed, how to become the best possible governor'.[2] For Foucault it was not accidental that these matters emerged at that time, as it was the temporal crossroads of two processes: the establishment of the centralised territorial, administrative and colonial states which ended feudalism; and, with the Reformation and Counter-Reformation, the question of how one must be spiritually ruled. For him, unlike the argument being put here, these were separate movements but they were the source of the new questions about government.

For Foucault it was *The Prince*, published in 1532, which catalysed these questions. Being without theological foundation and taking the Prince as transcending his territory, it was the subject of strident critique, expectedly from Catholics.[3] Their rejection was reinforced by the implication of the fragility of the connection between the prince and both his territory and subjects, causing him to act constantly to reinforce that connection.

The anti-Machiavellians did want an art of government but of a different kind. They recognised a notion of government that saw the plurality of its forms across society, including the head of a family or a convent superior and all of which are immanent to the State. This plurality fits within an art of government that comprises an upwards and downwards continuity of self-government, governing a family and ruling the State,[4] the former representing the view that morality in self-government brings success in governing the State, the latter that a well-run State provides guidance for the head of the family in dealing with his family, goods and wealth. The latter is the notion of *police*; the former, centred on governing the family, is *economy*, so the main concern for the emerging art of government is how to bring economy into the political management of the State. It remained a problem through to the eighteenth century, although during this time the word slowly acquired a modern meaning, signifying a real field of intervention rather than a form of government.

The anti-Machiavellians emphasised that government was the disposition of a multiplicity of things, contrasting Machiavelli's concern with the sovereign matters of territory and subjects. They were concerned with the complexity of men in their relations with wealth, subsistence, the land in all its features, customs, famines, epidemics and so on. This is a 'taking charge' of all things within a territory and with their various interconnections.[5] As with a family, this is a general form of management. Property and territory are among the variables, but were not pre-eminent.

This form of government has a finality of its own, distinguishable from sovereignty. For Foucault, sovereignty is circular in that, finally, it comprises a common good that is no more than obeying the law, with individuals practicing the trade they are assigned and respecting the established order by being submissive to sovereignty. But with government there lies a multitude of ends, such as producing wealth, providing subsistence, promoting the growth of the population. For this, things need to be disposed tactically, without the central sovereign concern to impose the law. The final attribute of the good ruler, as opposed to the sovereign's wrath, is the patience and wisdom of the tactics of disposition and a willingness to serve the governed. This new concept was made practical, from the sixteenth and seventeenth centuries, through the administrative apparatus and *savoirs* of the territorial monarchies and through mercantilism and the Cameralist science of *police*.[6] This was far from Machiavelli.

But a new *raison d'etat*, where the State was increasingly being governed by intrinsic rational principles rather than drawn from natural or divine law, was for Foucault an obstacle to the fuller emergence of the art of government, since this art increasingly found its principles within this reality of the State. His explanations for this are various but include such seventeenth century crises as the Thirty Years War, along with the consequent social and financial upheavals. These tensions, and their continuing 'mental and institutional structures,' affirmed the focus on the arrangements of sovereignty,[7] especially including the law. So the art of government was still caught between the large, abstract framework of sovereignty and an economy of enrichment based on the model of the family too weak to respond to the importance of territorial possession and royal finance. The impasse was resolved by the eighteenth century demographic expansion and its connection to an abundance of money and the expansion of agricultural production[8]: it was population that allowed the recentring of the economy on a different plane from that of the family, providing an opportunity for the development of the science of government, now incorporating mercantile statistical analysis, outside the juridical framework of sovereignty.

In fact, it was statistics that revealed the regularities and features of population separate from the family. These had economic effects not reducible to the family, which increasingly itself became an element internal to population, save for certain religious or moral themes, but which from the mid-eighteenth century becomes important as an instrument of the government of the population,[9] a form of government Foucault calls bio-politics. Managing the population now becomes the ultimate end of government. Unlike sovereignty, with its concern for the act of government itself, it is the wealth and welfare of the population which is the central concern of government. Without the full awareness of the people, in fact 'ignorant of what is being done to it',[10] new strategic and technical actions were undertaken regarding birth rates, distribution of activities and so on. Further, population becomes, from the eighteenth century, an object of the *savoir* of government and inseparable from the economy. So political economy emerges from the networks of relations between population, territory and wealth.[11]

But sovereignty doesn't diminish with the rise of the art of government. 'On the contrary, the problem of sovereignty was never posed with greater force than at this time',[12] essentially because it was no longer implicated, as in the sixteenth and seventeenth centuries, in the effort to source an art of government. Given that this art was now emerging on different grounds, there was an attempt to see 'what juridical and institutional form . . . could be given to the sovereignty that characterises a state'.[13] Foucault sees Rousseau as one asking how, using concepts like nature, contract and general will, there can be a general principle of government which allows for both sovereignty and the elements of an art of government.

To these two elements of the emerging modern landscape of political theory, Foucault adds a third, discipline. Although the institutions within which this technique spread were pillars of the administrative monarchies, its techniques also became important for managing a population in its depth and details. The result is that this is not a transition from sovereignty and discipline to the art of government but a triangle of these three elements, 'with its primary target the population and its essential mechanism the apparatuses of security'.[14] For him, this 'solid series' of eighteenth century government, population and political economy is not dissolved even today.

From all this, Foucault presents a definition of 'governmentality' with three elements: the ensemble of institutions, analyses, tactics that allow this form of power, the target of which is the population, the form of knowledge of which is political economy and the techniques of which are the apparatuses of security; the pre-eminence of this over such other forms of power as sovereignty and discipline and which has resulted in the formation of specific governmental apparatuses and *savoirs*; and the result of the process by which the State of justice in the Middle Ages, transformed into the administrative State during the fifteenth and sixteenth centuries, becomes governmentalised.[15]

Foucault then moves to the problem of the State, which for him is overvalued in two ways. The first is seeing it as a *monster froid* confronting us; the second is the reduction of the State to functions which, like the relation of productive forces, are important and so renders to the State a privileged position. Foucault denies it has this unity or functionality and so 'maybe, after all, the state is no more than a composite reality and a mythicised abstraction'.[16] For him, what is important is not the *etatisation* of society but the governmentalisation of the state, that is what has permitted the state to survive and what it is today is thanks to governmentality, 'which is at once internal and external to the state, since it is the tactics of government which make possible the continual definition and redefinition of what is within the competence of the state'.[17] These are arguments that will be contested in the mythological analysis which follows.

From this Foucault suggests that there is a global typology of forms and economies of power in the West: the State of justice, born of a feudal territorial regime, a society of laws; the administrative state, born of the territorial boundaries of the fifteenth and sixteenth centuries, a society of regulation and discipline; a governmental state, defined no longer by its territory but by its population. The latter, which makes use of an economic *savoir*, can also be seen as a type of society controlled by apparatuses of security.[18]

Foucault finishes by stating that governmentality was born out of Christian pastoral care and a diplomatic-military technique perfected with the Treaty of Westphalia, and that it assumed the dimensions it has only because of instruments contemporaneous with the art of government, known in seventeenth and eighteenth centuries as *police*. For Foucault, these are the three elements that made possible the governmentalisation of the state.[19]

This schema of governmentality will now be used to guide the elaboration of particular elements, and the cross-hatched connections between them, that are of interest for the account of the embedding of the idea of the State as mythological. Establishing that embedding has occurred requires that practices sponsored by and through the State have been adopted on the basis of claims that fear and sympathy are being conclusively addressed in return for the forgoing of self-responsibility. Understanding that fear and sympathy are addressed in practice by the manufacture of docility and productivity respectively, such practices should be seen to have been embedded by the combined effect of State pastoralism, police and discipline. Seeing this will also allow us to draw conclusions concerning the steps that will demonstrate the phased trajectory of these practices. Although these elements each have their own trajectory over time, their cross-hatching reflects the connections that Foucault makes within the triangle of sovereignty, discipline and governmentality. The shifting historical shape of this triangle, how these elements fit together into the phased trajectory of embedding, is the result of the critiquing and positive programming by liberalism as a broad mythological strategic methodology.

Pastoral Power

A central element of Foucault's account of governmentality is pastoral power and it turns out to be a principal means of the manufacture of docility and productivity. It appeared as the Christian idea of care given to members of the Church, especially the poor, in late antiquity. This was the relationship between the shepherd and his flock, the shepherd responsible for guiding and caring for the flock as a whole and for each individual. To fulfil his duties, the shepherd required in-depth knowledge of each individual, guiding him to work on areas of his own mortification so a state of grace could be achieved,[20] a theological normalisation. Even from this earliest period, there was a political dimension to this: in combination with the effect of this caring, the transparency that came from rooting out zones of negative privacy contributed, through normalising practice, to the social solidarity of what was, in early Christianity, a vulnerable and fractious group.

Foucault argues that these pastoral practices were ultimately assumed by secular authorities, for example, the State, private ventures, welfare societies or the family.[21] In saying so, he makes no comment concerning the dynamic inherent in or between these groups, that is regarding the pre-eminence that the State and its dominant interests increasingly had over the other means of embedding such practices. Irrespective, Dean indicates that it was during the Protestant-Catholic schisms of the seventeenth century that this adoption of welfare by secular authorities became a matter of general importance.[22] Foucault adds the further point that there was a change in the objective of pastoral power: 'It was no longer a question of leading people to their salvation in the next world, but rather ensuring it in this world . . . the word *salvation* takes on different meanings: health, well-being (that is, sufficient wealth, standard of living), security, protection against accidents. A series of "worldly" aims took the place of the religious aims of the traditional pastorate'.[23]

It was the theological crisis of early modernity that triggered this mirror image concern for the worldly well-being of people through the adoption of pastoral practices by secular authorities. To the considerable extent that this became a matter for the early State and philanthropic interests, this caring was an embedding of the idea of the mythological State and its dominant interests through their assumption of willingly forgone responsibility for dealing with the fear and conditions of existence of all individuals. This came through a deep intrusiveness in the form of the development of detailed knowledge of each individual by the post-theological pastoral authority. This knowledge was the ground for the imposition of normalisation as docility and productivity, framed by the promotion of the parallel development of the citizen-city model, built on its formal status of citizenship, with the shepherd-flock model of power. The latter is mythological practice, the former the embryonic modern ideas of equality and political participation which camouflage the latter and the status of which acts as an incentive to make oneself willingly subject to the latter. In short, the argument here is that pastoralism, with its strategies of care, of discipline and of normalisation, is a meta-theme that informs police, discipline, bio-power and ultimately governmentality in their embedding of the mythological idea of the State.

Reason of State, Police, Discipline and Bio-power

So pastoralism did not stand alone in this embedding of mythology through docility and productivity. It was elaborated through the practices of police, discipline and bio-power. But all three should be seen, initially, in the context of reason of state.

We have seen how for Foucault in the late sixteenth and early seventeenth centuries 'reason of state,' although an obstacle to the emergence of an art of government, is best seen as the State 'governed according to rational principles which are intrinsic to it and which cannot be derived solely from natural or divine laws of the principles of wisdom and prudence; the state, like nature, has its own proper form of rationality'.[24] The purpose was to increase the scope of power of the state 'for its own sake by bringing the bodies of the state's subjects under tighter discipline.' This saw the emergence of a new *savoir*, requiring information about the State's population, its resources and its problems.[25] This was in fact the early sign of an art of government.

The role of police in this was to enhance State control over its subjects. One means was to ensure increased provision of food, health, infrastructure and order to a growing population. The purpose was, during the seventeenth and eighteenth centuries, to fulfil the growing target of police on men and things in their relationship to property, what they produce, their coexistence and the market. It also included how they live and the diseases and the accidents which can befall them. State power had centred on men as subjects with rights and duties. Now the police targeted men in their everyday activities, the essential components of State strength and vitality.[26] These circumstances are characteristic of the decades-long period of religious conflict, so also featured a spread of indiscipline and insecurity. So police also emerged as the internal security component of reason of state,[27] and, connected to the ordering nature of discipline, slowly enhanced the embedding of the State as increasingly dominant and protective, in large part by making men docile and productive.[28]

Reason of state is thus founded on the problem of the security of the state.[29] Police became the means of its order and prosperity, through the issuing of a vast array of miscellaneous ordinances, intertwining morals and manners with governmental concerns. This was a coaching of individuals on how to behave, evolving from sumptuary laws to general morality as the estates devolved authority to the new municipal and central sovereign State structures.[30] We can see here an intersection here with the work of Elias.[31]

Following Foucault, Dean argues that these developments are best seen in the broader context of the development of State sovereignty and the flowering of forms of government rationality, examples of which include mercantilism, cameralism and the management of population. Here we see the emergence of political economy as the wide administration of the State, the encouragement of wealth and the provision for the wants of all members.[32] This included encouraging the growth of population but also its industriousness, mythologically its productivity.

This is the historical background to the ultimate emergence of a new political rationality of bio-power, focussing its attention during and from the eighteenth century on the growing population, which emerged and was connected to the nascent empirical human sciences, especially political economy.[33] From this 'there is no inherent limit to the possible strength a state might achieve.[34] Human beings were now considered a resource and the individual was of interest only as he could contribute to the strength of the State. The lives, deaths, activities and work of individuals were important to the extent that these everyday concerns became politically useful.[35] Essentially this was the evolution of the art of government, manifesting itself in the eighteenth century in new knowledge applied to the population as society and through political economy and respect of freedom through law, but still organised around *raison d'etat*.[36]

So a threshold was crossed with this phase shift which followed the establishment of the State on a firm footing. By the eighteenth century, population can no longer be understood as engaged in a struggle for survival, family is not a private sphere outside government, neither was economy an autonomous, quasi-natural reality to be respected by government or police as just one institution to enhance the security of the State.[37] Government had shifted from the disposition of things and people, that of humans in relation to a wide range of entities and movements within a territory, to one operating through social, economic and biological forces, in which population was a reality in itself, and with its own forces. This was the generalisation of the pastoral government of religious communities to the entire population, associated with but not the result of the exercise of the sovereign power of the State.[38]

Bio-power, now the companion to police by virtue of its management of the population as a global entity and in detail, is on the one hand a politics concerned with administering life and seeking to rationalise problems associated with health, economic growth, standards of living and so on.

This was the embedding of an entire range of new practices, each related to satisfying the desire for sympathetic conditions of existence and so with mythological import. It is for Dean thereby a 'broad terrain of governmental intervention' and is the field on which liberalism, as a critique of 'too much government' by the State, will be seen to operate.[39] This is not to deny other dimensions of government, for example the operation of the economy and the practice of sovereignty, which sustain and complement bio-power and which provide means by which this is contested by liberalism, as we shall see. But neither is it a denial of the function of the State as the framework for such interventions, by which its mythology is thereby embedded, as we shall also see.

On the other hand, bio-power also attempts to eliminate those groups, such as the criminal, the unemployable or imbecile, who threaten or constrain the general welfare. Although it had been connected with the police, this is the context in which Foucault's long interest in the techniques of discipline is best seen. This is not to say that only marginalised groups are its object, as discipline is also a primary technique for mainstream training and normalisation, but it is to say that it has been concerned with the elimination of crime and idleness. In this, its purpose has been to address fear and productivity through the assumption of responsibility. So it embedded the mythological idea of the State in the practices of increasingly disciplined individuals.

Although its roots were set in the devotional practices and architectural arrangements of medieval monasteries and from there gradually spread to other institutions, especially those of the State, only in the seventeenth and eighteenth centuries did disciplinary power begin to be fully realised as a technique of normalisation. The elementary goal of disciplinary power is the production of human beings who could be treated as a 'docile body,' which had also to be a 'productive body'.[40] This combination of docility and productivity has profound mythological significance, in particular since the manufacture of 'docility' is read here as representing the elimination of fear and 'productivity' is read as addressing the desire for sympathetic conditions of existence.

The paradigmatic form of discipline was to be found in the Benthamite Panopticon, where architecture produced not only a trained body but one of which there was a new, detailed, pastoral knowledge, the product of continuous surveillance and the basis of individualising, normalising judgment. Disciplinary control and the creation of docile and productive bodies are thereby connected to liberalism's freedom and security and to the rise of capitalism and its proliferating desires. The economic changes that resulted in the accumulation of capital and the political changes that resulted in the accumulation of power depended on each other for their spread, although discipline preceded the growth of capitalism.[41] So this became a technique of bio-power, whereby the population was managed in its detail, as much as globally.

Mythologically, bio-power required the fertile ground of the 'modern' populous State. As we saw in Parts I and II, the Protestant Revolution was the catalyst for widespread disruption and restructuring, including the creation of the idea of the modern State, and the start of the evolution of that idea and its location in institutional arrangements. The material we have just looked at affirms that response to the Revolution. A concept of the 'modern' State began to emerge, including a form that was absolutist and focused on its own interests and with its own rationality. Simultaneously, the new problem and opportunity of population emerged. This required a new strategy of government, a new form of government, which would not only bring order and security to this tumultuous period but would address the other mythological problem, the creation of sympathetic conditions of existence in the form of health, wealth and so on. This was the task beginning to be undertaken through bio-power, adding itself to that of police and then disciplinary techniques, each in the context of the generalisation of pastoral government. So we see the imagining and creation of the new mythological entity, with its own reason of state; the emergence of dominant interests; and the development of tactics that assumed responsibility for individuals in its claim to satisfy fear and sympathetic conditions.

Sovereignty, the State and Governmentalisation

The background to this dynamic of pastoralism, police, discipline and bio-power was the emerging bond between sovereignty and governmentality and the impact of this on the nature of the State.

For Foucault, sovereignty is founded on territory and the sovereign must always have as his aim the common welfare. Despite this positive scenario, sovereignty has for him as a circular notion, its purpose merely the exercise of its power so that all obey the law. Government, on the other hand, is distinguishable from sovereignty[42] and has positive implications. Two things flow from this difference: the nature of sovereignty which constitutes it as different; and the relationship it has with government. We shall examine these before considering Foucault's argument for the historical governmentalisation of the State.

Although sovereignty had been the mechanism of power effective under the feudal monarchy,[43] the Treaty of Westphalia (1648) was a trigger for the creation of the arrangement of the early modern, sovereign, absolutist States. The operational features of this form of power revolve around the actions and the person of the sovereign. It has its own history and effect, principally the power of death through the sovereign's exercise of ultimate authority over a territory and its subjects, and its own end in the form of its own survival.

The instrument of this right of death is the law, with its coercive sanctions, so it is a power that extracts products, wealth, services, labour and life[44] from its subjects and, at least, it strengthens the national treasury. Its law is displayed also by police regulations, for the purposes just examined. This also reinforced the patriarchal form of economy and family life, which came together within the territory in subjection to the royal sovereign household. There was no sense of population as we have just examined it, the basis of an evolving art of government, just a collection of individuals. What we have in Europe from the sixteenth to the eighteenth centuries is a patriarchalist, dispositional government of things being firmly established, featuring 'the dominance of the model of the family . . . , the subordination of the practice of government to the notion of sovereignty, and the use of law and regulation as the privileged instruments of government.'[45]

But once the sovereign form of State power was established, it began to change, although without losing its lawful fearsomeness. In the argument by Foucault, varied significantly in its presentation here, this was due to the emergence of the art of government and by which the State began to be governmentalised. We shall look at the argument for governmentalisation shortly, and the relation of the two forms of power that resulted, but first it is worthwhile reflecting on the changes that sovereignty underwent. The first was in its democratisation: its institutional form gradually began to adopt democratic, representative characteristics and a range of other, new constitutional features. We have extensively examined the evolution of the idea of these changes, essentially the establishment of an absolutist State and its gradual evolution into the supreme Constitutional State of separate powers and judicial independence, in Parts I–III but here is the corresponding change in institutional arrangements that reflect those ideas. A second change came from the relationship between sovereign power and the art of government. It was not that the latter replaced the former but that each became a condition of the other.[46] In this, sovereignty takes on new functions. For example, through the legal form of sovereignty, disciplinary practices acquire a theory of right, concealing its techniques,[47] a process which at the same time transforms the nature of sovereignty. We will look more closely at the relationship between sovereignty, discipline and government.

This brings us to the broader issue of Foucault's claims that what should concern us is not the *etatisation* of society but the governmentalisation of the State. It was the discovery of population which was the key to this emergence of a government rationality, as the basis of the move away from extractive sovereign power, from legalism and the model of the patriarchal family to a productive, scientific, strategic, economic approach. Understanding population transforms the governed from subjects into living social beings, transforms a collection of human beings into a living entity which is demographically manipulable with reference to norms and transforms awareness of individuals into knowledge of trends. It becomes an object for the positive productivity of bio-power. Society is separate from political institutions and authority.[48] The royal household is no longer the model of the government of the State and the family is reduced to an element of the population, albeit an important element. For Foucault, government takes place both outside and within the formal political institutional framework. One important feature of this is the emergence of means to secure these economic, biological and social processes.

There are other manifestations of emerging governmentality, including some which take advantage of sovereign arrangements by transforming them. We have just referred to the relationship between sovereign law and disciplinary practices. Others include the justification by sovereign arrangements of the practices of mercantilism and police. Yet another is the argument by Foucault that Hobbes' social contract theory can be understood as an attempt by the art of government to reconcile itself to the theory of sovereignty and that Rousseau sought in *The Social Contract* a general principle of government which allows for a juridical principle of sovereignty and for the elements through which an art of government can be characterised.[49] Another important but much later sympathy between sovereignty and the art of government will be seen to be the production of 'free, responsible individuals' by the processes of discipline and bio-politics, a process of production which is the result of the democratisation of sovereignty, that is in which sovereignty itself changed as a form of power.

In short, through the sixteenth and seventeenth centuries we have the dominant model of the family, the subordination of government to sovereignty, the use of law as a privileged instrument locking the government of the State into a patriarchal, dispositional form. However, with the establishment of the strong State, the concept of population, the discovery of the economy and the formation of society, a threshold is crossed beyond which government comes through economic, social, psychological and biological processes. This is the broad picture of governmentality, a new arrangement of institutions and tactics targeting the population with a new kind of knowledge and shored up in greater security. Now we see that the practices that reflect these broad changes are embedded in the lives and practices of individuals. Unlike the sovereign police fetish for regulation, which they join but do not displace, governmental regimes have individuals subjected to more intense education and training, have them brought to behave more tractably, required to live more healthily and work more productively. With the new awareness of the characteristics of population, there is thereby further assumption of individual responsibility and his practices become more closely prescribed and formed.

There are several points here of relevance to the mythological argument. First, the nature of sovereignty, particularly where it becomes closely connected to the Protestant Revolution and the consequential establishment of fearsome, absolutist States to which individuals were made widely subject, is the ground of the modern mythology of the State. Second, its subsequent democratisation into representative, constitutional arrangements tracks the evolution of the idea of the mythological State examined in Parts I and II of this work. Third, where sovereignty is connected to or camouflages the art of government, for example in the work of Hobbes and Rousseau regarding the social contract or regarding its relationship with mercantilism and discipline, it reveals its continuing presence within contemporary mythological arrangements. This applies equally to the manner in which its democratisation produces 'free, responsible individuals,' as we shall see. Finally, the regimes of welfare, training, productivity and punishment, of which police, discipline and governmentality are comprised and which are encouraged by its new understanding of population, are embedded in the individual, who has typically forgone his self-responsibility willingly. All this contributes to the assemblage of mythological arrangements and the practices which ground the claim that concerns about fear and sympathy are being conclusively addressed.

Sovereignty–Discipline–Government

As we have seen, Foucault brings these key historical elements together, stating 'So we should not see things as the replacement of a society of sovereignty by a society of discipline, and then of a society of discipline by a society, say, of government. In fact we have a triangle of sovereignty, discipline, and governmental management, which has population as its main target and apparatuses of security as its essential mechanism'.[50] He says that governmentality has pre-eminence over the others and has led to the development of apparatuses and *savoirs*.[51] Further, he adds that the State is overvalued and that its governmentalisation has 'been what has allowed the state to survive.[52]

Two points should be made about these statements. The first is the easy point that Foucault not only does not deny but in fact argues for a strong connection between sovereignty and governmentality. That is, along with disciplinary power, the democratised institutions of the constitutional State and the sovereign form of power it dispenses remain a principal means of determining the 'conduct of conduct.'

The second is more challenging, but fundamental to the mythological argument. It is that pre-eminence should be attributed to sovereign power and not to governmentality. It is the idea of the State as a fearsome, widely-empowered mythological entity, with its claims regarding fear and sympathy, which is the justification for the individual willingly complying with the embedding of practices which create him as docile and productive. These are the primary reference points and justification for forgoing self-responsibility and so for complying with prescriptions regarding conduct. Certainly, the strategies of governmentality, especially as they are applied to the phenomenon of population and how bio-political tactics are engaged, are important elements in this scenario but their primary function is to subversively affirm the idea of the mythological State and its claim to address the two primary mythological concerns. None of this precludes the argument by Foucault that there are activities which fall outside the direct action of the State or even that priorities of government determine their internal or external status but the mythological argument is that, even where the State stands back, it is required to ensure the satisfaction of the two primary mythological determinants either to retain responsibility through agents and allies, or as the legislative guarantor for example through a representative and legislative programme.[53] In short, Foucault has uncovered the complex of practices of modern power save for the mythological imperative, and so has misplaced his emphasis regarding priority.

The Long Phased Trajectory of Embodiment

It is worthwhile now to summarise the evolution of the strategies and tactics of embodiment uncovered by Foucault. As with the evolution of the idea of the mythological State canvassed in Parts I–III, the emergence of modern State practice is best seen to commence with the breakdown of the unitary theological myth due to the Protestant Revolution, which was thereby the catalyst for the creation of the modern form and structure of the European State system, initially with an absolutist theme. To establish itself, this State form, influenced by Machiavellianism, drew its own *raison d'état*, its own rationality, which required a new knowledge of its resources, problems, population. From this it developed its own sense of sovereignty, defining its territorial integrity, the supremacy of the prince and the wealth of the State, its law and policing, in effect its own constructive and extractive power. Through these the modern State began to be imprinted on individuals as a strong but increasingly fearsome entity. Following this was the emergence of the new phenomenon of population, growing in size and disorder but full of resource potential.

Sustaining this new entity of the State and its expanding population and wealth, over the long term and in a world without the imprimatur of a unitary theological myth, required new knowledge and a new strategy of management, exploitation and control. This strategy came substantially from the adoption by secular and commercial agencies of pastoral practices, with their concern for and knowledge of the characteristics of the population in breadth and in depth. This was a pre-eminently effective technique to exert more thorough control of individuals but by manufacturing their docility and productivity, thereby releasing the claims regarding the conclusive resolution of aspirations concerning sympathy and fear but at the heart of which lay a proto-typical strategy of normalisation. The ground for this was the typically willing forgoing of self-responsibility. Without losing the practices of sovereignty as a means of embedding of the idea of the mythological State, this was a phase shift in a new direction that provided a second layer of embedding. In all this, pastoralism should be seen as connected to the parallel techniques of police and discipline, reaching deep into the lives of individuals to train the body as docile and productive, and bio-power, to positively construct, control and exploit the population also down to the level of the individual. So did the new art of government, governmentality, emerge. Sovereignty also began to be gradually subject to democratisation under the influence of early liberal thought, what mythologically is the coming of the fate of the mythological magnitude into man's hands, beginning to bring it into a representative, Constitutional form. But this camouflaged the new governmentality, by which the 'free, responsible, autonomous' individual began to be manufactured, but only in the sense of the individual willingly seeking the status available in the city-citizen game on condition of subjecting himself to the shepherd-flock game, otherwise made subject by discipline as seen necessary.

Throughout this first interleaved phase shift, these elements persisted, finding the others as conditions of their own existence: Foucault's triangle of sovereignty, discipline and governmentality. For him, governmentality is pre-eminent but for the mythological argument it is only tactically pre-eminent and is so only because the former, sovereignty, remains strategically pre-eminent. Sovereignty, especially as it metamorphosed through democratisation into the 'modern' city-citizen game, is the incentive and camouflage by which individuals willingly comply with the shepherd-flock game and the bio-political, disciplinary regimes it employs. We explored this point variously in Parts I–III.

As this phase-shifted trajectory has emerged into contemporary history, there have been several endpoints in which it has become manifest, a range of not necessarily mutually exclusive State forms within which embedding has been fulfilled by further phase shifting: the welfare state, promoting fear elimination and sympathetic conditions but at the price of oppressive subjection; the liberal State in authoritarian uniform, coercive for those who do not demonstrate the capacity to become 'free, responsible, autonomous,' that is for those who do not or cannot play the city-citizen game by subjection to the shepherd-flock game; and the liberal constitutional State we examined in Parts I-III which has recently taken neo-liberal form, in which the State steps back to allow such agents as the market to impose the preferred practices and promote preferred outcomes. All are consistent with the mythological argument but, counter-intuitively for some, in the latter the State remains as guarantor, operating through its agents and allies but remaining the court of final appeal regarding fear and sympathy. This neo-liberal form has been subject to extensive examination in looking at Hayek's work. We shall take a closer look at the other two. However, it may be observed that these phase shifts together constitute a consistent, interleaved trajectory the effect of which is the subversive embedding of practices attributable to the idea of the mythological State.

In this broad context of embodiment, Foucault makes the interesting observations that the State should be seen as a mythicised abstraction and that the State would not be what it is without governmentality. However, in the context of political mythology, neither carries the truth Foucault intended. First, the transition of the State from absolutism to a democratic sovereign form and the application of pastoral power do ensure both the engagement and subjection needed to justify a claim regarding fear and sympathy, even though this is achieved through the manufacture of a docility and a productivity grounded in the willing forgoing of self-responsibility. It is thereby mythological. But it is not an abstraction. It is real in people's lives, actively validating pastoral or bio-political programmes and remaining vigilant as a court of appeal for issues associated with subjection, fear and sympathetic conditions. Second, governmentality has sustained the State but only to fulfil these mythological undertakings by the State regarding subjection, fear and sympathetic conditions. In doing so, it has shaped individuality but has integrated that individuality into the sophisticated structure of the modern state, the idea of which is thereby embedded by its bio-political tactics in the lives of individuals. Foucault himself acknowledges the State as a sophisticated structure, not above individuals and into which individuals are integrated but with a new form and under new patterns.[54]

It can now be said that, in terms of the steps identified at the beginning of this chapter necessary to demonstrate the full consistency of the idea and practice of the mythological State, beyond the demonstration of the corrective phase shifts in the trajectory of the idea of the State, the first group of two have been demonstrated. The embedding of mythological State practices, claiming to deal with fear and sympathetic conditions but undertaken through police, discipline and bio-power to manufacture docility and productivity and the premise of which is the willing forgoing of self-responsibility, have taken place across social space and deep into individual lives. We have also identified the first of a series of phase shifts in the trajectory of the practices by which this embedding of the mythological State has taken place. We have seen with Hayek that neo-liberalism subsequently brings another, through its critique of the democratic Constitutional State. The phase shift in practice promoted by that ideational form is constituted by the State's empowerment of the market and by the demands that the market makes on individual performance. In particular, it determines what are preferred conditions of existence and what therefore should be sought and how, thereby contracting specific behaviours of subjection by which the market itself is sustained. In short, there has been an embedding of mythological practice and this is best seen through its own interleaved phased shifted trajectory.

Liberalism

Now that the argument has been put regarding the first pair of steps necessary to affirm the account of the embedding of the mythological State in practice, the second can be put in place, that is the arguments for the inextricable connection between the two trajectories of idea and practice in liberalism and its location in the thought of particular thinkers of the tradition.

To this point we have alluded to but not presented a case that there is a conceptual framework within which these trajectories fit together. We will now argue that liberalism is such a framework, although republicanism would be another. We have considered a range of questions regarding liberalism, however questions remain about this political paradigm and how it is connected to the two trajectories, and their shifted phases, that we have been considering. A particular question is whether liberalism can be seen as a guiding force, as a corrective when its mythological programme strays too far from its purpose, so with a positive programme that redesigns the form by which individuals become subject in return for the claims regarding fear and sympathetic conditions. The question is whether liberalism, understood differently, is itself a face and force of political mythology, whether it can be seen as a conceptual template within which all these elements can find a place. I argue that it should be seen in this way, that is as much a principal reference point for the embedding of mythological practices through the strategies and tactics camouflaged by the idea of the mythological State as it has been of the evolution of that idea from Hobbes to Hayek.

Foucault and Liberalism

What has only been suggested in the several Parts of this work is that we can look to liberalism as a strategy driving both of the two major themes considered here, that is the emergence and repeated work on the idea of the mythological State from Hobbes to Hayek and on the practices through which this idea is embedded in the lives of individuals, uncovered by Elias and Foucault. What will now be clarified is the manner in which liberalism connects these two major themes. Doing so will show how the strong partnership between idea and practice works. It will thereby demonstrate the full coherence of the mythological account of the State.

We have seen that Foucault's account of liberalism, adopted here but extended and varied, is that it is not usefully seen merely as a political philosophy of individual freedom, nor as a set of policies, nor a way that society may represent itself. It should be viewed as a principle and method for the rationalisation of the exercise of government, a rationalisation which obeys the internal rule of maximal economy.[55] This is not an anarchic exercise but one in which the serious question is constantly asked 'what makes it necessary for there to be a government, and what ends should it pursue with regard to society in order to justify its existence?' He goes on to say that liberalism is a tool for criticising a previous governmentality to be shed, a current one to be reformed or one whose abuses must be limited. It is a scheme of governmental practice and a theme of opposition.[56] Governmentality is a pre-condition of liberalism, which stands as its pre-eminent critique.[57]

The questions raised by this are whether liberalism is best seen as a shadow of government, as Foucault suggests, providing a critique of whatever form it has taken over three centuries, or whether there is also implicit in these critiques a positive programme, as he also suggests, but a particular positive programme which is mythological in nature, which he would deny. Rejecting the characterisation of liberalism as an ideology of individual liberty, Foucault emphasises the former not the latter but it will be the argument here that we can answer each of these questions in the affirmative. Although he identifies much of the materiality of political mythology, Foucault's argument regarding the nature of liberalism as a critique of government is correct but ultimately limited.

Broadly, he sees liberalism as the veridiction of the market and as limitation by the calculation of governmentality.[58] It must know and understand the mechanisms of the economy so that this limitation of its power is not about individual freedom but is the acting on the evidence regarding these mechanisms. In this, he correctly sees that liberalism, as a general style of thought and imagination, is concerned with the positive programme of creating utopias.[59] In this context, he considers American neo-liberalism and its theory of human capital. Thereby, as machines that produce earnings,[60] individuals are subjected to training as infants[61] and to the broad mechanisms of control, constraint and coercion that disciplinary panopticism brings,[62] the purpose of which is greater productivity.[63] This is the taking charge of individuals and their well-being, health and work, their way of being, behaving and even dying.[64] It manages the conditions of what it is to be free[65] in this sense. In this, he has much to say about Hayek as a bridge between German ordo-liberalism and American anarcho-liberalism.[66] Here, freedom is, at least, to work and to consume.[67] He also sees liberalism as a means of responding repeatedly to crises in governmentality,[68] its critique, and thereby as a key strategy and tactic of government intervention.[69]

Foucault has no reference point of a practical mythology and so is without any sense that individuals might typically subject themselves to this taking charge of them in the hope that their fear and desires will be addressed. Nonetheless, although he does not provide it, his work allows an argument regarding the thoroughgoing mythological status of liberalism, even if this is against the grain of his thought.

Liberalism and Mythology

The argument here is that liberalism is an active promoter of positive programmes, and ultimately a single positive programme, and for a particular purpose which is mythological. The first evidence for this is displayed in the serial critiques presented in Parts I–III regarding the evolving idea of the State. What can be detected there, say of the critique of Hobbesian absolutism by Locke or of the 'Hobbesians' by Rousseau or of the contemporary democratic Constitutional State by Hayek, is that the critiques were in effect all intended to better realise by positive proposal the mythological idea of the State. Critique and positive reprogramming are closely linked in that the critiques have been undertaken to acknowledge weaknesses in the idea of the State, which are then corrected by the establishment of new, serial, preferred ideas for arrangements. If liberalism is a critique, it is also a positive reprogamming for the purpose of better promoting the idea of the mythological State.

The complementary evidence for this has been shown by the phase-shifting of the embedding of mythological practices along the trajectory by critique and positive programming from the individual as subject to police, discipline, bio-power and finally as the self-creating, neo-liberal 'free, autonomous, responsible individual.' Further, beneath the broad sweep of all this evidence, such writers of the Scottish Enlightenment as Adam Smith addressed a liberal critique at police and reason of state, claiming that the prosperity available from improved economic and other freedoms is not possible through a detailed knowledge of the reality to be governed, of the State itself, and that this was a desire for obsessional regulation of all aspects of life. For Smith, liberalism is a doctrine of the wise limitation and restraint on the exercise of authority by sovereign bodies.[70] Further again, under the guise of early liberal democratic thought, say of Locke, absolutism was seen as incapable of promoting the peace and prosperity—in the form of universally moral behaviour, hard work and property—which were fundamental practices of the liberal idea of freedom. That is, it failed in, in fact was itself a threat to, the manufacture of docile and productive individuals. Further still, one of the key State forms into which this form ultimately evolved, the democratic Constitutional Welfare State, was itself seen by neo-liberals to have failed in that same manufacture. The result is the claimed metamorphosis of the free, autonomous, responsible individual into the self-creating, free and flourishing individual who is argued to exist in spaces allegedly external to government, such as civil society and, especially, the market,[71] but who, as we saw with Hayek, is intended to be thereby normalised in the practices of docility and productivity.

The consequence of the totality of these interventions is the embedding of mythological ideas and practices in the lives of individuals, at two connected levels. The idea is embedded in the shared culture of ideas of which individuals are a part, always claiming that this latest version of the myth of the State will deliver greater outcomes regarding fear and sympathetic conditions, latterly through the establishment of the conditions for 'freedom, autonomy and responsibility,' on condition of forgoing self-responsibility. Second, it is this forgoing, typically willing in response to such a claim, which consequentially delivers the practices of police, discipline and bio-power, which will affirm this forgoing and the claims regarding fear and sympathy. That is, such ideas are thereby embedded in the sweated lives of individuals as docility and productivity. So these trajectories are not separate. They are fused, sharing the endpoint of promoting a more effective but debilitating myth of the State. The ideas of Hobbes, Locke, Rousseau and Hayek are reflected darkly in the practices of police, discipline, bio-power and the market.

Broadly, the conclusion to be drawn from this dual function is that the interventions of liberalism, both regarding its critiques and its positive programmes, are not merely circumstantial or fortuitously complementary but have the intended effect of allowing better claims regarding the reduction of

Governmentality, the Market and Liberalism 243

fear and the realisation of sympathy in return for the forgoing of self-responsibility. That is, liberalism is properly seen as a principal *persona*, a face and force, of the mythology of the State, operating through the phase-shifted trajectories of idea and practice. Whenever it is argued that either the idea or its embedding is failing to sustain the myth, that is regarding the State and the subjection-fear-sympathy nexus, liberal interventions will be engaged to critique the failing aspect of government so that it can then offer a new positive programme. So is the myth of the State sustained.

These trajectories are thereby functionally connected in that it is liberalism which guides the repeated repairs and supposed improvements of the idea of the mythological State, which act as a camouflage or disguise for the evolved embedding of this idea in practice through subversive strategies: the touchstone of the liberal State is the idea of freedom, which requires the claims about the elimination of fear and the creation of sympathetic conditions, which are in turn based on the requirement of subjection; it is this subjection which is the ground for embedding of practices that manufacture docile and productive individuals. Without the seduction of the idea, the practices would not be realised.

It can now be stated that the third of the steps outlined at the start of this chapter as necessary to complete the mythological account of the State and its embedding in practice, and demonstrate its coherence, has been satisfied. That is, this parallel series of phase shifts, these two trajectories, are integrally connected, and so form a coherent whole comprised of idea and practice.

Before we conclude this work by addressing the fourth and final step, there are two related issues that need to be dealt with, issues that elaborate further the nature of liberalism and the institutional forms it assumes. The related liberal notions of freedom, responsibility and autonomy have already featured variously in our consideration of the thought of the 'Hobbesians,' Kant, Hayek and Foucault. This party is an uncomfortable one on this issue, so some residual issues regarding their respective positions need to be clarified. Then finally, to emphasise both the diversity and the dark side of liberalism, that is to emphasise that liberalism does not merely take a form to promote the purity of freedom, responsibility and autonomy, two State forms which were referred to earlier, the liberal authoritarian and Welfare States, will then be examined.

Freedom, Responsibility and Autonomy

The discussion of liberalism has revealed the intimate connection between the two broad themes with which this work has been concerned, the idea of the mythological State (Parts I–III) and the subversive creation of the mythological subject (Part IV), how that idea is embedded in individual practice. However, there is an issue that needs to be dealt with, so that presumptions about it do not erroneously disturb the explanation of that ultimate connection. This is the issue of the 'free, autonomous and responsible' individual, the proud boast of popular liberal thought. But it is also significant for the notion of liberalism preferred here, this time at the micro level of the individual.

One can say that the effect of discipline and governmentality is generally contrary to the claim that there is an autonomous, consenting individual behind arrangements of the State, since individuals are significantly impacted by such forces as the powerful effect of such rationalities and so are not autonomous.[72] Such a claim about individual autonomy and consent is important because, on the one hand, the tradition of the social contract, from Hobbes at least to Kant, relies upon it and, more generally, it is the argument of this work that a social contract plays a central role in the mythological account of the State. On the other hand, the view of power as resting on autonomous consent is seen, for example by Hindess, to have no place in Foucault.[73] If Foucault's thought is to be compatible with the mythological account as is being proposed here, these disparate points, say between Hobbes and Foucault, need to be related.

The position adopted in this work is that mythology recasts the relationship between Hobbes and Foucault somewhat. Certainly, discipline and governmentality are important strategies by which mythological ideas are embedded in the practices of individuals, so there can be no autonomous individual in the sense of a person unaffected by the heteronymous features of existence, including the effects of political power, who simply makes rational political decisions. But here lies the difference from the position that sees Foucault as radically different from Hobbes. Whether because of the individual's own existential fear or because the exercise of political power by dominant interests has artificially generated fear and desire to secure their own advantage, the repeated instances of forgoing of his self-responsibility by each non-autonomous individual is in a clear sense a consent to the existence of the thereby empowered political magnitude, conditional upon that entity claiming to satisfy its responsibilities regarding fear and sympathy. This is so despite the fact that the individual is already disposed to create and affirm archetypal mythological entities and irrespective of the training to which an individual is subjected to regard the State as a realisation of the archetype. The primal nature of fear and desire for sympathetic conditions of existence are consciously held, even if their realisation in the State form is the result of disposition and training. Hence the consent to the validity of the mythological State, while not by autonomous individuals, is real.

Such consent, generated by this real or induced fear and affirmed by training, recognises that each will subject himself to the change in ourselves needed to establish a regime which addresses fear and sympathetic conditions. It is even willingly accepted by consenting individuals that the State should be colonised by dominant interests, who will make the claims regarding fear and sympathetic conditions, even if the change to which we subject ourselves will be somewhat against our individual interests. The problem that arises, as it must with the forgoing of self-responsibility in the first instance, is that dominant interests push these regimes more widely and deeply into social space and attempt to cause change that is mostly against individual interests. They do so by ensuring compliance through artificial generation of fear and inducement of desire for what is presented as improved conditions of existence. Even if there is benefit from it for some, there is more than some exploitation: there is Foucauldian governmentality, discipline and subjectivation. By forgoing self-responsibility, individuals are ensnared in an arrangement significantly of their own making, to which they are disposed and with which they typically willingly comply. In essence, the non-autonomous consenting individual is the mythological individual. In this, Hobbes and Foucault are not on the same ground but neither are they so far apart as is commonly argued.

There is a related argument regarding this ground that finds a place for both autonomous and non-autonomous consent within the mythological arrangements. This is that the claims about autonomous consent are just the public face of political arrangements that allow a claim of legitimacy but mask a form of consent which is non-autonomous and which is the foundation of the political mythology. That is, there was increasingly the public, popular liberal myth of institutions of true representation of autonomous individuals in a social contract, fair judicial interpretation of the law and the execution of popularly determined policy, each reflecting the preference of the autonomous, consenting individual, that is over which he has some real control. This Foucault might justifiably describe as related to 'a mythicised abstraction,' even though it persists as a salve to what lies beneath. What does lie beneath is the real mythology of a fearsome legislature of dominant interests, of hard justice that especially protects those interests and its dispersal through strategies that embed practices that promote global management and detailed discipline, almost universally embraced by non-autonomous individuals on the promise that the fear-sympathy nexus is being addressed. Control, to the extent that it exists, only relates to the interests to which individuals will make themselves subject in the hope that their concerns about fear and sympathy will be addressed. Seen in this light, Foucault's work is compatible with a mythological interpretation of Hobbes and his successors in the tradition. That is, individuals are more ready to accept the forgoing of their self-responsibility if they can claim that they do so by their own decision as autonomous persons, even if their consent is of a different kind, of subjection motivated by fear and desire. Both of these are reason in the service of mythology.

In essence, being 'free, autonomous and responsible' is a condition without fear and of sympathetic conditions. That is the ideology of the liberal myth. But this condition camouflages and is realised by the governmental creation of docile and productive individuals. This, not 'freedom, autonomy and responsibility,' is what the absence of fear and the creation of sympathetic conditions means. This is the practice of liberal mythology, in which 'free, autonomous consent' is only to the subjection that will return those conditions. It is the function of the mythological liberal State to ensure the realisation of the latter but relying on the guise of the former.

The Liberal Authoritarian and Welfare States

We will now briefly examine the two contemporary State forms referred to earlier, the liberal authoritarian and welfare states. The first is relevant because it shows the wider ground occupied by the particular account of liberalism preferred here, that is rather than merely being an ideological reference point. The second is relevant because it is background to the appearance of neo-liberalism, and especially Hayek, whose work we will revisit shortly. Each has mythological significance. In this we will refer to, but at times being critical of, the work of Dean and Donzelot but each should be seen as related to or extensions of the thought of Foucault. However, the broader point made by this examination is that liberalism is the ground on which has been constructed a range of State forms. These include forms that display such characteristics as authoritarianism and oppression as readily as they claim to protect individual freedom and autonomy and to promote and recognise responsibility.

Liberalism should not be associated simply with the idea of the representative, constitutional, democratic State which it tends to claim as its own. This complements the point repeatedly made throughout Parts I–III, that the constitutional democratic State itself features foundational characteristics of submission that lead to the practices of discipline and bio-power, transparently veiled in these two forms, as the price of forgoing self-responsibility.

The Liberal Authoritarian State

The question here is the relationship between authoritarianism and the liberal State and, in particular, whether these are compatible notions. Dean presents arguments that fulfil the thought of Foucault in the affirmative. However, as with Foucault himself, there are some issues here that need to be addressed. We shall consider and clarify these within the mythological context. The position in this work is that there is certainly no inconsistency between the notions of liberalism and authoritarianism, even where the latter takes an extreme form.

Dean's broad argument is that authoritarian governmentality, like liberal rule, is assembled from bio-politics and sovereignty, and, also like liberalism, coheres with the governmentalisation of the State.[74] It encompasses those liberal practices that are applied to populations who do not display responsible freedom and it also refers to non-liberal rule that operates through obedient rather than free subjects. Liberalism is a form of the shepherd-flock and city-citizen games, that is a combination of bio-political pastoral power and sovereignty that justifies bio-politics and discipline. In this context he says that liberalism can't check these elements and that much that is illiberal is done with the best of bio-political intentions.[75]

To examine this illiberality, Dean focuses on the liberal programme's appeal to a free subject active in his own government.[76] The illiberality comes in the form of either a division that excludes certain categories of individuals from the status of the autonomous and rational individual or one by which the individual is divided against himself in striving to realise these prescribed characteristics. Referring to Mill's argument regarding the capability of the subject being improved through education, including in an inter-cultural context, Dean sees liberal rule as consistent with authoritarian colonial rule. Similarly, those groups argued to be bereft of autonomy or responsibility have long been subjected to liberal disciplinary or bio-political programmes.[77] But he draws the line at eugenics, as an ultimate form of improving the population as a whole, denying that it can be accommodated within a liberal rationality.[78] This is because, for him, liberalism depends on a bio-politics of the population which is combined with a democratisation of sovereignty, thereby resolving the shepherd-flock and city-citizen games.[79]

Dean then considers non-liberal rule. Although he sees both liberal and non-liberal forms of rule as based on the combination of bio-politics and sovereignty and allows that the technologies of the latter were present in the former,[80] he categorically separates liberalism, as a democratised sovereignty founded on the liberty of the juridical subject[81] making choices or having aspirations, from non-liberal forms of sovereignty, such as the authoritarianism of Nazism. The result is that for him bio-politics can have a light side and a dark side.[82] Further, liberal government necessarily contains a division between those capable of being responsible and free and those not, the latter requiring despotic rendering to develop these characteristics. The latter justifies the 'good despot' but who is in danger of transforming into the patron of containment and coercion.[83] Hence Dean's warning for liberals to be ever alert, protecting government limited by the rule of law that secures the rights of citizens and which optimise the processes of life.[84]

The mythological account of liberalism, as opposed to this post-Foucauldian account, agrees with such arguments regarding the danger posed by liberal forms of government, but applies much wider caveats. In fact, it views a number of these arguments differently. First, liberal rule does not operate through free subjects but through obedient subjects, in that the forgoing of self-responsibility is heavily disposed to the acquisition of characteristics of docility and productivity. Second, for Dean the shepherd-flock and city-citizen games have equivalent status, whereas in the mythological account there is a more strategic relationship between the two: the former, the practical mythological process, is camouflaged by the latter, the process which is claimed to create conditions of freedom and autonomy and which thereby acts as the seductive force in relation to claims regarding fear and desire for sympathetic conditions.

Further, mythology sees liberalism as comprised of, and so could not ever check, pastoral power and sovereignty. Consequently, bio-political strategies cannot have any 'best intentions' or have a light side. Regarding the issue of eugenics and the incompatibility of that with liberal principles, democratisation is seen mythologically as only the metamorphosis of absolutism, so, when combined with bio-political management of the population, is capable of a eugenic programme, as colonial racial policy demonstrates. In relation to the liberal rule of law and individual rights, the mythological account regards these, when conditioned by the forgoing of self-responsibility that liberalism entails, as a demonstration that the fate of the magnitude has come into man's hands and thereby as the talisman of docility and productivity.

More broadly, even though Dean argues for conditions under which there is a separation of liberal from non-liberal rule, he still displays a questionable sympathy for the former. As we saw in the Introduction, 'raison d'état, will, decision, friend and enemy' are on the same mythological continuum as 'contract, consent, liberty, law, rights.' In fact, the difference between them is only the extent to which the magnitude has been delivered into the hands of man whereby he is willingly seduced into forgoing self-responsibility in return for the claim that fear and desire will be dealt with through 'freedom, autonomy and responsibility,' when in fact it is dealt with thru 'docility and productivity.' That is, liberal and non-liberal rule are both authoritarian but at different locations along the mythological axis. So, when self-responsibility has been forgone, there can be no good despot, no optimising of the processes of life and ultimately no separation of liberal from non-liberal rule. Accepting that the practices of pastoralism are a common element between them, as in Dean, mythology goes further and understands them as having this deeper, single root in the basic instincts of humanity.

The Welfare State

The Welfare State, as Dean indicates, 'was more an ethos of government or its ethical ideal and much less . . . a set of accomplished reforms and completed institutions. Above all, the welfare state was to be the *telos* . . . of particular problematisations, interventions, institutions and practices concerning unemployment, old age, disability, sickness, public education and housing, health administration, and the norms of family life and childrearing.'[85]

The roots of the Welfare State can be argued to go back to the ancient notion of pastoral care and to the sovereign notion of police, as well as to the notion of managing a population productively, with the emergence of government. It has a long history, coextensive with government in its varying forms. Its purpose was increasingly the provision for both general and individual subsistence, health, well-being, wealth and so on. But the Welfare State, an emanation of the late modern era of government, employs the new marker of totality, at least conceptually and significantly in policy and practice. It was this totality that generated the neo-liberal response that we shall revisit shortly.

Governmentality, the Market and Liberalism 249

For Donzelot, the problem of the State emerged with the 1848 revolution and its fracturing of right which had centred the republican ideal and eliminated enemies of the Republic on the left. Rights were to have ended despotism and installed a reign of harmony.[86] This fracture was between the right to work and right to property and its solution was the notion of solidarity, distinct from sovereignty. Solidarity accorded well with the new State interventions into the family through schooling, protection of minors and divorce provisions. But breaking into this sphere of natural association, seen by liberals and traditionalists as taking precedence over the State due to its prior existence, needed a criterion. The concept of organic solidarity justified this intervention.[87] The critiques of this State form from the Left were based on the arguments for social and cultural emancipation, that the welfare State was paternalistic social control that relied on the uniformity of hierarchy and bureaucracy, sometimes coercive and oppressive but often unresponsive to the needs of individuals and communities.[88]

The mythological implications of the welfare state are clear. It is an arrangement which could claim to provide for optimal security and to address the irrationalities of the impact on the individual of the economic. On the condition of individuals making themselves subject to Rousseauean social solidarity under the guarantee and intervention of the State, it would address fear and the creation of sympathetic conditions of existence for all. However, the level of its intrusion invited liberal critique and positive reprogramming.

The point to be drawn here is that the liberal State can and has adopted a range of forms, from those which emphasise an authoritarian approach to those with strong welfare credentials and those which promote neo-liberal principles. Each of these, upon close examination, reveals mythological presumptions, as we have argued in Parts I–III.

FOUCAULT, HAYEK AND THE INTEGRATED TRAJECTORIES OF THE LIBERAL MYTHOLOGICAL STATE

We are now in a position to take the final step, reaffirming the connection of the dual phase-shifted liberal trajectories and their mythological function regarding the State, by briefly revisiting their association in the thought of key figures in the tradition, especially Hayek. This latter connection may seem counter-intuitive, in that the liberal idea of the State comprises the repeatedly reinvented ideas of freedom, autonomy and responsibility and the neo-liberal idea presents these in a radically individualist form. However, as we have seen, they disguise the liberal practice of manufacturing docility and productivity and this disguise plays a key role in inducing individuals to forgo their self-responsibility, thereby ensuring their willing participation in sustaining the mythological State.

Employing Foucault's identification of the techniques of governmentality but extending these and using them in a fresh manner, we have traced the subversive embedding of the idea of the modern State within the practices of individuals, arguing that governmentality emerged and was sustained by its association with the mythological State. There are lateral arguments that reinforce this position. These include that, better than Foucault's own notion of governmentality, mythology explains both the ongoing agonistic process of politics, particularly in regard to the emergence of dominant interests; the willingness of individuals to forgo their self-responsibility to the governmental processes, whereas in Foucault the individual seems characterised by passive subjection; and that there is a dynamic among the secular authorities that adopted pastoral practices, a dynamic that favours the State and its dominant interests.

Broadly, the trajectory of this embedding has paralleled in practice the movement of the idea of the State through a series of phase shifts and has similarly been guided by a notion of liberalism not merely as an ideology nor even only as a critique but also as a means of positive programming. This reveals liberalism as a key *persona* of mythology, since its interventions have been concerned with the promotion of both the idea and these practices such that there can be claims regarding fear and sympathetic conditions. The endgame of this liberal strategy regarding the fear-sympathy nexus has been the creation of docile and productive individuals while presenting them as 'free, autonomous, responsible' citizens. We referred to the evidence for this in the analyses of Locke, Rousseau and Kant but Hayek brings together these two trajectories even more strongly, thereby making transparent through embedded market practice the inherent ideas of liberalism which the liberal State was unable to effect.

Through this trajectory there has been an implicit admission that the modern State, from its early sovereign form and by its subsequent long association with the techniques of governmentality, has failed to realise these aspirations, both in its idea and in its practices. This failure is recognised, despite the State retaining its ultimate fearsomeness through realigned functions, by Hayek's programmed transfer of more of its fate into man's hands in the form of a market. This market, agent and partner of the State, takes on a function of creating docile and productive individuals through its own internal dynamics. This is so even though it is likely to increase fear, adding the market to the State as a source of fear, and more distant as it is from the final court of appeal in the form of the mythological State. It is an attempt, disguised by the idea of the liberal State of freedom, to eliminate fear and satisfy desire by, respectively and subversively, making the individual docile and productive. Hayek does this by critiquing the idea of the established democratic Constitutional State, arguing that it has been overtaken by dominant interests, especially by organised labour, and is set firmly on the path towards socialism and totalitarianism, State forms which promote docility but not productivity. He then suggests a reforming, or reprogramming, of its institutions that will better realise the ideology of freedom, autonomy and responsibility. At the same time, he argues for the market as the dominant economic and social forum, through which will be realised peace and prosperity, but the dynamics of which require the individual to acquire personal practices typified by docility and productivity. In his full integration of the idea and practice of the mythological State, his is therefore a paradigm case, among such others as Locke, Rousseau and Kant, for the camouflage of the trajectory of practice by the trajectory of the idea.

We can say now that we have addressed the fourth of the steps outlined at the start of this chapter as necessary to demonstrate the full coherence of the mythological account of idea of the State and its embedding in practice, that is, the two trajectories are not only integrally connected but this connection is evident in the thought of key political theorists of the tradition.

CONCLUDING REMARKS

Foucault does open the door to how this process of embedding has occurred across both geographical and social space and even deeper into the lives of men and women. This is a matter of how, in Blumenberg's terms, there has been a dispersal of myth and how Wittgenstein's notion of normalisation works. Yet this is not a simple embedding of mythological practice by conscious learning. Rather, it is one in which the ideas, which in return for forgoing self-responsibility claim to address the fear-sympathy nexus, disguise practices that are systematised to produce docility and productivity, respectively. The State has failed by itself to realise these practices, despite the disguise, so has more recently through liberal critique and re-programming aligned itself with the market as agent to do so.

We have said that this is all part of the performance of a tradition which has since Hobbes promoted two bound ideas and sought to give these ideas consistency: one, that it is possible to be free of fear and have one's desires for sympathetic conditions satisfied; two, that the price of these freedoms is the forgoing of self-responsibility to the mythological magnitude of the State and the dominant interests which will claim to assure these aspirations. Hayek takes his place within the company as an active contributor to the trajectory of this long liberal tradition as part of its latest phase of critique and positive programming, the ultimate purpose of which is to sustain the idea of that magnitude. Foucault's work, extended and varied here, has been used to show that Hayek, apart from being a recent contributor to the trajectory of the liberal idea of the State, has promoted a new method to embed it in practice. But in doing so, he has merely offered the latest version of the strategy by which individuals are induced to make themselves subject, now more directly to an agent of the State than to the State itself, in return for claims that fear and desire can be addressed.

We can now say that we have not only satisfied the four steps outlined as requirements at the beginning of this chapter but have also fully explored the three-part proposition with which this entire work commenced: first, that strategic variations in the application of liberal principles have sustained the idea of the mythological State, the foundation of this idea being that forgoing responsibility for oneself to the State will ensure that our fear and desire are dealt with through the creation of freedom, autonomy and responsibility to others; second, that, while the variations in that idea have been pursued over time, strategic variations in the application of liberal practices have actually dealt with fear and desire through the manufacture of docility and productivity; and third that individuals typically forgo their self-responsibility willingly and submit to such practices due to the seductive power of the mythological idea of the State.

So we can now make more interesting final statements and make them more forcefully. That is, the ontologies of Blumenberg and Wittgenstein not only intersect with the rationalities of Foucault, but that the ontology of Blumenberg, as amended here, and that of Wittgenstein are complementary and both are materialised through the civilising practices revealed by Elias and by the liberal rationalities unmasked by Foucault, as extended and varied here, although not in a straightforward way. What this intersection reveals is that the strategy of liberalism, operating in the dual fields of idea and practice, repeatedly repairs and positively reprogrammes, and thereby sustains, the mythological State, subversively creating mythological individuals.

This intersection also helps us resolve the puzzle of the apparent flaw in the mythology raised in the early chapters, that is that the magnitude tasked to eliminate fear is flawed because it is itself created as a source of fear. We can now make sense of this apparent contradiction through this subversion: the State may claim to deal with fear and desire by establishing conditions of individual freedom, responsibility and autonomy but this is not contradicted by its continuing fearsomeness. This fearsomeness is the means by which it deals with fear and desire for sympathetic conditions, that is by manufacturing docility and productivity, principally through the strong inducement of the willing but by imposition on the unwilling. These are the inseparable dual trajectories of liberalism, working publicly and ideologically at one level but subversively at another so that the mythological State will be sustained, even though the archetype will never be realised.

Notes

NOTES TO CHAPTER 1

1. It is not common to see Locke as a figure of the Enlightenment, a cultural and intellectual current typically regarded as gaining influence from the 1680s to the 1780s. However, the *Essay Concerning Human Understanding* was published in 1690 and the *Two Treatises of Government* in 1689. This at least puts him on the cusp of the Enlightenment and certainly locates him as a figure of modernity.
2. Beyond these external criticisms, important work has been done concerning the internal dynamics of the Enlightenment. Ian Hunter, for example, argues that it is important to distinguish between Kantian political metaphysics and the civil philosophy of Pufendorf and Thomasius. Hunter's work will be considered below.
3. H. Blumenberg *The Legitimacy of the Modern Age*, Introduction by translator Robert Wallace pp. xxv–xxx and p. 97, 99.
4. I. Kant, 'An Answer to the Question: What Is Enlightenment?' in *The Cambridge Edition of the Works of Immanuel Kant—Practical Philosophy*, pp. 17–18.
5. R. A. Nisbet, *The Sociological Tradition* (Heinemann, 1966) p. 10.
6. Ibid., p.14.
7. Ibid., pp. 24–29.
8. Ibid., pp. 36–42.
9. I. Berlin, *The Roots of Romanticism* (Chatto and Windus 1999), p. 58.
10. Ibid., p. 68.
11. Ibid., pp. 69–70.
12. Ibid., pp. 77–78.
13. Ibid., p. 79.
14. Ibid., p. 81.
15. H. Blumenberg, *The Legitimacy of the Modern Age*, p. 429.
16. Ibid., p. 433.
17. Berlin, *The Roots of Romanticism*, pp. 146–147.
18. H. Blumenberg, *Work on Myth* (MIT, 1985), Translator's Introduction, pp. xix–xxiii.
19. Op. cit., pp. 116–117.
20. Ibid., pp. 119–120.
21. In exploring this and some other questions, we will consider certain propositions by Blumenberg, including his response to Lowith and Schmitt, but the emphasis given to these propositions is not a Procrustean presumption in their favour. It is an examination of whether they are affirmed by the

evidence presented in this work. In fact, the arguments presented here are at variance with his propositions.
22. Blumenberg *The Legitimacy of the Modern Age*, p. 90.
23. Ibid., p. 479.
24. Ibid., pp. 27–29.
25. Ibid., Introduction, p. xxiii.
26. Ibid., pp. 96–97, 99, 138; see also Elizabeth Brient *The Immanence of the Infinite—Hans Blumenberg and the Threshold to Modernity* (Catholic University of America Press, 2002), p. 75.
27. The notion of tradition used here is drawn from the Platonic concept of *pheme* as a form of speech which is collective in nature and sustained over the long term, the object of which is to set the past apart and make it paradigmatic for the present and future; see Luc Brisson *Plato the Myth Maker* (Chicago 1998) pp. 32–33. It is as fabricators and transmitters of such collective speech that the political theorists examined here will be considered. In effect, this is an examination of what it means to work within a political tradition. In that context, it is not necessarily the specific intentions of the theorist, psychological or historical, that are to be examined but what their work amounts to, individually and collectively. This is not merely the effect of them considering certain questions in historical, political context but also how doing so has connected them to traditions other than the political. One such other tradition is the mythological and the coincidence of these two traditions is the central focus here.
28. Governmentality is Foucault's understanding of the process of government as institutions, apparatuses and *savoirs*. It is dealt with at length in Chapter 11.

NOTES TO CHAPTER 2

1. L. Brisson, p. 13; see also p. 17, where Brisson makes the related point that myths never relate to an actual or recent experience, and so can never be validated, but are intended to evoke a recollection preserved in the collective memory of the community over a long period of time.
2. Ibid., p. 32.
3. In doing so, writing presents itself as complete reality although it is merely a copy, ibid., pp. 33, 36, 37.
4. Ibid., p. 45, where Brisson refers to the *Timaeus* at 21c4–d3 (see Plato *The Collected Dialogues* (Bollingen, Princeton 2002) p. 1156).
5. Ibid., p. 55.
6. Ibid., pp. 67, 69, 73.
7. Ibid., p. 75, 74.
8. Ibid., p. 78, where he refers to the *Phaedo* at 77d5–78a2 (see *Collected Dialogues*, p. 61), also Brisson, p. 117.
9. Ibid., p. 99.
10. Ibid., p. 109, where Brisson refers to the *Republic*, III 379a1 (*Collected Dialogues*, p. 625).
11. Ibid., pp. 119–120.
12. Ibid., p. 121.
13. See Plato *Timaeus*, 26c7–d4 (*Collected Dialogues*, p. 1160).
14. Op. cit., p. 131.
15. Ibid., pp. 137–138.
16. Ibid., p. 131, the reference to the *Timaeus*, 26c7–d5 (see Plato, *Collected Dialogues*, p. 1160).
17. Ibid., p. 139.

18. H. Blumenberg, *Work on Myth,* pp. 3–4.
19. Ibid., pp. 13–14.
20. Ibid., pp. 37, 42.
21. Ibid., pp. 142, 120.
22. Ibid., p. 31.
23. Ibid., pp. 124–125
24. This engagement is achieved through 'reverence,' 'seeking favour,' 'provocation,' 'forcing commitment,' 'even of malicious cunning,' 'good conduct,' 'absolute obedience' as wilful surrender, 'efforts to obtain favour,' 'compensatory actions' and 'exchange of gestures.' These are strategies that 'belong to the repertory of ways of coercing a power that it is all-important to make sure of,' ibid., pp. 16, 20, and 22.
25. Ibid., pp. 19, 20, 23.
26. Ibid., p. 21.
27. Ibid., p. 4.
28. Ibid., pp. 30, 135.
29. Ibid., p. 5.
30. Ibid., pp. 5–6.
31. Ibid., pp. 42–43.
32. Ibid., pp. 34–35.
33. Ibid., pp. 31, 62–64.
34. Ibid., pp. 26, 118.
35. Ibid., pp. 68–69.
36. Ibid., p. 67.
37. Ibid., p. 124.
38. Ibid., p. 64.
39. Blumenberg *Legitimacy of the Modern Age,* Introduction, pp. xxiv–xxv.
40. Op. cit., p. 32.
41. Ibid., pp. 113–114.
42. Ibid., p. 67, see also p. 160.
43. Ibid., p. 291.
44. L. Brisson, p. 55.
45. See B. Hindess, *Discourses of Power* (Blackwell, 2001), pp. 14–15, 25.
46. Blumenberg *Work on Myth,* pp. 6–7.

NOTES TO CHAPTER 3

1. The word 'modern' is used here although this is not the place to trace the elements common in the political tradition back to Plato which Hobbes then reassembled in a manner that would resolve the problems with which he was confronted. However, any examination of the history on the idea of the State reveals that, although he assembled these ideas in a particular manner, he was working with ideas that generally were well established in a long tradition of theorising about the State. His ideas were not *sui generis.* See O. Gierke, *Natural Law and the Theory of Society* (Beacon 1957) especially pp. 50–61, and Q. Skinner, *The Foundations of Modern Political Thought—Volume II, The Age of Reformation* (Cambridge 1996) pp. 184, 287.
2. See Q. Skinner, *Visions of Politics—Volume III, Hobbes and Civil Science* (Cambridge 2002) p. 329.
3. Ibid., p. 323.
4. H. Blumenberg, 'An Anthropological Approach to the Contemporary Significance of Rhetoric,' in *After Philosophy—End or Transformation* (MIT 1989) p. 438.

Notes

5. Ibid., p. 438.
6. H. Blumenberg, *Work on Myth*, p. 333.
7. Ibid., p. 6.
8. H. Blumenberg, "An Anthropological Approach to the Contemporary Significance of Rhetoric", pp. 438–439.
9. M. Oakeshott, Introduction to T. Hobbes, *Leviathan* in *Hobbes on Civil Association* (Liberty Fun 1975) p. 8
10. Ibid., pp. xi–xii.
11. Q. Skinner, *Visions of Politics—Volume III, Hobbes and Civil Science*, pp. 19, 33, 80, 204, 270, 285, 287.
12. T. Hobbes *Leviathan* (Cambridge 1991) p. 3.
13. Op. cit., p. 238ff.
14. Hobbes *Leviathan*, p. 491.
15. Ibid., pp. 88, 120, 128.
16. Christopher Hill, *The Century of Revolution 1603–1714* (Routledge, 1989), pp. 150–151.
17. Op. cit., p. 154.
18. Ibid., p. 153.
19. Hobbes, *Six Lessons to the Professors of Mathematics*, p. 336, quoted by Skinner in *Visions of Politics*, p. 306.
20. Skinner, op. cit., pp. 8–9.
21. Hobbes *Leviathan*, pp. 70, 117.
22. Ibid., p. 60.
23. Skinner, *Visions of Politics*, pp. 80–85; see Hobbes *Leviathan*, p. 483, regarding both reasoning and eloquence.
24. Op. cit., p. 92.
25. Ibid., pp. 32–33.
26. Ibid., p. 120.
27. Ibid., p. 9.
28. Ibid., p. 231.
29. Ibid., pp. 112, 92.
30. Ibid., p. 120.
31. B. Kriegel, *The State and the Rule of Law* (Princeton 1995) pp. 39–40.
32. Op. cit., p. 93.
33. Skinner, *Visions of Politics*, p. 207.
34. Ibid., p. 192.
35. Hobbes *Leviathan*, p. 113.
36. Ibid., p. 120.
37. Ibid., p. 129.
38. O. Gierke, *Natural Law and the Theory of Society 1500–1800*, pp. 60–61.
39. Op. cit., p. 120.
40. Ibid., p. 491
41. Ibid., pp. 120, 219.
42. Ibid., p. 91.
43. Ibid., pp. 89–90.
44. Ibid., p. 148.
45. Ibid., pp. 149, 150.
46. Ibid., pp. 484, 491.
47. Ibid., pp. 120–121, 148.
48. Ibid., p. 231.
49. 'he hath the use of so much Power and Strength conferred on him, that by terror thereof he is inabled to conforme the wills of them all, to Peace at home, and mutuall ayd against their enemies abroad,' ibid., pp. 120–121.
50. Ibid., pp. 86–87.

51. L. Brisson, *Plato the Myth Maker,* specifically his comment regarding myth, p. 17.
52. Skinner, *Visions of Politics,* p. 218 at note 67.
53. Hobbes *Leviathan,* p. 204.
54. Ibid., pp. 119–120, 146.
55. Ibid., p. 89.
56. Ibid., pp. 120–121.
57. Ibid., p. 469.
58. Ibid., p. 230.
59. O. Gierke, *Natural Law and the Theory of Society 1500 to 1800,* pp. 60–61.
60. Op. cit., p. 231.
61. Ibid., p. 186.
62. This will be against the sense of the argument by J. Dunn in *The Political Thought of John Locke* (Cambridge, 1995). Dunn claims that Locke 'merely and blandly ignored' Hobbesian arguments in the *Two Treatises of Government* (see p. 83). Although Dunn, like Laslett, is correct in asserting that Filmer and not Hobbes was Locke's target, it is enough for this work to argue that Locke's target was absolutism, an enthusiasm that Hobbes and Filmer shared. As Laslett states: 'Nevertheless Hobbes and Filmer shared nearly every one of the attributes of absolutism as it was rejected by English parliamentarians—will as the source of all law and the form of all authority, the necessity of perpetual and absolute submission to the arbitrary dictates of an invisible sovereign, the impossibility of mixed government. In so far as Locke's writing was directed against these things, it would not seem to have mattered whether it was Hobbes or Filmer he had in mind,' in P. Laslett, Introduction to Locke's *Two Treatises of Government* (Cambridge, 1988), p. 70. But Filmer constructed no political society from his absolutist views, and therefore had no direct political mythology. Hobbes did. It is the political society of Hobbes, drawn from the absolutism he shares with Filmer, which is of mythological interest, so it is proper to look at the mythological implications of Locke's rejection of absolutism by looking at that rejection in the context of Hobbes, more so than Filmer.
63. L. Strauss, *Natural Right and History* (Chicago, 1965), pp. 221, 222, 227–229, 231–233 (especially), 249, 250 (especially).
64. Dunn *The Political Thought of John Locke,* p. 158, 219.
65. Op. cit., p. 233, where Strauss talks of Locke's construction of his own 'leviathan,' and p. 250, where he states that Locke 'Moved by the same spirit [as Hobbes] identifies the rational life with the life dominated by the pain which relieves pain.'
66. Certainly Dunn thinks so. See pp. 132, 215, 217, 219, 221–222, 228, 233–234, 250, 262–265.
67. Waldron emphasises Locke's Christianity rather than his specific Calvinism in *God, Locke and Equality,* p. 12.
68. Op. cit., pp. 256, 258, 259.
69. *Two Treatises of Government,* II s.134, p. 355.
70. Ibid., II s.12, p. 275.
71. Ibid., II s.41, pp. 296–297.
72. Waldron *God, Locke and Equality* pp. 5, 12.
73. Dunn, pp. 249–250.
74. *Two Treatises,* I ss.41, 42, pp. 169, 170.
75. Dunn, pp. 252–253.
76. Ibid., p. 61.
77. R. Filmer, *Patriarcha and other Political Works of Sir Robert Filmer* (Oxford 1949) p. 71.

78. *Two Treatises*, I ss.41–43, pp. 169–171.
79. Dunn, p. 67, where he refers to *Patriarcha*, pp. 273, 157; see also *Two Treatises*, II s.25, p. 286.
80. Dunn, p. 68.
81. Filmer *Patriarcha*, pp. 232, 233, 234.
82. Op. cit., p. 73.
83. *Two Treatises*, II ss.224, 225, pp. 414–415.
84. Op. cit., pp. 44–46, for Locke's views, and regarding which see *Two Treatises*, ss.159–168, pp. 374–380; see also Waldron, p. 135.
85. *Two Treatises of Government*, II s.209, pp. 404–405.
86. Ibid., II s.134, pp. 355–356.
87. Ibid., II s.198, pp. 397–398.
88. Ibid., II s.205, p. 402.
89. Ibid., II s.138, p. 361.
90. Ibid., II s.158, p. 373.
91. Dunn, p. 89, but Waldron, at p. 54, argues that the direct relevance of the 'Great Chain of Being' argument for Locke is exaggerated, if not wrong.
92. Ibid., p. 94.
93. *Two Treatises*, II s.145, p. 365.
94. Waldron, pp. 5 and 12.
95. Op. cit., II s.14, p. 276, and s.100, p. 333.
96. Ibid., II s.14, p. 276.
97. Ibid., II s.172, pp. 382–383.
98. Ibid., II s.19, p. 280.
99. Ibid., II s.105, p. 336, and s.74, p. 316; see Waldron, p. 39, regarding Locke's view of the equal importance of the authority of mothers.
100. Dunn, pp. 117–119.
101. *Two Treatises*, II s.54, p. 304.
102. Although Waldron does argue that Locke's sentiments were more democratic than has been generally accepted, see J. Waldron, pp. 84, 116.
103. Dunn, pp. 122–125; Waldron emphasises that in Locke there is a strong link between basic equality and religious doctrine, p. 19.
104. Dunn, pp. 126–129; Waldron argues that Locke's views about consent cannot be read to exclude those without property, for example, from the political process, pp. 120, 125–126, 136.
105. *Two Treatises*, II s.119, p. 347, and s.122, p. 349.
106. Ibid., II s.119, p. 347.
107. Ibid., II s. 61, p. 308, and s.62, p. 309.
108. Dunn, p. 140.
109. Op. cit., II s.151, p. 368.
110. Ibid., II s.192, p. 394.
111. Ibid., II s.192, p. 394.
112. Waldron argues that majority consent does not deny equality in the process of participation (p. 130), although he struggles heroically in arguing that Locke did not intend to exclude such groups as married women from such participation (p. 124); cf. *Two Treatises of Government*, II s.2, p. 268.
113. Op. cit., II s.7, p. 271.
114. Ibid., II s.164, p. 377, ss.143–148, pp. 364–366.
115. Dunn, p. 153.
116. *Two Treatises*, II ss.158, p. 373, and s.164, p. 377.
117. Ibid., II ss.162–166, pp. 376–378.
118. Ibid., II s.158, pp. 373–374.
119. Ibid., I ss.86 and 88, pp. 205–207, II s.6, pp. 270–271.

120. Ibid., II s.11, pp. 273–274.
121. As Dunn argues: 'It was because Locke so readily felt the structures of social control in the society in which he lived to be legitimate that he rejected their abuse with such intensity. They were so stable, so sheltering, so reassuring. . . . The withdrawal of security was unendurable not only because men had come to depend so completely upon its existence, but because their dependence had itself conferred such deadly power upon their rulers . . . the trust which men instinctively feel towards the good ruler is so complete that the force which they consign to him (which is in its physical composition and its moral status their own force) comes to be overwhelming. The trust which they feel derives from the peace which he provides for them. The "trust" with which he is "entrusted" is the preservation of this peace. Law, consequently, is the antithesis of force. It represents ease as against anxiety, liberty as against subjection. It is the guarantor of all the elements of a fully human life in the complex societies of Locke's day. If the guarantee is reneged on, the betrayal is total,' Dunn, pp. 167–168, where he refers to *Two Treatises*, II s.209, pp. 404–405.
122. *Two Treatises*, II s.8, p. 272, and s.11, pp. 273–274.
123. Ibid., II s.17, p. 279, and s.20, p. 281.
124. Ibid., II s.198, pp. 397–398.
125. Ibid., II s.242, p. 427. This is the 'appeal to Heaven' reference, which Dunn claims can only mean the judgement of the Houses of Parliament (see p. 182, footnote 1); cf. Waldron, p. 226.
126. Ibid., II s.224, pp. 414–415.
127. P. Laslett, Introduction to *Two Treatises of Government*, pp. 23–24.
128. Ibid., II s.6, pp. 270–271.
129. Dunn, pp. 261, 260.
130. Waldron rejects Macpherson's claim that Locke is to be read as allowing economic inequality in such a manner that he could not take seriously the equal humanity of those experiencing that inequality (see p. 174). This rejection is consistent with his broad argument that Locke's Christianity is the ground for his radical egalitarianism (see p. 6).
131. Waldron, p. 5, and Dunn, p. 58ff.
132. *Two Treatises,* II s.140, p. 362, and s.138, p. 360.
133. Ibid., II s.35, p. 292.
134. Ibid., I s.45, pp. 172–173.
135. Ibid., II s.41, pp. 296–297.
136. Dunn, p. 231.
137. Op. cit., II s.208, p. 404, and s.223, p. 414.
138. This is a claim against Waldron in that, although he rightly argues Locke's tolerance for representative government (see Waldron, p. 116), there is little evidence that Locke himself supported anything like universal suffrage; see *Two Treatises,* II s.132 (p. 354), also Dunn, pp. 146, 225, 250, 265. Either way, it is not at all a litmus issue for the major theme of this work. Even if Waldron were right and Locke's egalitarianism extended to a tolerance of something approaching universal suffrage, all it would mean is that Locke actually trod further down the road of refining the absolute Hobbesian magnitude, to bring it into the hands of man, than I am arguing he did.
139. *Two Treatises* II s.123, p. 350.
140. Locke saw the state of nature more as a state of hunger than one of violence. From this derives the inalienable right of every individual to property; ibid., II ss.6 and 8, pp. 270–272; see also Gierke, *Natural Law,* pp. 101, 103.
141. Ibid., II s.49, pp. 301.
142. Dunn, p. 211.

143. Ibid., II s.50, pp. 301–302.
144. It is not being fastidious or anachronistic to note that Locke was a stockholder in the slave-trading Royal Africa Company, despite his claim that slavery was the antithesis of legitimate political authority; see Waldron, pp. 204–205.
145. L. Strauss, *Natural Right and History*, p. 231.
146. Neither did he argue for any equal access to property, Dunn, p. 266.
147. See Dunn, p. 146.
148. *Two Treatises*, II ss.149, 150, pp. 366, 367.
149. Ibid., II s.147, p. 365.
150. Ibid., II s.150, p. 367; s.153, p. 369.
151. See H. Blumenberg, *Work on Myth*, pp. 13–14,18.
152. *Leviathan*, pp. 53, 70.
153. Charles-Louis de Secondat, Baron de Montesquieu, *The Spirit of the Laws* (Cambridge, 1989), bk.11.4, p. 155.
154. Ibid., p. 155.
155. Ibid., bk.11.6, pp. 159–160.
156. Ibid., bk.19.27, pp. 325–333, 325; also p. 326.
157. P. Manent, *An Intellectual History of Liberalism* (Princeton, 1995), p. 60.
158. This is the position adopted by Manent, ibid., p. 63.
159. Ibid., pp. 63–64.
160. Ibid., p. 62.
161. Ibid., p. 62.
162. B. Kriegel *The State and the Rule of Law* p. 76.
163. Elie Halevy, *A History of the English People in the Nineteenth Century*, trans. E. Watkins and D. Barker (New York, 1949), 1:35.

NOTES TO CHAPTER 4

1. J.-J. Rousseau, *The Social Contract*, in *The Social Contract and Other Later Political Writings* (Cambridge, 1997), p. 146.
2. J.-J. Rousseau, *A Discourse on the Origin of Inequality*, in *The Discourses and Other Early Political Writings* (Cambridge, 1997), p. 135.
3. Ibid., p. 151.
4. Ibid., p. 152.
5. J. J. Rousseau, *Discourse on the Sciences and Arts*, in *The Discourses and Other Early Political Writings*, pp. 25–26.
6. Op. cit., p. 151.
7. *Social Contract*, p. 58. Regarding his reference here to 'politicians,' the editors observe that 'politicians' is now commonly translated 'political theorists.' The editors of the Everyman edition state that 'Rousseau is referring to those seventeenth century political theorists, Hobbes and Pufendorf in particular (but not Locke), who had thought of sovereignty as consisting in a number of distinct rights, which must, if they are to be effective, be in the hands of the same person or body (or else, in the view of some others, need not be so).' See especially Hobbes *Leviathan*, ch.18, and see J.J. Rousseau *The Social Contract and Discourses* (Everyman 1990), p. 350.
8. Manent makes the point, interesting at least for the broad argument here that Locke and Rousseau should be seen in the context of the Hobbesian enterprise; *An Intellectual History of Liberalism*, p. 37.
9. Regarding the need for legislators, see *Social Contract*, p. 68; regarding the disorder in the natural state, ibid., p. 49.
10. Ibid., pp. 54–55.

Notes   261

11. Ibid., p. 67.
12. Ibid., *Letter to D'Offreville*, in *The Social Contract and Other Later Political Writings*, p. 262.
13. *Discourse on the Origin of Inequality*, p. 144.
14. Ibid., p. 175; *Social Contract*, p. 41.
15. *Letter to Franquieres*, in *The Social Contract and Other Later Political Writings*, p. 279.
16. *Geneva Manuscript* of the *Social Contract*, p. 155; *Government of Poland*, in *The Social Contract and Other Later Political Writings*, p. 226.
17. *Discourse on the Origin of Inequality*, pp. 187–188.
18. *Political Economy*, in *The Social Contract and Other Later Political Writings*, pp. 9, 29.
19. *Social Contract*, p. 61.
20. Although acknowledging the independence of the concept of order, Rousseau sees its realisation as possible only through the establishment of law; *Social Contract*, pp. 66–67.
21. *Discourse on Inequality*, p. 127; *Discourse on the Sciences and Arts*, p. 28.
22. Ibid., p. 186.
23. Ibid., p. 170.
24. Ibid., p. 183.
25. Ibid., p. 170.
26. Hobbes, *Leviathan*, pp. 71, 119.
27. Rousseau, *Government of Poland* in *Social Contract and Other Later Political Writings*, p. 188.
28. *Discourse on Inequality*, p. 218.
29. Rousseau outlines the kind of life this could be, although man misused the opportunity, in his description of the evolution into society; ibid., p. 164.
30. *Social Contract*, p. 83.
31. Ibid., p. 57.
32. See Introduction by Victor Gourevitch to the *Discourses and Other Early Political Writings*, p. xviii.
33. 'Now it is solely in terms of this common interest that society ought to be governed,' op. cit., p. 57.
34. Ibid., p. 67.
35. *Discourse on Inequality*, p. 166.
36. Op. cit., p. 61.
37. Ibid., p. 124.
38. Ibid., p. 78.
39. Hobbes *Leviathan*, pp. 145–148.
40. Op. cit., pp. 53–54.
41. Ibid., p. 54; *Political Economy*, in *The Social Contract and Other Later Political Writings*, p. 13.
42. Ibid., p. 67.
43. Cf. *Social Contract*, p. 108, and Montesquieu, *Spirit of the Laws*, 11.4, p. 156.
44. Hobbes *Leviathan*, pp. 184, 224.
45. *Political Economy*, pp. 8–9, and *Social Contract*, p. 95.
46. *Social Contract*, p. 67; *Political Economy*, p. 10.
47. Ibid., p. 149.
48. This is the complement to the obedience of the individual to a law he gives himself, see ibid., p. 50.
49. Ibid., p. 69.
50. *Discourse on Inequality*, pp. 183–184.
51. Op. cit., p. 107.
52. Ibid., p. 86.

53. Ibid., pp. 69, 71.
54. Ibid., p. 69.
55. Montesquieu, *Spirit of the Laws*, p. 114.
56. Op. cit., p. 141.
57. Ibid., p. 229.
58. *Discourse on the Sciences and Arts*, pp. 13 and 56, respectively; *Discourse on Inequality*, p. 164.
59. *Government of Poland*, p. 193.
60. Viroli adopts such a generous interpretation in *Jean-Jacques Rousseau and the 'Well-ordered Society'* (Cambridge, 1988), pp. 205–206.
61. Montesquieu, *Spirit of the Laws*, Bk.19, Ch.12, p. 314.
62. *Social Contract*, pp. 141–142.
63. Ibid., p. 150.
64. Ibid., p. 78.
65. *Political Economy*, p. 18; *Social Contract*, p. 57.
66. *Discourse on Inequality*, p. 152.
67. *Social Contract*, p. 124.
68. Ibid., p. 69.
69. Ibid., p. 124.
70. *Geneva Manuscript*, p. 156.
71. Op. cit., p. 69; P. Manent, *An Intellectual History of Liberalism*, p. 77.
72. Ibid., p. 84.
73. Ibid., p. 69.
74. Ibid., p. 61.
75. Ibid., p. 150.
76. I. Berlin, *Two Concepts of Liberty*, in *Liberty*, ed. Henry Hardy (Oxford, 2002), p. 208.
77. Constant quoted in P. Manent, *An Intellectual History of Liberalism*, p. 87.
78. *Social Contract*, p. 115.
79. Ibid., pp. 51, 52.
80. Ibid., pp. 83, 84.
81. Ibid., p. 49; *Discourse on Inequality*, pp. 167–170.
82. Ibid., p. 71.
83. Montesquieu, *Spirit of the Laws*, pp. 310, 169.
84. That is, where the individual comes, or is brought, to understand that his personal interests are the common interests of the general will.
85. *Geneva Manuscript of the Social Contract*, p. 159.
86. Ibid., p. 161.
87. *Discourse on Inequality*, pp. 126–127.
88. *Letter to Mirabeau*, in *The Social Contract and Other Later Political Writings*, p. 270.
89. *Geneva Manuscript*, p. 155.
90. *The State of War*, in *The Social Contract and Later Political Writings*, p. 166.
91. *Letter to Mirabeau*, in *The Social Contract and Later Political Writings*, p. 270.
92. *Discourse on the Sciences and Arts*, pp. 102–103.
93. *Social Contract*, p. 150.
94. B. Constant, *Principles of Politics* in *Benjamin Constant: Political Writings* (Cambridge, 1988), pp. 175, 177.
95. *Geneva Manuscript*, p. 156, 157; *Social Contract*, p. 150.
96. *Social Contract*, pp. 109, 106, and 108.
97. *Essay on the Origin of Languages*, in *The Discourses and Other Early Political Writings*, p. 254.
98. Ibid., p. 267, and *Discourse on Inequality*, p. 127.

99. *Social Contract,* p. 124.
100. *Political Economy,* p. 9.
101. Op cit., pp. 60, 121, 155.
102. See M. Viroli, *Jean-Jacques Rousseau and the Well-ordered Society,* p. 227.

NOTES TO CHAPTER 5

1. H. S. Reiss, Introduction to I. Kant, *Political Writings* (Cambridge, 2002), pp. 21, 22, 24, 26, 27, 28.
2. P. Manent, *An Intellectual History of Liberalism* pp. 66–67 (his italics).
3. The following analysis has benefitted not only from direct consideration of the Kantian text but also, among other sources, from the analysis of by Ian Hunter in *Rival Enlightenments* (Cambridge, 2001).
4. I. Kant, *Groundwork of the Metaphysics of Morals* in *Practical Philosophy,* ed. Mary Gregor (Cambridge, 1996), at p. 47. Unless otherwise stated, subsequent references to Kant are from this source.
5. Hunter, p. 294.
6. Ibid., p. 302.
7. Ibid., p. 306.
8. Ibid., p. 303, where Hunter refers to the *Groundwork of the Metaphysics of Morals,* in *Practical Philosophy,* at p. 73.
9. Ibid., p. 333, where Hunter refers to the *Metaphysics of Morals,* in *Practical Philosophy,* at p. 459.
10. Ibid., p. 334, where Hunter refers to the *Metaphysics of Morals,* at ibid., p. 480.
11. See I. Kant, *On the Common Saying: That May Be Correct in Theory, But It Is of No Use in Practice*––Section II, 'On the Relation of Theory to Practice in the Right of a State (Against Hobbes),' pp. 290–304.
12. Ibid., p. 302.
13. I. Kant, *Metaphysics of Morals,* p. 565.
14. J. Rawls, *A Theory of Justice,* p. 256.
15. Ibid., p. 264.
16. Ibid., p. 264; W. Kersting, 'Kant's Concept of the State,' in *Essays on Kant's Political Philosophy,* (Chicago 1992 H. Williams, ed.) p. 149.
17. I. Kant, *Groundwork of the Metaphysics of Morals,* pp. 92–93.
18. J.J. Rousseau, *A Discourse on the Origin and Foundations of Inequality,* p. 140.
19. Ibid., p. 141.
20. I. Kant, *Groundwork of the Metaphysics of Morals,* pp. 43, 44.
21. I. Kant, *On the Common Saying: That May Be Correct in Theory,* pp. 291–292.
22. I. Kant, *Metaphysics of Morals,* pp. 415–416.
23. Ibid., pp. 457–458.
24. I. Kant, *On the Common Saying: That May Be Correct in Theory,* p. 291 (his emphases); see also *Metaphysics of Morals,* pp. 457–459.
25. Kant *Metaphysics of Morals,* pp. 451–452.
26. Ibid., p. 456 (his emphasis).
27. Ibid., p. 455 (his emphasis).
28. Ibid., pp. 456–457.
29. Ibid., pp. 458–459.
30. I. Kant, *On the Common Saying: That May Be Correct in Theory,* p. 295.

31. See, respectively, *Metaphysics of Morals*, pp. 457–458, 459, 462; *Social Contract*, pp. 110, 112, 114, and 115.
32. Ibid., p. 459.
33. Ibid., p. 459.
34. Ibid., pp. 461–462.
35. Ibid., p. 462.
36. Ibid., p. 463.
37. *Social Contract*, p. 112.
38. I. Kant, *On the Common Saying: That May Be Correct in Theory*, pp. 296–297.
39. *Metaphysics of Morals*, p. 468.
40. Ibid., p. 469.
41. Ibid., p. 469.
42. Ibid., p. 470.
43. Ibid., pp. 473, 474, 476.
44. J.J. Rousseau, *Political Economy*, pp. 9, 13, and *Social Contract*, pp. 60, 62, 124; and I. Kant, *Groundwork of the Metaphysics of Morals*, pp. 67, 82.
45. J.J. Rousseau, *Social Contract*, p. 60, and I. Kant, *On the Common Saying: That May Be Correct in Theory*, pp. 294–295.
46. I. Kant, *Groundwork of the Metaphysics of Morals*, pp. 64, 65, 76, 90, 372, and 582.
47. Ibid., pp. 95, 166, where Kant states that 'lawgiving of its own is freedom in the positive sense.'
48. G. Hegel, *On the Scientific Ways of Treating Natural Law*, in *Political Writings* (Cambridge, 1999) pp. 122–123.
49. F. Nietzsche, *Human, All Too Human*, in *On the Genealogy of Morality* (Cambridge, 2003), pp. 133–134.
50. I. Hunter, *Rival Enlightenments*, pp. 23, 306.
51. H. Blumenberg, *An Anthropological Approach to Rhetoric*, in *After Philosophy—End or Transformation*, p. 450.
52. I. Hunter, *Rival Enlightenments* pp. 28, 34, 37ff., 58–59, 65, 148ff., 274ff.
53. Rousseau, *Social Contract*, pp. 49–50.
54. Kant, *Metaphysics of Morals*, p. 459.
55. Ibid., p. 461.
56. *Social Contract*, pp. 50, 122, see also pp. 58, 123.
57. Ibid., p. 56.
58. *On the Common Saying: That It May Be Correct in Theory*, p. 295; *Metaphysics of Morals*, p. 458.
59. *Metaphysics of Morals*, p. 458.
60. Ibid., p. 459.
61. S. Mendus, *An Honest But Narrow-Minded Bourgeois?* in *Essays on Kant's Political Philosophy*, p. 174ff.
62. Rousseau, *Political Economy*, pp. 19–20.
63. Kant, *On the Common Saying: That May Be Correct in Theory*, p. 292 (my emphasis).
64. P. Pettit, *Republicanism*, p. 19.
65. Kant, *Towards Perpetual Peace* in *Philosophical Writings*, p. 324.
66. Kant, *Metaphysics of Morals*, p. 457.
67. W. Kersting, 'Kant's Concept of the State,' in *Essays on Kant's Political Philosophy*, p. 156.
68. *Social Contract*, p. 120.
69. *Metaphysics of Morals*, pp. 463, 465.
70. W. Kersting, 'Kant's Concept of the State,' in *Essays on Kant's Political Philosophy*, p. 163.

71. Op. cit., p. 378.
72. Kant is not fully committed to the principle of equality, as he makes special concessions for the 'sensibilities of the upper classes,' giving extra weight to the hurt to their pride if one has to kiss the hand of one from a lower class or regarding the painful effect on the vanity of one such person, ibid., pp. 473–474.
73. Ibid., p. 474.
74. Ibid., p. 476.
75. Ibid., p. 474 (my emphasis)
76. Ibid., p. 474.
77. Ibid., p. 473
78. See O. Gierke, *Natural Law and the Theory of Society 1500 to 1800*, pp. 135, 153.
79. *On the Common Saying: That May be Correct in Theory*, p. 306ff.
80. See H. Blumenberg, *An Anthropological Approach to Rhetoric* in *Philosophy—End or Transition*, p. 449.
81. See Kant, *Religion and Rational Theology*, quoted in I. Hunter, at p. 354
82. Rousseau *Discourse on the Origin and the Foundations of Inequality among Men*, in *The Discourses and Other Early Political Writings*, pp. 140, 141.
83. *Groundwork of the Metaphysics of Morals*, p. 98.
84. See S. Smith, *Defending Hegel from Kant*, in *Essays on Kant's Political Philosophy*, p. 273.
85. Ibid., p. 274.
86. I. Hunter, *Rival Enlightenments* pp. 184ff and 333.
87. Ibid., p. 278.
88. Ibid., p. 365, see also p. 277.
89. Ibid., pp. 303, 336, 375.
90. Ibid., p. 23.
91. Ibid., p. 300.
92. Ibid., p. 354, where Hunter also refers to Kant's *Religion and Rational Theology*, at p. 129.
93. Ibid., pp. 308–309.
94. *Groundwork of the Metaphysics of Morals*, pp. 79–80.

NOTES TO CHAPTER 6

1. C. Kukathas and P. Pettit, *Rawls—A Theory of Justice and Its Critics*, p. 8.
2. J. Rawls, *A Theory of Justice*, pp. 4–5
3. S. Mulhall and A. Swift, *Liberals and Communitarians*, pp. 3–33, especially pp. 10ff, 21ff, and 25ff.
4. Op. cit., pp. 137, 138.
5. Ibid., p. 5.
6. Ibid., p. 128.
7. Ibid., p. 139.
8. J. Rawls, *Collected Papers*, pp. 257–258.
9. Op. cit., p. 235ff.
10. Ibid., p. 145.
11. *Collected Papers*, p. 260.
12. Op. cit., p. 143.
13. Op. cit., p. 59.
14. *A Theory of Justice*, p. 302; *Collected Papers*, p. 227.
15. Ibid., p. 122.
16. Ibid., p. 153.

17. Ibid., pp. 167, 168, 171. This principle is used otherwise in this work, that there need not be any exhaustive rational process before decisions are made but, accepting that reasons are diffuse and that non-rational factors influence decisions, there is a wager that engaging positively with others is more likely to produce mutually acceptable results. See H. Blumenberg, *An Anthropological Approach to Rhetoric, in After Philosophy—End or Transformation*, p. 447. See pp. 448 and 449.
18. Ibid., pp. 151, 177.
19. *Collected Papers*, p. 180.
20. Op. cit., p. 224.
21. *Collected Papers*, p. 277.
22. Op. cit., p. 275.
23. Ibid., p. 298.
24. Ibid., p. 212.
25. *Collected Papers*, pp. 122, 126.
26. Ibid., p. 183ff.
27. *A Theory of Justice*, p. 391.
28. Ibid., p. 396.
29. *Collected Papers*, p. 304.
30. Ibid., p. 319.
31. Ibid., p. 451.
32. Ibid., p. 449.
33. Ibid., p. 241.
34. Ibid., p. 233.
35. *A Theory of Justice*, pp. 571, 572.
36. Ibid., p. 574.
37. R. Nozick, *Anarchy, State and Utopia*, p. 10.
38. Ibid., p. 155.
39. Ibid., p. 163.
40. M. Sandel, *Liberalism and the Limits of Justice*, pp. 127, 129, 132, 161, 164.
41. M. Walzer, *Spheres of Justice*, pp. 313, 314; and A. MacIntyre, *After Virtue—A Study in Moral Theory*, pp. 244–245.
42. Sandel, *Liberalism and the Limits of Justice* pp. 164, 103.
43. Ibid., p. 172.
44. *Collected Papers*, pp. 431–432 footnote 17.
45. *A Theory of Justice*, p. 137.
46. Ibid., p. 200.
47. *Collected Papers*, pp. 305–306.
48. Sandel, p. 152.
49. Op. cit., p. 306.
50. *A Theory of Justice*, p. 581.
51. *Collected Papers*, pp. 307–309.
52. Ibid., pp. 319, 331.
53. Ibid., pp. 388–389, including footnote 2.
54. Ibid., p. 389.
55. Ibid., p. 421.
56. Ibid., pp. 426–427.
57. Ibid., p. 395.
58. Ibid., p. 427.
59. Ibid., p. 306.
60. Ibid., p. 494.
61. Ibid., pp. 449.
62. Ibid., pp. 316, 319.

63. Ibid., p. 450.
64. *A Theory of Justice*, pp. 167–171.
65. Ibid., p. 224.
66. *Collected Papers*, pp. 179–180; see *A Theory of Justice*, p. 224.
67. See T. Hobbes, *Leviathan*, p. 120; see also the consideration of Aquinas and Dante by O. Gierke, *Political Theories of the Middle Age*, pp. 8–9.
68. *A Theory of Justice*, p. 520.
69. *Collected Papers*, p. 470; *A Theory of Justice*, p. 527; see also O. Gierke, *The Political Theories of the Middle Age*, p. 26, for the detail of this and at p. 27 for reference to the influence that the organic analogy had on Dante, Nicholas de Cusa and others.
70. O. Gierke, *The Political Theories of the Middle Age*, pp. 27–29, where the genesis of the elements of these concepts is to be found *inter alia* in Aquinas and Marsilius of Padua; then see *A Theory of Justice*, pp. 212, 456, 457, 458, 527, 528, 529.
71. *A Theory of Justice*, p. 15.
72. Ibid., p. 574.
73. Ibid., p. 575.
74. Ibid., p. 575.
75. Blumenberg *The Legitimacy of the Modern Age*, p. 179.
76. *A Theory of Justice*, p. 62.
77. Ibid., p. 153.
78. Ibid., p. 153.
79. See Blumenberg, *An Anthropological Approach to the Contemporary Significance of Rhetoric*, pp. 447–449.
80. Ibid., pp. 435–436.
81. Ibid., p. 449.
82. *A Theory of Justice*, p. 153.
83. Ibid., p. 139.
84. My emphasis, as it is my interpretation of the role of the malevolent opponent.
85. *Collected Papers*, p. 615.
86. *A Theory of Justice*, p. 11.
87. Ibid., p. 252.
88. Ibid., p. 256.
89. *Collected Papers*, p. 512.
90. Op cit., p. 253.
91. Ibid., p. 561.
92. Ibid., p. 560.
93. Ibid., p. 254.
94. Ibid., p. 253.
95. Ibid., p. 252.
96. Ibid., pp. 195, 274, 265.
97. Ibid., p. 252.
98. W. Kersting, 'Kant's Concept of the State,' in *Essays on Kant's Political Philosophy*, p. 153.
99. Op. cit., p. 253.
100. Ibid., p. 62.
101. Ibid., p. 260.
102. S. Smith, 'Defending Hegel From Kant,' in *Essays on Kant's Political Philosophy*, p. 270.
103. Op. cit., p. 256.
104. Ibid., p. 224.
105. Ibid., p. 259.

106. M. Sandel, *Liberalism and the Limits of Justice*, p. 62.
107. A. MacIntyre, *After Virtue*, pp. 232–233.
108. *A Theory of Justice*, pp. 522, 259–263.
109. *Collected Papers*, p. 582.
110. *Political Liberalism* (Columbia 1993) p. 146.
111. M. Walzer, 'Philosophy and Democracy,' in *Political Theory* 9, 3 (1981): p. 395.
112. M. Walzer, *Spheres of Justice*, p. 5.
113. J. Rawls, *Political Liberalism*, p. 189.
114. Ibid., p. 14.
115. *Collected Papers*, p. 451.
116. Stephen Mulhall and Adam Swift, *Liberals and Communitarians*, p. 222.
117. *Political Liberalism*, p. 64.
118. Ibid., pp. 100–101.
119. Ibid., p. 216.
120. Ibid., p. 97.
121. *Collected Papers*, pp. 305–306.
122. Ibid., p. 305.
123. Ibid., pp. 307, 306.
124. Ibid., p. 319.
125. *A Theory of Justice*, p. 447.
126. Ibid., p. 92.
127. Ibid., pp. 433, 425.
128. Ibid., pp. 275–277.
129. Ibid., p. 298.
130. Ibid., p. 351.
131. Ibid., p. 355.
132. *Collected Papers*, p. 451.
133. Ibid., p. 424.
134. *Political Liberalism*, pp. 139–140.
135. Ibid., pp. 143–144.
136. *A Theory of Justice*, pp. 407–416.
137. *Political Liberalism*, pp. 143–144.
138. *Collected Papers*, p. 395.
139. Op Cit., p. 68.
140. See Mulhall and Swift, *Liberals and Communitarians*, p. 225.
141. Op Cit., pp. 31, 146.
142. M. Sandel, *Liberalism and the Limits of Justice*, p. 211.
143. See O. Gierke, *Natural Law and the Theory of Society*, pp. 134–135.
144. *Political Liberalism*. pp. 139–40; see also *Collected Papers*, p. 578.
145. See Mulhall and Swift, *Liberals and Communications* p. 238.
146. Op Cit., p. 215.
147. Ibid., p. 62.
148. Ibid., p. 152.
149. *A Theory of Justice*, p. 253.

NOTES TO CHAPTER 7

1. E. Feser, Introduction to *The Cambridge Companion to Hayek* (Cambridge University Press, 2006), p. 2.
2. B. Caldwell, 'Hayek and the Austrian Tradition,' ibid., p. 18.
3. R. Scruton, 'Hayek and Conservatism,' ibid., p. 229.

4. F. A. Hayek, *Law, Legislation and Liberty*, 3 Volumes (Routledge, 1998), 2:100.
5. Ibid., 2:132.
6. Ibid., 2:166 at note 19.
7. Ibid., 1:17–18; 2:4, 5, 21, 42.
8. Ibid., 1:17, 82; 2:22.
9. Ibid., 2:37–38.
10. Ibid., 2:123.
11. Ibid., 2:2, 31.
12. Ibid., 2:23.
13. Ibid., 1:113–114.
14. Ibid., 2:22.
15. Ibid., 1:19.
16. Ibid., 1:135.
17. Ibid., 2:21.
18. Ibid., 2:5.
19. Ibid., 2:24, 27, 54.
20. Ibid., 3:5; 2:34.
21. Ibid., 3:130.
22. Ibid., 2:35, 36, 38.
23. Ibid., 2:41.
24. Ibid., 1:72
25. Ibid., 1:113.
26. Ibid., 3:111.
27. Ibid., 1:112–113.
28. Ibid., 2:5, 22.
29. Ibid., 1:90.
30. Ibid., 1:131.
31. Ibid., 1:73.
32. Ibid., 1:114.
33. Ibid., 1:132.
34. Ibid., 1:134.
35. Ibid., 3:111.
36. Ibid., 3:3.
37. Ibid., 1:17.
38. Ibid., 2:36.
39. Ibid., 2:31.
40. Ibid., 1:132; 2:34.
41. Ibid., 1:142; 3:41.
42. Ibid., 1:132–134.
43. Ibid., 1:36.
44. Ibid., 1:36.
45. Ibid., 1:35.
46. Ibid., 1:37, 38.
47. Ibid., 1:39, 47–48.
48. Ibid., 1:45.
49. Ibid., 1:45.
50. Ibid., 1:45.
51. Ibid., 1:41; see also his comment that the operation of the market, an emblematically spontaneous order for Hayek, exemplifies this: 'The market order in particular will regularly secure only a certain probability that the expected relations will prevail,' ibid., 1:42.
52. Ibid., 1:44, 51.

53. Ibid., 1:47.
54. Ibid., 1:50.
55. Ibid., 1:50.
56. Ibid., 1:48, 49.
57. Ibid., 1: 51
58. Ibid., 1:50.
59. Ibid., 1:46, 48.
60. Ibid., 1:47.
61. Ibid., 1:48.
62. See L. Wittgenstein, *On Certainty* 95; also M. Kober, 'Certainties of a World Picture,' in *Cambridge Companion to Wittgenstein,* pp. 418, 420, 423, 424–425.
63. See Wittgenstein *Nachlass* MS 124 213–221; MS 165 103–104; MS 166 4
64. Hayek 1:47.
65. Ibid., 3:99, 100.
66. Ibid., 1:131; 3:46
67. Ibid., 3:131.
68. Ibid., 2:2.
69. Ibid., 3:130.
70. Ibid., 1:51; 2:106.
71. Ibid., 2:142–143; 2:87.
72. Ibid., 3:54.
73. Ibid., 1:131.
74. Ibid., 3:41, 47.
75. Ibid., 1:47.
76. Ibid., 3:22.
77. Ibid., 3:22.
78. Ibid., 3:25, 26.
79. Ibid., 2:6.
80. Ibid., 2:6.
81. Ibid., 3:90; 2:7.
82. Ibid., 2:95.
83. Ibid., 3:96, 144, 90.
84. Ibid., 3:89.
85. Ibid., 1:130, 138, 143, 144; 3:105.
86. Ibid., 3:12.
87. Ibid., 3:32, 129.
88. Ibid., 1:2; 3: 151,
89. Ibid., 3:110, 111.
90. Ibid., 2:101, 102.
91. Ibid., 3:10; 2:9, 64, 67–70, 99; 1:2, 142.
92. Ibid., 2:106.
93. Ibid., 1:33; 3:94, 166; 2: 72.
94. Ibid., 3:167–168.
95. Ibid., 2:107.
96. Ibid., 2:2.
97. Ibid., 3:74.
98. Ibid., 2:9; 3:124, 166.
99. Ibid., 2:99.
100. Ibid., 2:124
101. Ibid., 2:72, 91, 120.
102. Ibid., 3:93.
103. Ibid., 2:119.

104. Ibid., 2:74.
105. Ibid., 3:81.
106. Ibid., 3:77.
107. Ibid., 3:84.
108. Ibid., 3:83.
109. Ibid., 3:80.
110. Ibid., 3:85.
111. Ibid., 3:57.
112. Ibid., 2:98.
113. Ibid., 2:115.
114. Ibid., 2:72.
115. Ibid., 2:75.
116. Ibid., 2:81.
117. Ibid., 3:89.
118. Ibid., 2:95, 107; 3:77.
119. Ibid., 2:71.
120. Ibid., 2:99.
121. Ibid., 2:95.
122. Ibid., 3:61.
123. Ibid., 2:84.
124. Ibid., 2:103–104.
125. Ibid., 2:131.
126. Ibid., 2:131.
127. Ibid., 3:151.
128. Ibid., 2:104.
129. Ibid., 1:48.
130. Ibid., 2:41.
131. Ibid., 3:123, 131.
132. Ibid., 1:91.
133. Ibid., 3:129.
134. Ibid., 1:91.
135. Ibid., 1:72.
136. Ibid., 3:31.
137. Ibid., 3:22, 111, 151, 152; 2:37, 65, 87.
138. Ibid., 3:5.
139. Ibid., 2:37.
140. Ibid., 2:73.
141. Ibid., 3:166; 2:71, 72.
142. Ibid., 2:144.
143. Ibid., 2:99.
144. Ibid., 2:2, 3.
145. Ibid., 3:132, 109, 123, 129, 22, 24.
146. Ibid., 3:5.
147. Ibid., 1:47.
148. Ibid., 3:55.
149. Ibid., 1:48.
150. Ibid., 3:77.
151. Ibid., 2:95.
152. Ibid., 3:88.
153. Ibid., 2:107.
154. Ibid., 2:112.
155. Ibid., 3:89, 96; 2:99.
156. Ibid., 3:166.
157. Ibid., 3:77, 80, 81, 86.

158. Ibid., 3:77, 144; 2:71, 82, 99.
159. Ibid., 2:117, 144.
160. Ibid., 3:90.
161. Ibid., 3:55.
162. Ibid., 2:83.
163. Ibid., 2:68, 69.
164. Ibid., 2:71, 72, 74, 75, 81, 94.
165. Ibid., 2:101, 102, 103, 104.
166. Ibid., 2:104.
167. Ibid., 2:91.
168. Ibid., 2:24, 25, 42.
169. Ibid., 1:17, 18, 44.
170. Ibid., 1:135.
171. Ibid., 1:135.

NOTES TO CHAPTER 8

1. P. Pettit, *Republicanism*, (Oxford, 1997) p. 10.
2. Ibid., p. 23.
3. Ibid., p. 18.
4. Pettit argues that it is possible to be dominated without being interfered with. For example, that I may be a slave but with a benign master who doesn't interfere or 'that I am cunning or fawning enough to be able to get away with doing whatever I like.' The problem with such an argument is that if I can get away with whatever I like, that is if I can do anything I like including leaving his household and wandering the earth, I am not a slave. If I'm prevented from doing such things, then I am being both dominated and actually interfered with; ibid., pp. 22–23, 97, 132, 138, 141, 142, 145; this distinction is the subject of similar analysis by Quentin Skinner in his essay *'Liberty Before Liberalism,'* in particular at pp. 36–41.
5. Ibid., pp. 81–82.
6. Ibid., p. 27.
7. Ibid., pp. 84–85.
8. Ibid., p. 85.
9. Ibid., pp. 67–68.
10. Ibid., p. 81.
11. Ibid., p. 193.
12. Ibid., p. 188.
13. Ibid., pp. 27, 28, 85, 263, 89, 132, 68.
14. Pettit includes in this category, along with slaves, such others as certain wives, employees, debtors and welfare dependants, ibid., p. 5.
15. Ibid., pp. 67, 68.
16. Ibid., p. 92.
17. Ibid., p. 94.
18. Ibid., pp. 6, 104, 207, 78.
19. Ibid., pp. 177–180, 191–192.
20. Ibid., p. 67.
21. Ibid., pp. 84, 86, 93, 230.
22. Ibid., p. 36.
23. Ibid., pp. 38, 39.
24. Ibid., pp. 78, 150.
25. Ibid., pp. 150–170.
26. Ibid., p. 23.

27. Ibid., p. 56.
28. Ibid., pp. 81, 260.
29. Ibid., p. 108.
30. In this context, 'responsible' is first meant to indicate 'being the primary cause for the nature of,' although the further sense of 'liable to be called to account for' also applies.
31. Ibid., p. 23.
32. As was indicated in the Introduction, 'respectful' is intended to indicate action that does not assume responsibility for other individuals, either by force or inducement, and so reveals an awareness of the other's right to self-responsibility.
33. Ibid., p. 23.
34. Ibid., p. 35.
35. Ibid., pp. 36–37.
36. Ibid., pp. 56, 68.
37. Ibid., p. 65.
38. Ibid., p. 181.
39. Ibid., p. 39, where Pettit quotes Harrington in this regard.
40. Ibid., p. 174.
41. Pettit does state that, for him, 'an act of interference will be non-arbitrary to the extent that it is forced to track the interests and ideas of the person suffering the interference,' but qualifies that to say that 'my relevant interests and ideas will be those that are shared in common with others, not those that treat me as exceptional, since the State is meant to serve others as well as me,' ibid., pp. 55–56.
42. Ibid., p. 86.
43. Ibid., p. 177.
44. Ibid., p. 181.
45. Indicative features of a non-Republican, in fact non-mythological, State were provided in Chapter 1.
46. Ibid., pp. 151.
47. Ibid., pp. 122–123.
48. Ibid., p. 125.
49. Ibid., p. 188.
50. Ibid., p. 193.
51. Pettit places considerable emphasis on the necessity for 'a minimum statistical representation for the major stakeholder groupings,' ibid., p. 192.
52. Ibid., pp. 137, 138.
53. Ibid., pp. 138, 140.
54. Ibid., pp. 141, 142.
55. Ibid., p. 145.
56. Ibid., pp. 191, 192.
57. Ibid., pp. 214, 221.
58. Ibid., p. 234.
59. Ibid., p. 217.
60. Ibid., p. 235; see also p. 223.
61. Ibid., p. 197.
62. Ibid., pp. 152–153.
63. Ibid., p. 199.
64. Ibid., pp. 199–200.
65. Ibid., p. 63; see also Q. Skinner, *Liberty before Liberalism*, p. 30 ff.
66. Ibid., p. 184.
67. Ibid., p. 188.
68. Ibid., p. 186.

69. Ibid., pp. 252–253.
70. Rousseau *Social Contract*, p. 69.
71. We have seen how Rousseau was ultimately forced to acknowledge that the acquisition of such characteristics can only come from a culture which promotes this and not through coercion.
72. Op. cit., pp. 56, 68, 232, 118, 120.
73. Ibid., p. 232.
74. Ibid., p. 107.
75. Ibid., p. 202.
76. C. Kukathas and P. Pettit, *Rawls—A Theory of Justice and Its Critics*, (Polity 1990) p. 140.
77. Op. cit., pp. 245, 251, 253.
78. Ibid., p. 266.
79. Ibid., p. 262.
80. Ibid., p. 251.
81. Ibid., p. 263.
82. Ibid., p. 268.
83. Ibid., p. 161.
84. Ibid., p. 161.
85. Ibid., pp. 118–119.
86. Ibid., p. 118.
87. Ibid., p. 118.
88. Ibid., p. 205.
89. Ibid., pp. 255–256.
90. Ibid., p. 236.
91. Ibid., pp. 236–237.
92. Ibid., p. 236.
93. Ibid., p. 237.
94. Rousseau *A Discourse on the Origin of Inequality*, p. 166.
95. P. Manent, *An Intellectual History of Liberalism* p. 65.
96. *Republicanism*, pp. 186, 251.
97. Ibid., p. 59.
98. Ibid., p. 60.
99. Ibid., p. 52.
100. Ibid., p. 159.
101. P. Manent, p. 62.
102. Op. cit., p. 35.
103. Ibid., p. 22.
104. Ibid., p. 51ff.

NOTES TO CHAPTER 9

1. I. Loader and N. Walker, *Civilizing Security* (Cambridge, 2007), p. 44.
2. Ibid., p. 35.
3. Ibid., p. 36.
4. Ibid., p. 57.
5. Ibid., pp. 58–59.
6. Ibid., pp. 40–43.
7. Ibid., pp. 61–64.
8. Ibid., p. 51.
9. Ibid., p. 35.
10. Ibid., p. 36.
11. Ibid., pp. 69–70.

12. Ibid., p. 70.
13. Ibid., pp. 68–69.
14. Ibid., p. 60.
15. Ibid., p. 49.
16. Ibid., p. 73.
17. Ibid., pp. 75, 79.
18. Ibid., p. 76.
19. Ibid., p. 79.
20. Ibid., p. 74.
21. Ibid., p. 75.
22. Ibid., p. 84.
23. Ibid., p. 79.
24. Ibid., p. 83.
25. Ibid., p. 87ff.
26. Ibid., p. 89.
27. Ibid., p. 92.
28. Ibid., p. 91.
29. Ibid., p. 92.
30. Ibid., pp. 86–87.
31. Ibid., p. 93.
32. Ibid., pp. 94–95.
33. Ibid., p. 97.
34. Ibid., p. 99.
35. Ibid., p. 100.
36. Ibid., pp. 102–103.
37. Ibid., pp. 105–106.
38. Ibid., p. 107.
39. Ibid., pp. 108–109.
40. Ibid., pp. 110–111.
41. Ibid., p. 110.
42. Ibid., pp. 111–112.
43. Ibid., pp. 113–114.
44. Ibid., pp. 117–118.
45. Ibid., pp. 118–119.
46. Ibid., pp. 121–122.
47. Ibid., pp. 124–125.
48. Ibid., p. 127.
49. Ibid., p. 128.
50. Ibid., p. 129.
51. Ibid., p. 145.
52. Ibid., p. 148.
53. Ibid., p. 149.
54. Ibid., p. 151.
55. Ibid., p. 161.
56. Ibid., pp. 162–163, 166.
57. Ibid., p. 167.
58. Ibid., p. 171.
59. Ibid., pp. 173–174.
60. Ibid., p. 183.
61. Ibid., p. 189.
62. Ibid., p. 191.
63. Ibid., p. 193.
64. Ibid., p. 195.
65. Ibid., p. 198.

66. Ibid., p. 202.
67. Ibid., p. 204.
68. Ibid., p. 207.
69. Ibid., p. 208.
70. Ibid., p. 209.
71. Ibid., pp. 210–211.
72. Ibid., p. 213.
73. Ibid., pp. 214–215.
74. Ibid., p. 216.
75. Ibid., pp. 220–221.
76. Ibid., p. 223.
77. Ibid., pp. 224–225.
78. Ibid., p. 228.
79. Ibid., pp. 229–230.
80. Ibid., p. 44.
81. Ibid., p. 228.
82. Ibid., p. 230.

NOTES TO CHAPTER 10

1. L. Wittgenstein, *Philosophical Investigations* (Blackwell, 1995), p. 225e.
2. L. Wittgenstein, *Zettel* (Blackwell, 1998), pp. 541, 545, 587.
3. M. Kober, 'Certainties of a World-picture: The Epistemological Investigations of *On Certainty*,' in the *Cambridge Companion to Wittgenstein*, (Cambridge 1996) pp. 420–421.
4. *Philosophical Investigations*, p. 198.
5. L. Wittgenstein, *On Certainty* (Blackwell, 1998), p. 283.
6. L. Wittgenstein, *Philosophical Occasions 1912–1951* (Hackett, 1993), p. 377 (his emphasis); *On Certainty*, p.160 (his emphasis), p. 143.
7. M. Kober, p. 427, where he refers to *On Certainty*, pp. 205, 321, 54, and 454.
8. *On Certainty*, p. 167.
9. Op. cit., p. 422, referring to *On Certainty*, p. 416.
10. *Philosophical Occasions*, p. 395.
11. *On Certainty*, p. 298.
12. M. Kober, p. 424.
13. Ibid., p. 416, where he refers to Wittgenstein's *Last Writings on the Philosophy of Psychology, Vol. 1*, p. 892; *On Certainty*, pp. 360.
14. *On Certainty*, pp. 414, 446.
15. M. Kober, p. 418 (my emphasis).
16. Op. cit., p. 95.
17. L. Wittgenstein, *The Blue and Brown Books* (Blackwell, 1980), p. 13.
18. *Philosophical Investigations*, pp. 199, 202.
19. Op. cit., p. 206; see also Wittgenstein *Nachlass* MS 124 213–221; MS 165 103–104; MS 166 4.
20. *The Blue and Brown Books*, p. 98 (at 41).
21. S. Loyal and S. Quilley, *The Sociology of Norbert Elias* (Cambridge, 2004), pp. 12, 16.
22. Ibid., p. 10.
23. Ibid., pp. 5–7.
24. N. Elias, *The Civilising Process*, (Blackwell 2003) p. 419, 420, 421, 441 ff.
25. Ibid., p. 373.
26. Ibid., pp. 104–105.

27. Ibid., pp. 162–164.
28. Ibid., p. 166.
29. Ibid., pp. 168–169.
30. Ibid., pp. 419–420.
31. Ibid., pp. 421.
32. R. van Krieken, *Norbert Elias*, (Routledge 1998) p. 47.
33. Ibid., p. 47.
34. Elias, *The Civilising Process*, p. 456.
35. Op. cit., pp. 86–89.
36. Ibid., pp. 90–91.
37. Elias, *The Civilising Process*, p. 441.
38. Ibid., pp. 441–443.
39. Ibid., Chapters 4–9, pp. 72–142.
40. Ibid., p. 367.
41. R. van Krieken, p. 69.
42. Ibid., pp. 70–71.
43. Elias, *The Civilising Process*, pp. 169–170; for accounts of this process which emphasise the warlike nature of State formation in Elias and thereby both its internal and external field of operation, see S. Mennell, 'State Formation in America,' and P. Kapteyn, 'Armed Peace: On the Pacifying Condition for the "co-operative of States"', in *The Sociology of Norbert Elias*, pp. 159–161 and 175–177, respectively.
44. Ibid., p. 369.
45. Ibid., p. 271.
46. Ibid.,. p. 337.
47. Ibid., pp. 349, 351, 353, 354, 355.
48. Ibid., pp. 356, 360.
49. See S. Mennell, 'State Formation in America,' in *The Sociology of Norbert Elias*, p. 161.
50. See C. Wouters, 'From Disciplining to Informalizing,' ibid., p. 210.
51. See T. Scheff, 'Elias, Freud, and Goffman: Shame as the Master Emotion,' in *The Sociology of Norbert Elias*, p. 229.
52. No claim is in fact made by Elias in *The Civilising Process* that shame is the master emotion nor is there any significant inference of that kind.
53. In *The Civilising Process*, Elias himself does not understand anxiety in the sense argued here. For him it is social emotion. See pp. 114, 121, 172, 385, 392, 415 in particular.
54. R. van Krieken p. 60.
55. Elias, *The Civilising Process*, p. 479.
56. Ibid., pp. 258–260.
57. Ibid., pp. 170–171.

NOTES TO CHAPTER 11

1. M. Foucault, *Governmentality*, in *The Foucault Effect—Studies in Governmentality*, ed. G. Burchell, C. Gordon, and P. Miller (Harvester Wheatsheaf, 1991), p. 87.
2. Ibid., p. 87.
3. Ibid., p. 89.
4. Ibid., p. 91.
5. Ibid., p. 93.
6. Ibid., p. 96.
7. Ibid., p. 97.

8. Ibid., p. 98.
9. Ibid., p. 99.
10. Ibid., p. 100.
11. Ibid., p. 101.
12. Ibid., p. 101.
13. Ibid., p. 101.
14. Ibid., p. 102.
15. Ibid., pp. 102–103.
16. Ibid., p. 103.
17. Ibid., p. 103.
18. Ibid., p. 104.
19. Ibid., p. 104.
20. M. Dean, *Governmentality* (Sage, 2006), p. 75.
21. M. Foucault, 'The Subject and Power,' in H. Dreyfus and P. Rabinow, *Michel Foucault—Beyond Structuralism and Hermeneutics* (University of Chicago Press, 1983), p. 215.
22. Op. cit., p. 74.
23. Op. cit., p. 215.
24. M. Foucault, *Governmentality*, p. 97.
25. H. Dreyfus and P. Rabinow, 'From the Repressive Hypothesis to Bio-power,' op. cit., p. 137.
26. Ibid., p. 139.
27. M. Dean, *Governmentality* p. 88.
28. M. Foucault *Security, Territory and Population* Palgrave 2007 pp.312-26, 334-5, 340.
29. Op Cit., p. 87.
30. Ibid., p. 91.
31. Ibid., p. 91.
32. Ibid., p. 93.
33. H. Dreyfus and P. Rabinow, pp. 137–138.
34. Ibid., p. 138.
35. Ibid., p. 139.
36. M. Foucault. *Security, Territory and Population,* pp.348–354, 378; also M. Foucault *The Birth of Biopolitics*, p. 21.
37. M. Dean, *Governmentality*, p. 95.
38. Ibid., p. 96.
39. Ibid., p. 99.
40. Dreyfus and Rabinow, 'From the Repressive Hypothesis to Bio-Power,' p. 135.
41. Ibid., p. 135.
42. M. Foucault, *Governmentality*, pp. 93, 94, 95.
43. M. Dean, p. 103.
44. Ibid., p. 105.
45. Ibid., p. 111.
46. Dean argues this at p. 106. Although his argument relates to international relations, the argument to be put here extends that argument to the internal operation of forms of power but will shift the rationale for this point.
47. See M. Foucault, *Power/Knowledge: Selected Interviews and Other Writings 1972–1977* (Brighton: Harvester, 1982), p. 105.
48. Op. cit., p. 107.
49. Ibid., p. 109.
50. M. Foucault, *Security, Territory, Population*, p. 108.
51. Ibid.
52. Ibid., p. 109.

53. This is complemented by the statement by J. Donzelot in 'The Mobilisation of Society' in *The Foucault Effect—Studies in Governmentality,* p. 173.
54. Dreyfus and Rabinow, 'From the Repressive Hypothesis to Bio-Power,' p. 214.
55. M. Foucault, 'The Birth of Biopolitics,' in *Michel Foucault—The Essential Works 1, Ethics* (London: Allen Lane/Penguin Press, 1994), pp. 73–74.
56. Ibid., p. 75
57. M. Dean, *Governmentality,* p. 103.
58. M. Foucault, *The Birth of Biopolitics,* p.61.
59. Ibid p. 219.
60. Ibid p. 224.
61. Ibid p. 229.
62. Ibid p. 67.
63. Ibid p. 231.
64. Ibid p. 62.
65. Ibid p. 65.
66. Ibid pp. 79, 92, 104, 132, 161, 171-2, 218-219.
67. Ibid p. 68.
68. Ibid p. 68.
69. Ibid p. 193.
70. Ibid., pp. 49–50.
71. N. Rose, 'Governing "Advanced" Liberal Democracies,' in *Foucault and Political Reason,* ed. A. Barry, T. Osborne, and N. Rose (Routledge, 2005), p. 45; see also B. Hindess, 'Liberalism, Socialism and Democracy: Variations on a Governmental Theme,' ibid., p. 65.
72. Or, at the most, that sovereign power based on consent is but one of a range of rationalities that operate within the field of government. See B. Hindess, *Discourses of Power,* pp. 145, 157, 16–17, 96. As we saw in Chapter 3, autonomy and consent are also central to the Hobbesian conception of power.
73. Ibid., p. 151.
74. M. Dean, p. 130.
75. Ibid., p. 132.
76. Ibid., p. 132.
77. Ibid., pp. 132-3.
78. Ibid., p. 137.
79. Ibid., p. 138.
80. Ibid., pp. 140–143.
81. Ibid., p. 140–141.
82. Ibid., p. 139.
83. Ibid., p. 146.
84. Ibid., p. 147.
85. M. Dean, *Governmentality* p. 55.
86. J. Donzelot, *The Foucault Effect* p. 170.
87. Ibid., p. 172.
88. M. Dean, pp. 153–154.

Bibliography

Atkinson, A. *The Europeans in Australia—A History. Volume 1.* Oxford, 1998.
Barry, A., Osborne, T. and Rose, N. *Foucault and Political Reason.* Routledge, 1996.
Bentham, J. *Works. Volume 4.* Ed. Bowring. 1843.
Berlin, I. *The Roots of Romanticism.* Chatto and Windus, 1999.
Berlin, I. *Liberty.* Ed. H. Hardy. Oxford, 2002.
Blumenberg, H. *An Anthropological Approach to the Contemporary Significance of Rhetoric.* In *After Philosophy—End or Transformation.* Ed. K. Baynes, J. Bohman, and T. McCarthy. MIT Press, 1989.
Blumenberg, H. *The Legitimacy of the Modern Age.* MIT, 1985a.
Blumenberg, H. *Work on Myth.* MIT, 1985b.
Braithwaite, J., and Pettit, P. *Not Just Deserts.* Oxford, 1998.
Brand, I. *The 'Separate' or 'Model Prison,' Port Arthur.* Jason Publications, 1985.
Brient, E. *The Immanence of the Infinite—Hans Blumenberg and the Threshold to Modernity.* Catholic University Press, 2002.
Brisson, L. *Plato the Myth Maker.* University of Chicago Press, 1998.
Burchell, G. *Civil Society and 'The System of Natural Liberty.'* In *The Foucault Effect.* Ed. G. Burchell, C. Gordon, and P. Miller. Harvester, 1991.
Cassirer, E. *The Myth of the State.* Yale, 1974.
Chesterman, J., and Galligan, B. *Citizens without Rights—Aborigines and Australian Citizenship.* Cambridge, 1997.
Clendinnen, I. *Dancing with Strangers.* Text Publishing, 2003.
Commonwealth of Australia. *Report of the Royal Commission into Aboriginal Deaths in Custody. Volumes 1 and 2.* 1991.
Constant, B. *Principles of Politics* in *Benjamin Constant: Political Writings.* Cambridge, 1988.
Cowling, M. *Mill and Liberalism.* In *Mill—A Collection of Critical Essays.* Ed. A. Rorty. MacMillan, 1969.
Dean, M *Governmentality—Power and Rule in Modern Society.* Sage, 2006.
Dreyfus, H., and Rabinow, P. *Michel Foucault—Beyond Structuralism and Hermeneutics.* Chicago, 1983.
Dunn, J. *The Political Thought of John Locke.* Cambridge University Press, 1995.
Elias, N. *The Civilising Process.* Blackwell, 2000.
Feser, E. Ed. *The Cambridge Companion to Hayek.* Cambridge University Press, 2006.
Filmer, R. *Patriarcha.* Oxford, 1949.
Fitzpatrick, P. *The Mythology of Modern Law.* Routledge, 1992.
Foucault, M. *Discipline and Punish.* Vintage, 1979.

Foucault, M. *Ethics*. In *The Essential Works*. Volume 1. Ed. P. Rabinow. Penguin, 1994.
Foucault, M. *Governmentality*. In *The Foucault Effect*. Ed. G. Burchell, C. Gordon, and P. Miller. Harvester, 1991.
Foucault, M. *History of Sexuality*. Volume 1. Vintage, 1990.
Foucault, M. *Power/Knowledge: Selected Interviews and Other Writings 1972–1977*. Ed. C. Gordon. Pantheon, 1980.
Foucault, M. *Security, Territory, Population*. Palgrave, 2007.
Foucault, M. *The Subject and Power*. Afterword. In H. Dreyfus and P. Rabinow, *Michel Foucault—Beyond Structuralism and Hermeneutics*. Chicago, 1983
Foucault, M. *The Birth of Biopolitics* (Palgrave Macmillan 2008).
Fox, L. W. *The Modern English Prison*. Routledge, 1934.
Gierke, O. *Natural Law and the Theory of Society*. Beacon Press, 1957.
Gierke, O. *Political Theories of the Middle Age*. Cambridge, 1996.
Gordon, C. *Governmental Rationality—An Introduction*. In *The Foucault Effect*. Ed. G. Burchell, C. Gordon, and P. Miller. Harvester, 1991.
Grant, D. *Prisons—The Continuing Crisis in New South Wales*. Federation Press, 1992.
Haebich, A. *Broken Circles*. Fremantle Arts Centre Press, 2000.
Haebich, A. *For Their Own Good—Aborigines and Government in the Southwest of Western Australia, 1990–1940*. University of Western Australia Press, 1988.
Haferkamp, H. "Beyond the Iron Cage of Modernity? *Theory, Culture and Society*, Vol. 4 (1987).
Halevy, E. *A History of the English People in the Nineteenth Century*. New York, 1949.
Hampton, J. *Hobbes and the Social Contract Tradition*. Cambridge, 1995.
Hasluck, P. *Black Australians—A Survey of Native Policy in Western Australia 1829–1897*. Melbourne University Press, 1970.
Hayek, F.A. *Law, Legislation and Liberty*. Routledge, 1998.
Hegel, G. *Philosophy of Mind*. Oxford, 1971.
Hegel, G. *Political Writings*. Cambridge, 1999.
Heidegger, M. *An Introduction to Metaphysics*. Yale University Press, 1959.
Hill, C. *The Century of Revolution 1603–1714*. Routledge, 1989.
Hindess, B. *Discourses of Power*. Blackwell, 2001.
Hindess, B. *Liberalism—What's in a Name*. Electronic Papers 2002. Political Science Program, RSS, ANU.
Hindess, B. "Neo-liberal Citizenship." *Citizenship Studies*, Vol. 6, No. 2 (2002).
Hobbes, T. *Leviathan*. Basil Blackwell, 1946. Reprint. Cambridge, 1991.
Hunter, I. *Rival Enlightenments*. Cambridge, 2001.
Kant, I. *The Cambridge Edition of the Works of Immanuel Kant—Practical Philosoph*. Cambridge, 1996.
Kant, I. *Philosophical Writings*. The German Library, Vol. .13. Ed. E. Behler. Continuum, 1993.
Kant, I. *Political Writings*. Cambridge, 2002.
Kober, M. 'Certainties of a World-picture: The Epistemological Investigations of *On Certainty*'. *Cambridge Companion to Wittgenstein*. Cambridge, 1996.
Kriegel, B. *The State and the Rule of Law*. Princeton, 1995.
Krieken, R. van. *Norbert Elias*. Routledge, 1998.
Krygier, M., and Krieken, R. van. *The Character of the Nation* in *Whitewash*. Black Inc. Agenda, 2003.
Kukathas, C., and Pettit, P. *Rawls—A Theory of Justice and Its Critics*. Polity, 1990.
Lemke, T. 'The Birth of Bio-politics': Michel Foucault's Lecture at the College de France on Neo-liberal Governmentality.' *Economy and Society*, Vol. 30, No. 2 (May 2001): 190–207.

Lindahl, H. "Democracy and the Symbolic Constitution of Society." *Ratio Juris*, Vol. 11, No.1 (March 1998).
Llewellyn, K.,and Hoebel, E. *The Cheyenne Way*. University of Oklahoma, 1961.
Loader, I., and Walker, N. *Civilising Security*. Cambrudge University Press, 2007.
Locke, J. *Two Treatises of Government*. Cambridge University Press, 1988.
MacIntyre, A. *After Virtue—A Study in Moral Theory*. Duckworth, 1986.
Manent, P. *An Intellectual History of Liberalism*. Princeton University Press, 1995.
Margalit, A. *The Ethics of Memory*. Harvard University Press, 2002.
Marshall, T. H. *Citizenship and Social Class. Citizenship—Critical Concepts, Volume 2*. Ed. B. Turner and P. Hamilton. Routledge, 1994.
Mill, J. S. *On Liberty*. Penguin Classics, 1974.
Montesquieu, Charles-Louis de Secondat, Baron de. *The Spirit of the Laws*. Cambridge University Press, 1989.
Mulhall, S., and Swift, A. *Liberals and Communitarians*. Blackwell, 1997.
Nietzsche, F. *On the Genealogy of Morality*. Cambridge University Press, 2003.
Nisbet, R. A. *The Sociological Tradition*. Heinemann, 1966.
Nozick, R. *Anarchy, State and Utopia*. Basic Books, 1974.
Pasquino, P. *Theatricum Politicum: The Genealogy of Capital—Police and the State of Prosperity* in *The Foucault Effect*. Ed. G. Burchell, C. Gordon, and P. Miller. Harvester, 1991.
Pearson, N. *Freedom, Capabilities and the Cape York Reform Agenda*. Cape York Institute for Policy and Leadership, 2005.
Pearson, N. *Our Right to Take Responsibility*. Noel Pearson and Associates, 2000.
Pettit, P. *Republicanism*. Oxford University Press, 1997.
Plato. *The Collected Dialogues*. Bollingen Series. Princeton University Press, 2002.
Rawls, J. *Collected Papers*. Harvard University Press, 2001.
Rawls, J. *Political Liberalism*. Columbia University Press, 1993.
Rawls, J. *A Theory of Justice*. Oxford University Press, 1973.
Rousseau, J-J. *The Discourses and Other Early Political Writings*. Cambridge University Press, 1997.
Rousseau, J-J. *The Social Contract and Discourses*. Everyman, 1973.
Rousseau, J-J. *The Social Contract and Other Later Political Writings*. Cambridge University Press, 1997.
Rowley, C. D. *The Destruction of Aboriginal Society*. Penguin, 1983.
Sandel, M. *Liberalism and the Limits of Justice*. Cambridge University Press, 1982.
Skinner, Q. *Liberty before Liberalism*. Cambridge University Press, 1998.
Skinner, Q. *The Foundations of Modern Political Thought3 Volume 1, The Renaissance*. Cambridge University Press, 1994.
Skinner, Q. *The Foundations of Modern Political Thought—Volume 2, The Age of Reformation*. Cambridge University Press, 1996.
Skinner, Q. *Visions of Politics—Volume 3, Hobbes and Civil Science*. Cambridge University Press, 2002.
Strauss, L. *Natural Right and History*. Chicago, 1965.
Taylor, C. *Foucault on Freedom and Truth. Foucault—A Critical Reader*. Ed. D. Hoy. Blackwell, 1987.
Thomas, J., and Stewart, A. *Imprisonment in Western Australia—Evolution, Theory and Practice*. University of Western Australia Press, 1978.
Turner, B. *Outline of a Theory of Citizenship. Citizenship—Critical Concepts, Voume I*. Ed. B. Turner and P. Hamilton. Routledge, 1994.
Viroli, M. *Jean-Jacques Rousseau and the 'Well-ordered Society.'* Cambridge University Press, 1988.

Waldron, J. *God, Locke and Equality*. Cambridge University Press, 2002.
Walzer, M. 'Liberalism and the Art of Separation.' *Political Theory*, Vol.12, No. 3 (1984).
Walzer, M. *Spheres of Justice.* Blackwell, 1983.
Williams, H., ed. *Essays on Kant's Political Philosophy*. University of Chicago Press, 1992.
Windshuttle, K. *The Fabrication of Aboriginal History--Volume 1, Van Dieman's Land*. Macleay, 2002.
Wittgenstein, L. *The Blue and Brown Books*. Blackwell, 1980.
Wittgenstein, L. *On Certainty*. Blackwell, 1998.
Wittgenstein, L. *Culture and Value*. Blackwell, 1994.
Wittgenstein, L. *Philosophical Investigations*. Blackwell, 1995.
Wittgenstein, L. *Philosophical Occasions 1912-1951*. Hackett, 1993/
Wittgenstein, L. *Remarks on the Philosophy of Psychology, Volumes 1, 2*. Blackwell, 1990.
Wittgenstein, L. *Zettel*. Blackwell, 1998.

Index

Items in bold indicate the principal pages relating to each particular theorist.

A

absolutism, 13, 14, 18, 24, 26, 28, 29, 30, 31, 36, 38, 44, 45, 46, 47, 48, 50, 51, 52, 53, 55, 56, 57, 58, 59, 60, 62, 64, 65, 67, 68, 69, 70, 71, 72, 74, 75, 93, 95, 98, 109, 112, 145, 158, 194, 202, 203, 204, 215, 219, 220, 221, 222, 233, 234, 235, 237, 238, 241, 248

absolutism of reality, 23, 24, 27, 28, 34, 44, 49, 149, 162, 180, 217

allies and agents (of the State), 139, 154, 155, 160, 161, 164, 182, 189, 204, 207, 212, 217, 218, 224, 237, 238, 250, 251

amour de soi, amour propre, 81

anchored pluralism, 193, 195

arbitrary interference, 166, 167, 170, 171, 172, 173, 183, 185

aristocracy, 84, 85, 109, 217

artifice, 43, 46, 47, 48, 50, 51, 52, 78, 79, 80, 82, 85, 89, 92, 94, 115, 139, 150, 245

Ascham, 45

authoritarianism, 243, 246, 247, 249

autocracy, 109, 128

automatic pilot, 181

autonomy, 3, 5, 10, 14, 16, 18, 71, 102, 123, 125, 127, 128, 129, 133, 134, 135, 136, 153, 154, 155, 163, 165, 166, 181, 207, 222, 223, 225, 238, 241, 242, 243, 244, 245, 246, 247, 249, 250, 251, 252

B

basic structure (of society), 123, 124, 134, 138, 140, 141, 144

Berlin, 7, 88, 95

bill of rights, 173

bio-power, 221, 227, 230, 231, 232, 233, 234, 235, 236, 237, 238, 239, 241, 242, 246, 247

Blumenberg, 3, 4, 8, 13, 14, 17, 19, 20, **22–32**, 33, 39, 40, 43, 52, 53, 152, 231, 222, 250, 251, 252

bodily functions, 214

bourgeoisie, 216, 217, 219, 220

Boutmy, 76

Brisson, 19, 20, 21

C

calling, 55, 56, 57, 65, 66, 68, 69, 70, 71, 164

cameralism, 226, 231

capitalism, 213, 232

Cassirer, 19, 20

categorical imperative 102, 103, 104, 105, 106, 107, 109, 110, 111, 112, 113, 115, 116, 117, 119, 129, 133, 135, 140, 141, 142

certainty, 10, 34, 152, 204, 205, 206, 207, 208, 210

Christianity, 6, 13, 14, 37, 41, 46, 55, 56, 58, 59, 60, 62, 63, 64, 65, 66, 68, 69, 70, 75, 76, 84, 85, 89, 100, 106, 108, 115, 118, 128, 136, 139, 164, 203, 207, 208, 217, 219, 220, 225, 226, 229, 230, 231, 232, 233, 235, 237

Cicero, 89, 166

citizens, 21, 22, 33, 36, 37, 38, 40, 46, 47, 48, 73, 74, 77, 82, 83, 84, 88, 90, 91, 92, 96, 97, 101, 102, 103, 104, 105, 106, 108, 109, 110, 111, 112, 115, 117, 118, 125, 127, 132, 134, 135, 136,

137, 139, 142, 148, 154, 159, 164, 166, 170, 171, 176, 177, 179, 182, 183, 184, 188, 190, 194, 195, 197, 201, 202, 204, 211, 221, 230, 238, 247
citizen-city model, 230, 236, 246, 247
civilisation, 37, 38, 144, 157, 158, 187, 189, 201, 203, 205, 206, 210, 212, 213, 214, 216, 217, 218, 219, 220, 252
civility, 178, 181, 183
common good, 79, 80, 82, 83, 84, 85, 87, 88, 90, 91, 92, 93, 94, 95, 96, 106, 107, 108, 124, 125, 148, 156, 172, 174, 177, 182, 186, 189, 192, 195, 196, 197, 226, 233
communalism, 6, 21, 78, 82, 101, 102, 104, 108, 112, 116, 125, 126, 137, 144, 145, 152, 157, 172, 179, 187, 189, 193, 194, 196, 204, 206, 207, 208, 216, 249
communitarianism, 11, 107, 125, 127, 128, 135, 143, 145, 164, 173, 191
complicity, 17, 201
consent, 55, 57, 59, 61, 62, 63, 64, 69, 70, 71, 101, 105, 112, 117, 118, 119, 128, 141, 156, 175, 176, 177, 181, 183, 184, 197, 204, 206, 207, 209, 243, 244, 246, 247
Constant, 88, 89, 91, 96
constitution, as constitutionalism, 17, 22, 30, 34, 36, 37, 38, 39, 40, 60, 62, 63, 64, 65, 67, 75, 76, 82, 83, 84, 91, 92, 100, 101, 104, 105, 109, 112, 117, 124, 128, 129, 130, 134, 137, 138, 139, 140, 141, 142, 145, 148, 162, 164, 167, 168, 169, 173, 178, 184, 186, 188, 189, 190, 202, 204, 222, 236, 238, 239, 241, 245, 250
constraint, contesting the State, 171, 172, 173
constructivism, 124, 145, 196
contract, 6, 13, 14, 16, 22, 24, 26, 27, 28, 29, 30, 32, 35, 36, 37, 43, 44, 48, 50, 52, 56, 57, 61, 67, 70, 75, 79, 80, 81, 82, 83, 84, 85, 87, 88, 90, 91, 92, 94, 96, 97, 100, 101, 102, 104, 105, 106, 112, 118, 123, 130, 132, 133, 141, 158, 160, 197, 202, 204, 217, 219, 224, 227, 235, 239, 243, 245, 248
corporatism, 11, 156, 157, 160, 161, 167, 173, 177, 178, 181, 183, 184, 186, 197, 207
court society, 211, 213, 221
critique and reprogramming, 4, 15, 18, 54, 77, 99, 118, 129, 134, 135, 144, 145, 155, 159, 161, 162, 163, 165, 186, 197, 221, 224, 229, 239, 240, 241, 242, 248, 249, 250, 251, 252
custom, 78, 86, 91, 98, 107, 108, 111, 113, 124, 126, 127, 128, 129, 134, 135, 136, 137, 138, 140, 141, 145, 147, 150, 151, 152, 153, 205, 208, 226, 242, 247, 249

D

Dean, 245, 246, 247, 248
democracy, 85, 110, 117, 119, 124, 128, 129, 130, 136, 137, 138, 139, 140, 142, 144, 145, 148, 156, 159, 160, 162, 175, 188, 189, 190, 191, 192, 194, 195, 196, 203, 204, 215, 222, 223, 234, 235, 236, 237, 238, 239, 241, 245, 246, 248, 250
Descartes, 135
desire, 3, 4, 9, 10, 14, 18, 26, 70, 71, 72, 73, 74, 98, 113, 114, 116, 117, 119, 125, 133, 139, 145, 150, 153, 154, 155, 163, 165, 189, 190, 196, 201, 203, 205, 207, 220, 221, 241, 244, 247, 251, 252
despotism, 110
discipline, 4, 37, 66, 157, 203, 205, 206, 220, 221, 223, 227, 228, 229, 230, 231, 232, 233, 234, 235, 236, 237, 238, 239, 241, 242, 243, 245, 246
dispersal, 28, 29, 30, 32, 36, 37, 38, 40, 51, 52, 53, 67, 76, 94, 95, 96, 97, 99, 106, 115, 130, 133, 144, 147, 169, 170, 185, 204, 217, 220, 222, 245, 251
disposition to myth, 18, 19, 33, 51, 75, 93, 203, 206, 218, 219, 244, 247
docility, 3, 5, 14, 18, 72, 99, 117, 119, 152, 154, 162, 163, 165, 213,

Index 287

220, 221, 222, 223, 225, 228, 230, 231, 232, 236, 237, 239, 241, 242, 245, 247, 249, 250, 251, 252
dominant interests, 84, 10, 11, 12, 14, 15, 17, 26, 27, 29, 31, 32, 35, 37, 38, 39, 40, 44, 51, 67, 69, 70, 76, 82, 87, 88, 89, 92, 93, 95, 96, 97, 99, 100, 105, 116, 117, 119, 123, 124, 130, 142, 143, 144, 145, 156, 157, 159, 160, 161, 162, 164, 165, 174, 176, 177, 180, 181, 182, 183, 186, 187, 189, 190, 196, 197, 201, 202, 204, 205, 207, 209, 212, 215, 216, 217, 229, 230, 233, 244, 245, 249, 250, 251
Donzelot, 246, 249
doubt, 205, 206, 208
Dunn, 54, 61, 65, 69

E
economy, 211, 213, 214, 226, 227, 228, 231, 232, 233, 235, 249, 250
education, 124, 158, 161, 247, 248
Elias, 4, 18, 33, 71, 202, 203, 204, 205, 206, **210–220**, 231, 240, 252
embedding, 16, 17, 18, 22, 37, 71, 91, 128, 130, 135, 136, 137, 138, 149, 190, 202, 203, 204, 208, 217, 220, 221, 222, 223, 224, 225, 228, 229, 230, 231, 232, 235, 236, 237, 238, 239, 240, 241, 242, 243, 245, 249, 251
engagement, 18, 24, 28, 30, 35, 40, 44, 51, 55, 61, 74, 77, 93, 97, 98, 100, 104, 105, 108, 109, 111, 112, 117, 118, 119, 129, 133, 134, 141, 162, 163, 164, 188, 195, 196, 202, 203, 210, 216, 230, 238,
Enlightenment, 4, **5–8**, 9, 12, 13, 17, 26, 39, 53, 93, 94, 242
equality, 60, 61, 62, 65, 66, 69, 70, 71, 78, 80, 83, 85, 87, 94, 95, 96, 97, 98, 100, 102, 103, 104, 106, 109, 111, 112, 113, 117, 118, 123, 124, 127, 130, 133, 134, 135, 137, 139, 141, 143, 158, 161, 164, 179, 189, 196, 230
eugenics, 246, 248

F
false negatives and positives, 195

family, 226, 227, 231, 233, 234, 235, 249
fear, 3, 4, 9, 10, 11, 14, 15, 17, 18, 21, 22, 25, 26, 27, 28, 29, 30, 31, 32, 34, 35, 36, 37, 38, 39, 40, 44, 46, 48, 49, 50, 51, 52, 53, 54, 55, 57, 59, 65, 66, 67, 68, 69, 70, 71, 72, 73, 74, 75, 77, 82, 87, 92, 93, 94, 95, 96, 97, 98, 110, 111, 112, 113, 115, 116, 117, 118, 119, 125, 128, 131, 132, 133, 134, 135, 137, 138, 139, 140, 141, 142, 143, 144, 145, 150, 152, 153, 154, 155, 159, 160, 162, 163, 164, 165, 168, 171, 172, 178, 181, 182, 183, 185, 186, 189, 190, 191, 194, 196, 197, 201, 202, 203, 204, 205, 206, 207, 208, 210, 211, 212, 213, 214, 215, 216, 217, 218, 219, 220, 221, 222, 223, 224, 228, 230, 232, 233, 234, 235, 236, 237, 238, 239, 240, 241, 242, 244, 245, 247, 249, 250, 251, 252
fear, existential, 5, 12, 22, 23, 24, 25, 27, 28, 29, 30, 32, 34, 35, 36, 37, 39, 44, 53, 55, 64, 67, 68, 69, 71, 72, 73, 74, 75, 104, 115, 118, 119, 130, 167, 168, 187, 189, 192, 193, 194, 196, 197, 202, 203, 204, 205, 206, 210, 212, 214, 217, 218, 243, 244
Ferguson, 179
feudalism, 225
figurational sociology, 211
Filmer, 56, 57, 58, 59, 61, 62, 63, 64, 65, 68, 70
force, 125, 139, 141, 142, 143, 144, 147, 148, 150, 152, 153, 155, 156, 157, 159, 161, 162, 163, 168, 169, 170, 172, 173, 189, 190, 191, 193, 194, 195, 196, 211, 214, 216, 217, 218, 219, 233, 238, 247, 249
form of life, 139, 152, 208
Foucault, 4, 15, 18, 33, 71, 202, 203, 204, 205, 206, 210, 220, **221–252**
freedom, 3, 5, 7, 13, 14, 15, 16, 18, 48, 55, 58, 60, 64, 66, 68, 69, 71, 72, 73, 74, 75, 83, 84, 85, 87, 91, 95, 96, 98, 100, 101, 102, 103, 104, 105, 107, 110, 112, 124, 125,

127, 131, 133, 134, 137, 138, 139, 141, 147, 148, 149, 155, 156, 157, 158, 159, 161, 162, 163, 164, 165, 166, 167, 170, 171, 177, 178, 182, 183, 184, 186, 188, 189, 193, 197, 201, 222, 223, 225, 235, 236, 238, 240, 241, 242, 243, 245, 246, 248, 249, 250, 251, 252
French Revolution, 6
general will, 18, 52, 79, 80, 82, 83, 84, 85, 87, 88, 89, 90, 91, 92, 93, 94, 95, 96, 97, 98, 99, 101, 102, 103, 104, 105, 106, 107, 108, 111, 113, 115, 116, 119, 164, 177, 178, 182, 186, 227

G

Genesis, 57, 59
Gierke, 50, 52
goods, 124, 132, 134
Good, 123, 124, 126, 127, 128, 129, 130, 133, 136, 137, 139, 141, 142, 143, 144, 145
government, 18, 146, 147, 148, 149, 151, 153, 154, 155, 156, 158, 159, 161, 162, 163, 164, 193, 197, 204, 206, 207, 208, 210, 213, 217, 231, 234, 236, 238, 240, 241, 243, 247, 248
governmentality, 4, 15, 37, 202, 203, 205, 211, 220, 221, 222, 223, 224, 225, 226, 227, 228, 231, 232, 233, 234, 235, 236, 237, 238, 239, 240, 241, 243, 244, 245, 246, 249, 250

H

Habermas, 196
habitus, 211, 212, 213, 219
Halevy, 76
Hayek, 3, 12, 14, 15, 16, 18, 33, 37, 72, **146–165**, 191, 201, 203, 204, 212, 221, 222, 223, 224, 225, 238, 239, 240, 241, 242, 243, 246, 249, 250, 251
Hegel, 107
Herder, 7
heteronomy, 10, 133, 244
Hindess, 244
Hobbes, 3, 10, 12, 13, 14, 15, 16, 17, 18, 19, 33, 40, 41, **43–54**, 62, 63, 64, 65, 66, 67, 68, 69, 70, 71, 72, 73, 74, 75, 76, 79, 80, 81, 82, 84, 92, 93, 95, 96, 97, 98, 99, 100, 101, 102, 105, 108, 109, 114, 115, 116, 117, 118, 124, 128, 129, 130, 132, 133, 134, 135, 137, 138, 139, 140, 142, 143, 144, 145, 154, 155, 158, 162, 163, 164, 165, 166, 168, 169, 171, 177, 178, 182, 183, 185, 188, 197, 201, 203, 204, 212, 219, 221, 224, 235, 240, 241, 242, 243, 244, 245, 251
human nature, 46, 51, 101, 103, 107, 113, 114, 115, 118, 119, 126, 131, 133, 134, 231, 248
Hunter, 101, 102, 107, 108, 115, 117

I

inclusion-exclusion, 174, 175
indigenous people, 11,
individualism, 6, 100, 109, 123, 146, 219, 249
individual interest, 78, 83, 84, 87, 100, 104, 106, 107, 108, 109, 112, 113, 119, 124, 125, 152, 155, 157, 161, 164, 167, 169, 171, 173, 174, 177, 178, 179, 180, 181, 183, 184, 188, 197, 244, 245
inducement, 206, 251
Industrial Revolution, 6
instincts, 3, 4, 15, 16, 17, 80, 90, 117, 153, 154, 159, 161, 196, 197, 248
insufficient reason, principle of, 112, 114, 124, 130, 132, 135, 140
intangible hand, 178, 180, 183
interdependence, 211, 212, 216
interest groups, 174
invisible hand, 146, 180

J

judicial decisions, 143
justice, 11, 100, 112, 118, 124, 125, 126, 127, 128, 129, 131, 132, 133, 135, 136, 137, 138, 141, 142, 143, 145, 146, 148, 155, 156, 158, 161, 228, 245

K

Kant, 5, 6, 7, 8, 10, 12, 15, 16, 18, 52, 53, 72, 77, 98, 99, **100–119**, 123, 126, 127, 129, 132, 133, 134, 135, 137, 138, 139, 140,

141, 142, 143, 144, 145, 161, 164, 168, 172, 176, 177, 178, 186, 209, 222, 243, 250
Kober, 205, 206, 207
Kriegel, 76

L

labour, 65, 66, 68, 70, 71, 86, 89, 98, 100, 157, 158, 210, 213, 216, 235, 241, 242, 249
language games, 206, 207, 208
law, 13, 16, 21, 22, 24, 25, 33, 39, 46, 48, 49, 50, 53, 55, 58, 60, 61, 62, 63, 64, 65, 69, 70, 72, 73, 78, 79, 80, 82, 83, 84, 85, 86, 87, 88, 89, 90, 91, 92, 93, 94, 95, 96, 98, 99, 100, 102, 103, 104, 105, 107, 111, 112, 116, 118, 124, 133, 138, 147, 148, 149, 150, 152, 155, 156, 158, 159, 162, 168, 169, 171, 172, 178, 182, 183, 186, 189, 192, 193, 196, 213, 226, 227, 231, 233, 234, 235, 237, 242, 248
legitimacy, 4, 5, 13, 45, 46, 49, 50, 55, 58, 59, 60–61, 62, 63, 64, 65, 66, 68, 70, 82, 139, 147, 163, 167, 169
liberalism, as mythological, 219, 232, **239–243**, 245, 249, 251, 252
liberalism, also as non-interference, 3, 4, 5, 6, 12, 13, 15, 16, 17, 18, 36, 65, 70, 71, 74, 77, 94, 98, 99, 123, 124, 125, 127, 136, 139, 141, 142, 143, 144, 145, 146, 150, 154, 155, 158, 159, 161, 162, 163, 165, 166, 167, 182, 184, 185, 186, 188, 197, 202, 203, 220, 221, 222, 223, 224, 225, 238, 242, 245, 246, 247, 248, 251
liberalism, as neo-liberalism, 35, 188, 194, 197, 220, 222, 223, 224, 229, 238, 239, 241, 242, 246, 248, 249
libertarianism, 179
life plan, 124, 140
Loader and Walker, 18, **187–197**
Locke, 5, 12, 14, 15, 16, 17, 18, 52, 53, **54–72**, 74, 75, 76, 84, 92, 93, 94, 96, 97, 98, 99, 101, 108, 109, 110, 111, 112, 115, 118, 125, 132, 134, 135, 137, 140, 145, 146, 159, 164, 166, 176, 178, 183, 185, 188, 209, 222, 241, 242, 250
Lowith, 13

M

Machiavelli, 84, 86, 166, 182, 225, 226, 237
MacIntyre, 136
Macpherson, 54, 61
malevolent opponent, 123, 124, 126, 130, 132, 134, 135, 141, 146
Manent, 54, 73, 74, 100, 181
manners, 213
market, 15, 139, 146, 147, 149, 150, 153, 154, 155, 156, 157, 158, 159, 160, 161, 162, 163, 164, 179, 180, 188, 191, 194, 195, 196, 197, 221, 222, 223, 224, 230, 238, 239, 241, 242, 250, 251
maximin strategy, 132
Mendus, 109
mercantilism, 226, 231, 235
Mill J.S., 247
Mirabeau, 91
mirror-image, 13, 229
modernity, 3, 4, 5, 13, 14, 15, 16
monarchy, 93, 159, 227
monopoly, 154, 157, 160, 162, 193, 214, 215
Montesquieu, 5, 12, 17, 18, 71, **72–77**, 84, 85, 86, 89, 92, 93, 94, 101, 109, 110, 111, 115, 118, 119, 135, 143, 164, 166, 168, 183, 185, 188
morality, 101, 103, 104, 105, 106, 107, 108, 109, 110, 111, 112, 113, 114, 116, 117, 118, 119, 123, 124, 125, 127, 129, 133, 134, 135, 136, 137, 140, 143, 145, 151, 158, 164, 165, 188, 226, 231, 242
myth, theories of, 19, 20–32, 217–218
myth, as archetype, 29, 31, 33, 34, 35, 37, 38, 50, 51, 54, 63, 67, 94, 95, 202, 204, 206, 207, 208, 210, 216, 218, 219, 242, 244, 252; finally its fate into man's hands, 26, 27, 29, 32, 36, 38, 44, 51, 52, 53, 55, 57, 65, 67, 69, 70, 95, 96, 97, 98, 119, 133, 159, 160, 163, 164,

290 *Index*

194, 202, 220, 221, 238, 248, 250
mythological magnitude, 11, 14, 19, 22–32, 33, 34, 36, 38, 39, 40, 41, 44, 51, 53, 69, 70, 92, 93, 96, 98, 100, 114, 115, 116, 119, 133, 134, 138, 158, 159, 161, 162, 163, 164, 165, 172, 174, 185, 190, 191, 194, 202, 203, 204, 205, 206, 207, 208, 210, 212, 216, 219, 220, 223, 228, 233, 235, 236, 242, 251

N

naturalism, 101, 103, 113, 227
Nazism, 247
Nedham, 45
neutrality, 31, 37, 39, 123, 128, 139, 141, 142, 143, 144
Nietzsche, 107, 114
Nisbet, 6
normalisation, 4, 10, 22, 145, 150, 151, 152, 178, 186, 189, 191, 193, 196, 197, 203, 204, 205, 208, 209, 210, 222, 229, 232, 234, 237, 242, 248, 251
Norman Conquest, 45, 62
Nozick, 125

O

Oakeshott, 45
order, as spontaneous or made, 147, 149, 150, 151, 152, 153, 154, 155, 156, 157, 158, 160, 161, 162, 163
order, as stability, 57, 60, 63, 64, 65, 66, 69, 78, 79, 80, 84, 85, 86, 87, 89, 91, 92, 93, 94, 97, 106, 110, 112, 124, 127, 132, 136, 140, 150, 151, 153, 158, 190, 191, 226, 231, 233, 237
organic conception (of society), 130, 133, 135
organisation, 147, 148, 155, 158
Original Position, 123, 125, 126, 127, 128, 130, 132, 133, 134, 135, 137, 138

P

Panopticon, 232
Parliament, 45, 46, 55, 57, 58, 61, 64, 65, 68, 69, 70, 93, 143, 145, 148, 153, 161
passions, 84

pastoralism, 15, 221, 223, 228, 229, 230, 231, 233, 237, 238, 239, 246, 247, 248, 249
patriarchalism, 6
peace, 155, 160, 163, 164, 201
personal interest, 73, 98
Pettit, 3, 12, 14, 16, 18, 33, 77, 98, 115, **166–186**, 187, 195, 196, 197, 203, 204, 209, 210, 212
phase shifts, 155, 165, 221, 223, 225, 229, 231, 237, 238, 239, 240, 241, 243, 249, 251
Plato, 17, 19, **20–22**, 23, 25, 26, 32, 33, 38, 40
pluralism, 140, 141
police, 187, 188, 189, 190, 191, 194, 195, 221, 223, 226, 228, 229, 230, 231, 233, 235, 236, 237, 239, 241, 242, 248
political, notion of the, 127, 136, 142, 143, 152, 163, 207
population, 211, 216, 226, 228, 230, 231, 232, 233, 234, 235, 236, 237, 246, 247, 248
postulates, Kantian, 108
power, 211
practice, 197, 204, 205, 206, 207, 208, 209, 211, 213, 214, 215, 216, 218, 219, 220, 221, 222, 223, 224, 232, 236, 238, 241, 242, 243, 248, 249, 250, 252
prerogative, 55, 57, 58, 61, 62, 63, 69
productivity, 3, 5, 14, 18, 72, 99, 117, 119, 154, 157, 158, 161, 162, 163, 165, 212, 213, 218, 220, 221, 222, 223, 225, 228, 230, 231, 232, 234, 236, 237, 239, 241, 242, 245, 247, 248, 249, 250, 251, 252
progress, 6, 27, 28, 30, 37, 39, 54, 112, 215, 218
property, 12, 55, 56, 57, 59, 61, 64, 65, 68, 69, 70, 71, 79, 95, 104, 109, 110, 123, 125, 134, 164, 189, 230, 242, 249
psychogenesis, 211
Pufendorf, 108, 115, 116, 117, 119
punishment, 86, 87, 88, 91, 95, 97, 98, 101, 106, 107, 110, 111, 112, 113, 118, 119, 129, 141, 233, 236

R

raison d'etat, 13, 17, 226, 231, 237, 242, 248

rationalities, 210, 222
Rawls, 12, 14, 15, 16, 18, 77, 98, 115, 119, **123–145**, 146, 164, 178, 201, 224
reason, 3, 4, 5, 6, 8, 9, 16, 17, 18, 20, 37, 44, 45, 46, 48, 49, 50, 56, 68, 71, 79, 82, 83, 87, 90, 91, 94, 95, 96, 97, 98, 99, 101, 102, 103, 104, 105, 106, 107, 108, 109, 110, 111, 112, 113, 114, 115, 123, 124, 125, 127, 128, 129, 131, 132, 134, 135, 136, 137, 138, 139, 140, 141, 142, 143, 144, 145, 161, 163, 164, 193, 195, 196, 207, 213, 214, 226, 230, 233, 234, 244, 245, 247, 249, 252
Reformation, as Thirty Years War, 6, 71, 108, 115
reoccupation, 13, 26
republicanism, 3, 4, 12, 13, 17, 18, 77, 79, 84, 91, 95, 96, 97, 98, 102, 109, 110, 115, 116, 117, 164, 166, 167, 168, 171, 172, 173, 175, 178, 179, 180, 181, 182, 183, 184, 185, 186, 195, 197, 201, 203, 224, 240, 248
resistance, 55, 57, 58, 60, 62, 63, 64, 66, 69, 70, 71, 101, 102, 105, 110, 111, 112, 113, 115, 117, 118, 119, 124, 128, 129, 169, 209
responsibility, 3, 4, 9–12, 14, 16, 18, 71, 102, 103, 104, 109, 114, 158, 161, 162, 163, 165, 206, 222, 223, 235, 236, 238, 241, 242, 243, 245, 246, 247, 249, 250, 251, 252
rights, 13, 14, 16, 31, 36, 39, 47, 48, 49, 51, 52, 58, 59, 60, 61, 62, 63, 64, 65, 67, 68, 69, 70, 71, 73, 75, 92, 104, 108, 123, 124, 125, 130, 132, 134, 135, 138, 145, 154, 156, 158, 160, 161, 162, 186, 195, 196, 219, 221, 230, 247, 248
Right, 57, 100, 102, 105, 110, 111, 112, 118, 124, 126, 127, 128, 129, 133, 137, 139, 142, 143, 144, 145, 148, 234, 249
Rousseau, 5, 12, 15, 16, 18, 50, 52, 53, 72, 76, 77, **78–99**, 100, 101, 103, 104, 105, 106, 107, 108, 109, 110, 111, 113, 114, 115, 117, 118, 125, 129, 132, 133, 135, 137, 143, 164, 166, 168, 172, 177, 178, 179, 181, 183, 222, 227, 235, 241, 242, 249, 250
rules of just conduct, 146, 147, 148, 149, 150, 151, 152, 153, 154, 155, 156, 157, 158, 159, 161, 162, 163, 164
rules, 149, 158, 160

S
salvation, 229
Sandel, 126, 136
savoir, 191, 211, 228, 230, 232, 235, 236, 237
Schmitt, 13
Schiller, 8, 189
Schopenhauer, 27
screening, 180, 183, 186
scrutiny of private life, 86, 87, 88
secession, 176
secularisation, 13
security, 187, 189, 190, 191, 192, 193, 194, 196, 197, 228, 230, 231, 233, 235, 249
self-responsibility, as respectful responsibility to and for oneself, 3, 4, 5, 6, 9–12, 13, 14, 15, 22, 27, 32, 36, 38, 39, 40, 71, 74, 75, 76, 81, 91, 96, 98, 110, 112, 113, 114, 128, 130, 132, 137, 138, 139, 140, 143, 155, 162, 168, 172, 179, 181, 183, 192, 197, 201, 207, 210, 216
self-responsibility, forgone or assumed, 3, 12, 17, 29, 30, 32, 34, 35, 37, 38, 39, 40, 48, 51, 53, 65, 71, 77, 93, 95, 96, 114, 115, 116, 117, 119, 130, 131, 133, 134, 135, 138, 142, 144, 145, 154, 155, 159, 163, 164, 165, 167, 168, 170, 171, 173, 174, 175, 178, 183, 184, 185, 186, 203, 204, 205, 207, 208, 209, 211, 212, 216, 218, 219, 220, 221, 222, 228, 230, 232, 233, 235, 236, 237, 239, 242, 244, 245, 246, 247, 248, 249, 251
separation of powers, 24, 25, 36, 40, 72, 74, 76, 93, 110, 164, 173
shame, 216, 217
shepherd-flock model, 230, 238, 246, 247

292 Index

Skinner, 44, 45, 47, 48, 49, 166
Smith, Adam, 146, 242
social imaginary, 188, 196, 197
social justice, 156, 161, 162
social space, 160, 162, 170, 185, 193, 202, 204, 218, 221, 222, 224, 239, 244, 250
socialism, 146, 156, 161, 179, 250
society, as spontaneous order, 155, 158
sociogenesis, 210
solidarity, 249
sovereignty, 6, 13, 17, 29, 34, 46, 47, 48, 49, 51, 52, 57, 59, 61, 62, 69, 74, 75, 78, 80, 82, 83, 84, 85, 87, 88, 89, 90, 91, 92, 93, 94, 95, 96, 97, 99, 104, 105, 108, 109, 113, 118, 148, 158, 162, 195, 204, 208, 214, 218, 223, 224, 226, 227, 228, 231, 232, 233, 234, 235, 236, 237, 238, 242, 246, 247, 248, 250
State, as empowered central authority, 3, 4, 5, 9, 10, 11, 12, 13, 15, 17, 18, 19, 23, 29, 32–40, 43, 44, 45, 46, 48, 49, 50, 51, 52, 53, 54, 55, 67, 69, 70, 72, 73, 74, 75, 76, 79, 89, 92, 93, 99, 100, 101, 102, 103, 104, 105, 107, 108, 109, 110, 111, 112, 113, 115, 116, 117, 118, 119, 123, 125, 128, 129, 131, 133, 136, 138, 139, 141, 143, 144, 145, 149, 158, 159, 160, 161, 162, 163, 164, 165, 167, 168, 169, 170, 177, 179, 180, 182, 185, 187, 194, 196, 201, 202, 207, 208, 210, 211, 212, 214, 215, 216, 217, 218, 219, 221, 222, 223, 224, 226, 228, 229, 230, 231, 233, 234, 235, 236, 238, 241, 245,249
State as freedom, 169, 170
State as institutional arrangements, 33, 34, 36, 37, 39, 44, 47, 51, 58, 61, 62, 63, 64, 68, 69, 70, 71, 72, 73, 74, 75, 76, 84, 85, 88, 89, 92, 93, 94, 95, 97, 99, 100, 101, 102, 104, 105, 106, 109, 110, 111, 112, 113, 114, 117, 118, 123, 124, 125, 126, 127, 128, 129, 130, 131, 134, 135, 136, 137, 138, 140, 141, 142, 144, 145, 147, 148, 153, 154, 156, 158, 159, 160, 162, 164, 165, 167, 173, 174, 177, 178, 180, 181, 182, 183, 185, 190, 192, 195, 196, 197, 201, 202, 204, 205, 206, 207, 208, 209, 210, 215, 216, 217, 219, 226, 231, 233, 234, 235, 237, 238, 242, 243, 244, 246, 248, 250
State, as Leviathan, 43, 44, 51, 65, 67, 74, 95, 97, 98, 204
State, as mythological idea and practice, 170, 197, 201, 207, 230, 232, 237, 239, 240, 243
state of nature, 24, 26, 27, 34, 44, 48, 49, 50, 55, 57, 58–60, 64, 68, 69, 70, 71, 72, 73, 74, 75, 78, 80, 82, 89, 90, 101, 104, 108, 112, 113, 118, 119
State scepticism, 188, 191
statism, as empowerment, 174, 175, 176, 177, 179
statistics, 227
Strauss, 54
subjection, 13, 14,17, 24, 28, 29, 30, 31, 32, 35, 36, 38, 39, 48, 51, 52, 57, 60, 62, 67, 69, 75, 76, 80, 83, 87, 88, 93, 94, 95, 96, 98, 105, 112, 116, 119, 131, 143, 150, 152, 153, 155, 157, 159, 160, 161, 162, 163, 164, 188, 189, 191, 194, 196, 201, 202, 211, 215, 216, 217, 218, 219, 223, 224, 226, 234, 235, 238, 239, 240, 241, 243, 244, 245, 246, 247, 250, 251
subjectivication, as subjectivity, 160, 162, 245
subversion, as disguise, 14, 15, 16, 18, 58, 66, 71, 154, 159, 162, 163, 165, 224, 235, 238, 242, 243, 245, 247, 249, 250, 251, 252
sympathetic conditions of existence, 3, 9, 10, 11, 14, 17, 18, 23, 24, 26, 27, 28, 30, 31, 32, 34, 35, 36, 37, 38, 39, 44, 51, 52, 53, 67, 70, 71, 76, 77, 87, 93, 94, 95, 96, 97, 98, 106, 109, 111, 113, 115, 117, 118, 119, 123, 124, 129, 130, 132, 133, 134, 135, 138, 139, 143, 144, 145, 146, 150, 152, 153, 154, 155, 157, 158, 159, 160, 161, 162, 163, 164, 165, 168, 178, 179, 180, 182, 183, 185, 190, 193, 194, 195, 196, 197, 201, 202, 203,

204, 205, 206, 207, 208, 209, 210, 211, 212, 215, 216, 217, 218, 219, 220, 221, 222, 224, 226, 227, 228, 229, 230, 231, 232, 233, 236, 237, 238, 239, 240, 241, 242, 244, 245, 247, 248, 249, 250, 251, 252

T

taxation, 106, 125, 156, 193, 215, 218
territory, 61, 66, 225, 226, 227, 231, 233, 237
Thomasius, 108, 115
totalitarianism, 12, 146, 148, 154, 155, 156, 161, 250
trade unions, 156, 157, 160, 161, 162, 250
tradition, political, 3, 4, 5, 14, 15, 16, 17, 19, 22, 26, 29, 31, 33, 34, 40, 41, 44, 53, 54, 93, 94, 97, 101, 113, 114, 115, 129, 137, 143, 144, 145, 162, 163, 164, 165, 166, 167, 203, 204, 222, 239, 244, 245, 249, 250, 251
training, 117, 118, 205, 206, 207, 208, 210, 211, 216, 218, 236, 241, 244
trajectories of idea and practice, 4, 14, 15, 16, 17, 18, 71, 72, 77, 98, 99, 119, 135, 145, 155, 162, 163, 165, 219, 220, 221, 222, 223, 225, 229, 238, 239, 240, 242, 249, 250, 251, 252
transformation, as training, 81, 85, 86, 87, 88, 89, 90, 91, 94, 95, 96, 97, 98, 107, 116, 117, 118, 119, 152, 157, 159, 160, 161, 177, 186, 210, 211, 213, 214, 216, 218, 231, 235, 239, 247
triangle of sovereignty, discipline and art of government, 227, 229, 238
trust, 178, 179, 183
Two Principles, 130, 132, 133, 134, 141, 164

V

veil of ignorance, 126, 133, 137, 141

W

Waldron, 54, 65
Walzer, 136
Welfare State, 162, 238, 242, 243, 246, 248, 249
Westphalia, Treaty of, as European State system, 12, 211, 228, 233, 237
Wittgenstein, 4, 18, 71, 151, 152, 202, 203, **204–210**, 211, 214, 216, 222, 251
women, 104, 105, 112, 115, 129
world picture, 206, 207, 208